BORIS

GODUNOV

BORIS

Transpositions of
a Russian Theme

GODUNOV

Caryl Emerson

BLOOMINGTON AND INDIANAPOLIS *Indiana University Press*

Manufactured in the United States of America

Library of Congress Cataloging-in-Publication Data

Emerson, Caryl.
  Boris Godunov : transpositions of a Russian theme.

  Bibliography: p.
  Includes index.
  1. Boris Fyodorovich Godunov, Czar of Russia, 1551 or 2-1605. 2. Boris Fyodorovich Godunov, Czar of Russia, 1551 or 2-1605, in fiction, drama, poetry, etc. 3. Karamzin, Nikolaĭ Mikhaĭlovich, 1766–1826. Istoriia gosudarstva rossiĭskogo. 4. Pushkin, Aleksandr Sergeevich, 1799–1837. Boris Godunov. 5. Mussorgsky, Modest Petrovich, 1839–1881. Boris Godunov. 6. Opera— Soviet Union. 7. Soviet Union—Kings and rulers— Biography. I. Title.
DK109.E44   1986   947'.044'0924 [B]   85-45772

ISBN 0-253-31230-2

1 2 3 4 5 90 89 88 87 86

To my parents, Bonnie and David Geppert,
who have been (for as long as I can remember)
a spectacular source of ideas, support, and creative dialogue

CONTENTS

ACKNOWLEDGMENTS   ix

CHRONOLOGY   xi

GENEALOGY   xii

I. *Boris Godunov* and a Poetics of Transposition   1

    The Translatability of Narrative   3
    Boris Godunov and the False Dmitri: An Overview   11
    Aestheticizing the Boris Tale   14
    Trapping a Hero inside a Genre:
        Four Questions to Ask of the Boris Tale   25

II. Boris in History: *Karamzin*   30

    Double Response to Double Text   33
    History Before Karamzin: Two Categories   35
    Karamzin's History: "Purposeful" Narrative,
        "Truthful" Apparatus   37
    Defining Karamzin's Chronotope   43
    The Layering of a Source   46
    The Historical Boris   48
    The Boris Tale Matures   53
    The History of the History   57
    Karamzin's Boris in the History:
        Two Episodes and a Moral   61
    Civil Disobedience and Silence   70
    Boris the Usurper   76
    Historian and Poet   82

III. Boris in Drama: *Pushkin*   88

From Romantic History to "Romantic Tragedy"   91
The Chronotope of Boris   96
Boris the Pretender   99
Pushkin and Uglich   103
For and Against a Playable Boris   105
Some Formal Considerations   107
The Shakespeare Connection   110
Pimen   119
Endings   131
The Narod as Hero   135
Karamzin and Pushkin: Closing Down the Tale   137

IV. Boris in Opera: *Musorgsky*   142

Transposition into Opera   143
Three Principles for Adapting Texts   147
Is the Libretto Literature?   152
Russian Music in the Reform Decade: Two Schools   155
Musorgsky's Musical Aesthetic   157
From Pushkin to Gogol: Setting the Prose Word   159
From Gogol Back to Pushkin: Sung Speech into
     Historical Opera   162
The Chronotope of a Libretto in Prose   165
Musorgsky's Prose Line   168
The Boris Tale as Libretto: Musorgsky's Two Versions 170
Romantic Tragedy into Realistic Opera:
     General Principles of Transposition   175
The Narod as Operatic Hero   180
Tsar Boris's Great Monologues:
     The Return to Karamzin   184
Pimen   192
Endings: Transcending Karamzin, Rethinking Pushkin   198

Concluding Remarks   207

NOTES   212
INDEX   263

Acknowledgments

O<small>F THE MANY</small> who have responded to this text during the eight years of its evolution, several deserve special mention. Sidney Monas of the University of Texas at Austin has been with the Boris project since its inception, and his wise commentary on successive drafts has been indispensable to the shape of the book. Donald Fanger made some luminescent suggestions on the final manuscript that rescued me from dead ends I did not even suspect; William Mills Todd, Robert Louis Jackson, Stephanie Sandler, Walter Pintner and J. Thomas Shaw tactfully combined support for the whole with corrections in detail. The Karamzin chapter owes a special debt to Judith Vowles of Yale University, and the section on Pushkin's "Shakespeare Connection" to Phyllis Rackin of the University of Pennsylvania. Moscow friends on Boris Watch for a decade now can at last gratefully let down their guard.

For the Musorgsky chapter I am much indebted to the scholarly generosity of Richard Taruskin of Columbia University, whose detailed scrutiny of a final draft (and relentlessly right advice) pulled me back from several brinks and pointed the way toward a richer interpretation of my material. That chapter also benefited greatly from careful readings by Robert Oldani and David Geppert—who shared with me their spirited first reactions as well as their final reservations. To Christopher Been, composer, pianist, and long-time partner in recitals of Musorgsky's chamber songs, a special thanks for making the performance ethic of the *kuchkisty* more than a theory. That my husband "can't understand why he should be thanked for anything" is characteristic of him and of his steadfast support, so taken for granted by us both. And finally, in a category of its own: my debt to Gary Saul Morson, friend and colleague, who read all the final drafts and cajoled, prodded and inspired me with his commentary from start to finish, is beyond adequate acknowledgment.

This book was completed during my sojourn as a Mellon Fellow at the University of Pennsylvania, 1984–85. I thank its Humanities Coordinating Committee and its Department of Slavic Languages and Literatures for that indispensable gift of time and place. Indiana

University Press sustained over five years an enthusiasm for this project that brightened the dreariest moments of doubt. The Soviet Studies Committee of Cornell University kindly subsidized a portion of the costs of manuscript preparation. And I am still seeking a way to thank Deone Terrio, who keyed on draft after draft of this book with such skill, patience and presence of mind that I experienced none of the frustrations (and all of the pleasures) of a flexible yet ever-authoritative manuscript.

Portions of chapters 1, 3, and 4 appeared in earlier draft or in compressed form as the following articles: "Bakhtin and Intergeneric Shift," *Studies in 20th Century Literature* 9, no. 1 (Fall 1984): 145–67; "Real Endings and Russian Death: Musorgskij's 'Pesni i pljaski smerti,'" *Russian Language Journal* 38, nos. 129–30 (1984): 199–216; "Pretenders to History: Four Plays for Undoing Pushkin's *Boris Godunov*," *Slavic Review* 44, no. 2 (Summer 1985): 257–79. My discussions in this book sharpen the issues (and, to the best of my ability, correct misconceptions) laid out in those earlier versions of the argument. I have, in addition, visited "Boris talks" on easily a dozen conferences and institutions in the last five years. From each of them—and in particular from Yale University and Moscow's Gorky Institute—I came away much enriched by the feedback of students and colleagues. Even with the best dialogic intentions, it always seems something of a miracle when long-term research avoids being a lonely thing.

Chronology

1580	Marriage of Ivan IV (The Terrible) to a seventh wife, Maria Nagaia Marriage of Ivan IV's younger son, Fyodor, to Irina Godunova
1581	Ivan IV kills his elder son and heir
1582	Maria Nagaia gives birth to a son, Dmitri
1584	Death of Ivan IV; ascension of Fyodor De facto rule of Fyodor's brother-in-law, Boris Godunov
1589	Establishment of a Russian patriarchate
1591	Death of Tsarevich Dmitri in Uglich
1592	Birth of Tsarevna Feodosia, daughter of Tsar Fyodor and Irina Godunova
1594–97	Conventional starting-point of serfdom (legislation restricting peasants' right to leave their landlord)
1598	Death of Tsar Fyodor; end of Riurikovich dynasty *Zemsky sobor* elects Boris Godunov tsar
1601–1603	The great famine
1604	Dmitri the Pretender invades Moscovy from Poland
1605	Death of Boris, ascension of Fyodor Borisovich
1605	Triumph of the Pretender; Fyodor Borisovich and Maria Godunova put to death Ascension of the False Dmitri
1606	Dmitri deposed and put to death Ascension of Vasily Shuisky
1607	Appearance of the second False Dmitri
1610	Death of Tsar Vasily; invasion of Muscovy by Poles and Swedes with their own candidates for the Russian throne
1612	Liberation army gathers in the hinterland and expels the invaders
1613	Election of Michael Romanov as tsar

Genealogy

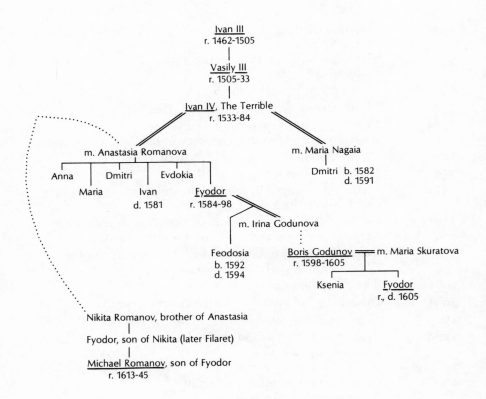

Ivan III
r. 1462-1505

Vasily III
r. 1505-33

Ivan IV, The Terrible
r. 1533-84

m. Anastasia Romanova

m. Maria Nagaia

Anna

Maria

Dmitri

Evdokia

Ivan
d. 1581

Fyodor
r. 1584-98

Dmitri b. 1582
d. 1591

m. Irina Godunova

Feodosia
b. 1592
d. 1594

Boris Godunov
r. 1598-1605

m. Maria Skuratova

Ksenia

Fyodor
r., d. 1605

Nikita Romanov, brother of Anastasia

Fyodor, son of Nikita (later Filaret)

Michael Romanov, son of Fyodor
r. 1613-45

BORIS

GODUNOV

I

Boris Godunov and a
Poetics of Transposition

THE RUSSIAN AESTHETIC IMAGINATION has often
turned for inspiration to its troubled past, but few
images in the nineteenth century achieved the visibility, and notoriety, of Boris Godunov. His story,
and that of his political rival Dmitri the Pretender,
inspired dozens of dramas, musical settings, poetic
sketches, historical novels, and tales. In this he resembles other mythic personalities in Russian history—Ivan the Terrible, Peter the Great, Pugachev.
What distinguishes Godunov, however, is the quality
and placement of the major versions of his story.

Boris Godunov figures prominently in the work
of Russia's first great popular historian, her greatest
poet, and one of her greatest composers. At the time of his death in
1826, Nikolai Karamzin had carried his *History of the Russian State* up
through the Time of Troubles. Its treatment of Boris Godunov became an exemplar for biography in this new "romantic-national" type
of history designed to ennoble a specifically Russian past. Out of
Karamzin's portrait Alexander Pushkin created his "romantic tragedy" *Boris Godunov* (1825)—a work Pushkin considered his masterpiece, and which was perceived by him as a self-consciously national,
Russian response to imported neoclassical norms in drama. Modest
Musorgsky adapted both Pushkin's and Karamzin's texts for the libretto to his greatest opera, *Boris Godunov* (1869–72)—which he offered as a national alternative to Western operatic models, his first step
toward a specifically Russian "people's musical drama." Each chose to
link the story of a famous national figure with an innovative, pur-
posely national form of art.

1

In its three greatest expressions, then, the Boris Tale was a vehicle for generic innovation. Each version asserted a specifically Russian concept of genre in opposition to the borrowed European models then reigning in the three disciplines: German historiography, French tragedy and melodrama, and Italian (or French-Italianate) opera. Each innovator hoped to find a new tradition, creatively transformed, in his respective discipline. As regards this final goal they did not succeed, at least within their own century. Karamzin's *History* was read by generations of literate Russians, its ideology held sway for a century, and its apparatus was indispensable for later historical research—but in terms of methodology there is no "Karamzin School" in Russian historiography. Pushkin's *Boris* went essentially without imitators and, even after the ban on stage performance was lifted in 1866, almost without successful productions. Musorgsky's *Boris* reached the larger world only through Rimsky-Korsakov's conservative reworking of both music and libretto in 1896 and 1908. The attempt to lay the foundation for a new Russian tradition resulted in each case in a brilliant cul-de-sac, a curiosity, and an occasion for spirited debate.

So popular did the saga of Boris Godunov become in the arts that only much later, and with some difficulty, was his image reconstituted on the basis of historical evidence. But this evidence, often contradicting the canonized biography, did not liberate Boris Godunov from his traditional plot. Paradoxically, it was often claimed that the truth of his story could be found precisely in art.

This argument, of course, has ancient credentials. At least since Aristotle, poetry has had a good defense in its debate with history. Art, so the argument runs, is not less true than history, but more universal. Whereas historians are limited by the particularity of found events, poets work with laws of plausibility—and thus the poeticized event is not just *different* from real experience but also more durable, and perhaps more valuable, as well. Literary works, in this construct, are also forms of knowledge.

In nineteenth-century Russia, this dialogue between history and poetry was recast by realist theorists of the novel. As Leo Tolstoy argued in his article on *War and Peace,* there could be no single standard to judge "historical" and "artistic" accounts of the same event.[1] But where the Aristotelian distinction privileged poetry as open, philosophical, of more serious import than history because it dealt with the general, Tolstoy sympathized with poetry for very different reasons. The historian, Tolstoy conceded, must select and arrange data from the outside world just like any other writer of narrative. But Tolstoy then argued that historians, although indeed limited by verifiable facts and "evidence," were nevertheless on balance *more* free, more arbitrary, than poets. Historians are permitted to assign significance to events, to draw abstractions, and to manipulate plot accordingly. True poets, on the other hand, must think away future significance. Contrary to Aristotle and Sidney, Tolstoy contended that it is the poet rather than the historian who must attend to the *truly* particular; the poet's task is to invent a world where, by its own inner logic, only certain things can happen.

What Tolstoy suggests here is that different genres, fictional *and* nonfictional, contain hidden assumptions about the nature of historical causality. For this and similar reasons, Tolstoy was often reluctant to designate the genres in which he worked: he realized that to label a genre was already to prefigure the field, to restrict the options of both author and reader in relation to the text.[2] The very choice of genre was a choice among various notions of plausibility, and each predetermined the value of actions occurring within its borders.

The twentieth century has had many articulate spokesmen for this idea, including Carl Becker, Erich Auerbach, Hayden White, and, among the Russians, Dmitri Likhachev and Mikhail Bakhtin. There is a link, these theorists argue, between the shape of a history and the shape of a narrative. The very mode of telling functions as a concealed vehicle of morality, causality, and value—and thus the choice of a genre already implies a conception of the historical process. Likewise, to make a point about history means to choose a genre that can tell the story in a particular way. Even in the earliest data-gathering stages, documentary evidence cannot be invoked as a *fact* (in the Rankean sense) but must be interpreted as a *text*.[3] And in the final stages, when a historical narrative is sufficiently well integrated into a culture to inspire counterversions, imitations, fictionalizations, and parodies, that narrative is the closest to functioning as a literary artifact. When the "same" story is retold in another genre, the meaning of events and personalities within it is transformed.

The Translatability of Narrative

This retelling of a narrative in different genres we will call transposition. In recent years, transposition and generic border-crossings have been the subject of many excellent studies—of history becoming drama, verbal narrative becoming opera, short story or novel becoming film.[4] But no real discussion of method has followed, and basic questions remain provocatively open. How do stories cohere as recognizable wholes in the process of a radical shift to a new language, genre, or medium? What sort of cumulative awareness of earlier versions is ascribed to the implied audience? And how does one celebrate a debt, but not necessarily a fidelity, to earlier versions—

which is to say, how does one create an *in*clusive unity among competing versions?

For several reasons, these questions resist an easy methodology. First, there is the inevitable confusion over the *status* of competing versions. In recent years, critical attention has shifted away from the intentionality of individual authors and toward questions of transmission, reception, and interdependence of texts. In influence studies where authors are working in closely kindred or identical genres—say, Gogol and Dostoevsky in the short prose narrative—techniques of criticism are quite sophisticated. In those instances we readily admit that to "copy" or "draw upon" another's words or plot is not necessarily to endorse them; quotation is not identification but more often stylization or parody.[5] Where generic conventions shift, overlap, and recombine in a single work, however, genuine coauthorship can make us uncomfortable. As Yuri Tynianov has argued in his essay on illustration,[6] an art form is excruciatingly specific. What makes verbal art concrete is quite different from, and often inimical to, the concreteness of visual or musical art. When the medium of telling shifts radically, criteria for evaluating the transposition and the nature of its coauthorship break down. If Makar Devushkin, hero of Dostoevsky's *Poor Folk,* is now seen as a comment upon and not a copy of Gogol's Akaky Akakievich, this is in part because the distance between short story and novel-in-letters is a negotiable one, well within the fictional and verbal realm. But broaden the gap in genre or medium, introduce thereby widely differing conventions and standards of validation, and comparison becomes increasingly arbitrary. With historical themes that have received masterly treatment in another medium— say, music or dance—the matter is further complicated by the prejudices we bring to quasi-fictional genres like sentimental history and quasi-literary genres like the libretto.

The critical history of transpositions and "adaptations" thus tends to be recriminatory. The most influential social critic of the 1830s and forties, Vissarion Belinsky, accused both Karamzin and Pushkin of misinterpreting sources to construct their versions of the Boris story; later, Mikhail Pogodin criticized Pushkin for repeating in his play the absurd slander of the chronicles, and still later Nikolai Strakhov lambasted Musorgsky for the violence he did to Pushkin. To this day, Tchaikovsky is accused of "destroying" Pushkin with his musical *Onegin* and Prokofiev of "insulting" Tolstoy with his operatic *War and Peace.*

There is a second problem with intergeneric comparisons, and this has to do with a confusion of "different kinds of differences."[7] Among the distinctions most often blurred is that between medium and genre. Problems ascribed to the one are often problems of the other. Discussions of transposition often delineate, for example, the move from novel to film.[8] But to see the shift along that axis is misleading. Film, unlike the novel, is not a genre but a medium. Its equivalent would be print, or marble, or the acoustic building blocks of music—not a sonata or a sonnet. Genre has its conventions, medium its material constraints. And thus analysis of a given narrative as short story and as adapted for film would have to take into consideration more than the brute move from print on a page to celluloid on a screen. That move itself can be inter- or intra-generic. Instances of a media shift within the same genre would be the move of a nineteenth-century novel into historical or romantic film, or the move from newspaper article to film documentary. Medium merely provides the material within which genre operates; genres themselves cross the medium barrier with little or no friction.

For the purposes of this study, then, some definition of genre is necessary that is essentially *conceptual,* not oriented toward medium. In narrative art forms this would be genre understood as a sort of prestructural matrix determining how an event is conceived, and how it is transmitted in stories. The literary theorist who has done the most to develop this understanding of generic specificity is Mikhail Bakhtin.

In his early writings of the 1920s, Bakhtin had already dismissed the traditional notion of genre as a hierarchy of literary forms embedded in a poetics. In its place he offered a concept both more comprehensive and less exclusively aesthetic. "Every genre represents a special way of constructing and finalizing a whole," Bakhtin wrote. "One might say that human consciousness possesses a whole series of inner genres for seeing and conceptualizing reality."[9] Genre, in this sense, is a category of consciousness. It is this category that governs what Hayden White deems the "essentially poetic acts" of the nineteenth-century historians discussed in his *Metahistory,*[10] and what (this present study will argue) governs the overtly poetic acts of all other transposers as well. In an essay from the 1930s Bakhtin gives this new concept of genre a name, *chronotope.*

The term itself, a post-Einsteinian neologism meaning "time-space unit," is a sort of shorthand for the conviction that the very structure of narrative carries within itself laws of causality and plausibility. Prior to every representation of reality, Bakhtin argues, the author of any form of narrative makes an assumption about the workings of time and space. These time-space matrices determine the kinds of events that can happen within their borders. Unlike time-space categories in Kantian thinking, the chronotope is not transcendental; on the contrary, it makes "narrative events concrete, makes them take on flesh, causes blood to flow in their veins. An event can be communicated, it becomes information, one can give precise data on the place and time of its occurrence."[11] Chronotopes can never be abstract. Therefore every chronotope inevitably contains an *evaluation*—that is, it inevitably delimits and individualizes the perspective from which the story is told. It constitutes a justification for the unstated causality that joins a series of events into a plausible narrative. As illustration of Bakhtin's technique, we might consider his treatment of the novel of the ancient world, the so-called Greek romance.

These are boy-meets-girl love stories with the love (at the beginning) and the marriage (at the end) interrupted by a vast number of adventures, often thousands of pages of them. None leaves any trace on the bodies or psyches of the heroes. Any number of improbable adventures can be included because, in the biographical sense, time does not add up; adventures are clocked only internally. Events are linked together not with any organic cause and effect but with a "suddenly," for the sequence of adventures is governed by pure chance. Human beings exercise no initiative in this world; they either endure or run. This Bakhtin calls "adventure time," and it requires a certain type of space. This space must be vast (for all the kidnappings and escapes), it must be abstract (since its link with time is purely fortuitous and mechanical), and it must be *strange*. This does not mean exotic; the exotic would engage too much of our attention and encourage us to think up our own, potentially logical stories. It must be simply strange, alien. An adventure-time world cannot be our own familiar world, because anything recognizably real might enter history, and anything historical restricts the power of chance. What, indeed, can be described in such a space? Only rarities, wonders, isolated curiosities. Things can have no consequences. Fifteen pages might be devoted to describing a crocodile, but then the crocodile is not heard of again.

What sort of human being could live in this time and space? A passive and unchanging one, whose primary task is "enforced movement through space"—that is, catching up or escaping. Bakhtin points out that such a hero, while passive, *is* alive and does endure; at the novel's end his identity, although not changed, is at least affirmed. But it is affirmed in a vacuum. Such heroes are all isolated private persons. There is no country or clan to occupy them, nothing larger than their private interests, and these are usually limited to being in love. The chronotope of Greek romances is a lonely one: "adventure time in an alien world."

The idea that spatiotemporal representation is linked in some way with genre does not, of course, originate with Bakhtin. But to Bakhtin belongs perhaps the boldest attempt to link types of action and forms of personal identity or biography with the various "chronotopic possibilities" available in a given cultural era. *Space* and *time* are the basic coordinates. But other contingent categories follow in close order. It is evident, for example, that a given sense of space and time is always accompanied by a particular concept of *action*. What can or cannot be done, what seems plausible or logical from within the narrative, what it means to *act* upon the environment are all functions of the spatial-temporal matrix. This specification of action, in its turn, carries assumptions about personality and the development of character. How does the passage of time affect the formation of a self?

This question was addressed in several distinct chronotopes in antiquity, Bakhtin notes, from the earliest Greek romance (where passage of time had no effect on personality at all) to later, more elaborate models for conceptualizing the lives of great men. Each model possessed, in addition to a temporal logic organizing its events, its own special space—a space at first exclusively public and proclaimed from the *agora,* but then increasingly private. Starting with the random "suddenlys" that linked biographical moments in the Greek romance, moving through the idealized images of rulers in Plutarch and Suetonius, and ending on the carnivalized rogues and fools of the Renaissance, Bakhtin shows how narrative heroes slowly accumulate linear paths, societal slots, private lives. As we shall see, the complex images of Boris Godunov and the Pretender partake of these chronotopic models for biography and the lives of kings, juxtaposing them in impossible ways to raise questions about the very nature of public greatness and a private self.

Not only genres, but even single works can have multiple chronotopes. It is through this "play of chronotopes," in fact, that an image of man emerges in a given work of art. "Chronotopicity" itself—that is, the degree to which events, plots, and motifs are related to the particular time and place of their occurrence—can be strong or weak in different authors, and in different periods of literary history. In Greek romance, as we have seen, chronotopicity is minimal. In Goethe, on the other hand, "everything [Bakhtin claims]. . . is time-space, authentic *chronotope.*"[12] Thus do time, space, action, and character condition and delimit one another in a given narrative. This complex whole is *perceived* as whole because the sum of these four factors implies an integrated sense of how things happen—that is, a sense of historical process.

In what other ways might Bakhtin's genre/chronotope framework be useful in studying transposed images in art? First and most generally, the chronotope makes sensible the constraints that operate on a given version of a story. If miracles occur in a medieval chronicle account of the tsarevich Dmitri's death at Uglich, this hardly attracts attention; a Saint's Life, after all, is a genre where miracles are normal, *real,* like talking animals in a beast fable. But if Karamzin relates that miracle as a seamless part of his historical narrative, or if Pushkin permits his fictive chronicler Pimen, while posing as a vehicle of truth in the play, to endorse this miracle and even to elaborate on it, then these are clues to a chronotopic complexity that must be sorted out before we can experience the artwork in any coherent way. Further, if we conceive of genre in terms of chronotope, then a shift in medium may or may not occasion a shift in genre. The important changes in a narrative take place not when the medium shifts but when the chronotope changes. Within a new chronotope the events may be the same, but the probability and significance of events happening in a certain way will have changed. There is a change in the evaluative aspect, the moral quality, of the narrative.

This is not, again, merely a matter of adjusting to the new prerequisites of a different medium. The famous nineteenth-century transpositions of the Boris Tale did, of course, involve replacing scholarly footnotes with stage directions and the pages of a book with the performance of musical spectacle. Singing a line is very different from reading it aloud, or to oneself. But in terms of the chronotopes governing those three versions, different cross-patternings emerge. Karamzin's concept of the hero appears to overlap with Musorgsky's; his Boris *can* be sung, while Pushkin's cannot. On the other hand, the sense of history that informs Musorgsky's opera seems to take its cue from Pushkin and not from Karamzin. The three works overlap in intriguing ways when considered as complex narratives, each combining elements of the other to create new fields of time and space within which action makes sense, or resists making sense, and value is created.

Transposition might in fact be the most vigorous commentary possible on another's work of art. It is that one category of "translation" where coauthorship is not hidden but rather celebrated, where the independence of the second voice is guaranteed by the new genre or medium, and where dialogue among versions is inevitably explicit. A good part of the audience's interest lies precisely in watching a multiple *co*authorship at work.

A study of the Boris transpositions—these three major statements, and the many dozens of minor versions—suggests that the changes each author wrought on his predecessors were indeed complex and calculated. Plot was not at issue; the audience was presumed to know the story. Karamzin's *History* provided an account of the Russian past that was as universally read as any the nineteenth century was to know. Variants on events contained in that *History* were no more responsible for "telling the whole story" than illustrations to a novel are meant to be read separately from the verbal text. The appeal was precisely in experiencing a familiar story under radically new conditions.

If Karamzin served as the historical source for innumerable "poeticizations" in the nineteenth century, then Pushkin became the poetic source for later and equally numerous transpositions. His texts were continually reworked as stage spectacle, opera, dance, dramatic dialogue. But whereas Karamzin was rifled for plots with relative impunity, Pushkin has found his angry defenders. His transposers are accused of "misunderstanding," "destroying," "violating" his texts. These charges are interesting, for they bear witness to our discomfort in evaluating reframed, reconceptualized versions. There is no reason, of course, why a derived text need be perceived as a threat or a distortion of an original. Pushkin is put in no danger by the existence of sentimental libretti drawing on his characters and occasionally on his verse. It could even be argued that Tchaikovsky, far from "misreading" Pushkin to create his operatic *Eugene Onegin,* in fact intended his composition to say something about the incompatibility of opera and novel. His subtitle to *Onegin,* "lyrical scenes," in fact suggests just that: portions of Pushkin's novel reworked in the lyric mode.[13] The existence of the opera *reconfirms* the uniqueness of Pushkin's novel, it does not undermine it.

Transposed versions compress intergeneric dialogue into a single multiply coded space. And thus, Bakhtin urges, one must not be reluctant to read out of context.[14] The full potential of artistic works, as well as their power to inspire new works, is only realized out of their original contexts and refracted through other visions. Masterpieces in a genre, powerful conceptualizations of a certain sort of time and space, always contain more than a given epoch can absorb. When these works are built upon in later times, different aspects of form emerge as significant and thus encourage different patterns of response, specific "counterversions." A theme is *freed* from one context into another, and this liberation is the first step in transposing a theme.

Across genres, in response to changing political needs and changing concepts of art, a known story accumulates new contexts and yet remains recognizably of one piece. The story of Boris Godunov, closely tied to problems of Russian national identity, has proved curiously central in the Russian attempt to achieve specifically Russian forms of art. It was one of the first historical tales to capture the imagination of the nineteenth-century reading public, at a time when Russia as a whole was witnessing an explosive interest in national history. Chronicles and state documents were being published in unprecedented quantities. The invasion and defeat of Napoleon had

promoted a vigorous and self-conscious patriotism, which was reinforced by the romantics' call for *narodnost'*, or national consciousness,
in art. In the 1830s Russia's first generation of professional historians,
alert to the expanded role of Russia in Europe, sought heroic figures
from their own national past that might elevate the image of Russia in
the eyes of their own people as well as the West.

This search for a national identity through a re-creation of the
past was, to be sure, a general European project. But it was pursued
with particular intensity in Russia, where there has always been a
special orientation toward historical experience. The past has weighed
heavily on Russia's present. In part this is a function of official censorship; a common mode of talking about the present has been by
talking about the past, and this allegorical imperative imposes itself as
vigorously on audiences as on authors. There is also the general
preoccupation of the Russian intelligentsia with their nation's identity,
and the presumption that certain historical periods hold the key. But a
larger reason embraces all of these: to a much greater extent than
Americans, Russians have tended to believe in a closed future. What a
nation can become is dependent upon what it was. Thus history is a
passionate and sometimes dangerous pursuit, taken very seriously,
and rewritten (often on command) in the faith that the shape of the
past can determine the possibilities for the future. Events of a distant
time—the role of the Normans in founding Kievan Rus, for example,
or the authorship of the twelfth-century epic "Lay of the Host of
Igor"—become urgent *contemporary* issues.[15] Their integration into
some larger historical scheme takes on an immediate and practical
significance.

When a historical event becomes the theme of a poetic retelling,
other conventions come into play. Poetic works have always fulfilled
many nonaesthetic functions in Russian culture. The poet has been
not just artist but also prophet and spokesperson for the nation. And
thus artistic representations of the past are doubly burdened with
significance: as history they answer to the future, and as art they
continually call into question their own fictionality and become commentary on the present. One can hardly imagine *Ivanhoe* being debated in England in a way that would have had significance for Whigs
and Tories. Such, however, is the common fate of Russian works of
historical fiction. The story of Boris Godunov, belonging equally to
history and to art, has been the uneasy beneficiary of both these
powerful traditions of reception.

The three major nineteenth-century retellings of the Boris Tale
thus constitute a case study in the problem of versions. Considerable
scholarship has already been devoted to documenting "who got what
from whom" in the Boris Tale; the critical literature is rich in scene-by-

scene comparisons. That work, while indispensable, will not be repeated here. The focus will be rather on the dialogue between the works, and on the possibility of devising meaningful grounds for relating them to one another. Moving a single story through different genres over time has been seen, by Roman Jakobson and others, as a category of translation.[16] And indeed, students of intergeneric shift could learn from recent developments in translation theory. Researchers in translation have begun to shift their attention from objective linguistic structures toward more intersubjective factors, or norms; in a similar way, one might study cultural artifacts for their "translatability" into different systems, and for their capacity to survive in different eras as contextually sensitive concepts.[17] This is not to suggest that designed, authored versions of a familiar plot can be treated, say, as folklorists treat found versions of a folktale. But it is to suggest that plots and texts survive in a culture because they have *currency*. This is currency in both senses of that word: wide circulation and value. Texts live only as they are cited, recited, republished, and as they become a source of allusions and shared metaphor. Perhaps even more than the telling of a new story, the retelling of an old familiar story is perceived as context-specific. In Russia especially, with its traditionally high expectations of art, of history, and of the public's power to make art politically meaningful, a reason would always be found for reminding us of that story *just now*. The audience, freed from the necessity of wondering "what will happen next" or "how it will end," inevitably reads through the plot to some other text—and, remembering that text, recasts it in light of contemporary needs.

Boris Godunov and the False Dmitri: An Overview

In 1580, Tsar Ivan the Terrible celebrated a double wedding: his own to Maria Nagaia, who became his seventh wife, and his younger son, Fyodor's, to Irina Godunova. Irina and her brother, Boris, were wards of the tsar and intimates of the royal family. A year later Tsar Ivan killed his elder son and heir in a fit of rage; the following year, Maria gave birth to a son, Dmitri. When Tsar Ivan died in 1584 there were thus two claimants to the throne: Fyodor, who was feeble-minded, and a two-year-old infant.

Fyodor assumed the throne with the understanding that his competent and ambitious brother-in-law, Boris, would rule. Boris did rule for fourteen years—and, in the assessment of most contemporary chroniclers and current historians—with intelligence and foresight. He made peace with Lithuania, created a Russian patriarchate, strengthened Russia's diplomatic ties with Europe, and kept in check the Tatar raids from the south. Halfway through Fyodor's reign, in 1591, the tsar's nine-year-old half-brother, Dmitri, in royal exile in Uglich, was found one May day in the palace courtyard with his throat slit. The boy was an epileptic. An official commission investigated and attributed the death to self-inflicted wounds during a fit that came upon the child while he was playing with knives.

Irina Godunova bore Tsar Fyodor only one child, a girl (1592) who did not survive her second year. When Fyodor died in 1598, the Riurikovich dynasty therefore came to an end. After some delicate maneuvering among the boyars and a show of reluctance on the part of Boris, an Assembly of the Land elected Boris tsar. For three years his reign was relatively peaceful. It was marked, however, by the perpetual scheming of the princely families (the Shuiskys and Mstislavskys), many of whom resented an untitled boyar on the throne of Russia.

In 1601, a series of natural disasters—floods and a killing frost in August—ruined the harvests throughout Russia. In Muscovy of the time, crop failure was hardly uncommon. But in a normal cycle bad years alternated with good ones, permitting the poor peasant to sustain losses and still not be ruined. In the early seventeenth century all of Europe suffered a general cooling of the climate for several consecutive years. For Russia, with her subsistence agriculture and already marginal growing season, this spelled disaster. By 1603, Russian villages had nothing to sow. It was the first major famine to occur in conjunction with enserfment, that is, after the Decree of 1597 anulling the traditional right of peasants to leave their masters on St. George's Day. Starvation was coupled with immobility. According to accounts of contemporaries, something like one-third of the population of Muscovy perished.

This social crisis coincided with Boris's tenure on the throne. He did what he could to alleviate the suffering, opening state coffers of grain and severely punishing hoarders. Boris also took measures against many princely and boyar families, especially the Romanov clan, accusing them of witchcraft and treason. Many were exiled to Siberia, forbidden to marry, or forcibly tonsured. As peasant unrest rose, Boris strengthened his internal police with a wide network of informers.

At some time in the early spring of 1602, a young man turned up in Poland claiming to be the tsarevich Dmitri, miraculously saved from the attempt on his life at Uglich in 1591. This Pretender, identified by the Muscovite authorities as the runaway monk Grigory Otrepiev, had apparently been at one time in the service of the Romanovs. He was also the veteran of several monasteries, where his skill at transcribing books and composing sacred canons had attracted some attention; in the prestigious Monastery of the Miracles he had even served for a year as deacon. Once across the border, Grigory had some initial difficulty finding a patron. But historical circumstances came to his aid. The southern reaches of Muscovy were on the brink of peasant war; the countryside was demoralized, the Don Cossacks in open revolt. In Poland—a traditional rival always ready to exploit Russian weakness—enough ambitious parties were found willing to make of this Pretender a pretext for war. Grigory gained the sympathy of a portion of the Polish diet, as well as the unofficial support of King Sigismund. On both sides of the border, then, the Pretender found himself riding a wave of anti-Godunov sentiment.

In 1604 the False Dmitri, with a Polish fiancée and newly converted to Catholicism, invaded Muscovy with a motley crew of Polish adventurers, Cossacks, and disgruntled peasants. The forces of Tsar Boris, vastly superior in arms and men, defeated the Pretender—who fled and hid in Putivl, expecting the worst. But the tsar's army failed to follow up on its victory, and Cossacks continued to capture towns in the name of the Pretender. Dmitri survived the winter and was reinforced in the spring by a full-scale peasant uprising in the south. Town after town declared for the Pretender, and key leaders in Boris's own military staff defected.

As the Pretender was marching on Moscow, in April 1605, Boris suddenly died. His family and his dynasty could not have been left in a more precarious position. Sixteen-year-old Fyodor Borisovich, the tsarevich, ascended the throne, only to be mutilated and strangled by victorious rebel troops two months later. His sister, the tsarevna Ksenia, was, according to popular legend, raped by the Pretender and then shorn as a nun. This violation and murder of children—Dmitri of Uglich in the beginning, the Godunov adolescents at the end—became a central motif of the Boris Tale.

The False Dmitri reigned for scarcely a year. He antagonized the Russians with his pro-Polish sentiments, Catholic masses in the Kremlin, and his scandalously non-Orthodox wife. Then he too was put to death, his ashes shot from a cannon in the direction of Poland, and Prince Vasily Shuisky crowned. Domestic chaos invited foreign intervention; both Poland and Sweden invaded with their own candidates for the Russian throne. A second False Dmitri appeared and full-scale civil war raged. After half a dozen years of devastation, in 1612, a "national liberation" army coalesced in the hinterland and, at great cost, drove out the invaders. This *Smuta*, too palely rendered as a "Time of Troubles," did not come to an end until the election of Michael Romanov in 1613. The new dynasty—founded on the ashes of a decade of pretenders, invasion, peasant revolt, and famine—survived until 1917.

Aestheticizing the Boris Tale

This complex and colorful time has appealed powerfully to artists, both in Russia and elsewhere. Over a hundred dramas have survived on the Boris/Demetrius theme alone.[18] Curiously, the first was written by Lope de Vega (*El Gran Duque de Moscovia*, 1607–13), while news of Tsar Dmitri's ultimate fate was still wending its way to Spain. The Germans have been particularly attentive to the Pretender; at least since Schiller's fragment *Demetrius* (1805) they have considered him to a certain extent their own.[19] German playwrights tend to see Dmitri, not Boris, as the hero of the tale. Dmitri is perceived less as the Russian Pretender than as a universalized romantic rebel—an incarnation of Faust. His pretense is read as positive heroism, for through it man becomes free to *assume*, not merely passively accept, his identity.

This aspect of Dmitri's pretendership received eloquent treatment in German literature as late as Rilke. *Die Aufzeichnungen des Malte Laurids Brigge* evokes, in fact, an almost classic German image of the Russian Pretender. Dmitri would have survived, Rilke writes, if he had refused to recogize the nun Marfa as his mother, if he had had the strength to continue being "no one's son":

> . . . But did not his uncertainty begin with the very fact that she acknowledged him? I am not disinclined to believe that the strength of his transformation lay in his no longer being anyone's son.
>
> The people, which defined him without picturing anyone in particular, made him only more free and more unbounded in his possibilities. But his mother's declaration, even though a conscious deception, still had the power to belittle him; it lifted him out of the fulness of his inventions; it limited him to a weary imitation; it reduced him to the individual he was not, it made him an imposter.[20]

The Russians, on the other hand, have preferred Boris as hero. While Russian Demetrius-dramas do exist—Khomiakov, Ostrovsky, and Suvorin wrote excellent ones[21]—their Dmitris tend not to be heroic pretenders in the German sense. They are trapped and tormented tsars, variations on Boris. Representative of this overlap are the two character sketches of Boris and the Pretender (#60 and #61) by Pushkin's contemporary Kondraty Ryleev in his *Dumy* or "Reflections."[22] The two portraits are almost identical: two conscious-stricken monarchs, kept awake nights by dreams of shed blood. More central to the Russian view of Boris, it seems, has been a suffering tsar caught between personal guilt and an enlightened rule unable to cancel out that guilt.

This theme figured prominently in nineteenth-century Slavophile ideology. Slavophiles frequently perceived tsars as secular

Christs who assumed the guilt of the world, thus removing from the people the compromising responsibilities of power. Boris, in so many ways a gifted ruler, was thus doubly burdened. He was perceived not only as tsar, but as tsarecide. The death at Uglich, which made possible the glory of his reign, also poisoned that reign. From here it is a short step to that larger category soon to prove so congenial to Russian literature, the theme of the great man who commits a crime for a Christian purpose. Boris Godunov is thus linked with Napoleon (viewed as another "false tsar" and destroyer of dynasties) and with those later distinguished protagonists of ends justifying means, Raskolnikov and the Grand Inquisitor. In his person, Boris paradoxically joins an ancient, Orthodox defense of autocracy with the more contemporary image of Napoleon the Usurper.

This rich blend of traditional and contemporary motifs might explain why the Boris Tale is so often rewritten in the nineteenth century. But there are other, more directly sociohistorical reasons for its peculiar resonance. As a historical phenomenon, Boris is something of a bridge figure, reigning at a time when the very idea of secular history was being born in medieval Russia.[23] He does not fit comfortably into any of the categories created by the three major periods of reassessment in Russian historical thought: the sifting of the chronicles after Ivan IV, the utilitarian history of the Petrine era, or the nineteenth-century efforts toward a scientific and national history. Caught between the two great mythic forces of Ivan the Terrible and Peter the Great, between oriental despot and westernizing monarch, the received image of Boris combines elements of both. Boris was married to the daughter of Tsar Ivan's henchman Maliuta Skuratov, dread commander of the *oprichniki* or secret police, but at the same time he sent young men abroad to study and dreamed of founding a Russian university. This progressive aspect of Godunov's image has been canonized in scenes of Boris with his children: the tsarevna Ksenia lamenting the death of her Danish bridegroom, the tsarevich Fyodor studying a map. But the *oprichnik* element is always present. It is forcefully spoken by Prince Shuisky in the bitter lines on Boris that open Pushkin's play:

> Yesterday's slave, Maliuta's son-in-law,
> The son-in-law of a hangman and himself a hangman at heart. . . .

And Boris's wife, Maria Skuratova, by most historical accounts a modest and virtuous woman, is depicted in some chronicles and in Aleksei K. Tolstoy's drama *Tsar Boris* as a torturer, who throws a burning candle into the nun Marfa's face when the latter refuses to disavow the Pretender as her son.[24]

The complex image of Boris Godunov complements another watershed in Russian historiography just predating the Time of Troubles: the emergence of individual personality in the biographies of tsars.[25] It is of course true that the relationship between a life as lived and as narrated by a given biography is always tentative, reflecting the interests and values of the biographer and his times. The tale of Boris Godunov, however, was victim to a series of quite special constraints and filters. As we shall see in chapter 2, historical evidence now suggests that Boris was probably innocent of the death of the tsarevich in Uglich. But powerful political and religious forces conspired early in the seventeenth century to "confirm" Boris's guilt. Dmitri of Uglich was canonized by Tsar Vasily Shuisky in 1606, and henceforth Boris Godunov became, in the eyes of the church, both tsarecide and *sviatoubiitsa,* murderer of a saint. Civilian authorities were equally ungenerous to his memory. Once on the throne the Romanovs, persecuted by Tsar Boris, lost no time in proscribing the Godunov name. It is hardly surprising that Karamzin, working with two centuries of chronicles and state documents for his well-annotated *History,* ended his chapter on the Fall of Boris with the cry: "Thus was God's punishment brought to bear on the murderer of the True Dmitri, and a new punishment began for Russia under the scepter of a False one!"[26]

One task of scholarship has indeed been to recover the historical Boris Godunov from the legends canonized by chronicle and song. It is a task to which Sergei Platonov, early twentieth-century revisionist historian of the Time of Troubles, devoted a good part of his career. But of equal interest are the reasons why Boris's story lent itself to such elaboration, and why, after more reliable data became available, the presumption of guilt persisted. In part, of course, his traditional biography reflected a popular romantic plot: the tragic hero or hero-villain, tormented by a terrible crime on his conscience, is pursued by the avenging image of his innocent victim. In part, too, the authority of the three great artistic treatments preempted any merely documented account of the theme. The tale had become legitimate as more than a fiction. To understand its peculiar durability in Russia, however, we must also look at one of the governing metaphors for the entire Time of Troubles: *samozvanstvo,* "self-calling" or pretendership.

By the end of the sixteenth century, Muscovy had begun to shift from governance by the royal family to governance by a central political power. The Russian peasant was being fastened to the land; decrees restricting peasant movement were issued in the late 1580s and nineties during Godunov's regency. The years following were fraught with popular unrest. During this period, Boris held the unhappy distinction of being Russia's first elected tsar. Not born to the throne, not even of princely blood, he had to create his own legitimacy at every step—and be created by others. His biography was inevitably more secular, more political, than that of the earlier Muscovite rulers, and thus it was uniquely available for psychological individuation. What picture does Karamzin cull from the sources? As we shall see, it is the portrait of a lonely, ambitious man, raised from obscurity by a violent and suspicious tsar, who was throughout his life (but especially at the end) deeply superstitious and dependent on sorcery and denunciation when crisis struck or when faith in his own rightness to rule abandoned him. It is no accident that Boris Godunov, the first elected Russian tsar, was challenged by Dmitri, the first pretender to the Russian throne. Both tsar and people were undergoing a crisis in identity.

During such times, ancient formulas and popular prototypes are activated to anchor incomprehensible events. Several have held sway over the biography of Boris, uneasily coexisting and shifting from century to century as his story is progressively transposed. There is, first, the general appeal of pretendership on Russian soil. "*Samozvanstvo,*" the Soviet scholar Vladimir Turbin has written, "is a profoundly Russian phenomenon, in art and in life."[27] Certain classes of Russians—especially Cossacks and peasants of the southern and southeastern steppe—have shown a predictable willingness to follow pretenders, and pretenders of a special sort. The most successful imposters, for all their courtly pretensions, have been creatures of wide open spaces, wanderers who ignite the countryside against the city. The city ultimately defeats them (the dominant image remains Pugachev, carried to the capital in a cage), but even when failure is inevitable, a stratified and enserfed Russia has tended to honor caprice, escape from identity, miracles. Boundless hope is combined with boundless pity, a profoundly Orthodox fusion.

Such pity underlies the second prototype at work in the Boris Tale, the myth of the passion-sufferer (*strastoterpets*) and its companion myth of the Saintly Prince. Dmitri of Uglich came to be viewed as the last of the martyred princes in an Orthodox pantheon stretching back to Boris and Gleb, Andrei Bogoliubsky, and Michael of Tver.[28] It was this lineage, as much as the fact of being Ivan IV's son, that eventually provided the organic link with the past so desired once the ancient dynasty became extinct. The life of Dmitri mattered less than the ritual spectacle of his nonresisting, inevitable death.

At the time of his appearance in Russia, the False Dmitri drew on another and incompatible myth. This was the legend of the "True Deliverer," the man of royal birth who emerges from exile or disguise to reverse a wicked policy and save his people.[29] Clearly, both myths could not function simultaneously as "true": Dmitri could not be murdered at Uglich and then return later as the True Dmitri, the living son of Ivan. It is not so much Dmitri, therefore, as it is the very plot that is a pretender. Keeping its incompatible parts together requires a leap of faith, a unifying of opposites characteristic of supernatural explanations and resurrections.

Russia was, and remained into the nineteenth century, fertile ground for this sort of faith. It is worth noting that in the century following the French Revolution Russia was the last remaining major European nation where a pretender to the throne could still have real political consequences. This could be seen as an inevitable factor in a state system where absolute power had always been vested in individual personality. Pushkin finished his *Boris* during 1825, a year rife with rumors of anointed tsars having died, having feigned death, having left no clear successor.[30] The Decembrist Revolt, it must be remembered, was triggered by confusions about legitimacy.

Other reasons for the appeal of *samozvanstvo*, especially among cultured Russians of the period, have been suggested by Yuri Lotman.[31] By the late eighteenth century, Lotman argues, the growth of a money economy, the phenomenon of favoritism at court, and the social mobility made possible by civil service had effected a great change in the psychology of ambition. New models of behavior emerged for both real-life and literary heroes. Unlike the picaresque protagonist, whose ambition was limited to changing his own status in an unchanging world, the modern hero now saw his personal activity capable of changing the world. Chance, and all games of chance (gambling), enjoyed new authority. Characteristic of this behavioral model were a short memory, a dislike of one's own biography, and a privileging of others' space. In the society of Nikolaevan Russia, where social fictions and "pretendings" played such a large role, *samozvanstvo* was almost first nature.

These sociopolitical factors left their mark on the literature of the period, where the theme of pretendership began to be associated with the theme of identity. The great prototypes are Gogol's "Diary of a Madman" and Dostoevsky's "The Double"; in the second half of the century, the themes of False Napoleon and False Tsar found their culmination in Raskolnikov and in the "Ivan the Tsarevich" chapter of *The Possessed*. It had become routine to explore personal identity through metaphors of political imposture.

Pretendership is indeed at the center of most versions of the Boris Tale. Part of the obsessive attraction of this tale in Russia has been its plot with a triple identity crisis. Boris the Usurper, the False Tsar, is challenged by a False Dmitri. But even the real tsarevich of Uglich is something of a false tsarevich, being the son of Ivan IV's seventh wife and thus technically illegitimate by Orthodox church law, which sanctioned only three marriages. Everywhere one turns in this tale authority begins to slip, and the inevitable question must be confronted: what constitutes a true sanction to rule? Is a usurper of a usurper a restorer, or just another usurper? A related complication arises in the very person, or rather the personality, of the False Dmitri. Most historians concur that he was indeed a pretender; but many also contend that he genuinely believed himself to be the son of Ivan the Terrible. Can we become what we believe ourselves to be? The complex issue of guilt, long canonic for the tale, is thus modified and undermined by the problem of identity.

Both Boris and Dmitri seek confirmation of "who they are" in outside forces. But Boris is the most complex loser in this legitimacy crisis, and therein lies the particular richness of his fate, its potential psychologization. The terrible lesson of the Boris story is that he loses both ways. If the tsarevich was indeed murdered at Uglich, then Boris (as the only party who stood to gain) is presumed guilty, and subject to hallucinations of the slain child. If, on the contrary, Dmitri escaped death at Uglich, then Boris is at least innocent of tsarecide—but nevertheless stands to be deposed by a rightful heir to the throne. The myth of Boris has thus lent itself to a sort of Freudian reading that draws no distinction between deed and intent to deed: we are punished for our guilt all the same.

This painful quest for personal identity, culminating in a revelation of past crimes that are then projected onto all of society, gave the Boris Tale the static completeness of a Greek tragedy enacted on Russian soil. The Slavophile Ivan Kireevsky observed precisely this about Pushkin's *Boris*.[32] Two filicides frame the story, the death of Tsarevich Dmitri at the beginning and of young Fyodor Borisovich at the end. Trapped between the murders of these child-tsars is the tormented father, pursued by fate, dimly aware that his willingness to die is not enough; innocent blood can only be redeemed by more innocent blood, and the death of Tsar Ivan's son in Uglich will require the sacrifice of his own son. Godunov's fall makes possible the House of Romanov. Beneath this somber plot, then, is the ancient myth of the founding of states on the blood of innocent child-martyrs.[33] Perceiving the story as in fact another Theban tragedy, the German dramatist Paul Ernst set his *Demetrios* (1905) in Ancient Greece, with the death of the tyrant Nabis (Boris), and later of Demetrios, dramatizing the fall of the ruling house of Sparta.[34]

We see, therefore, that the basic elements of the Boris story can be fitted into a number of different genres and conventions of telling: Saint's Life, Greek tragedy, romantic melodrama, political allegory. Competition between these different chronotopic images was a matter of some import for several nineteenth-century minds. There is the curious phenomenon of Karamzin's treatment, of which more in the following chapter, where two incompatible purposes come into conflict in a single history: documents conscientiously cited in the *Primechaniia* (Notes) do not always affect the moral shape of the actual narrative. It has thus been possible to draw two distinct histories from Karamzin's text, and in fact this is routinely done: historians use the notes, poets the narrative. Pushkin, significantly, drew on both—and perhaps the notes were for him the more important. Other writers, responding to Karamzin, have hesitated among traditionally fictional or nonfictional modes for retelling the tale. Mikhail Pogodin, for example, emerged in the 1830s as the historian most committed to opposing Karamzin's (and Pushkin's) image of Boris. As a nine-year-old boy reading Karamzin, he had suddenly been struck with the necessity of Boris's innocence.[35] Communicating this conviction ultimately became a question of genre. Noting in his diary that "he had begun to write a scholarly article . . . but tragedy rose to the top,"[36] Pogodin eventually found a compromise between drama and historical monograph in a "history in voices," *Istoriia v litsakh o Borise Godunove*.[37]

As with so many frequently transposed themes, the tale seemed to contain a truth and a potential that begged to be set free from the documented facts of historical narrative. It encouraged generic innovation, threshold treatment. At the end of the century, Aleksei Suvorin, amateur historian, wrote several essays and monographs on the Time of Troubles—and then finally a play on the Pretender and Ksenia Godunova. In one of his early essays on the Pretender,[38] Suvorin specifically recommended to students of *samozvanstvo* that they look at history *as* literature. Suvorin was convinced that Dmitri, alis Otrepiev, was in fact the son of Ivan the Terrible. Putting together his case for the escape from Uglich (which includes some provocative thoughts on the nature of epilepsy and "temporary death"), Suvorin admitted that he lacked the necessary documented proof (5–6). But what are documents? Suvorin asks. Chronicles, government reports, memoirs—is this evidence reliable? Documents are merely traces of "the life of the time, so full of whim and violence . . ." (96). Suvorin intended his own play, *Tsar Dmitri Samozvanets i Tsarevna Ksenia* (1904), to be a sort of pyschological document exploring the effect on Ksenia of Dmitri's conviction that he was the true tsarevich. To understand the Pretender, Suvorin argues, read the play—or, better still, read the earlier play that had elevated pretendership into an art, Gogol's *Inspector General*. Dmitri was Russia's first Khlestakov.

Historians will resist this methodology, he admits.

History is a serious science . . . but all the same I say that *The Inspector General* will be read when no one any longer reads serious historians and their very names are forgotten. An artistic work is distinguished from a historical work by precisely this: it lives much longer, becomes general property, and preserves in itself, alongside its poetic merits, a historical significance as well. . . ."(2)

Suvorin's celebration of literary "truth" and his scepticism toward the objectivity of all sources is a characteristic feature of the Boris Tale, where the theme of pretendership so often implicates the very form and status of historical fact. In effect, the "pretender"—fiction—has achieved legitimacy.

The innovative genre Pushkin devised for *his* retelling of the tale, "romantic tragedy," was both an irritant and a stimulant to nineteenth-century dramaturgy. The play's apparently eccentric defiance of all canon became a challenge to subsequent playwrights. Dozens of dramas on the Boris/Dmitri theme were written in Russia after 1830, and each entered into its own eerie dialogue with Pushkin. Each was bent inevitably by ideological currents in the particular decade of its retelling. Aleksei Khomiakov's 1833 *Dimitrii Samozvanets,* for example, was conceived in the heat of the Polish Uprising and presents a Slavophile-chauvinist perspective on events, the grim portrait of an idealistic Dmitri amid hostile and conniving Polish Catholics. Mikhail Lobanov's 1835 *Boris Godunov* is a monarchist version, written in angry answer to Pushkin, with Romanovs in the role of hero and a holy fool who delivers rhetorical speeches on Russia's glorious destiny. Aleksei K. Tolstoy's *Dramatic Trilogy* of the 1860s—and especially its final play, *Tsar Boris*—is a Westernizer's Boris, a product of the Emancipation decade and a meditation on the possibilities of progress for Russia. Aleksandr Fedotov's little-known play *The Godunovs* (written 1868, published 1884) is a mystical-Christian Boris play for a more reactionary era: in its final scene, the tsareva Ksenia witnesses the death of her family and awaits her own awful fate with a prayer on her lips: "Forgive them, for they know not what they do."[39]

Any accumulation, through time, of reworkings on the same theme suggests larger questions about the general nature of cultural tradition. On what grounds does a work enter a tradition, and by what mechanism does the tradition evolve? How closely is national tradition tied to national language? A good case is provided by the dramatist Henry von Heiseler, Russian-born and educated but living and writing in Germany, who began in 1911 to translate Pushkin's dramatic works into German.[40] In 1922 he wrote his own version of the Boris Tale, *Die Kinder Godunofs,* a play with complex bonds to Tolstoy's and Fedotov's images of Boris as well as to Pushkin's. The German tradition—harking back to Schiller and celebrating the tragic heroism of the Pretender—is little in evidence. Heiseler wrote in German but he must be considered part of the Russian tradition, and part of the evolution of Pushkin's *Boris*.

What an audience is presumed to know, and its attitude toward translation procedures, can profoundly change the nature of the tradition in which a work is perceived.[41] Consider, for example, two plays by Aleksandr Sumarokov, his *Hamlet* (1748) and his *Dmitrii Samozvanets* (1771), a version of the Boris Tale. The former has little in common with Shakespeare's text, the latter even less in common with the facts (as then known) of the Time of Troubles. But the two plays greatly resemble each other; they are variations on a single plot familiar and readily acceptable to audiences of the eighteenth century.[42] That age had its own understanding of both translation and borrowing. Borrowing was so widespread that there was almost no concept of plagiarism,[43] but at the same time translation was a much more creative category than we know it today. Translators were expected to adapt and alter the text, bearing as they did a moral responsibility to transmit, via received texts, the values appropriate to their society. Sumarokov's *Hamlet* is read today as an absurd distortion of Shakespeare; in its own time, however, it was attacked as too derivative, too similar to Elizabethan models and insufficiently imbued with the spirit of the Greek and Roman classics.[44] Sumarokov was *proud* of the fact that his text did not resemble Shakespeare's.

Likewise, Sumarokov produced for the eighteenth century a thoroughly acceptable re-creation of history in his *Dmitrii Samozvanets*. It was only fifty years later, with the vast movement of Shakespeare into French and German and with the advent of Karamzin's and Pushkin's powerful versions of the Boris Tale, that both Sumarokov's dramas entered new traditions. Sumarokov's *Dmitrii* became the first in a long list of Russian Boris/Dmitri dramas. It was retroactively reclassified, almost re-authored, and—in the light of its illustrious successors—invariably discredited.

Determining the chronology of this tradition of Boris transpositions is not always an easy task. Consider just one example, Pushkin's *Boris Godunov*. This problematic literary version of the tale emerged, in effect, three times, and *into* three different times. It was written in 1825, published in 1831, and first staged (although incompletely) in 1870. The play was received differently at each juncture, and against very different political and social events that tended to highlight different aspects of the work; the Decembrist Revolt of 1825, the Polish Uprisings of 1830 and 1863, the Emancipation of the serfs and rise of terrorism in the 1860s and seventies.

As permanent background to the century's culture there was, in addition, the factor of censorship, and the interaction of plagiarism with political power. Faddei Bulgarin, minor novelist, government censor, and employee of the Third Section, was effective in "delaying" the publication of Pushkin's *Boris Godunov* for six years. Bulgarin's own historical novel *Dimitrii Samozvanets* (1830) was published, with no delays, one year before Pushkin's play appeared. It was widely believed at the time that Bulgarin drew heavily on Pushkin's characterizations for his own version—embodying them, of course, in his own uninspired prose.[45] The play that was actually published in 1831, moreover, was not the one Pushkin had written in 1825. There was a different ending; Pushkin himself omitted two scenes, and the censor suppressed one entire additional scene as well as many individual lines.[46] Reprintings of the play in subsequent collections of Pushkin's works (1838, 1855, 1859) restored some of the material, either in the text of the play or in notes. Each of these new and slightly different editions became "the play," and the starting point for new commentary and public response.

Alongside, then, the genuine reworking of a theme—that is, the phenomenon of a Khomiakov or Lobanov supplementing or refuting an earlier version with a new composition—there is also the more subtle "re-authoring" that occurs when a text is reissued or read in a newly receptive context. These contexts had complicated effects on later transpositions of the theme. The fate of Boris Godunov in music offers one instructive example.

Musorgsky began work on his opera *Boris Godunov* in 1868, two years after the lifting of the ban on stage performances of Pushkin's play. Very likely he was encouraged in this operatic project by the loosening of censorship toward his source text. But the actual production of Pushkin's play was delayed four years (prohibitions had to be surmounted concerning patriarchs and monks appearing on stage), and the premiere performance of the play on 17 September 1870— cut to sixteen scenes—was a failure.[47] When Musorgsky submitted his opera to the Mariinsky Theater in October 1870, that theater was still smarting from the debacle of Pushkin's play a mere month earlier. Its Repertory Committee was justifiably suspicious of a libretto based on the same unpromising text. What had been a spur to action, the new "legal" status of Pushkin's play, now became an impediment.[48]

The committee rejected Musorgsky's opera (although not, of course, for that reason alone) and this sent the composer back to work on his score. In his revised version Musorgsky incorporated more scenes from Pushkin's original, but preserved much less of Pushkin's actual text. The debate among musicologists, unresolved and unresolvable, over Musorgsky's "original" intentions is in part a function of this shifting status of earlier versions.

The ultimate triumph of Musorgsky's musical *Boris* raises other interesting issues. By the second decade of the twentieth century, the operatic version of the Boris Tale had eclipsed all others.[49] Beginning in 1908 with Diaghilev's production of the Rimsky-Korsakov version in Paris, and aided by the vocal magic of Fyodor Chaliapin, *Boris Godunov* quickly became for the Western world a work that had always been sung. The musical *Boris* profoundly penetrated Russian contexts as well. It has proved almost impossible to peel away the ponderous sets and majestic music of Musorgsky's operatic *Boris* and get back to Pushkin's play. One who tried was the great theater director Vsevolod Meyerhold; in 1925–26, and then again in 1936, he rehearsed two productions of Pushkin's play.

High on Meyerhold's list of priorities was to de-operatize the play, to give it the swiftness, lightness, and loneliness of Pushkin's text.[50] He had his actors moving impetuously through a stripped-down set, their faces appearing sometimes at a window, their torsos at a door. A small and wiry Pimen relished retelling the Uglich murder while yawning and scratching himself in his bright, cozy monk's quarters. Boris appeared in his famous scene in a dirty smock, exhausted (there had been no time to wash, things were falling apart), surrounded by wailing soothsayers, hunchbacks, magicians, hot metal hissing in water, all sorts of prophetic rituals and chants. The tsar's famous monologue on "achieving supreme power" could hardly be heard above the clamor.[51] Meyerhold was waging war against the grandeur and heroicization of the operatic *Boris*.

Sergei Prokofiev was commissioned to compose incidental music for Meyerhold's 1936 production.[52] The composer greatly admired Musorgsky, but was determined to return *Boris Godunov* to Pushkin's pre-Musorgsky text. Could Pushkin's theme be transposed into a *non*operatic musical genre without reference to the canonized setting? Could quoting be avoided, by imitation or by omission? When confronted that same year with a similar task (a commission from the Kamerny Theater for incidental music to a stage production of Pushkin's *Eugene Onegin*) Prokofiev evaded Tchaikovsky by providing music for precisely those episodes that do *not* occur in the opera.[53] But evasion does not eliminate dialogue. A familiar version is always in the background of audience perception, inviting comparison. If Musorgsky had provided the canonized musical texture for a nineteenth-century Boris, Prokofiev's eerie, open sound suggests a Boris of and for the twentieth. The theme of a supreme ruler with blood on his conscience, impotent before the specter of popular revolt and foreign invasion, was a bold theme indeed for the Stalinist 1930s. This performance of Pushkin's *Boris* was never realized. Meyerhold's theater was closed by decree in 1938; Meyerhold himself was arrested, and in 1940 put to death.

The political potential of the Boris Tale remains acute to this day. One need only recall Yuri Liubimov's ill-fated production of Pushkin's *Boris* at the Taganka Theater in December of 1982. His was a fast-moving, vibrant *narodnoe zrelishche* (popular spectacle) quite in Meyerhold's spirit, with an omnipresent chorus that sometimes echoed, sometimes ironically commented upon, the action of the players.[54] At the dress rehearsal, an actor descended into the audience after the final scene and addressed Mosalsky's words directly to the spectators: "Chto zh *vy* molchite?" (Why are *you* silent?). The performance was banned, and early in 1983 Moscow theaters were criticized in the official press for ideological untrustworthiness.

Liubimov himself was in London, in March 1984, when he heard the news of his dismissal as director of the Taganka Theater.[55] He explained to the Western press that he had written a letter to Andropov soon after *Boris* was banned. In it he protested censorship of his productions and promised, should the ban on *Boris* not be removed, that he would quit the theater. The letter was not answered, and Andropov himself soon passed from the scene. *Boris Godunov*, with its generic and ideological indeterminacy, has a long history of distressing politicians, and this could be one reason why the 350-year-old story has remained so thoroughly contemporary.

Trapping a Hero inside a Genre: Four Questions to Ask of the Boris Tale

The chapters that follow cannot pretend to be a comprehensive treatment of the Boris transpositions. They will, however, attempt an analysis of select themes in the three major statements—themes recurrent in the generic debates surrounding these works, and echoed in the post-Karamzin histories and post-Pushkin dramas. These will be limited to four, and they might serve as examples of the sort of questions one can ask of transpositions.

What is, first, the chronotope of the work? What constitutes plausible action for the participants, what time and space are real for them, and how is the audience positioned in relation to that reality? Is there, embedded in the telling, a voice that speaks to the form of the story? Pimen in Pushkin's *Boris* is the most obvious instance of such a voice, the chronicler who talks the history that Grigory wants to make. In Karamzin's *Boris Tale*, Pimen does not exist at all—or rather a monk so named is mentioned in connection with the Pretender's escape from Russia, but he plays no real part in the narrative. Musorgsky's Pimen, a complicated amalgam, fills a larger structural role in the libretto, but there is less of the metaliterary element in him than in Pushkin's chronicler. Are the respective weights of the various Pimens relevant to the degree of generic self-consciousness present in each transposition?

Second, how does each Boris treatment end, and when is the

story considered closed? Dramatists have tended to take on the Time
of Troubles in multiple parts, and there is a tradition of "completing"
Pushkin's *Boris* with a Dmitri play. Internally, artistic closure of the tale
has occasioned real polemic. Karamzin left the twelfth volume of his
History unfinished at his death. But the fall of Boris is clearly the
climactic prototype for all the lesser falls that follow, of young Fyodor,
the False Dmitri, Shuisky. The death of Boris midway through Pushkin's drama was, for its time, a bold innovation; in his revised version
Musorgsky followed it. The ends of both opera and drama, of course,
differ profoundly from Karamzin's closure to chapter 3 of volume 9
of the *History:* "Thus was God's punishment brought to bear on the
murderer of the True Dmitri. . . ." All three tellings of the tale are to
a certain extent end-determined fictions, that is, their beginnings and
middles are reflections of their ending modes. Here much centers
on the definition of heroes: who they are, and how they die or fall
silent.

Third, how is material from earlier statements of the tale quoted
or incorporated into various later versions? As we noted above, research into direct quotation is the best-documented aspect of work on
the Boris Tale. But much of this analysis tends to be rather mechanical. Details from separate works are extracted and displayed
alongside one another as if on some neutral territory. An artistic
element, however, fits first of all within its *own* system, and transposed
tales must be read with some awareness of chronotopic shift. Pushkin
does indeed "copy" a great deal from Karamzin. But the closeness of
the copy must not obscure the fact that the poet is working in a very
different genre, one quite alien to Karamzin's romantic-didactic purpose. It could in fact be argued that the closer the quotation, the more
pointed the parody. Some quotation is explicit. Characters are occasionally expected to survive moves from one work to another with
personality and memory intact: Khomiakov's Dmitri, for instance,
actually remembers his earlier meeting with Marina Mniszech the
previous year among the lime trees of Pushkin's Polish scene.[56] But
other quotation is not so innocent. This subtle reaccentuation of
quotations primarily affects Boris himself, the real victim of the identity crises that fill this story.

The fourth question, then, concerns the character and historical
awareness of the doomed tsar in the title role. In two of the most
famous retellings, Pushkin's and Musorgsky's, Boris *as tsar* is defeated—but his transposer in each case uses that defeat to score a
victory for the new generic statement he is trying to make. Consider
Pushkin. He copied almost exactly Karamzin's presumptions and plan
in the Boris Tale—withdrawing, however, the high diction from the
hero's lines at the crucial points, and abandoning altogether Ka-

ramzin's moral framework. To quote extensively, but in a new context, is perhaps the most effective way to disappoint generic expectations— and thus to achieve that authentic "new work," which was, for Push- kin, the prerequisite for *true* romanticism. In keeping with the chro- notope Pushkin had devised for his drama, Tsar Boris knows less about his role the longer he lives it. This is not the well-motivated plot of classical tragedy, where actions may be misguided but are always *significant,* able to shape events. "Verisimilitude of situations and truth of dialogue," Pushkin wrote in 1825, "that is the real rule of trag- edy."[57] The implications of this "verisimilitude," for the theater in general and for Russian historical drama in particular, will be ex- plored in the third chapter. Pushkin was seeking a sort of reality for his characters that had no precedent on the Russian stage, and he achieved it through a cunning interplay of genres. His Boris is a realistic hero trapped in a sentimental plot.

In September 1825, near the end of his life, Karamzin suggested in a letter to Viazemsky that Pushkin give his Boris a "wilder mixture" of emotions—more piety and more criminal passion. "He was forever re-reading the Bible, seeking there some justification for himself," wrote Karamzin. "There's dramatic contrast for you!" To this advice Pushkin wryly responded that he thanked the historian, and would make haste to "sit his Boris down with the Gospel, force him to read Herod's Tale, etc."[58] Pushkin's irony is rarely simple, but this would seem to be a reference to the celebrated opening sentence in Ka- ramzin's Foreword to his *History:* "In a certain sense, history is the sacred book of peoples." History was not that for Pushkin, and *his* Boris, forced to secularize his role, to make sense out of his fate in everyday language, to work within that limited perspective which is all individuals can claim on great events, clashes with every sentiment that had been canonic for the Boris Tale since the time of the early chronicles. A new dramatic contrast is indeed born—although not the one Karamzin probably had in mind—as we watch Pushkin's Boris strain against Karamzin's plot.

In Musorgsky's second transposition of the theme we have another polemic and another new generic model. The libretto achieves its own peculiar noncoincidence of hero with expected setting, albeit quite different from Pushkin's. The composer's expansive *re*-psychologiza- tion, re-heroicization of Boris is wonderful theater. All traces of Push- kin's awkward and misinformed tsar have disappeared. It is good theater precisely because this is Karamzin's Boris back again, with crimes and passions bigger than life.

But this ruler is not allowed, as he is in Karamzin, to assume any responsibility for the tragic events of history. His is an image of nightmarish suffering, of apocalyptic rhetoric, but he does not carry any real political or social power. Amid the musical and theatrical daring of the opera—bells, drunken monks, ragged masses, a live horse, crowds of children and a holy fool on stage—this Boris plays the part of a hero who sees only himself and his own internal torment. His hallucinations are straight out of the romantic cliché that was his canonized story, that of a murderer noisily pursued by the ghost of his victim. This huge and immobilized presence dominates the work.

Yet Musorgsky, in his revised version of the opera, declined to end the work with the end of Boris. The romantic hero was not allowed to take the world with him when he died. So the operatic Boris, so different from his counterpart in Pushkin, suffers from a similar incongruity. The popular choruses that open and close the work literally trap and silence the fated romantic Boris, who dies without delivering the last word. Musorgsky's Boris is a sentimental hero trapped, as it were, in a realistic opera. The peculiar frame of this operatic *Boris* might be seen as an attempt to approximate, through unconventional closure, the real experience of "heroes" and the real, invisible processes of history.

In both drama and opera, then, we recognize the familiar Russian tendency to distrust narrative as such, to challenge its neat openings and closures and its claim to transmit truth in any conventionally acceptable way. This distrust has become almost a trademark of Russian literature, best summarized, perhaps, by Tolstoy's celebrated statement that no great Russian work of art comfortably fits into any preexisting generic classification.[59] Ninteenth-century Russians were particularly self-conscious about the forms, received or native, of their nation's art. The aggressive influx of foreign texts—first scientific, then literary and philosophical—that began with Peter the Great was yet to be absorbed a century later, and this multitude of alien forms in the culture created a rift between ideas and their exposition. It fostered the suspicion that all narrative modes were unreliable and arbitrary. As suggested earlier in this chapter, many artists responded with an aggressive laying bare of the chronotope. No forms were simply *there* to be used; genre was not a neutral vessel but a challenge. Here Russian intellectuals often contrasted their young nation with the culture of Western Europe, so apparently comfortable in reproducing itself according to a time-honored poetics. Out of Russia came a spectrum of dramatic overstatement, from Belinsky's and Chaadaev's lament that Russians had no culture at all to Dostoevsky's later boast that only the Russians had a truly comprehensive culture: we can translate the French and the German, he intimates, but they cannot translate us.[60] Between these two extremes lay a restless, and radical, scepticism toward all received norms in art.

Thus the frequency of mystifying subtitles and polemical forewords: *Dead Souls* is a poem, the formally perfect cantos of *Eugene Onegin* are a novel, *War and Peace* is not. The Boris Tales of Karamzin, Pushkin, and Musorgsky participate in this iconoclastic tradition; they are an expression of this same impulse to undo narrative and discredit secure genres. And here we have an interesting paradox. All three major statements work within the same traditional biography of a guilty Boris, one quite suspect today. The *content* of the Boris Tale from one transposition to the next is quite conservative. But its generic expression is in each case complex and even contradictory. Karamzin wrote a romantic history, but one with a scholarly apparatus that Schlözer and his school would (and indeed did) admire. Pushkin wrote a "romantic tragedy" that by consensus of a baffled public was neither romantic nor feasible on the tragic stage. Musorgsky wrote a musical drama that challenged most of the operatic conventions of his time, and which to this day is rarely performed as he wrote it. Something in these works did not fit. And it could be precisely the rub, the misfitting of part to whole, that carries the message.

We cannot of course speak here for creative genius, nor presume to have "decoded" Pushkin's or Musorgsky's intent. Artistic intent is not so easily extracted, and in any case is rarely singular. But we *can* speak to effect, to methods of innovation that consciously or unconsciously create generic confusion and break new ground. Incompatible elements are combined within the work itself. A character is set against the canons of the genre in which his story is embedded, or he is confronted with an earlier "authoritative" version of his own biography. One or the other is exposed as inadequate, ludicrous, artificial—and the story, as it were, bursts apart from within. We are forced to see the relationship of part to whole, of individual to history, in a new way.

The Boris Tale has thus proved a rich vehicle for certain recurring themes in Russian culture. Among these are the appeal of pretenders, the paralyzing effects of power, the impulse to deform and mystify genre, and the radical doubt generations of Russians have raised over the very possibility of historical "truth." Both conception and reception of these Boris versions have been closely tied to political and national consciousness. This complex of factors is already clearly present in our first case study, Karamzin's treatment of the theme.

II

Boris in History: *Karamzin*

Thus Russia prepared long and well for the most terrible event of her history: with the vile tyranny of Ivan's twenty-four years, with the infernal game of Boris's ambition, with the calamities brought on by vicious famine and widespread brigandage, with the hardening of hearts and corruption of the people—with everything that must precede the collapse of states condemned by Providence either to perish, or to be painfully reborn.[1]

THE APPEARANCE, in 1818, of the first eight volumes of Karamzin's *History of the Russian State* was a major cultural event. No Russian history before or since— with the possible exception of Stalin's "Short Course" during the darkest years of Soviet rule—knew so instantaneous a success, or had so concentrated an impact on a reading public. The entire printing of 3,000 copies, almost three times larger than the printings standard for the times, sold out in less than a month.[2] Literary figures of the day greeted the work enthusiastically. Vasily Zhukovsky, after hearing Karamzin read a description of the taking of Kazan, wrote to Dmitriev in a sort of ecstasy:

> What perfection! And what a new epoch has opened up for Russians with the appearance of this history! What a treasure-house for language, for poetry, not to mention all the activity it will generate in the intellect. This history could be called the resurrector of the past centuries of our people's existence. Previously, these centuries had been no more than mummies for us. . . .[3]

Prince Pyotr Viazemsky called Karamzin "our [General] Kutuzov," the man who "saved Russia from an invasion of forgetfulness, called her to life, showed us that we have a fatherland—as many had discovered

30

in 1812."[4] And Pushkin, several years later, recalled in his reminiscences how he had devoured the first volumes of the *History* as a nineteen-year-old: "It was for us a new discovery. Ancient Russia, it seems, was discovered by Karamzin as America had been by Columbus."[5]

This initial enthusiasm, so resonant with patriotic self-consciousness, was in good part a response to the type of history Karamzin had composed. His foreward to the first eight volumes makes explicit the duties of a historian. "History," Karamzin writes, "is in a certain sense the sacred book of peoples, their main and indispensable book" (I, xvii). Its purpose is organic, to "unify what has been handed down to us by the centuries into a system clear and coherent in the harmonious correlation of its parts" (xxvi). Such correlations could be made only by a mind gifted with historical insight, which is a function of the rational patriotism of the historian: "The feelings of 'we,' 'our' enlivens the narrative; and while crude partiality—the result of weak reasoning or a weak soul—is intolerable in a historian, love of country gives his brush ardor, power, appeal" (xxv–xxvi).

The dividing line between patriotism and partiality is a subjective one. Applying to the art of history the same synthesizing criterion that the Abbé Batteux had applied to aesthetics,[6] Karamzin argues that rationalism and sensibility could be coordinated through taste, which is both a sensible decision and a sentiment. The most perfect among modern historians, Karamzin writes, would have been Hume, had he not "unnecessarily prided himself on his impartiality, and thus chilled down a fine creative work" (xxv). One should *feel,* as well as demonstrate, that history is moving in the right direction.

That "right direction" for history was perhaps clearer for Karamzin than for many of his contemporaries.[7] Successful and aggressive revolution in France had sensitized all of Europe to the idea of sudden change, and had made more urgent the historians' search for cause and effect. But 1789 found Karamzin already well formed in other, earlier traditions. For him the French Revolution was a stain on the eighteenth century, a disaster whose sole beneficial result would be to demonstrate irrefutably the sanctity of civil order—even in the presence of social injustice. Karamzin was committed to a Rousseauism without the revolutionary consequences. He insisted upon the authority of personal sentiment without the accompanying social or political rule of the middle class—that very class, in fact, which had championed the claims of individual pathos against the aristocratic criteria of birth and rank. Thus not only the *History* but its author as well was something of an anachronism. In the Age of Napoleon, Karamzin combined a very *ancien-régime* understanding of political virtue with both sentimentalism and faith in Divine Providence; two decades into the French Revolution he could still speak of history as a "*sacred* book." This soothing blend of old and new was not lost on his readers. In November 1853, the twenty-five-year-old Leo Tolstoy jotted down in his diary that he had been browsing on and off in Karamzin's history. "The style is very fine," he wrote, "and the Foreword evoked a mass of good feelings in me."[8] That was exactly what Karamzin had intended his *History* to do.

Patriotically inspired narrative was not, however, the whole of the *History*, nor the whole reason for its success. The documentation authenticating the narrative was collected in the back of each volume in a section entitled *Primechaniia* (Notes). *Primechaniia* are clearly more than footnotes—they almost constitute a second text.[9] Several volumes allot more space to them than to the text itself. Sources are not just cited but verified, compared with one another, ranked for reliability, and extensively quoted; Karamzin noted discrepancies among the source material and offered his own resolutions. His sophistication in working with original texts was, for the time, considerable. Many later historians even ranked Karamzin's bibliographical and critical skills superior to those of the meticulous eighteenth-century German scholars who had worked on Russian documents; the historian Nikolai Polevoi, for one, regretted that this aspect of the *History* could not be easily appreciated or verified abroad and in translation.[10]

The *primechaniia* took on new significance after Napoleon's invasion of Russia. In the burning of Moscow in 1812, Musin-Pushkin's magnificent library, as well as Karamzin's, was reduced to ashes.[11] Many original documents would have disappeared without a trace had they not been cited in, or incorporated into, the early and still unpublished drafts of the *History*. Perhaps in response to this abrupt object lesson in the perishability of sources, Karamzin, starting with volume V, supplemented each chapter with lengthy extracts from unpublished material—even when they did not bear directly on his text.

This last aspect of the notes raises an interesting theoretical question. Not only is some of the documentation not relevant to the main text but it is on occasion in direct opposition to it. Among the more celebrated incompatibilities are Karamzin's suggestion, in the narrative, that the name for the Slavs had its origin in *slava* (glory) (I, 13), a thesis that is then refuted in *prim.* #42; and, in volume II, his claim that Vladimir Monomakh received his crown from a Byzantine emperor (II, 100), a story discredited at length in the accompanying *prim.* #220 and #221. In these instances the superscript, which usually binds authority to the narrative, actually directs the reader to data that undo the intention of the text. Clearly there was a tension between telling the right story and objectively citing the source.

Double Response to Double Text

Karamzin himself admitted, with disarming lightheartedness, that his huge amount of documentation did not make things easier or clearer for the reader. "I am myself aghast at the number of my footnotes and excerpts," he wrote in the foreword (xxvii). "The ancients were more fortunate. They did not know this trifling work, in which half the time is lost, while the mind is bored and the imagination withers. This painful sacrifice offered to authenticity is, however, unavoidable."

Karamzin hoped that his readers would feel free to dip at their own discretion into that "motley jumble, which at times serves as evidence, at times as explanation and supplement" (xxvii).

Part evidence, part explanation, part supplement: so ambivalent is the status of the *primechaniia* that they more resemble the marginal gloss than the conventional footnote today.[12] Their very bulk in the *History* inevitably raises the issue of the nature and location of the historian's voice—and makes problematic the authority (or authorship) that voice commands. Which text can be said to authenticate the other? Can a tendentious narrative, provided with extensive documentation, reap the benefits of both objective scholarship and creative storytelling? One scholar of the *primechaniia* has resolved the issue bluntly: "Karamzin . . . had no intention of allowing the results of his research to interfere with the socially and politically derived premises on which he built the narrative of the *History*."[13]

The issue, however, is considerably more complex and interesting than such a dismissal suggests. As subsequent theorists have pointed out, since Karamzin's time not much progress has been made toward defining exactly what it is that a "reference to a source" is supposed to document:

> No historian in our time can allow himself the luxury of constructing footnotes in the way Karamzin did—putting into them, in extenso, the text of the source utilized. But even when we find a reference to a concrete source in a [contemporary] historical study, we are not always able to tell what the value of the source is (whether it is contemporaneous with the event or written later, tendentious or objective) and whether the point made in the study is stated directly in the source or is a deduction from the source based on a whole series of collateral references.[14]

The respectable way out of this dilemma—at least as regards Karamzin's *History*—has been simply to separate the narrative from the notes. This separating activity began soon after the *History* appeared. Poets delighted in the wealth of newly available plots. Professional historians quickly repudiated the sentimental story line of the main text, while admiring (and frequently consulting) the apparatus. The bifurcated, ambivalent generic identity of the *History* continued to emit contradictory signals to successive generations of readers, and has thus provoked an especially rich and varied critical response.

The opening moves in that response give us some idea of its range and rhetoric. The first eight volumes of the *History* were praised as literature—at least among the advocates of Karamzin's stylistic reforms—and hailed as a monument to Russian culture. But they were criticized, by and large, as ideology. Karamzin's acquaintances among the Masons accused him of being an unbeliever and a Jacobin; the future Decembrists, not surprisingly, labeled him a reactionary.[15] Pushkin, just graduated from the Lycée and already long on intimate terms with the Karamzin family, wounded the Historiographer with his famous epigram:

> With elegance and simplicity his *History*
> Proves to us, utterly impartially,
> The necessity of despotism
> And the charm of the knout.[16]

But the ninth volume (1821), dealing with Ivan IV's "bad years," was received with excitement for both its literary merits and its political boldness. The first eight volumes had been folklore and heroics; volume 9 was about the abuse of power. Karamzin spared nothing in his exposure of Ivan the Terrible's crimes. Kondraty Ryleev, future Decembrist, wrote to Faddei Bulgarin in July 1821: "So that's the Terrible! So that's Karamzin! I don't know what to marvel at more, the tyranny of our Ioann or the talent of our Tacitus."[17] No doubt it was the spirit of this volume that Pushkin had in mind when he wrote his defense of Karamzin in the mid-1820s:

> Our Jacobins are displeased: a few individual observations on the benefit of autocracy, eloquently refuted by the story of events, seemed to them the height of barbarism and humiliation. They forgot that Karamzin printed his *History* in Russia, that having freed him from censorship the sovereign, by this sign of confidence, placed upon Karamzin the obligation of all possible modesty and moderation. He told his story with all the truthfulness of a historian, he everywhere referred to the sources—what more can be demanded of him? I repeat that the *History of the Russian State* is not only the creation of a great writer but the heroic deed of an honorable man.[18]

Few pursued at the time Pushkin's suggestion that there might be a dialogue, and possibly an ironic one, between Karamzin's ideological generalizations and the hard data of his sources. But most critics, in Pushkin's century and in our own, have noted an overall lack of organic unity between the two parts of the *History,* each of which possesses a certain autonomy and historiographical style of its own.[19]

One clue to this peculiar "separability" might be sought in the pre-history of the text, that is, in the state of history-writing before Karamzin.

History before Karamzin: Two Categories

The great impact of Karamzin's *History* on the Russian public was due to a fortunate confluence of circumstances, some created by Karamzin himself and others the product of the political and cultural climate of early nineteenth-century Russia. The rise of Napoleon, and the sacrifice his invasion exacted, stimulated an appetite for heroic stories from the national past. This popular awareness of history, alongside Russia's emerging sense of herself as a major world power, coincided with and reinforced a change in the professional status of history. Encouraged by the liberal atmosphere of Alexander I's early years, historical societies were organized and journals founded. Count Rumiantsev headed a campaign to get chronicles and government documents into print. But this new quantity and visibility of sources did not yet constitute a history. In fact the very profusion of historical materials made all the more plain their lack of coherence. A vivid, if somewhat rhetorical, picture of the state of historical resources in Russia at the time has been provided by Karamzin's first biographer, Mikhail Pogodin:

> Libraries had no catalogues; no one had gathered together the sources, no one had organized or put them into order; chronicles were not researched, explicated, even published in a scholarly way; *gramoty* lay scattered about the monasteries and archives, no one knew the chronographs; not a single part of history had been worked out, neither of the Church, nor of law, literature, trade, customs; no preparation had been made for an ancient geography, chronology was confused, genealogies not studied. . . . Distant European travelers to Russia were known only by rumor; the works of foreign scholars, containing many scattered judgments on ancient Russia, had not been dealt with at all; not a single question out of thousands had been completely resolved, not a single contradiction reconciled.[20]

Russian histories had of course been written in the eighteenth century. But they had not been designed for a general reading public. Before Karamzin, historians of Russia could be divided into two basic categories—and neither particularly attended to the literary aspects of their enterprise. The "monarchical school" (Tatishchev, Lomonosov, Shcherbatov) wrote ideological tracts that breathed love of country but lacked objectivity and anything like a scientific methodology. The "Germans" (Bayer, Müller, Schlözer) were familiar with scholarly method, with Byzantine history and with Western Europe, but often lacked a thorough knowledge of Russian sources and (as in the case of Bayer) of the Russian language as well.[21] At the end of the nineteenth century, the liberal historian Paul Miliukov offered a neat formulation for these two trends in Russian historiography of the preceding age. The monarchist school, he maintained, was governed by *pol'za*, benefit or purpose, and the Germans by *istina*, scientific truth—and this meant truth taken in a rather narrow sense.[22]

These terms were Miliukov's shorthand for the larger nineteenth-century debate over the purpose and method of history. At one "utilitarian" pole, history was seen as a didactic art form. Its purpose, like Voltaire's "philosophy teaching by example," was to tell a story or stress a moral. The duty of the historian, therefore, was to make details cohere and transmit a strong, positive national image. At the other, "truthful" pole, history aspired to science, to something distinct from art. Documents were expected to speak for themselves, and when they did not, scholars were to keep a source scrupulously separate from their commentary on it. In the Russian eighteenth century both schools produced texts for specialists, or for special purposes. Yet the need for a general and readable survey of Russia's national experience had been recognized throughout Catherine II's reign. The moral benefit of such a history was a central tenet in Enlightenment philosophy. Thus Karamzin set to writing his *History* at a time when both poles in Russian historiography—the "monarchists" and the "Germans"—appeared increasingly inadequate.

This inadequacy was not due to a lack of talent or energy on the part of the early practitioners. It was due, rather, to a lack of audience, and to a lack of appropriate language. The Russian eighteenth century did not possess in its native tongue a narrative style flexible enough to transmit the emerging secular national consciousness. Just as Karamzin had found no native vehicle for Russian sentimentalism in the 1780s, so at the turn of the century he found no domestic vehicle for popular history; the secularized, yet thoroughly sophisticated, Russian lexicon and diction of the *History* was largely Karamzin's own creation.[23] We may appreciate the enthusiasm of his readers and the significance of his accomplishment when we realize that his history was not only a model for future historical scholarship but also an exemplar for discursive prose.

In his foreword Karamzin noted the historians he most admired. They included the English (Gibbon, Hume) and the ancients; conspicuously absent were the two nationalities that had tried their hand at writing specifically *Russian* histories, the German and the French. In that area the models available to Karamzin were either Le Clerc's scurrilous and ill-informed *Histoire physique, moral, et politique de la Russie ancienne et moderne* (1783–94) or, on a much more respectable level, the works of the German School in and outside Russia.[24] With the latter school Karamzin took special issue. In a memorable phrase, Schlözer had stated—with Lomonosov in mind—that "a short history of 600 years of truth" was preferable to "a long one of 3,000 years of fables."[25] And Karamzin, as if in response, commented on Schlözer in a letter to Aleksandr Turgenev by noting regretfully that the German seemed to admire those historians who "only recognized dates, and hardly ever reflect." In the same letter Karamzin expressed doubts that Schlözer would ever finish his *Nestor*. "What for?" he asked. "For seven or eight people? That's hardly worth doing. The explanations and translation of the text are very poor and often ridiculous. . . ."[26] Karamzin set himself the task of writing a historical narrative that would not only be more "useful," but also more truthful—with a different sort of truth.

This broader truth would include, first, a great deal more than earlier historians had ever admitted as evidence. In his official capacity as historian of the empire, Karamzin had access to many previously closed state and church archives, and could requisition foreign holdings as well. He drew on forty chronicles (twice as many as the previous record, set by Shcherbatov), and ultimately cited 350 authors and titles.[27] Karamzin enlarged not just the quantity but the very quality of the evidence. He treated ritual, legend, and historical song not as "fables" but as documents, whose admittedly unscientific content did not preclude a scientific investigation—and appreciation—of their role in transmitting history.[28] Second, Karamzin openly endorsed Lomonosov's partisan approach to writing about the national past. He intended his *History* to be in part a response to Lomonosov's complaint that Russian history lacked fame and glory only because it had not yet been properly embodied in art.[29] But Karamzin aimed to realize this artistic embodiment with greater factual accuracy than Lomonosov could muster, and within a much more broadly defined historical field.[30] As Karamzin wrote in an 1802 essay outlining events and characters most appropriate as subjects for the arts, "One must know what one loves, and in order to know the present we must have information about the past. . . . Not only the historian and the poet but also the painter and the sculptor can be organs of patriotism."[31] It was possible, Karamzin believed, to produce a work that was at the same time partisan, artistic, *and* true.

Karamzin's History: "Purposeful" Narrative, "Truthful" Apparatus

According to Miliukov, a "scientific" history did not become possible in Russia until the 1820s, the first time the word *nauka* (science) was linked with history in a printed text.[32] But Miliukov insists that Karamzin was not the cause of this new development. Summing up half a century of praise and criticism for the *History*, Miliukov argues in fact the contrary, that Karamzin merely combined (and rather irresponsibly) the two earlier trends in Russian historiography. "Karamzin in all earnestness strove for truth—in his Notes. But this was involuntary tribute to that condition introduced by the Germans into Russian historical scholarship . . ." (143).

Since Miliukov's time, readers of histories have become more sceptical, and more aware of the complexities involved in gathering and representing historical data. As Hayden White has argued in a series of influential essays, the nineteenth-century belief in the radical dissimilarity of art to science no longer holds undisputed sway. Both writers and readers of history are more receptive to the idea that "facts" are not unambiguously given, not simply found, but are in part "constructed by the kinds of questions which the investigator asks of the phenomenon before him."[33] This is not to suggest, of course, that history is just another form of fictive narrative. Whereas historians may choose among facts and among modes of emplotment, *what* they choose is still subject to verification. But it is to suggest that history, understood as the changing conventions of a place and an age, affects historical writing itself—and this principle invites a more serious investigation of different forms of historiography. Thus an emphasis on disparities in "fact," between the two parts of the *History* and between the *History* and other versions of the past, has begun to give way to more productive inquiry into the possible ideology underlying Karamzin's vision of historical integrity.

Turning first to Karamzin himself, we find very little self-reflexive commentary on his own creative method. Except for that whimsical advice to his readers in the foreword—that they should "dip into this motley mass" of documentation at their own discretion—Karamzin left no more precise guidelines for integrating narrative and notes. On this and many other questions the Karamzin archive is sparse.[34] Early drafts of the *History* are few and fragmentary. So we can only conjecture about Karamzin's integrating techniques, or seek indirect evidence from contemporaries. Nikolai Polevoi provides a clue in a critical review written one year after Karamzin's death:

> We have heard that the publication of the twelfth volume, unfinished, is now detained by the compilation of notes (the most indispensable ones). The Historiographer usually carried out that portion of his work simultaneously, and on finishing each chapter would then turn to the supplementary explanations of the text; but in putting together the twelfth volume, as if sensing that his time was precious, he hurried to complete the narrative part and planned to deal with the notes afterwards.[35]

Composing text and notes simultaneously, Karamzin may have envisaged a dialogue between the two that was rather fresh, without privileging either side as more "true." This dialogue is worth considering, for it should not be forgotten that Karamzin, as an eighteenth-century man of letters, was quite sophisticated in matters of narrative voice and in the creation of divergent narrative perspectives. Karamzin wrote in an age when history was still perceived as part of literature. The flexibility that marked sentimental and romantic genres served to sanction a meshing of national and personal events, of public and private spheres. New generic hybrids—the novel-confession, the travel diary, the personal letter as public document—were all bringing the inner man into maximal view apart from his official roles, and self-consciously revealing the poeticality of everyday life. In the 1790s Karamzin himself had experimented with one such hybrid, the travel diary, in his semifictional *Letters of a Russian Traveler*. And long before his appointment as State Historian in 1803, Karamzin had been experimenting with the literary expression of themes from the Russian past.

These literary experiments have some relevance to the *History*. Two of Karamzin's historical tales—"Natalia the Boyar's Daughter" (1792) and "Marfa Posadnitsa" (1802)—are based on real historical events. But medieval Russian reality in them is little more than a backdrop, a visual ornament, and both language and psychological motivation belong fully to the genres of pastoral and love idyll.[36] Historiographical subtlety, such as there is, comes in the storyteller.

The teller of these historical tales is an active participant in the story, alternately asserting and then undermining its truthfulness.[37] While writing "Natalia," for instance, Karamzin was in the process of translating "The Story of Le Fever" from *Tristram Shandy,* and his own tale is full of Sternean digressions and parodic footnotes elucidating the "historical sources."[38] The text of "Marfa" is so saturated with epic rhetoric and Homeric epithet that the tone borders on irony. We will examine the complex Karamzinian narrator in more detail in the *History,* but here it is enough to note that quite early Karamzin developed a characteristic "image of the author" in his works—and an image, moreover, that implied a certain sort of reader. Author and reader in Karamzin's narratives are intimates, eager to further the same goals, and fully aware of the tricks literature can play.

The very "trickiness" of literature could well have been one reason behind Karamzin's decision to turn to history.[39] For if narrators can manipulate readers and render stories ironic, then authors—even as they orchestrate these effects—inevitably lose authority. Karamzin's literary activity took shape amid eighteenth-century debates over the effectiveness of fiction versus history as a means of moral instruction.

Having chosen history, Karamzin did not part with literary devices. But he did more openly acknowledge their power to corrupt and seduce, and stressed the boundary separating history from fiction. As he wrote in an essay of 1803, "In several years, history will occupy us considerably more than novels; for the mature mind, truth has a special charm which does not exist in fictions."[40]

The "mature mind," Karamzin implies, can confront the truth of history, honestly told in all its moral ambivalence. Readers of novels, on the other hand, are conditioned to distrust narrators—and to identify with, perhaps even to imitate, the heroes of fictional texts. But both categories of reader insist upon *charm*. In this sense Karamzin perceived his new task as an extension into historiography of the service he had provided for Russian fictional literature a decade earlier. It would become his goal to show that the real life of a nation, just like the real life of an individual, is filled with poetry.[41]

This romantic concept of history as heroic biography, as a story to be told through symbolic personalities like tsars, became Karamzin's dominant mode for telling Russia's story. In the *History,* of course, the characters of romance have a more complex role to play than did their counterparts in the historical tales. They are still engaged in a struggle of virtue over vice. But the characters now have their biographies documented by a massive scholarly apparatus, and are themselves subordinated to a suprapersonal national destiny. The author regains authority, yet the storyteller still enchants. Romantic emplotment thus loses romantic irony and begins to serve serious patriotic purpose.

This artistry and partisanship were not naïve. Karamzin constructed his image of a historian carefully amid various alternatives.[42] Throughout his life he remained convinced that a historian should be predominantly a moral, rather than a scientific or (for that matter) a mystical, force. When the quest for universal history created an enthusiasm for broad periodizations and "laws" of history, Karamzin remained unmoved. The so-called Sceptical School, which arose in the first half of the nineteenth century to challenge Karamzin's historical methodology, prided itself (and perhaps justly) on a more politically independent stance. But as Karamzin would have easily divined, its use of sources was hardly more objective.[43] Its "higher criticism," which subjected data to the so-called laws of history, embodied that very mysticism which Karamzin considered so disrespectful to the stories that the sources themselves told.[44] Karamzin's scholarship, in other words, was subjective, but the subjectivity was forthright, not concealed under cover of "objective" laws that presumed to transcend individual interpretation. As his foreword to the *History* intimated, the admission of subjectivity where it must exist was a part of true objectivity.

Not surprisingly, Karamzin's brand of sentimental-moral history has had its periods of greater and lesser favor. It should be remembered, however, that his work was not so much reevaluated critically as it was subjected to shifting definitions of what constituted proper history. Karamzin had written in the conviction that history was compatible with, perhaps even a part of, poetry—and therefore could combine in one organic whole the particular (in need of verification) and the universal, which was beyond notions of verification and causation. When history and poetry parted ways, Karamzin's type of history seemed anachronistic and improperly motivated. Nikolai Polevoi reviewed the *History* in *Moskovskii telegraf* (1829),[45] when Karamzin had been dead scarcely three years, yet the bulk of his review is taken up with a case for the historian's outdatedness. "For us, the new generation, Karamzin exists only in the history of literature and in his own literary creations. We can no longer be carried away by a personal passion for him, or by his passions . . ." (470). Among those passions, the most damaging was Karamzin's concept of history as a force residing entirely in the Personality. To Polevoi, the *History of the Russian State* was in effect a history of psychologized personalities, and this was intimately bound up with Karamzin's conception of autocracy as a personalized state.

Not until the Marxist historians, it could be argued, was this issue of personality decisively confronted.[46] And not surprisingly, the Soviet historical establishment has been for the most part unsympathetic to Karamzin.[47] Recently, however, there have been signs of new interest in and appreciation of Karamzin's work. In 1979 A. Gulyga lamented the fact that the *History of the Russian State* had been so long out of print, and that no scholarly Soviet edition had yet been published.[48] History, Gulyga insisted, need not be "documentary." Karamzin performs another service; he reminds us that both art and history routinely violate their own definitions. "History," Gulyga wrote, "is the science which forever exceeds its own limits, literature is the art which always oversteps its own boundaries . . ." (215).

Generic flexibility is but one step away from ideological flexibility, and that step was in fact taken in a recent popular Soviet treatment of Karamzin's career as historian. The study concludes by invoking Collingwood, with this observation:

Every historian is limited by the facts which come down (or do not come down) to him . . . Karamzin writes less than did later historians on economic questions, on the importance of popular resistance, etc. And why? Because with utter sincerity he believes, in the spirit of his upbringing, position, world outlook, that those questions are not that important; we do not agree with him today, but it is quite possible that we ourselves are relegating to the sidelines as secondary something that the twenty-second or twenty-fourth century will talk about most of all.[49]

Such relativism in history is not, certainly, an approved position in the Soviet historical establishment. But the fact that Karamzin provides an occasional opportunity to raise this issue makes his further fate in Soviet historiography worth following.

One aspect of this increased interest in Karamzin's historical method is of special importance to this study. For it could be argued that the most productive feature of Karamzin's system is not its play with the status of historical fact per se—that ground, however reworked, is the familiar one of hostility between text and notes. More useful for a reading of the Boris Tale is an approach exploring the principles by which Karamzin integrated "fact" into the fabric of his narrative.

Such techniques of integration have recently received considerable attention from the new generation of Soviet Karamzin scholars, most notably L. N. Luzianina.[50] One way of reshaping the inquiry, then, would be to assume that many potential narratives lurk in the *primechaniia*. Whereas Karamzin fully realized only one, that one narrative was a complex hybrid, with multiple ties to its source material. This complexity was noticed a century ago by Mikhail Pogodin. In the 1860s he wrote (already somewhat defensively) that

> Karamzin presented many events as if they were truly re-created in our imagination: he portrayed a number of figures [under discussion are Boris Godunov, the Pretender, and Ermak] in such a way that they actually come to life before us, if not always in their own life then at least in that life which the artist imparted to them at various moments of their activity.[51]

Pogodin is suggesting here that several different levels of authenticity coexist in any history. A historical event can "come to life" in a number of ways: by appearing real to a current generation of readers, or real to the recorder of the event ("the spirit of the source"), or real to the historical participants themselves.

Karamzin does not attempt to re-create the last authenticity, a version of the event as it might have been experienced in its own time. By our standards, Karamzin is in fact quite ahistoric, even anachronistic. He underestimates change and historical specificity on both the individual and cultural planes. But this is not surprising. The generally accepted timetable for universal history (7000 years since the creation of the world, 5000 years of human history since the Flood) made available much less time for change and encouraged a static conception of human nature. As a matter of course Karamzin assumed an unchanging universal psychology and a stable set of motivations for all people in all situations.[52]

We do, however, get the first two authenticities in the *History:* a spirit true to the source, and a spirit true for the early nineteenth-century reader. In fact, the dialogue between these two realities constitutes the key to Karamzin's style. This dialogue is an uneasy one.

Never does Karamzin work out a stable relationship between his own "historian's" viewpoint and the viewpoints embedded in the sources. The boundaries of his own narrative voice are unstable, at times penetrated by the voices of the documents he cites and at other times impermeable to them. Karamzin's own aesthetic principles were in continual flux during his twenty-five years' work on the *History;* he constructed and amended his methodology as he went along. The twelve volumes as a whole therefore reflect, in the terminology offered at the beginning of this study, a set of shifting chronotopes— that is, a set of different realities transmitted by a narrative voice that changes perspective on the time and space of the telling.

Defining Karamzin's Chronotope

Karamzin's various chronotopes are related to one another in a sequence that reflects the historian's evolving attitude toward his sources—and most particularly, his attitude toward the medieval chronicle. As Luzianina has shown in her investigation into the *History*,[53] Karamzin draws on chronicles in two quite different ways. First, he incorporates and comments upon the past events recounted there from the perspective of the present—that is, he objectifies the event as a historian of his own time. Second, he embeds the chronicle account directly in his narrative, fuses his own authoritative voice with the voice of the chronicler, and thus achieves an integrated picture that breathes "the spirit of the time"—which is to say, the time of the chronicler, and, from the perspective of the chronicler, the time of the event as well.

The first approach dominates the early volumes. There, Karamzin keeps the chronicler's voice and the historian's voice carefully separate. Accounts are clearly marked as authored versions by such closing tactics as "Thus our chroniclers tell us . . ." (I, 110) or such opening phrases as "Writers who have seen this with their own eyes have preserved . . ." (I, 58). Chronicle accounts are set off as such by quotation marks, which are visibly repeated (according to the printing conventions of the time) at the beginning of each line. And they are often prefaced with elaborate disclaimers, as in the case of Nestor's manifestly formulaic account of Olga's Revenge against the Drevlia- nians (I, 108–10):

Here the chronicler tells us many details incompatible with both the probabilities of reason and the dignity of history, taken, without a doubt, from a popular *folktale;* but as a true event must lie at their base, and since ancient fables are themselves of interest to the inquiring mind as a portrayal of the customs and spirit of the time, we will repeat Nestor's simple tale.

Because Karamzin distances his own time from the time he describes, in these early volumes he rarely censures the Kievan princes morally. Their sins are accepted as sins of the age—although the chronicles upon which the accounts depend often openly lament the internecine strife. Legend, myth, and folklore freely enter the narrative, bracketed by a neutral and uncritical voice and justified as *kolorit*, "local color"—or, rather, temporal color. In this technique lies an implicit appreciation of changing moral standards, a sense of anachronism, and perhaps a kind of incipient historical relativism as well.

Starting with volume VII, and specifically with the subjugation of Pskov, there is a change in the way the chronicle material is integrated. Factual data from later sources begin to be woven into the laments of the chroniclers. Thus their special tone is no longer isolated but begins to penetrate the larger narrative, participating as a seamless part of the text and thereby partaking of a portion of the historian's authority. The narrative purpose is no longer to juxtapose various accounts of an event from an outside and later perspective but to recreate in the text a "chronicle view of the world."[54] When in 1806 Karamzin wrote, apropos of the *History,* that he had begun to "freely transmit the spirit,"[55] this shift in chronotope must have been already well under way.

As Luzianina demonstrates, the ninth volume (1821), on the tyrannical years of Ivan IV, achieves a significant new synthesis.[56] Karamzin assumes the perspective of the times, partially impersonating its values, and so allows himself to enter the minds of the people he describes. Opening his description of the Terrible Tsar, Karamzin writes:

> History does not resolve the question of man's moral freedom. But by putting forth its own judgment on actions and characters, it clarifies, first, various inherent qualities of people, and, second, the circumstances or impressions of objects that act on the soul. (IX, 5)

This new psychological mode of analysis ("clarifying. . . what acts on the soul") was familiar to readers of sentimental fiction. It permitted Karamzin to expose, even to exaggerate, Ivan the Terrible's crimes, while at the same time motivating those crimes with intense inner soliloquies that serve to "explain" the action—however apparently mad. The reader would feel, perhaps even sympathize with, the *intimacy* of the horror. A suffering soul that had become so spectacularly available would doubtless be censured, but it would also be "understood." Thus Karamzin could reveal and condemn the crimes of an individual monarch while retaining an emotional sympathy for the pain, and burden, inherent in the institution of the monarchy as a whole.

This perspective required, however, some major reworking of chronicle material. Karamzin's medieval sources did not approach the inner world that way. The narrative voice of the *History* had begun, we recall, by bracketing the chronicler, and then gradually had absorbed the chronicler's moral tone and world view into itself. Now the narrator had to transcend that perspective. Somehow a thoroughly romantic emplotment would have to be grafted onto the original "chronicle chronotope," where it had little organic place. Karamzin signals the shift in his introductory remarks to Ivan's first mass tortures and executions:

> His soul, once desirous of good, did not of course turn vicious overnight: the achievements of good and evil are gradual. But the chroniclers could not penetrate into that soul's interior, they could not see in it a conscience struggling with turbulent passions; they saw only terrifying deeds, and called Ioann's tyranny an *alien storm*, sent from the depths of Hell to torment and torture Russia. (IX, 13)

Karamzin's narrative voice has now gained indiscriminate access to both external and internal perspective. In effect, he combines the psychological perspective of his own time with the events and perspectives of the chronicles, in order to narrate what a chronicler might have seen if he had asked nineteenth-century questions.

Among these "nineteenth-century questions" the most prominent was the question of moral choice. The story of Boris Godunov is in fact structured around this issue, but traces of the older chronicle perspective persist. Although Boris is presumed free to choose—that freedom alone justifies a psychological narrative—the plot prepared for him by the chroniclers makes no provision for this freedom of choice. Thus chronicle accounts take on yet a further authority: fused with the general narrative, they determine not only the "spirit of the times" but also the details of individual moral character. This new fused narration is most evident during descriptions of the Time of Troubles, and especially whenever Karamzin touches upon the death of Dmitri of Uglich. As Luzianina observes, by this point in his writing of the *History* Karamzin had "erased the boundary between an analytical and an emotional attitude toward the facts of history."[57]

In the early volumes of the *History,* then, chronicle narration is introduced to invoke *its own time.* This is the time of the recorder, which is presumed contemporaneous with the event and kept in check by external commentary. By the final volumes, chronicle interpretation is itself a primary source for the psychologized motivation of heroes and villains, and the exemplary victim of this new methodology is Boris Godunov. The portrait that emerges is not Boris in his own time, not even Boris in the chroniclers' time, but Boris as an eternal psychological type, for *any* time, including the time of the historian's writing and of the reader's present. This shift in the chronotope of chronicle material, from limited and encapsulated to essentially universal, is perhaps the single most significant feature in the evolution of Karamzin's historical style.

The Layering of a Source

Today it can easily be shown that Karamzin was naïve in his use of the medieval chronicle.[58] Although he knew that chroniclers did not tell everything,[59] he apparently believed that they "did not, at least, make anything up either,"[60] and thus could be used as reliable building blocks to reconstruct a historical event. What made a source truthful for Karamzin was its age. In the words of one modern scholar, Karamzin's internal criticism ceased as soon as he had access to "the indubitably authentic, the most ancient (preferably *kharateinye,* parchment) manuscripts, closest to the times described in them."[61] Apart from the manifestly miraculous or fairy-tale aspect of some early chronicle accounts, Karamzin assumed that "a true event lay at the base" of a chronicle view of the world. Thus the distinctiveness of the chronicle, in Karamzin's view, was not to be found in the degree of its veracity but in its special sense of time, its chronotope. "The historian is not a chronicler," Karamzin wrote in his foreword (xxvi–xxvii). "The latter considers only time, while the former considers the affinity and interconnectedness of events."

This view is, of course, a considerable oversimplification. It is true that the organizing principle of Muscovite chronicles remained simple chronology; the sixteenth-century chronicle compilation was conceptually rather primitive as a history-bearing genre.[62] To this extent Karamzin was correct in his claim that chronicles "considered only time." Events of several years' duration were cut up and distributed so that any internal cohesion or thematic unity was lost. As Edward Keenan has colorfully expressed it, ". . . scraps of *vitae,* accounts of miracles and hailstorms, martial tales and fragments of diplomatic correspondence were hung on the 'years,' like a shapeless pile of clothing on a coat rack. . . ."[63]

But even with their coat-rack organization, these "omnibus chronicles" were quite thoroughly ideological. Aleksei Shakhmatov, pioneering Russian philologist, demonstrated at the turn of this century that the language of the chronicles was a carrier of political passions and worldly interests.[64] Soviet scholarship has followed this line, assigning chronicle compilations to medieval genres of literary—and political—creativity.[65] The greatest Soviet medievalist, Dmitri Likhachev, assures us that the famous literary image of Pushkin's Pimen, casting "an indifferent eye on good and evil," was not an accurate representation of the typical chronicler.[66] Chroniclers recorded their accounts in the heat of the moment. It was the later compiler, "mechanically unifying a series of chronicles," who lent them an air of impartial authority. The appearance of objectivity was bestowed by the very process of becoming old, of being recopied and collated by later hands. In effect, therefore, chronicles can only be understood by presuming a double author for each passage: the one who recorded it, and the one who lent the tone of the whole to each part that he compiled.

Karamzin's *History* thus achieves a wonderful irony. By assuming the nonpartisan legitimacy of his sources and then blurring the line between his own critical voice and the voice of the chronicler, Karamzin in effect returns the chroniclers to their original partisan stance. He becomes a later compiler but in reverse, bestowing authority with the increasingly subjective intervention of a narrative "I." It is an "I," furthermore, that pretends to full access and full historical perspective. This constitutes "pretense" because Karamzin could not really return to the original perspective of each passage. He could only add yet another perspective layer—a sort of negation of the negation—which actually complicated perspective under the guise of apparent simplicity.

This chronotopic approach to the *History* makes possible a more historically responsive criticism than the work has usually received. Without a doubt, the two-part text of the *History* is internally contradictory and double voiced. But the confusion in it comes not merely because two voices, historian's and chronicler's, coexist in a single work. Confusion comes when the boundaries between voices begin to disappear, when the principle for incorporating source material into the narrative begins to shift or change focus. It was this threshold quality of the text that Pushkin surely had in mind when he called Karamzin "our first historian and our last chronicler."[67]

Pushkin, in fact, was among the first to appreciate Karamzin's *History* not for its facts but for its "chronicle style."[68] This style, at its most intense in the final volumes and exemplified by the story of Boris

Godunov, raises important questions about the nature of narrative responsibility in the writing of history. As we shall see, that same story serves Pushkin in his investigations of authorial responsibility in the writing of historical drama. Since the Boris Tale in Karamzin's hands became the canonical version, a close look at two of its central moments—the death of Dmitri of Uglich in 1591 and the election of Tsar Boris in 1598—will serve to sensitize us to Karamzin's chronotope in its most evolved form. These two events are also the pivotal ones for Pushkin and Musorgsky in their retellings, so a close reading of Karamzin (and a consideration of some of his sources) will prepare us for those later and even more complex transpositions of the theme. But first, a look at the Uglich events and the election of Boris as modern historians have reconstituted them.

The Historical Boris

A good example of the current state of Godunov scholarship is Ruslan Skrynnikov's 1978 monograph *Boris Godunov*.[69] It is a modest work meant for a lay audience, but nevertheless a model of cautious archival research—and structured, as most works on Boris have been, in the shadow of the great art preceding it. As if to free himself from that burden, Skrynnikov is polemically nondramatic. The one chapter dealing with events central to all artistic accounts, the death of Tsarevich Dmitri in 1591, is entitled "The Uglich Drama"—and Boris plays almost no part in it.

Skrynnikov argues that Boris was not powerful enough at the time to have arranged the murder, even had he wanted to. And had Boris in fact been strong enough to arrange the murder, he would not have needed to. The year 1591 was an inappropriate and dangerous time for such inflammatory gestures. Both the Swedes and the Tatars were planning attacks on Muscovy. For two years Boris's rivals at court had been maneuvering to increase their influence, and the death of Dmitri could easily have been used against the Godunovs. The murder, in any case, would have scarcely been worth the risk, for at that time the elimination of Dmitri by no means cleared Boris's way to the throne. The tsaritsa Irina was still in her childbearing years, and her several miscarriages did not preclude the eventual birth of an heir; Boris in fact argued precisely this point when he refuted, in 1586, a crude petition gotten up by the Princes Shuisky and Mstislavsky to divorce Fyodor from Irina on grounds of barrenness. But even had the murder of Dmitri been both possible and advantageous, and had Boris somehow arranged for it, a politician of his experience would have never botched the job so badly. The Godunovs had been under attack for a long time. Boris knew how to fight and he did so quietly, without witnesses and never at high noon.

Yet even in the unlikely case that the above suspicion was true, Skrynnikov claims, Boris—and this is of great importance for later transpositions of his story—would never have suffered any guilt. In the sixteenth century, eliminating political rivals was dangerous, but hardly to the soul. It is unwise to psychologize Boris, Skrynnikov warns. In those days men kept no diaries to record the torments of their hearts. The place to look is at lists of donations to monasteries: "like many other men of his time, he entrusted his troubles not to a diary but to monks" (21). Depositing money in a monastery both mollified a conscience and guaranteed a family's income if the head of household was disgraced. There had been years of great giving, such as 1585, the first year of Fyodor's reign and a time of great insecurity for Boris. But there were no special donations for 1591.

Skrynnikov thus joins his great revisionist predecessor Sergei Platonov[70] in insisting that Dmitri's death in 1591 was simply not the scandal that it later became. Dmitri was technically illegitimate, not even called Tsarevich by many but merely Grand Prince. His funeral was held in Uglich, not in Moscow. His grave was forgotten or abandoned by the Uglich townsfolk themselves, who, when asked to lead the clergy to the site of the newly sainted martyr's grave in 1606, found it (after a long search) in the side of a ditch. Tsar Fyodor Ioannovich, whose life was largely taken up with religious observances and holy pilgrimages, never once saw fit to go to Uglich and visit his half-brother's grave. And when Muscovy negotiated with the Poles in 1609, it was revealed that the Muscovite government did not remember the most elementary facts about Dmitri's death, including the year in which it occurred.[71]

Dmitri's death, however it came to pass, was a catastrophe for the Uglich court. The Nagoi brothers, ambitious uncles to the tsarevich, had long chafed under Moscow's supervision and inadequate subsidies. The crown secretary Mikhail Bitiagovsky, assigned to Uglich from the Moscow chancery, routinely resisted their demands for more money; a violent argument had occurred the very morning of the death. With Dmitri's passing the entire Nagoi power base had collapsed, for now the family had no claim to special treatment. Their fury, fueled by hard drink and the hysterical grief of the tsaritsa, touched off a general uprising against Muscovites in Uglich. Over a dozen government officials were massacred by the mob. When this news reached Moscow two days later, the Boyar Duma appointed an investigatory commission headed by Vasily Shuisky, an enemy of the Godunovs. This commission issued an official statement, known as the *Sledstvennoe delo*, within two weeks of the event.

Skrynnikov (62–63) credits the commission with an accurate picture of the massacre of May fifteenth. There was no torture of informants; the commission was unarmed. Principal witnesses were questioned in the presence of the tsaritsa Maria (who had the right to object to false testimony), but even she ceased insisting that her son had been murdered, begging instead for mercy. Several men who had cooperated with the Nagoi brothers in falsifying evidence (laying bloodstained weapons alongside the victims) confessed to the deed. Dmitri's death was declared an inadvertent suicide by the will of God, and his uncles were charged with the murder of state officials.

The *Sledstvennoe delo* is the single surviving document contemporaneous with events in Uglich. There is no reason to believe that it was partial to any particular version of events. The commission was much more concerned with the threat of civil violence, and with the dangerous precedent of appanage subjects murdering representatives of the crown, than with the death of an Uglich prince.

Not only, then, was there no guilt for Dmitri's death; there was almost no interest in him. Although Boris most likely had no role in these events, Skrynnikov assures us that he did know how to exploit them (64–65). Appanage cities would not lightly decide to rise up against the center again. The dowager tsaritsa was forced into a convent and her brothers imprisoned. The population of Uglich was dispersed. And the town bell, which had sounded the alarm that roused the mob to vengeance, had its tongue ripped out and was exiled to a remote Siberian village.

The second defining event in the Boris Tale, Boris's "seizure" of the crown upon Fyodor's death in 1598, is no less in conflict with current scholarship. Chronicle accounts and seventeenth-century sources routinely call Boris a "usurper." But later research, especially Kliuchevsky's work on the composition of the medieval *zemsky sobor* or Assembly of the Land,[72] has demonstrated that Boris came to power in as legal a way as the times permitted. Of course, neither patriarch nor *zemsky sobor* could confer the sort of legitimacy that came as a birthright to heirs in an established dynasty. Boris, Russia's first elected tsar, could never escape the fact of his election—and certainly his passionate desire to display and promote his son as heir indicated an eagerness to return, as soon as possible, to more traditional means of succession. But the mere fact of being chosen, of having to court support among *all* classes in an effort to counterbalance the hostility of the princes and the jealousy of other high-ranking boyars, has given rise to the image of Boris as "people's tsar," a tsar elected in defiance of the old families. Through this door Boris has entered the pantheon of popular heroes reaccented for Soviet audiences, a sort of royal equivalent to Pugachev.

This is partially correct, says Skrynnikov (chapter 9), but the matter is much more complicated. Since Tsar Fyodor left no heir and no will, Muscovy suffered a severe succession crisis throughout 1598. The tsaritsa Irina nominally assumed authority after her husband's death, but there was no precedent for crowning a woman in her own name. Many months of desperate politicking and redefining of procedures followed. The maneuvering that, in the opening scene of Pushkin's play, recalls a crafty and theatrical Julius Caesar (Boris refusing the crown three times, hypocritically, like "a drunkard before a jug of wine") was really a life-and-death struggle for power that Boris very nearly lost.

Surviving official and eyewitness accounts provide conflicting testimony. Relying on documents that were altered, forged, or imprecisely dated, historians have long been confused about the politics of that interregnum year. In one (more pious) version of events, Irina withdrew into a monastery, invited Boris to follow her, and in an excess of humility both brother and sister refused even to consider the crown. In a tougher and more cynically political version, Irina— consigned to a convent by her dying husband but pressured by her brother to remain in control—was forced to abdicate in favor of the Boyar Duma. She then took the veil as a way of pacifying the mob, which was incensed at the very idea of an uncrowned tsaritsa following a consecrated tsar on the throne. Even in the monastery Irina, with Boris at her side, tried to rule Russia and issue decrees in her own name. Boris assured the hostile crowd, with perhaps more hope than confidence, that "everything would remain as before."

In fact, Skrynnikov explains, both versions of events occurred during 1598. Boris actively campaigned for the crown but then refused it when hostility to his candidacy persuaded him of the hopelessness of retaining it. Withdrawal to the well-fortified Novodevichy Monastery was for protection, not for prayer. Boris left behind in Moscow his benefactor and beneficiary the Patriarch Iov, who organized processions to Novodevichy in support of Boris. But Iov was no match for the rival nobles and boyar families. In fact the Poles, carefully monitoring the progress of the elections in Russia, gave Boris the lowest chance out of four aspirants to the throne.

Moscow was being whipped into a frenzy of anti-Godunov sentiment. Rumors were sown that Boris had poisoned Tsar Fyodor. From this time, it seems, also date the first rumors that Boris had a hand in the death of Dmitri of Uglich seven years earlier.[73] It is, as we shall see, no accident that Pushkin opens his play on Prince Shuisky, whispering about the Uglich "murder" to a fellow malcontent precisely in 1598, during the heat of the interregnum. That is most likely when the "deed" was born.

The Boyar Duma failed, however, to capitalize on this anti-Godunov frenzy. It could not settle on a single candidate from among its own highborn, and bitterly divided, members. Boris's faction went to work among the gentry and townsfolk. The church organized more demonstrations to Novodevichy in support of Boris, enticing large crowds by bringing out the most sacred icons. Boris delayed calling a *zemsky sobor* until its support could be assured; he blocked the roads to Moscow so only his deputies could reach the capital. The Patriarch finally convened a *zemsky sobor* in February and it endorsed Boris. But that decision had to be approved by the Boyar Duma, as the most influential body in Muscovy outside the church, and the Duma was paralyzed.

In early spring, finally persuaded of mass support, Boris agreed to accept the crown. He was blessed by the Patriarch and escorted to the Kremlin. But the Duma continued to withhold its confirmation, and Boris again withdrew to the monastery. Another procession and assembly was organized; again Godunov protected himself by dramatically rejecting the throne. Fearing a prolonged boycott by the Duma and the specter of a leaderless state, the Patriarch asked Irina to command her brother's coronation, threatening them both with excommunication should he refuse. They relented, and again Boris moved to the Kremlin palace.

The Boyar Duma was finally roused to action. It agreed on a pliable countercandidate for the throne, the baptized Tatar khan Simeon Bekbulatovich, notorious in Ivan the Terrible's time and now living out his days old and blind in a remote province. At this point Boris played his most skillful card. He engineered rumors that the Crimean Tatars were about to attack, and then set up an elaborate tent-city south of Moscow as a site for mobilization. There he feasted the troops throughout the summer, distributing honors and largesse, until peace envoys arrived. Boris's popularity was now so great that he agreed, again, to take the crown. He hoped to buy off his remaining foes with promotions and gifts.

The September coronation was still so fraught with uncertainty, however, that rumors circulated in Poland of a tsar being crowned and then assassinated. Thoroughly aware of his vulnerability, Boris devised elaborate oaths of loyalty to his person and his family. Many contemporary accounts mention this obsessive swearing of loyalty oaths, in government offices, public squares, during church services— and not just by dignitaries but by the entire people. Again the opening scenes of the play and the opera ring true: regardless of Boris's virtues, an *elected* monarch could never rest in power. No display of support could ever seem sufficient.

Skrynnikov has nothing but praise for the role played by Boris during this difficult year:

Tradition posed overwhelming obstacles to Boris's rise to power and the interregnum threatened at any moment to collapse into a time of trouble. But Godunov succeeded in avoiding all pitfalls without once resorting to force. He had no peer in the art of forming political combinations. (104)

It must be admitted that Skrynnikov's and Platonov's revisionist treatments of the Boris Tale are not without their own bias and polemical intent. Their research was as predisposed to uncover an innocent Boris as earlier research had been to presume a guilty one. But they did demonstrate that the two great motifs in the tale—Boris as Tsarecide and Boris as Usurper—could not be documented historically, at least not in a way compatible with our current historiographical practice. Yet for reasons we will now explore in more detail, an innocent Boris has almost no embodiment in three centuries of artistic treatment.

The Boris Tale Matures

In the century closest to our own, the reasons for a guilty Boris are readily apparent. Soviet historians of the Time of Troubles in fact routinely hold Pushkin and Musorgsky responsible for our present inability to see the Boris Tale in its "true" historical light. One good case in point is the curious fate of the 1591 *Sledstvennoe delo*. Repressed after Boris's death, it was published only in 1819—and known, although somewhat abused, by Karamzin in the tenth volume of his *History*. Scholarly reconstruction of the actual document occurred only in the twentieth century.[74] But the events at Uglich are even now far from free of art. In 1963 the Soviet scholar I. I. Polosin published a historical monograph that painstakingly reviewed the material evidence on the *Delo,* again making a persuasive case for Boris's innocence and for the honesty of Shuisky's commission.[75] Why, he asks, is this evidence ignored, even today? In part, he claims, it is the fault of nineteenth-century historians like Kliuchevsky and Soloviev who, as believers, were unduly influenced by church canon and prejudiced in favor of the "pious" tsars Fyodor and Aleksei (243). But he then names the single most serious obstacle still facing Soviet historians in the Uglich affair: Pushkin's drama. His article ends with a highly curious reading of that work, one that attempts, as it were, to recover Pushkin for the cause of historical "accuracy" by proving that Pushkin too believed in Boris's innocence.[76] The temptation to produce such readings stems from Pushkin's dual status in Russian culture as poet *and* historian—although, to be sure, Pushkin never attempted a history of the Time of Troubles. To a degree that would have doubtlessly dismayed Pushkin himself, *Boris Godunov* has achieved canonical status as a historical (not just a literary) text, so much so that revisions of history have tended to include rereadings of the play. Even professional historians have felt a need to come to terms with the powerful *fictional* biographies of Boris.

In addition to aesthetic reasons there were powerful, and closely related, religious and political factors at work in the very recording of the "evidence." The critical documents in the seventeenth-century construction of a guilty Boris were scrutinized in the early part of this century by Sergei Platonov.[77] More recently a number of Soviet researchers, most ably K. V. Chistov and A. A. Rudakov, have investigated the "Legend of Saint Dmitri"—a legend that called into being an equally mythical biography of Boris.[78] Our interest in these documents and legends will be dictated largely by the use Karamzin later made of them, and the sort of authority he bestowed upon their authors.

Most significant is the fact that all surviving documents, excepting the *Delo* itself, date from (and none before) 1606. In that year Tsar Vasily Shuisky arranged for Dmitri to be canonized by the church and his remains brought to Moscow for consecration. This avowedly political act was designed to accomplish several tasks at once: to confirm the fraud of the False Dmitri, just deceased; to emphasize the evil of Boris Godunov (whose defeat by a pretender could thus be seen as divine punishment); and to discourage (as it happened, unsuccessfully) any further pretenders to Dmitri's name. The necessary miracles were produced. According to eyewitness accounts by foreigners, the fresh corpse of a priest's son was displayed as proof that the new saint's remains had not decomposed during seventeen years in an Uglich grave. Various afflicted persons, in Shuisky's pay, became whole at graveside.

When the written accounts of Dmitri's death and canonization began to appear, then, they were all thoroughly politicized. These written accounts were conditioned by other factors as well. As part of the medieval literary system, the historical material they contained was rigorously organized according to fixed stylistic stereotypes mandatory for certain types of events.[79] A brief survey of the major seventeenth-century treatments of Dmitri's death will serve to illustrate the larger shape, and fate, of the Boris Tale before Karamzin encountered it.

Two basic versions of Dmitri's fate can be detected in the sources. Both are anti-Godunov, but each served its own political purpose. Before and during the False Dmitri's actual reign, of course, the death-in-Uglich story had to be reworked into a miraculous salvation. According to popular rumor and to the False Dmitri's own decrees on his personal history, the murder attempt did not take place in the courtyard at all but in the royal bedroom, where, anticipating the intent of Boris's agents, a German doctor had long been putting the tsarevich to sleep alongside another boy. It was this boy, so the version goes, who was eventually murdered; the true Dmitri, smuggled out of Uglich, was raised in a distant village until his coming of age.

The basic format of this biography—with its folkloric motifs of substitution, sequesterment, and years of wandering in distant places—proved very popular during the Time of Troubles, when legends of the Returning Tsarevich-Deliverer were widespread. It nourished the movement for False Peter in 1606 (the supposed son of Tsar Fyodor, whom a jealous Boris had replaced with a girl in 1592) and the movement behind the Second False Dmitri as well. Significantly, the deaths of Tsar Fyodor and of Boris did not give rise to legends of miraculous return; the popular consciousness seemed to prefer an innocent child on whom to pin its unrealized hopes. Between 1607 and 1610 a large number of "tsarevichi" appeared in Russia and Poland under a profusion of names: Tsar Fyodor's supposed sons Peter, Fyodor, Klementy, Savely, Semyon, Vasily, Erofei, Gavrila, Martin, and Lavrenty; yet another (lost) son of Ivan the Terrible; and even a nonexistent son of Ivan the Terrible's eldest son (and victim), Ivan Ivanovich. A generation later, during the 1640s, three or four "sons of Dmitri" emerged briefly.[80] But by then the Romanov clan had given evidence of its political tenacity, and from then on pretenders claimed relationship to the new dynasty.

The second version of Uglich, relating the successful murder of Dmitri by agents of Boris, gained official status during Shuisky's reign and soon became the canonical account. The story underwent numerous transformations, each version vilifying Boris more energetically than the last. The first documents to emerge during 1606 with a version of Uglich were the official decrees on Dmitri's death issued by the boyars, Maria Nagaia, and Tsar Shuisky. The earliest decrees from that year did not mention Boris or murder at all; that detail entered only after Shuisky's coronation in May, by which time it had apparently become clear that Tsar Shuisky intended to repudiate the findings of the commission he had headed back in 1591. By June the death—now a murder—had accumulated details appropriate to a saint; a new decree spoke of Boris murdering an "innocent lamb," and miracles were noted during the ceremonial transfer of the tsarevich's remains to Moscow. All the decrees that dated from 1606, however, were rather sparse and formulaic in their mention of the crime at Uglich. The embroidery of details came later, when the event was no longer the province of eyewitnesses.

The next important stage in the evolution of the legend was

reflected in the *Inoe skazanie* of 1645, itself a compilation of earlier chronicle accounts. The *Skazanie,* immensely influential on later compilations, was apparently wholly a product of the Shuisky camp. Its "Tale of 1606" *(Povest' 1606 goda)* contained an account of Dmitri's death, in a version that smoothly integrated details from the earlier decrees into a single narrative and added some new information. The miracles at the grave were now specific. Boris was made responsible for a series of actions preliminary to the murder (exiling Dmitri to Uglich, attempting to poison him, dispatching agents with sinister intentions), and he was accused of subsequent murders as well, most spectacularly the murder of Tsar Fyodor. The soul of Boris was now identified with the serpent who tempted Eve, with Judas Iscariot, and with the ~~twelfth~~-century Kievan prince Sviatopolk the Accursed, murderer of Saints Boris and Gleb. The *Povest'* was more than a political pamphlet; it is, in the opinion of several current scholars, a superb example of anti-Godunov art.

Quite different in tone were the nonhagiographic tales of the period, especially the accounts of Avraam Palitsyn (1617) and Katyrev-Rostovsky (1630). Both were reasonably neutral about Boris's career, and free of irrational hatred toward the Godunovs. But new details continued to enrich the story. In Katyrev's account, for example, Boris was charged with setting fire to Moscow in 1591 to divert attention from Uglich—a detail, incidentally, that helped Katyrev account for the fact that the death of the tsarevich had passed almost unnoticed by the Muscovites at the time.

Beginning with the *Novy letopisets* (1630) the Uglich story became ever more internally contradictory, as chroniclers attempted to compile and splice variously embroidered versions. Boris, always so cautious and secretive, was now shown recruiting a large crew of murderers for Uglich. Persons close to the Romanov family began to be retroactively exonerated and excised from the plot. A more dramatic scenario was provided, with a fuller cast of good and evil characters: the tsarevich's nurse Volokhova became an accomplice in the murder, his wet nurse a heroic protector. For the first time bad conscience was ascribed to the murderers. A courier sent by the *Uglichane* to Tsar Fyodor with news of the murder was intercepted by Godunov (another ancient folkloric motif) and the message rewritten.

We arrive finally at the *Zhitie,* or Saint's Life, of Tsarevich Dmitri as it stabilized at midcentury. Since Dmitri's real biography was so brief and unexceptional, his Life was put together out of standard formulae. The death was the central event, and a ready vehicle existed in Russia's long tradition of martyred princes. The Uglich murder now took on a ritualized solemnity. The "murderers" of Dmitri were no longer pursued by an unruly mob but were killed on the spot, blinded by divine wrath. Lengthy laments by the tsaritsa, by the *Uglichane,* and by Tsar Fyodor were interpolated into the text. The Moscow fires, still set by Boris, now not only distracted from the murder but also became the reason why a grief-stricken Tsar Fyodor did not visit Uglich to take leave of his brother's body. The *Zhitie* mentioned the investigatory commission and its *Delo,* but then openly accused Boris of buying off its members and falsifying testimony. Shuisky, perhaps back in favor for his pivotal role in canonizing the victim, took no part in the commission's interrogations but only wept.

The last major seventeenth-century account, the *Skazanie o tsarstve Tsaria Feodora Ioannovicha* (1680–90s) already showed evidence of secular literary devices, including psychologized inner monologue. Boris was no longer prompted solely by the devil but by worldly ambition as well. Categories of time had begun to be exploited for suspense and pathos: Fyodor, for example, had premonitions that he would not see his brother alive again, and soothsaying (a play with present and future time) had become a major motif.

The Uglich story moved into the eighteenth century, then, in two basic forms. On the one hand, hagiographic accounts stressed miracle and divine wrath, describing Boris as an incarnation of the devil. Rudakov has called most of these accounts simply "fantasy"; Platonov considered the *Skazanie* "an interesting example of the literary devices characteristic for mytho-legendary *[basnoslovnyi]* narration."[81] More secularized accounts, on the other hand, had begun to develop personalities and patterns of inner motivation for the participants in the tale. Both forms stitched "known" details together in a way appropriate to the genre and purpose of the telling, and both presumed a guilty Boris.

These were the sources out of which Karamzin built his own story. But that story, too, went through several variants and was subject to changing criteria of validation. In fact, the evolution of Karamzin's relationship to the Boris Tale is a history in itself.

The History of the History

That relationship began in the early years of Karamzin's move from literature to history, with a brief piece entitled "Historical Reminiscences and Observations on the Road to Troitse" (1802).[82] "Troitse" was the Troitse-Sergeevo Monastery, where Boris had so often taken refuge and where the Godunovs are buried. Karamzin devotes the latter half of his essay to a meditation on that family's unjust fate. He begins by affirming the most generous verdict history could offer: "If Godunov had not cleared his way to the throne by murder, history would have acclaimed him a glorious monarch—and his services as Tsar were so important that a Russian patriot would like to doubt even that evil deed" (351). Karamzin then deflects this rebuke, already mild, away from Boris and redirects it against the documents that condemned him:

> What is accepted and confirmed by general opinion tends to become a sacred thing, and the timid historian, fearing to be found too bold, repeats the chronicles without criticism. In this way history sometimes becomes the echo of slander. . . . What a mournful thought! The cold ashes of the dead have no defender except our conscience: all is silent around an ancient grave! (351–52)

The chronicler has become the villain of the tale. Karamzin asks whether we, as modern readers, should believe "false opinion, incorporated into the chronicle through senselessness or malicious intent." Although the chroniclers, "unwillingly doing him justice," had admitted that Boris loved to rule justly, nevertheless "all that could have been said in praise of Godunov they passed over in silence" (359).

Karamzin does not deny Boris's guilt, nor his cunning (khitrost'). But he does recommend that they be seen in context, and measured against the good that Godunov hoped to accomplish as Tsar. "We, thank God, live in such times when man can and must use his reason; we explain the character of a man by the deed, and the deed by the character of the man. We know that the ambition of intelligent men is not always a stranger to evil-doing" (365).

Karamzin passes over Uglich and the 1598 elections with hardly a murmur. "Dmitri was no more. . . . For the first time, Russia elected herself a monarch, triumphantly and freely" (356). If such a tsar rarely showed himself to his people, Karamzin noted, this was understandable. Although generous and progressive, "Godunov the Tsar was afraid to remind the people, by his person, of Godunov the Subject. It is a terror unknown to hereditary monarchs!" (367).

Thus Karamzin's early portrait of the Tsar Boris is a spirited defense of the man against his detractors. Karamzin assures us in this essay that he is not "writing history"; consequently, he has "no need to resolve the matter [of Boris's guilt]" but merely "marvels at Divine Justice, that could punish this evil deed in such a terrible and even miraculous way" (352–53). Already present in microcosm here is the ethical imperative and larger moral logic that will later inform the *History*. But what is also present here, and removed from Karamzin's later accounts of the Boris Tale, is a suspicion of the source, an insistence that sources can be held morally responsible for the images they create and that later generations have an obligation to redress any imbalance.

It is intriguing to speculate—as Mikhail Pogodin did in print in 1829, and Wilhelm Kiukhelbeker did in his diary three years later[83]— why Karamzin's early image of Boris is so much more charitable than the harsh portrait in the *History* some two decades later. The year 1802, when the Troitse essay was published, had just witnessed the triumphant ascension of Alexander I to the throne. Karamzin was a fervent admirer of the new tsar, and he linked (as did many of his class) the early, more liberal years of Catherine the Great with this illustrious grandson. Between 1801 and 1803 Karamzin had written a lengthy eulogy to Catherine, and two odes to Alexander. It is in this context that we should read the Troitse piece on Boris.

Karamzin's 1802 Boris is no criminal. He is ambitious, Karamzin admits, and "the ambition of intelligent men is not always a stranger to evildoing." But to a certain extent great men write their own laws. A higher court will hold them accountable; meanwhile their fellow men must understand their errors in light of the larger earthly good they make possible. So while the murder of Dmitri is a constant subtext, it is also constantly qualified: "God judges secret villainies, but we must praise tsars for everything that they do for the glory and welfare of the Fatherland" (374). The "secret villainies" is clearly a reference to Uglich. But in 1802, any retelling of the death of Dmitri in Uglich would most likely also be an allusion to the death of Paul I in Petersburg. Alexander I, too, had come to the throne in a scandal-ridden succession, with tsarecide (and perhaps parricide) clearing the way for a competent ruler to assume power. Karamzin's enthusiastic support of the young tsar might well have motivated this charitable reading of events in Uglich, and of Godunov's dilemma. Paul I had been as disastrous for Russia at the end of the eighteenth century as Fyodor would have been, were it not for Boris, at the end of the sixteenth. Clearly, the "glory and welfare of the Fatherland" could not always be served by the same morality that governed private actions.

This implicit parallel—of Boris and Alexander transgressing personal morality on behalf of the greater good—was soon overtaken by events, and the Godunov saga was accordingly reshaped for a new function. Between 1802 and Karamzin's next statement on the Time of Troubles, the full force of Napoleon was felt on the European scene. In the early volumes of the *History* written during these years Karamzin refined his understanding of usurpation: it was a potentially legitimate route to power, but only for members of the reigning house.[84] By 1811 and the writing of his "Memoir on Ancient and Modern Russia," Karamzin had ceased to bring to his task the emotional sentiments of a man in love with a maligned tsar; his was now the perspective of a national historian during a time of crisis. In this memoir Karamzin created for Boris an almost programmatic role in the disintegration of the old dynasty, and it is this role that Boris plays, with some additional burdens, in the *History* as well.

The memoir is prefaced by a brief historical introduction surveying Russian rulers since the Kievan period. According to Karamzin, the lesson that history teaches us is this: "Russia was founded by victories and by monocracy, she perished from the division of authority, and was saved by wise autocracy."[85] Rulers who succeeded at Russia's great tasks—defense of the state from its enemies, and defense of the people from internecine strife—had all shared certain attributes. They inherited power in legitimate dynastic succession. That power was undivided. And rulers wielded it with firmness and restraint. From the 1580s to the end of the Riurikovich dynasty, five monarchs occupy the throne—and Karamzin reads the sequence as a gradual erosion of these desirable attributes.

Ivan IV, the Terrible, indeed ruled without restraint, but he was indisputably autocratic and legitimate. Thus his tyranny was "awe-inspiring" and his obedient subjects prayed for mercy rather than plotted against his rule. Loyalty was cruelly tested in those years, Karamzin admits, but "virtue did not even hesitate in choosing between death and resistance" (113). Boris Godunov, "a Tatar by origin, a Cromwell by disposition, assumed the throne with all the prerogatives of a legitimate monarch." But his ambition, his complicity in the murder of the true heir, and the very fact of his election weakened "the moral strength of tsardom": "This unfortunate man, overthrown by the shadow of the tsarevich he had slain, perished amid deeds of great wisdom and apparent virtue, the victim of an immoderate, illicit thirst for power, as an example for ages and peoples" (113).

In 1811, Karamzin would not have needed to make this point any more explicit. His "example for ages and peoples" was no longer a private individual whose fate moved the heart. It was a lesson to Napoleon's age, that the low-born cannot achieve political greatness except through crime. The point had to be made so strongly precisely because both Boris and Napoleon were *successful* rulers. The extraordinary diplomatic and domestic achievements of Napoleon and Boris in their respective times had to be placed in less dazzling context. Thus Godunov's virtue in the memoir is already only "apparent," his positive deeds an attempt to atone for hidden sins.

Karamzin easily dismisses the last two tsars who reigned before Russia's complete collapse. The False Dmitri, initially popular as the returning tsarevich, "more closely resembled a tramp than a king," and disregarded Russian custom (while demeaning the dignity of his office) by debating with his boyars in the Duma (114). His successor, Tsar Vasily Shuisky, further betrayed the autocratic mandate by promising, in an attempt to bolster his faltering reign, to "execute no one, to deprive no one of his property" (115). In this spectrum of tsars manqués, Boris is midway in the slide from flawed rule to failure. But we already see the larger purpose his biography will serve.

Karamzin's Boris in the History: *Two Episodes and a Moral*

We can now turn to the *History* itself. The fifteenth- and sixteenth-century chronicles upon which Karamzin drew for his final volumes differed substantially from the earlier historical writings of Old Russia. Muscovy had expanded enormously under the reigns of Ivan III and Vasily III. The church and the central power were firmly allied, and for the first time it seemed possible for Russia to confront—and match—the models of universal history offered by the Holy Roman Empire and Roman Christianity. Scribes ceased to be anonymous recorders of local events in isolated monasteries and began to function as authors inspired by an imperial vision. A desire for harmony and unity permeated secular as well as religious literary production. And the tenth volume of the *History,* which contains accounts of our two central events, reflects honestly the spirit of these sources.

The first story, Dmitri's death in Uglich, is the presentation of an event—and closely resembles the formulaic patterning in the Life (or rather the Death) of a Saint. The second story, Boris's rise as brother-in-law to Fyodor and his ultimate election as tsar, is the presentation of a personality—and has strong affinities with a morality play. Both accounts are marked by a distinctive chronotope that denies, in essence, any developmental potential to time. All characteristic features of the biography are present ready-made at the outset.[86] Telling the story, therefore, entails distributing static qualities along a sequence of events that are not, in themselves, allowed to participate in the formation of character. Events reflect character passively; they do not modify or challenge it.

To say that Boris's character does not develop is not, however, to suggest that it is *simple*. On the contrary, Boris's character is complex, and Karamzin brings different sides of it into play at different times. But this complexity is profoundly diminished by the fact that Boris remains, for Karamzin, essentially an *illustration.* The value Karamzin aims to transmit is not in the biography itself but in larger, impersonal categories: the need for legitimacy and the advantages of hereditary monarchy. The overwhelming presence of preconceived categories imparts a stasis to the developing life, however multifaceted and complex.

This nondevelopmental, "illustrative" chronotope is already clearly present in the very first mention of Boris in the *History.* Noble and base are, from the start, fully matured attributes:

> The love of the Tsar [Ivan IV] toward him [Maliuta Skuratov]—if tyrants are able to love!—was instrumental in the promotion of yet another noble youth, Maliuta's son-in-law, a relation of the first wife of Ioann's father, Boris Fyodorovich Godunov, in whom both great virtues of statecraft and a criminal ambition had already ripened. During this time of terrors the young Boris, endowed with the rarest gifts of nature, imposing, handsome, sagacious, stood near a bloodstained throne but was himself unstained by blood, with subtle cunning avoiding any part in the murders, awaiting better times, and amid the savage *Oprichnina* shone not only with beauty but with moral calm, outwardly compliant but inwardly steadfast in his far-sighted schemes. (IX, 131–32)

This preformed nature of Boris's character is reinforced in volume X, where the accession of Fyodor marks the *de facto* beginning of Boris's rule.

> That famous man [Boris] was then in the full flower of his life, in his full strength both bodily and spiritually, being at the time thirty-two years old. In regal beauty, in commanding visage, in a quick and profound mind, in a stunning eloquence (so speaks the chronicler) Boris surpassed the nobles, but he lacked only virtue. He desired and knew how to do good, but only out of a love for glory and power; he saw in virtue not an end but a means to the attaining of an end. Had he been born to the throne, he would have deserved to be called one of the best monarchs in the world; but born a subject, with an unbridled passion to rule, he could not resist the temptation when evil seemed to his advantage—thus the curse of centuries muffles Boris's positive reputation in history. (X, 7)

Karamzin models Boris's rise on that of Ivan the Terrible, that is, "good years" followed by "bad" (X, 15–16). But this parallel only serves to accentuate Boris's departure from the model on the crucial issue of illegitimacy. As in those morality plays where the sin is only gradually revealed to the sinner (and to the audience), Boris begins triumphant. No one in the kingdom is wiser, or richer, than Godunov (11–12). His generosity and mercy are unprecedented; when he discovers a plot to poison his own person he is satisfied by having a single prince shorn as a monk. Karamzin himself marvels at Boris's *umerennost'*, his measured responses and moderate temperament, comparing him to Ivan IV's levelheaded advisor Adashev (27–28).

Since this biographical mode does not allow personality to develop but only to be disclosed, change in character can be registered solely by revelation—that is, by a sudden confirmation of what was present, but hidden, all along. Like Macbeth, Boris turns out to be not the innocent flower but the serpent under it. What had once been moderation now turns out to be *khitrost'*, guile or cunning. Godunov, "despite all his skills in the art of charming men," is the continual target of hatred and evil plots (43). People begin to recognize him for what he *truly is*. "Not only many of the leading state figures but also ordinary citizens of the capital expressed a general dislike of Boris," Karamzin claims. And this is because the common people had an instinctive sense of proper hierarchy in matters of power and rank:

> . . . unlimited power in even the most worthy magnate is repellent to the people. Adashev at one time had power over Ivan's heart and over the fate of Russia, but he stood humbly behind an intelligent, impulsive, energetic monarch, disappearing, as it were, in his glory; Godunov reigned openly and magnified himself in front of the throne, covering with his arrogance the weak shadow of him who wore the crown. (43–44)

For this, Karamzin says, Boris was considered a *khishchnik*, a plunderer or bird of prey—one of several ugly words built off the adjective *khitry* (clever, cunning), which will become Godunov's special epithet. Although Boris has so far brought nothing but good to Russia, he begins to suffer a major shift in adjectives. "People remember" that Boris is Maliuta Skuratov's son-in-law, and a descendent of "Mongolian tribes" (44). Restraint on Boris's part is seen not as moderation but as failure of will; "Boris," Karamzin asserts, "is a tyrant, although still a timid one."[87] Good behavior has become cowardly or hypocritical; aggressive behavior is tyrannical. The turning point is Boris's retribution against the princes of the blood who plotted to divorce Irina from Fyodor: "Thus did the evil deeds begin; thus was the heart of Godunov laid bare. . ." (48).

Even Fyodor's incompetence is now somehow held against Boris. Chapter 1 ends with a lengthy passage describing the tsar's day: prayer, matins, naps, jesters, bear-fights, prayer, and bed. When petitioners came on state business, Fyodor, "who avoided the vanity of the world and its tedious requests, did not want to listen, and sent them to Boris." *Khitry* Godunov, "inwardly rejoicing at the trivial inactivity of the Tsar," tried to elevate his sister, Irina, in her own name and thus "to affirm his present grandeur and prepare for the future" (49).

Godunov's political rise is his moral fall. But since Boris's diplomatic triumphs and domestic projects are still so beneficial to Russia, Karamzin must find a focus, a dramatic event, to illuminate that fall. This is the Uglich murder.

Karamzin tells the story (X, 74–84) through a subtle alternation of techniques, and carefully prepares the ground. Two lengthy discussions precede the fatal year 1591: the first concerns Russia's wars and ceasefires with Poland and Sweden, the second (signaling a shift to more sacred matters), the establishment of a Russian patriarchate.

The latter achievement, of enormous significance for Russia, becomes in Karamzin's retelling a mere function of Godunov's ambition:

> In the eyes of Russia and of all states dealing with Moscow, Boris Godunov at this time stood at the very peak of greatness, as the full ruler of the Tsardom, a man who saw nothing around him except silent slaves or people noisily praising his lofty virtues. . . . Not one to praise too modestly his power and virtue, Boris, as ambitious as he was cunning, thought up the idea of imparting new glitter to his rule by means of an important innovation in the Church. (X, 69)

In fact, the demand for a Russian patriarchate long predated Godunov. Ever since the Council of Florence in the mid-fifteenth century—and the subsequent Turkish conquest of Constantinople, which Muscovy saw as divine retribution for the sin of attempted reunion with Rome—the Russian Orthodox Church had been pressing for a patriarch of its own. Russia was, after all, the sole surviving independent Orthodox nation. When, in 1588, the Byzantine patriarch Jeremiah visited Moscow on an alms-gathering mission, Boris maneuvered him into promising Russia her own patriarchate.

Karamzin interprets this move as a plot to install the Metropolitan Iov, Boris's trusted supporter, in that new high office. In the presence of the new patriarch, the tsaritsa Irina begs the Greek prelates to intercede for her with God, in hope that He might grant her a son and heir to the tsardom. At the end of his account, Karamzin compares Boris's establishment of a Russian patriarchate with Peter the Great's destruction of it a century and a half later:

> Peter reigned on the throne and wanted [around him] only servants; Godunov, still a subject, was seeking support, for he well foresaw circumstances under which kinship with the Tsaritsa would not be sufficient for his ambition and even for his salvation; . . . Godunov, in Peter the Great's place, could have also demolished the rank of patriarch, but being in different circumstances he wanted to flatter the ambition of Iov with a high title, so as to have in him a most loyal and distinguished accomplice: or had the decisive hour come, and the despotic powermonger at last dared for himself to lift the veil of the future? (X, 74–75)

These contiguous references, to a Royal House without an heir and to Godunov creating (in a move as aggressive as the Petrine reforms) an agent to legitimize his rule, are followed immediately by the Uglich murder.

> If Boris, having everything except Fyodor's crown, had wanted nothing more, would he have been able even in that position to enjoy peacefully his greatness, contemplating the near end of the Tsar who was weak not

only in mind but also in body, contemplating the legal heir, raised by his mother and kinfolk in obvious though honorable exile, in hatred toward the Ruler, in feelings of malice and vengeance? What, in such a case, awaited Irina? A monastery. And Godunov himself? Prison or the executioner's block. This for the man who had moved the Tsardom with a wave of his hand, who was pampered by monarchs of East and West! . . . Events had already exposed Boris's soul: those unfortunate men whom the Ruler had feared had already perished in the dungeons, on the *Lobnoe mesto*—and who was more dangerous to him than Dmitri? . . . Convinced that the scepter would be handed to him who had so long and so gloriously ruled without the name of Tsar, this greedy and ambitious man saw, between himself and the throne, only one helpless infant, just as a greedy lion sees a lamb. . . . The death of Dmitri was inevitable! (75–76)

This extended passage provides good evidence of that web of narrative technique and rhetoric commanded by Karamzin in the final volumes of the *History*. An inner perspective on criminal acts, first bestowed on Ivan the Terrible in volume IX, is enriched here with inner dialogue in a question-and-answer format. Significantly, the second voice is sympathetic to Boris's plight: "What, in such a case, awaited Irina? A monastery. And Godunov himself? Prison or the excutioner's block. This for the man who had moved the Tsardom with a wave of his hand. . . ." Mere condemnation of the murder could never have been as persuasive as this format of "reasonable inquiry," where Boris is portrayed as a man simply *not free* to act otherwise. He is not free because his character can react to circumstance in only one way. Whatever evidence might be later introduced for or against his guilt, none of it could be as strong as this preordained psychological imperative.

This imperative appears to dictate how Karamzin incorporates his sources into the main narrative. In one category of incorporation, common (as we have seen) in the early volumes of the *History*, Karamzin isolates a chronicle account specifically as a quotation and prefaces it with a disclaimer. This device is employed in the Boris Tale when chronicle information does not conform to the psychological prerequisites of the established portrait. A good example is the "curious but doubtful tale" that Karamzin cites concerning Boris and the soothsayers.

Although he had a keen intelligence, Boris nevertheless believed in the art of soothsayers. He summoned several of them in the dead of night and asked what awaited him in the future. The smooth-tongued sorcerers and astrologers answered: what awaits you is the crown. . . and then they suddenly fell silent, as if frightened by future prophecy. Impatient Boris ordered them to continue. When he heard that he was to be given only seven years to rule, he exclaimed with the most lively joy, embracing the soothsayers: Let it be seven days, if only to rule! (76)

One might ask why Karamzin considers this story, so correct in its moral and characterological profile, only "doubtful." Part of the reason, of course, is the reticence a nineteenth-century historian must bring to the prophecies of witches and astrologers. But this is not the only reason; elsewhere in the *History* Karamzin fuses the authoritative voice of his narrator with the most unlikely events, including the miraculous nondecomposition of Tsarevich Dmitri's corpse that Muscovites "witnessed" after the holy remains were moved from Uglich to the capital (XII, 9). In the soothsayer instance, Karamzin is in fact quite explicit why the chronicle account is unreliable: "As if Godunov would have revealed the inner workings of his soul so carelessly to the sham wise men of that superstitious age!" (76). To Boris in his own age, of course, soothsayers were hardly "sham wise men." But Karamzin, in keeping with his consciously chosen ahistoric narrative style, lifts Boris out of his medieval time and frees him of its grip over his psyche. Given the choice between medieval chronicle (which embraces superstition) and a psychologized narration (which resists it), Karamzin clearly favors the latter. Thus the chronicle can revert to its earlier status as "local color," as purveyor of the "spirit of the times."

When Karamzin utilizes a different category of source—say, contemporary accounts by foreigners—he has a different set of means for embedding authority. The use of Giles Fletcher in the Uglich Affair is one instructive example (76–77). Karamzin is understandably hostile to Fletcher's celebrated, and largely negative, picture of Russia in *Of the Russe Commonwealth* (1591); one of the few good things Karamzin writes about Queen Elizabeth is that she banned Fletcher's book (X, 123). But Karamzin does know how to utilize Fletcher as a pliable source. In describing the events preliminary to the Uglich murder, Karamzin lists several steps taken by Boris to prepare public opinion. First, Boris supposedly spread rumors that Dmitri, as the son of a seventh wife, was illegitimate (76–77). Fletcher is cited as the source for this rumor. But the quotation from Fletcher's text offered as documentation (*prim.* #222) does not actually accuse Boris of responsibility for the rumor; here is that familiar incompatibility between narrative text and notes. Karamzin employs a more aggressive tactic in Boris's alleged second step, the spreading of rumors that Dmitri resembled his father in cruelty and perverse delight in torture. Again Fletcher is the source,[88] but this time Karamzin, while confirming the reliability of Fletcher's account, discredits the rumor directly in the narrative text by calling it a "fairy tale" and "absurd slander":

In opposition to this absurd slander, many asserted that the young Tsarevich showed intelligence and qualities worthy of a child of royal blood; people said this with reverence and with fear, for they guessed the danger facing the innocent child, saw the aim of the slander—and were not deceived: if Godunov had ever struggled with his conscience he had conquered it now. Having prepared the gullible to accept evil-doing and feel no pity, Boris held in his hand both poison and the knife, seeking only someone to whom to give them, so that the murder might be accomplished! (77)

The sole source for the above interpretation of events (*prim.* #225) is A. I. Mankiev's *Iadro Rossiiskoi Istorii* (The nucleus of Russian history), written in 1713, published half a century later, and Karamzin's major source for the events at Uglich.[89] The *Iadro* has a rather unsavory reputation in Russian historiography.[90] Its Uglich story is a composite of late seventeenth-century versions, in which the murder has already moved from the rear courtyard to the main palace staircase for greater elegance and effect.[91] We noted earlier that Karamzin's usual evaluative criterion for a source was its age, its closeness to the events described within it. In the Uglich case, however, a different principle clearly applies. Here the most distanced and embroidered version is the favored one,[92] and this must alert us to some rearrangement of value within the chronotope.

Rumor and embroidery are not, to be sure, irrelevant to history. Even if false they may influence opinion and action; rumor may even be true, and with suitable qualification be used as a source. In Pushkin's drama, we recall, the evil machinations of Boris in preparation for Uglich are first voiced by Shuisky—a man we know to be craftier and less trustworthy than Boris himself. In Karamzin, likewise, rumors play a major role. But only in those instances where they discredit Godunov are they treated as true and presented without a qualifying frame.

Significantly, the last overt premurder instance of "indirect speech"—that is, the marker "in the words of the chronicler"—prefaces one patently miraculous detail: poison intended for the tsarevich "worked neither in his food nor his drink" (78). But this presumption—that the hand of God had intervened to protect Dmitri from lethal poison—could not be allowed to stand without comment in the *History,* however compatible it was with a chronicle view of the world. Verisimilitude was precisely what Karamzin had to create for his sources as he moved into the central event of the Boris Tale, yet he was writing for an audience no longer automatically persuaded by the reality of divine intervention against material cause. Thus the chronicle account of foiled poisoning is not discredited, not dismissed, but rather remotivated. A psychological explanation replaces the super-natural:

> Perhaps a conscience still functioned in the perpetrators of that hellish intention; perhaps a trembling hand carefully contrived to spill some of the poison, thus reducing the amount, to the irritation of impatient Boris, who decided to make use of other and bolder scoundrels. . . . (78)

Two faithful servitors, Vladimir Zagriazhsky and Nikifor Chepchugov, are offered the job but they decline; they would die for Boris, but not kill. Finally Boris settles on the reliable Bitiagovsky, whose scarred and evil face earns him Karamzin's epithet *izverg*, monster. Bitiagovsky's official role as crown secretary, responsible for financing and supervising the Uglich court, is mentioned only in passing. Karamzin attributes a singular purpose to the man, "not to let the ill-fated victim out of his sight, to seize the first favorable moment" (78).

> Some time passed; finally the murderers, not seeing a chance to get the evil deed done in secret, risked an open plot in the hopes that powerful and cunning Godunov would find some means for concealing it, for the sake of his own honor, from the sight of his speechless slaves. But the murderers were thinking only of men, and not of God! (79)

For the actual death scene, vividly replete with dialogue among playmates, Karamzin footnotes only one preliminary detail: the fact that the tsaritsa and her son had just returned from church at six P.M. on that fatal day, May fifteenth, and were preparing to dine. Expanding on the *Iadro* source, Karamzin narrates as if he had the testimony of eyewitnesses. The tsarevich is approached by his young playmates Osip Volokhov, Danilo Bitiagovsky, and Nikita Kachalov:

> [Osip], grasping Dmitri by the hand, said: "Sovereign! You have a new necklace!" The child, with a smile of innocence, raised his head and said, "No, it's an old one . . ." Then the murderer's knife glittered above him; it barely touched his larynx, then fell from Volokhov's hands. Screaming with horror, the wet nurse embraced her royal nurseling. Volokhov ran off, but Danilo Bitiagovsky and Kachalov snatched the victim, slit his throat, and rushed down the staircase, at the very moment when the Tsaritsa was coming from the entrance-hall out onto the porch . . . The nine-year-old Holy Martyr lay bloody in the arms of the woman who had raised him and who had wanted to protect him with her own breast; he *trembled like a dove*, expiring, and died, never hearing the shriek of his desperate mother. . . . (79; emphasis and ellipses in original)

We recognize here the diction and elevated rhetoric of a *Zhitie* or Life of a Saint. The general model would seem to be that of the first canonized figures in the Russian church, Boris and Gleb, younger sons of Vladimir, Grand Prince of Kiev. Both brothers were canonized for no other reason than that they died without resistance in a dynastic quarrel. Dmitri's fate recalls in particular that of Gleb, who had offered his throat "for Christ's sake" to the knives of his murderers, among whom he recognized a cook of his own household.[93]

The specific model, however, is clearly the Life of St. Dmitri in one of its mid-seventeenth-century versions. The link between Boris and Gleb and the death of Dmitri had been made, we recall, at least as early as the *Inoe skazanie*. As Skrynnikov sums up the evidence:

> The earliest lives of the new saint declared Dmitrii was attacked by wicked youths, one of whom snatched away his knife and cut his throat, but feeling this brief version unsatisfactory church propagandists composed an emotional narrative abounding in dramatic but entirely fictitious details: one of the wicked boys, seeing Dmitrii wearing a necklace, asked the latter to display it. When Dmitrii trustingly thrust out his neck he struck with the knife but missed the throat. The two other miscreants then slaughtered Dmitrii like a lamb. Those who contrived such a legend, disappointed in the prosaic details of the incident, tried to embellish it, moving the action from an unexciting location—the rear courtyard—to the Red Porch and ultimately to the main palace staircase. . . .[94]

In Platonov's opinion, these later seventeenth-century accounts achieved an unlikely synthesis: they "related the murder in a very lifelike way, and yet at the same time contained much that was historically imprecise and incompatible."[95] The chronicle account of Uglich that Platonov summarizes as "the most widespread" version (231–32) accords almost perfectly with the version in Mankiev's *Iadro*, and with Karamzin's account. Karamzin, it appears, had drawn on a variety of sources—each in turn synthetic and of diverse legend, genre, and chronotope—to create a picture rich in detail and marked by an aura of almost legendary holiness.

Once the death has been accomplished, Karamzin slowly repartitions narrative authority. He now intimates historiographical scepticism without, however, implying doubt of the main features of his account. Footnotes again appear, as well as the textual insertion of distancing and framing devices: "The villains [i.e. the murderers of Dmitri], expiring, lightened their conscience, *or so it is written,* by a sincere confession: they named the main party guilty in Dmitri's death: Boris Godunov" (80; emphasis added).

After the lofty religious tones of the death, unqualified by any concessions to documentation, some sense of displacement is inevitable in the transition to any merely profane interpretation of events. In this context Karamzin's treatment of the investigatory commission is instructive. Not surprisingly, the commission is discredited. The selection of Vasily Shuisky, enemy of the Godunovs, to head the group is explained as a function of Shuisky's own opportunism: "Cunning Boris had already made peace with this ambitious prince, frivolous, clever but without moral principles. . . . Godunov knew men, and he was not mistaken in Prince Shuisky" (82). Interesting here, however, is not so much the fact as the method of the discrediting. It is achieved more by a juxtaposition of two narrative modes—sacred versus profane, revelation against investigation—than by any systematic exposure of the commission's dishonesty. Karamzin ignores the variety and specificity of the commission's testimony, and makes a farce of its activities:

> [To Shuisky's question, How did Dmitri, due to the Nagois' negligence, stab himself?] the monks, priests, men and women, old men and youths, in one spirit and unanimously, answered: "The Tsarevich was murdered by his own slaves, by Mikhail Bitiagovsky and his minions, on the order of Boris Godunov." Shuisky listened no further, dispersed them, decided to interrogate secretly, not in public, in his own way through threats and promises; he summoned whom he wished, he wrote what he wanted, and finally . . . composed the following communication to the Tsar. . . . (82)

Where Karamzin excerpts from the *Delo* in his notes, he does so accurately.[96] The segment inserted into the main narrative text of the *History* is likewise intact and includes important details nowhere else discussed. Dmitri's affliction with the "falling sickness," epilepsy, is documented, as are the Nagoi brothers' demands for more funds and their falsification of evidence after the massacre (83). But precisely by separating the exact text of the *Delo* from the narrative voice surrounding it, Karamzin can more easily dismiss its mode of testimony. The *Delo* is not misquoted, but it is (in the most sinister sense of the word) framed. The diversity of its testimony disappears and its conclusions are replaced by the statement of a single witness, Volokhova, whose account functions as a summation of the entire investigation (83). Comments on the state of the tsarevich's health or temperament become slander; the Nagoi brothers' faked evidence loses credibility when Karamzin claims that high church officials had confirmed it only "out of timidity and cowardice; the evidence of truth, unanimous and of the people, was suppressed" (83).

Civil Disobedience and Silence

This question of the people's truth, expressed and suppressed, intimates a complex area in Karamzin's historical consciousness. A mob had stoned to death a crown secretary and murdered a dozen other government officials along with wives and children. Given Karamzin's monarchist convictions and his royal patron, civil disobedience (even from the best motives) is quite understandably a sensitive issue, and the historian treats it with care and ambivalence. Just as Boris had been provided with a psychological justification for murdering Dmitri (pardoning, and therefore confirming, his guilt), so now the rebellious people benefit from a psychological explanation of their mob murder. But here, psychology confirms their higher innocence:

> The people, illegally although justifiably having avenged themselves, out of hatred to the villains, out of love for Tsarist blood, yet still forgetting their civil duties . . . pardoned perhaps by a feeling of compassion, but still guilty before a court of state, came to their senses, quieted down, and with uneasiness awaited an order from Moscow. (81)

The self-cancelling charges and exonerations of the above passage (its "althoughs," "yets," "buts") speak to Karamzin's own uneasiness as well. His *History* as a whole demonstrates a rather complex attitude toward the anarchic impulses of the folk.[97] In describing Uglich, Karamzin can no longer invoke the simple rubric that had worked so well for rebellion in the early volumes—the courage and passion for freedom of the ancient Slavic tribes. For these are no longer ancient tribes; the people of Uglich are imperial subjects. Nor can Karamzin assimilate this incident comfortably to the later heroic popular resistance to false tsars and foreign invaders. The Uglich Affair, and the scourge of pretenders to Dmitri's name that became its troubled legacy, carries a more ambivalent message about the Russian people's role in their own political history. For if the people can vindicate legitimacy and punish crimes against the royal family, then they can endorse pretenders. Succession crises and conflicts within a reigning house raise troublesome questions for defenders of autocracy, because they so often involve the use of a power from outside the royal family. It is a problem that Karamzin may have considered when reading Gibbon. The English historian described popular intervention in succession crises as the worst possible combination of the excesses of both democracy and tyranny, and attributed Roman instability and civil wars to the precedent set by such interventions.

In exploiting his sources and apportioning his judgments, then, Karamzin maneuvers skillfully among various harsh and incompatible realities. In Uglich, it so happens, the tension between civil disobedience and righteous vengeance can be resolved in a relatively straightforward manner. The massacre becomes an arena for the struggle between earthly law and divine justice. Although the reader is given to believe that Providence will ultimately reward Russia for her abhorrence of tsarecide, the people of Uglich, "guilty before a court of state," would in the short term be forced to pay. That bill is presented with no delay. The description of the Uglich Affair literally ends with the end of Uglich: two hundred executed, mass exile to Siberia, and a town of 150 churches "emptied out forever, in memory of Boris's terrible rage against the bold exposers of his deed. There remained only ruins, which howled to heaven for vengeance!" (X, 85).

Throughout the remainder of the Boris Tale, the "ruins of Uglich" are often invoked, and always in connection with divine justice—that is, with Godunov's inability to expiate his crime. In July 1591, for example, rumors spread to the effect that the Khan, then preparing to attack Muscovy, had been invited by Boris to stifle the howl over Dmitri's murder. Karamzin admits this rumor to be "absurd in the extreme" (94). But then he offers reasons why Boris's response to the rumor was so unnecessarily swift and harsh:

> A Godunov with magnanimity and an innocent heart would have despised this course slander, blown in by the wind; a Godunov with an unclean conscience boiled over with rage; he sent his officials to various parts, ordered them to search, to interrogate, to torment poor people who from simplicity of mind had merely echoed slander . . . some died under torture, others were executed, others' tongues cut out—and many places, in the words of the chronicler, emptied out at that time in the Ukraine, an addition to the ruins of Uglich!

By extension Uglich has become Russia, and the death of Dmitri the starting point for the Time of Troubles.

Such a relatively schematic "religious" resolution is, however, insufficient to explain later consequences of the Uglich murder resulting in more sustained tension between the state and the folk. Matters become too internally conflicted, and no single logic seems capable of comprehending events. To make Karamzin's Boris Tale cohere, of course, two contradictory elements must both be "true." On the one hand, Boris must be a murderer (that is, Dmitri must be dead); on the other hand, Dmitri must be alive—for so many Russians of sound mind hailed him as the true tsar. Apparently the people, as Karamzin describes them, held these two incompatible beliefs simultaneously.[98] Karamzin makes this possible by a rhetorical device, innocent enough in itself but soon to become infamous by Pushkin's borrowing of it: the device of the people's silence.

In Karamzin's history as in Pushkin's play, the people are a huge and enigmatic force, available for both good and evil. Pushkin ends his drama on their stunned silence, that famous final stage direction, *narod bezmolvstvuet* (the people remain silent). Pushkin will not say what that silence means—and in this reluctance, as we shall see, rests a philosophy of history very foreign to Karamzin. The historian, however, would have us know from the start that the people's silence does in fact speak. As he describes the midpoint of Boris's reign:

> Many still glorified Boris: his followers, flatterers, informers, those who had fattened themselves on the winnings of those disgraced; the high clergy, or so it was said, still retained in its heart a zealous attachment to the Tsar, who had showered churchmen with signs of his generosity; but the voice of the Fatherland was no longer to be heard in personal, avaricious flattery. It was the silence of the people [*bezmolvie naroda*], serving as a clear reproach to the Tsar, which communicated an important change in the hearts of Russians: *they no longer loved Boris!* (XI, 65)

Here Karamzin is honing silence as a major tactical weapon, not on behalf of any special candidate (for all candidates are discredited) but in the interests of the people themselves, as a means for making their disastrous support of pretenders less culpable and their contradictory convictions less irrational.

> Peoples are always grateful. Leaving it to Heaven to judge the secret of Boris's heart, the Russian people genuinely glorified their Tsar when he seemed to them in his personal virtue to be a father to his people; but once having recognized the tyrant in him, they naturally began to hate him, for the present as well as the past: what they perhaps had wanted to doubt they were convinced of anew, and Dmitry's blood showed up all the more vividly on the royal purple of this Destroyer of innocent lives; they recalled the fate of Uglich . . . they were silent, but felt it ever more strongly as the number of informers increased. . . . (66)

This refrain—the people were silent, the people did not love Boris—is repeated throughout the eleventh volume, as the rebellion of the *Uglichane* slowly becomes emblematic for the gap opening up between state authority and the people's trust. Karamzin, of course, would like to portray the Russian people as instinctively sympathetic to autocracy and capable of acting reasonably to secure it. Yet in their acceptance of Grishka Otrepiev, Karamzin is faced with a delusion of enormous proportions. It could be made sensible only by appealing to those psychological determinants long in place in Boris's own biography, and now in the biography of the *narod* as well:

> God's judgment thundered over the Supreme Criminal. Not one Russian before 1604 doubted the fact that Dmitri had been murdered; Dmitri, who had grown up in full view of all Uglich, whom all Uglich had seen dead, whose body they had washed with their tears for a full five days—consequently the Russians could not have reasonably believed in the resurrection of the Tsarevich: but *they did not love Boris!* (94)

Karamzin works the Uglich story so he can have it, as it were, both ways. In the actual sequence of historical events, Dmitri receives his saint's death only in 1606. But he is canonized by the people of Karamzin's *History* in 1591, and thus the rest of the Rise (and Fall) of Boris Godunov can be constructed on this sacred and violated ground. The False Dmitri is therefore supported not so much in person as in name: however illegitimate, he is in fact a *symbol* of legitimacy. He is as real, as credit-worthy, as a dead soul.

Here we see most clearly the space separating Karamzin's Borises of 1802 and 1824. In the earlier "Troitse" piece, Karamzin had pointedly opened his account of Boris's career with a footnote: "The injustice of our chroniclers in assessing this tsar has impelled me to enter here into some detail."[99] Nowhere in the essay does he directly accuse Boris of the crime at Uglich; often and fervently does he draw attention to the anti-Godunov slander of Romanov apologists.[100] The people are presented as perhaps loving, and perhaps not loving, Boris Godunov; it was simply not a critical issue.

> As concerns the people's hatred of Tsar Boris at that time, of which Prince Shcherbatov has spoken, I do not see any conclusive evidence of it. The inconstancy of the people is well known: they could have been charmed by the miraculous news and followed the banners of the False Dmitri without any special hatred toward Boris, whose reign did not deserve it. (371)

In 1802, Karamzin encouraged Russians to accept even tsarecides on the throne if they could promise progress. After 1812, and the experience of Napoleon—whose legacy in Russia was to prove so ambivalent—the people's role in the Boris Tale was recast in more "orthodox" form. Now Karamzin took pride in the difference between the Russians and the peoples of Europe.

The Russian people, however, were not wholly different. Nor could they be, if Karamzin's *History* was to serve one of its larger purposes: to demonstrate to Europe that Russia *had* a history. This was to become a recurrent task in the nineteenth century, attracting spokesmen as mature and self-critical as Alexander Herzen.[101] Russia, so the argument went, should be exempt from judgment by European criteria on the grounds of her difference—those centuries of the Mongol yoke, Muscovy's isolation from both Renaissance and Reformation. Yet at the same time Russia should be seen as similar enough to Europe to qualify her as a source of moral lessons from which all humanity could benefit.

To recover a *Smuta,* a time of trouble, for any sort of reasonable or moral pattern was an accomplishment of no mean proportions. Karamzin created a framework in which even those chaotic events had coherence and could be seen to lead (although Karamzin did not live to describe it) to the resurrection of Russia after 1613. Its governing theme, Russia's great hunger for dynastic security, required that the guilt of Uglich be the dominant motif of the last two volumes of the *History*. When the choice reduced to one between people and their leader, then Boris, because he was illegitimate, was deemed the more appropriate sacrifice to human folly.

A few general remarks are in order about Karamzin's conclusion to his chapter on Uglich, for the events mentioned there lead directly into the second central event of the Boris Tale, the election of Boris as tsar seven years later. The Uglich chapter (X, ch. 2) ends on three crucial historical events, symbolically covering civil, military, and inti-mate-dynastic affairs: the Moscow Fires of May 1591, the invasion by the Khan in the summer of that same year, and, finally, the tsaritsa Irina's pregnancy (and successful delivery of a daughter) in 1592. A guilty Boris is linked to each of these events. After the fires Boris rebuilds homes and distributes money: "Was he not [Karamzin muses] taking advantage of the misfortune of the capital to gain the people's gratitude, or was he himself even guilty [of starting the fires], as the chronicler claims and as many contemporaries believed?" (86). Was not the invasion likewise "beneficial to Godunov," since it distracted the people from "Dmitri's terrible death"? (86). It is the pregnancy of his sister, however, that subjects Karamzin's Boris to his greatest temptation. The theme of children and the death of children is central to the Boris Tale, coexisting in a complex way with the well-documented image of Boris as loving father and protective parent. With the prospect of a new legitimate heir from his own—and yet not his own—family, the drama of Uglich is not only invoked; it is almost replayed.

> . . . Suddenly news spread from the Kremlin palace to the most distant regions of the state—filling everyone, from monarch to peasant, everyone except Boris, with joyful hope—the news that Irina was pregnant! Never had Russia, in the words of the chronicler, expressed so profound a joy: it was as if Heaven, offended by Godunov's crime but moved by the secret tears of her good sons, had made peace with Russia, and on Dmitri's grave had planted a new tsarist sapling, which with its branches would embrace the future generations of Russia. (95)

Karamzin then begins to interrogate Boris from an intimate inner perspective:

> The most heinous of murders had been in vain for the murderer: his conscience tormented him, his hopes had been eclipsed forever or at least

until a new crime was committed, one even more terrible for the villain; meanwhile Godunov had to endure the general joy, take an active part in it, deceive the court and his own sister! After several months of impatient waiting, Irina gave birth to a daughter, to the great relief of Boris's heart. . . . (95)

Even a daughter was cause for rejoicing, however, and the people rejoiced. "But some, inclined to suspicion and guessing the secret of Boris's soul, quietly spread doubts: could not Boris, by some deceit, have exchanged an infant boy—if the Tsaritsa had in fact given birth to a son—for Feodosia [the tsarevna]?" (96) Karamzin admits that this idea is "improbable." But he equivocates. In the peculiar psychologized world that has become Boris's plot, fact and rumor seem to have equal force. Such troublesome questions are resolved by the death of the infant tsarevna the following year. But then rumors begin to spread that Boris had poisoned little Feodosia. His dilemma, as later literary treatments will richly demonstrate, is a bad dream: acceptance of rumor is compliance, rejection of rumor is proof of a guilty conscience. Karamzin ends the chapter on precisely this double bind: "God knew the truth. But stained with the sacred blood of Dmitri, Boris did not have the right to complain of the people's slander and gullibility: even the most improbable slander served him as just punishment!" (96)

Boris the Usurper

This subjugation of external event to internal psychological imperative is the single most characteristic feature of Boris's elevation to tsar after Fyodor's death in 1598 (X, 132–41). Karamzin reduces the complicated political realities of that year to a linear unraveling, within Boris's soul, of ambition and bad conscience.

> He could no longer raise himself through the reign of Irina, having already enjoyed limitless power under Fyodor; he could not, at the end of his fifth decade of life, wait or postpone things any further; he had handed over the Tsardom to Irina in order to take it for himself, out of kindred hands and as if by right of inheritance, to occupy the throne in place of a *Godunova* and not a Monomakh. . . . (132)

Boris, as resolute externally as he was anguished within, organizes the popular and institutional support that in fact results in the first offer of the crown. His refusal of this offer is presented as a political tactic linked, in a way that the criminal will realize only gradually, to the horror of Uglich:

Thus the powermonger's wish had been accomplished! . . . But he knew how to deceive: he did not forget himself in the joy of his heart—and, seven years earlier having boldly plunged the murderer's knife into the throat of Saint Dmitri to seize the crown for himself, now he rejects it with horror, rejects the crown offered him triumphantly, unanimously, by the clergy, the council, the common people. . . . (134)

This stubbornness is all the more remarkable, for Karamzin pays almost no attention to other political factions competing for power during that turbulent year. Boris's desire for a broad mandate is solely the result of personal strife and bad dreams:

Godunov wanted not only the capital but all of Russia to recognize him on the throne, and he took measures to insure his success, everywhere sending his diligent slaves and courtiers: this appearance of a unanimous, free election seemed necessary to him—for the calming of his con-science? Or for the firmness and safety of his rule? (135)

Again this is a Russian Macbeth, offered to the Russian equiv-alent of the line of Banquo. Karamzin knew Shakespeare well. He had in fact translated *Julius Caesar* in the mid-1780s, and prefaced that translation with an enthusiastic defense of Shakespeare's dramatic imagination and psychological boldness. Boris's elevation to supreme power takes on powerful Shakespearean subtexts when the image of a guilty Macbeth is combined with the cold political calculation of a Julius Caesar hypocritically declining the throne. And most certainly also present here is Richard III, whose part in the death of the royal princes in the Tower has clear parallels with Uglich.[102]

To cast Boris's monstrous hypocrisy and ambition in greater re-lief—without, however, granting him splendid inner monologues in the style of Shakespeare's Richard—Karamzin overemphasizes the uniform eagerness of "all of Muscovy" to see Boris on the throne. "It seemed as if everyone [in the *sobor*] wanted one thing only: like orphans, they wanted to find a father as soon as possible—and they knew in whom to seek him" (136). The ancient princely families "did not even dare to think of their hereditary rights" (137). Thus the crowds that howl *"Slava!"* (Glory!) to Boris in the monastery court-yard—so familiar to us in the ironic mode from play and opera—are in Karamzin's narrative genuinely caught up in the fire of the mo-ment. "Sincerity triumphed over pretense; inspiration acted even on the indifferent and on the hypocrites!" (140).

The final scene, of a triumphant Boris and a triumphant people, cements this deceptive unity of the earthly realm, the realm of ap-pearances. All the dictates of reason and of emotion—all, in short,

that man alone has at his disposal—combine to hail this new tsar. All
the more terrible, then, will be the intervention of heavenly justice.
On that realm of higher reality Karamzin ends the chapter:

> What, by all appearances, could be more triumphant, more unanimous,
> more legitimate than this election? And what could be more reasonable?
> Only the name of the tsar had changed: state power remained in the
> hands of him who had long wielded it and who had ruled happily for the
> integrity of the state, for its internal welfare, for the external honor and
> security of Russia. That is indeed how it seemed: but this Ruler, so
> endowed with human wisdom, had reached the throne through evil-
> doing. . . . Heavenly punishment threatened the tsar-criminal and the
> unfortunate Tsardom. (141)

It is often said that the romantic hero holds the world within himself.
The world is *his* creation, a reflection of his bliss or his torment. In this
sense Karamzin's Boris is indeed a romantic figure: his psychology, or
rather the disintegration of his psyche, is fated to become Russia's
disintegration. If volume X of the *History* is an account of the Rise of
Boris and of his Fall at Uglich, volume XI projects Boris's fate onto
Russia at large. Early in chapter 2 of that eleventh volume Karamzin
fixes Boris in this new perspective:

> Even before the blows of Fate, before his good fortune and his subjects
> betrayed him, while he was still peacefully on the throne, sincerely
> glorified, sincerely loved, he already knew no spiritual peace . . . this
> internal agitation of the soul, unavoidable for a criminal, brought to the
> surface unfortunate traits of suspicion in the Tsar—which, alarming him,
> soon alarmed Russia as well. (XI, 58)

It is no longer enough for Boris to pay. He becomes the source
for a pollution that spreads throughout Russia. Unable to fulfill the
traditional role of tsar as Christ, tsar as intercessor for his people,
Boris suffers the additional burden of visiting his own sins upon the
nation. This is the tragedy, surely, in the refusal of the holy fool to
pray for Boris, a scene in Karamzin (X, 169) that was taken by Pushkin
and by Musorgsky as central to the tale—so central, in fact, that
Musorgsky eventually ends his opera on a version of it. As all Russia
comes to suffer from Godunov's paranoia, political criteria give way in
the *History* to religious or psychological ones. Karamzin presents the
purges of 1601–1602 not as part of a succession struggle or as response to treachery, but as extermination campaigns in which "not
only the Romanovs, but all their kinsfolk were to perish, so that no
one remained on earth to avenge innocent martyrs" (XI, 61). The
tsar's very generosity during the terrible famine of 1601–1603 is
interpreted as an attempt to "cover up this consequence of heavenly

wrath" (69). Less and less distinction is drawn between Boris's behavior and the people's fate. Thus the actual appearance and victorious campaign of the Pretender on Russian soil is inevitably
paralleled by his appearance, and victory, over Boris's soul. "Like
something supernatural, the shade of Dmitri arose from the grave to
strike terror in the heart of the murderer, to drive him mad, and to
bring confusion to all of Russia" (74).

The final months of Boris's life are described as a sort of paralysis—another allusion, perhaps, to Macbeth. To be sure, those months
are unclear in most histories, even today; Boris's sudden political and
physical collapse is one of the more confusing aspects of his brief
reign. Karamzin has a ready explanation for these obscurities. Had
this energetic tsar but mounted his horse and led his troops, his "great
boldness and confidence would doubtless have had their effect," but
Boris "did not dare to confront Dmitri's shade" (94). Karamzin's battle
scenes carry no suspense because we are dealing here with an internal
landscape, etched long ago in Uglich and now being revealed, quite
independent of external military events.

Unrelieved paralysis is death. Chapter 2 of the eleventh volume
ends with the death of Boris, which (while not quite a thunderbolt
from heaven) is interpreted largely in psychological terms. Boris had
long been ill with gout, and "already aging, he could have easily
exhausted his bodily strength with spiritual suffering" (108). The
terrible suddenness and vividness of the tsar's death struck many at
the time as something almost supernatural. He was with his boyars in
the Duma, receiving foreigners, when suddenly he rose from the
table:

> . . . blood poured from his nose, ears and mouth; it flowed in a river, and
> even the doctors whom he so loved could not stop it. He lost con-
> sciousness, but did manage to bless his son to the Russian state, to be
> accepted into a Holy Order under the name Bogolep, and after two
> hours expired, in the same chamber where he had feasted with his boyars
> and the foreigners. . . . Unfortunately, posterity knows no more about
> his end, so rending for the soul. (108)

Thus does Karamzin close on the facts of the case. But he puts this
strange and abrupt death to good purpose, with a sort of postmortem
questionnaire in which all possibilities are interrogated. Could it have
been suicide? No: would this "tender father of a family, this man so
strong in spirit, save himself from calamity and then in so cowardly a
way abandon his wife and children to almost certain destruction?"
Was the Godunov cause so hopeless that death was the only escape?
No: Boris was still tsar, treason was in the air but not yet an accomplished fact among his generals, and "only Boris's death decided the

success of the deceit." Boris dies, it turns out, because the larger shape of Russian history requires that death. His passing from the scene was both payment for Uglich and explanation for impending, inexplicable chaos. "Russia, deprived in him of an intelligent and solicitous tsar, became the prey of evil-doing for many years" (108–109).

Karamzin's closure here is highly characteristic. It combines the best of a morality play with the more contemporary device of a psychological portrait, a good man brought low by a single act that it was nevertheless his choice to commit. There is also an older dichotomy at work here, one as familiar to Muscovy as it was, in altered form, to the later romantics among whom and for whom Karamzin wrote his *History*. This is the opposition of the head—intelligent, cunning, *khitry*—to the heart, wherein lies virtue. In sixteenth-century terms this was the split between *khitrost'* and *blagochestie*, between "cunning" and "piety," which even in old Muscovy was analogous to the opposition of the West to Russia.[103] That parallel would certainly not lack resonance for the generation that had survived Napoleon. But Karamzin's achievement is larger than propaganda for legitimatist loyalties. He manages to fit motifs from stories of *blagochestie*— especially the Life of St. Dmitri of Uglich—together with a more secular language, one that claims to see the causes for events not in heaven but in the psyche. His is a romantic, not a divine, determinism. And on this plane Boris's worst enemy is always himself. His heart literally bursts apart from within; the tsarevich's blood so long contained finally flows forth in expiation, taking the life that had taken Saint Dmitri's. The name of Godunov should have been celebrated the world over, writes Karamzin in closing, but "posterity sees only the *Lobnoe mesto* crimsoned with the blood of innocent victims, Saint Dmitri expiring under the knife of murderers . . ." (XI, 109). Karamzin then translates this image into his second and more secular language. "The glitter [of Godunov's reign], while bright for the mind, proved cold for the heart."

To tell Godunov's story Karamzin wove a complex fabric. Through multiple chronotopes, judicious framings and quotings, varied emplotment from Saints' Lives to Shakespeare, and a continual allegorizing with events of his reader's present, Karamzin was able to blur the line between an event and its later reception. It could be argued, in fact, that Karamzin gives us in his Boris Tale not just a history of events but a history of *perception* of events. The integrity of such an account itself constitutes a sort of master-chronotope, whose essential contours we might now consider.

It is, as we noted above, basically nondevelopmental. Character is presented as something preformed; experience does not shape Boris but merely reveals him. In such a chronotope, chronological sequence is often arbitrary and anachronism loses its sting. Providing Dmitri with a martyr's death in 1591, sixteen years before his actual canonization, occasions no special awkwardness. Since time can only be measured by the changes that occur within it, the very sense of time's passing is weakened. Cause and effect, so problematic in other chronotopes, is a transparent process here, for events serve more as illustrations than as isolated willed actions. Events happen not because one precedes and occasions the other but because a pattern is made manifest.

Stasis of this sort is commonly sensed in providential histories. But it is important to note that Karamzin by no means cast his whole history in this chronotope. The tenth and eleventh volumes contain many descriptions of wars, diplomacy, trade, and popular life that are concrete in time and place, free of tendentiousness, and full of an immediate open present. But when dealing with certain historical figures—most especially Ivan the Terrible and Boris Godunov—different organizing principles seem to apply.

Ivan, as he emerges in the ninth volume, embodies absolute legitimate power gone wrong. His crimes are examined from the most intimate inner perspective. And yet, paradoxically, this inner irrationality and tyranny do not contaminate Russia as a whole. Ivan's excesses become the symbol of Russia's patience and suffering—and a measuring rod of her progress under later, more enlightened monarchs. "Glory to that time," Karamzin writes, "when, armed with the truth, a historian under an autocratic regime can expose such a ruler [as Ivan IV] to shame; may his sort never be seen again!" (IX, 274).

The chronotope of Boris Godunov is somewhat different, but equally constructed as a lesson to a later time. His crime is singular but awful: the crime against dynastic legitimacy. Thus his reign becomes the symbol of Russia's *im*patience, of bonds tested and broken, of suffering that was *not* made sensible. Although the reigns of Ivan IV and Godunov are contiguous and Ivan's is full of monstrous deeds, Karamzin will not blame Boris's failures on his predecessor's policies: Boris begins to fail at Uglich. His reign is all of a piece, and within it all times seem to exist at once. The narrator claims both the privilege of present-time experience (eyewitness reporting) and the benefit of more distant perspectives, where the future is already the past. Space becomes a generalized internal landscape, a "battleground for the soul" in which the outcome is already known, and time a mere chronological marker.

As a result, the Boris story causes a special aura in Karamzin's *History.* It coexists with other chronotopes. But it presumes a greater scope and flexibility than the others, combining in itself both the stature of romantic myth and a claim to factual accuracy. It is as if Karamzin were showing us that history, in this one case, just happened to take the form of myth, and for once could reveal its inner meaning.

Karamzin achieves in these portions of the narrative a sort of contrived primitivism that resembles naïve painting. The reader perceives a complex picture of reality from which something has been artfully taken away. This technique, which was typical for a type of Sternean narration, had skillful practitioners among the preromantics who were Karamzin's contemporaries. Their purpose was to filter the world in such a way that the reader was impressed not by the chaos of reality but by its rigor and irreversibility. And the result was an artful patterning, an undisguised form of literary plotting in which disorder was acknowledged but prudently resolved in a deliberate simplicity.

In summary, we might return to Miliukov's distinction between *pol'za* (benefit) and *istina* (truth), which has structured so much of our discussion of Karamzin as a historian. Miliukov claimed that Karamzin had merely joined together these two historiographical approaches in one single, and unpersuasive, text. But in light of the discussion above, other hybrid constructions are also possible—and ones more congenial than Miliukov's for the purposes Karamzin most likely had in mind. One such hybrid has been suggested by Rudolf Bachtold in his "Karamzins Weg zur Geschichte."[104] In Karamzin's view, Bachtold argues, history was not the conjunction of two forms but of three: art, science, and judge. It was History as Judge, in fact, that ultimately validated the other two:

> History as science and history as art were simply not Karamzin's main concerns. His intellectual development and his previous activities were nonetheless influential in forming his fundamental conception of "history" as a literary project. Literary and scientific values were important to him primarily because they increased the nonpartisan authority of his work and thus promoted his primary goal. (98)

This "primary goal," Bachtold reminds us, was always moral rather than artistic or scientific. "History as Judge" was the truth that Karamzin intended to transmit, and, as we have seen, he was roundly criticized for it. Among those who came to his defense, the most astute was Alexander Pushkin.

Historian and Poet

The relationship between Pushkin and Karamzin, between historically oriented poet and poetically inspired historian, was intricate and uneven. By the mid-twenties, however, Pushkin invariably defended the *History* against its detractors. He was immediately responsive to the tenth and eleventh volumes.[105] Yet Pushkin never solicited Karamzin's opinion of his own play-in-progress based on those volumes, *Boris Godunov*. Rather the contrary was true: when Karamzin, in the final months of his life, requested through Pletnev that Pushkin show him the entire finished tragedy, Pushkin put him off with sly quips and evasions.[106]

After Karamzin's death Pushkin complained that the eulogies were a disgrace, all "cold, stupid, condescending."[107] Pushkin himself, however, could not offer anything in their place—and his tribute, such as it was, remained largely a reaction to the judgment of others.[108] The posthumous relationship between historian and poet can be traced in the marginalia on others' essays, in polemical asides, and in the occasional rebuttal of unjust criticism. Much in these scattered statements is open to interpretation. One of the most telling remarks that Pushkin made about the *History*, and about what we have called Karamzin's mature chronotope, can be found in his marginalia to an article by Mikhail Pogodin on the death in Uglich.

Pogodin's essay, "On Godunov's Participation in the Murder of Tsarevich Dmitri," was first published in *Moskovskii vestnik* in 1829.[109] Pogodin was a great admirer of Karamzin, and his criticism is cast in the most respectful tones. But its basic intent is subversive. Using Uglich as a case study, Pogodin lays bare the discrepancies between Karamzin's documentation and the motivation supplied in the narrative text. As Karamzin himself had done in his initial portrait of Boris twenty-five years earlier, Pogodin outlines the political and religious factors shaping Boris's image in the seventeenth century, stressing the absurdity of the slander in the chronicles. But excepting a few harsh words on Karamzin's misuse of the *Delo*, Pogodin does not concentrate on errors of fact. He does not, likewise, undertake to de-psychologize Godunov's story. His tactic is rather to show how easily Boris Godunov can be *re*-psychologized, even in multiple biographies, on the basis of the same source material. Pogodin begins by presuming a Boris neither innocent nor guilty, but simply *sensible*. At each of the junctures where Karamzin presumed evildoing, Pogodin argues that Boris's interests might well have been better served by a living Dmitri, not a dead one. Moving through each major Uglich event, Pogodin makes the same point many times: if the event happened at all, it would never have happened as Karamzin described it. Or, to put the point differently, the shape of Karamzin's story—its plot or chronotope—was wrong, regardless of any demonstrated correctness of the facts.

Pogodin closes his essay with a rhetorical question that returns us to Bachtold's category of History as Judge.

> Now that I have brought together all my evidence for and against him [Boris], I submit the whole case to a criminal court to be judged by *today's* laws. Would not that court be obliged to place Boris only under suspicion, and under weak suspicion at that?
> So! Today's criminal court can do no more than place Boris under suspicion, but history, with twenty-five years of Boris's good deeds for Russia to its benefit, dares to pronounce a decisive sentence! No, no, we will be just to this great man who so well understood virtue, if not with his heart then at least with his fertile mind, the man whose brilliant rule raised Russia to the peak of greatness and glory, who at the triumphant moment of his coronation promised to give the last shirt off his back to his impoverished subject and never betrayed that solemn vow, who wanted to establish a university in Moscow in 1600, not in 1755—we will be just to him . . . and his shortcomings, amid such great prowess, we will ascribe to the frailty of the human vessel. Boris most likely heard with pleasure the news of Dmitri's death, since it furthered his own plans. But he has paid too dearly for this pleasure. . . . (304)

Pogodin's defense of Boris rests on three points. First, he exposes the bias of the documents; then he insists on recognizing the achievements of Boris's rule; ultimately, he will abide by the verdict of a court governed by "today's laws." From Pogodin's correspondence and certain entries in his diaries we know that Pushkin argued with Pogodin over the substance of this essay in the fall of 1829.[110] Pushkin's marginal comments to Pogodin's essay[111] read like a transcript of that argument, and constitute an unusual defense of Karamzin's historical method against this first generation of revisionists.

Pushkin, here as elsewhere, reveals a profound and almost superstitious awe at the power of dynastic legitimacy. As did Karamzin, he appeals to the chroniclers as to an ultimate authority.[112] Numerous marginal entries of "nonsense!" or "absurd!" discredit Pogodin's implicit remotivating of Boris's behavior—as if to show that the story Pogodin wanted to tell through the sources was just as subjective and *a priori* as Karamzin's. But the most substantive criticism comes in an extended marginal comment at the very end of the essay. Pushkin underscores Pogodin's words about submitting the case "to a criminal court governed by *today's* laws." And then he accuses Pogodin of anachronism: "That's simply stupid. A Criminal Court does not judge dead tsars by *today's laws*. History judges them, because there is no other court—for tsars or for the dead."

Here Pushkin understands the category of "history as judge" in a special and stark way that both enriches and complicates the chronotope of Karamzin's Boris Tale. The judgment passed on Boris is severe, Pushkin seems to suggest, not because God runs history. It is precisely because human beings run history—because history is recorded by men and this record is what judges "tsars and the dead"— that Boris stands so thoroughly condemned. As Boris Eikhenbaum has pointed out in an essay on "chronicle style" in nineteenth-century literature,[113] Pushkin took chronicles very seriously; for him they were not only "local color" (Karamzin's phrase) but also a way of reasoning historically, an insight into the popular mind of the time.

It might be helpful to recall here the larger context of Pushkin's remark that Karamzin was "our first historian and last chronicler." The statement constitutes the closest Pushkin ever came to a classification of Karamzin as a historian:

> In his criticism he [Karamzin] belongs to history, in his artlessness and aphorisms to the chronicle. . . . His moral ruminations, by their monkish simplicity, lend his narrative all the inexplicable charm of an ancient chronicle. He used those moral asides as color, but did not attach any essential importance to them.[114]

It can certainly be argued that Pushkin misreads here the part for the whole. Whereas "chronicle as local color" is indeed one of Karamzin's early chronotopes in the *History,* by the later volumes this "monkish simplicity" has become quite devious—as "monkish simplicity" so often is. Pushkin, it has often been noted, was reluctant to confront the tendentious and didactic thrust of the *History,* preferring instead to weigh it on the scales of literature.[115] The case can indeed be made that Pushkin's reading of Karamzin is as vulnerable to charges of naïveté as is Karamzin's own reading of the chronicles. But this flaw should not obscure the larger insight implicit in Pushkin's defense.

Karamzin, in Pushkin's view, did more than merely respect his sources. He limited himself by them, and in so doing admitted their power to shape, almost to create, a past event. Karamzin's narrative presented not only a closed future—a truism of all providential histories—but a closed past as well. The past, in other words, might be theoretically open to new readings, but those readings then accumulate an authority that can become almost unassailable. One crucial difference between Pushkin and Pogodin, in short, is that for Pushkin historiography was part of history, its organ of judgment, perhaps flawed but not to be simply thought away. We see in this defense of Karamzin a continuation of the debate that Pushkin had embedded in the image of his chronicler Pimen.

Indeed, the features most characteristic of Karamzin as a historian all had good precedent in the etiquette of his chronicler predecessors. Karamzin too displayed an exalted moral tone, a faith in the validity of the sources, a reliance on specific formulae for fixed types of events, and above all a passion for integrating earlier versions of an event into a coherent whole that would instruct his *own* generation. As Pushkin divined, the truth of Karamzin's account was not the truth of fact but the truth of judgment: of rumor, hope, anger, despair. Karamzin was providing not so much the truth about events as the truth about the perception of events; not the truth of time, but of chronicle. The Time of Troubles, with its scourge of pretenders and its progressive slandering of Boris, was the chaotic peaking of this popular judgment. It was fueled by a desire for scapegoats, not for truth, as God's grace seemed withdrawn from the Russian land.

This larger and more formidable truth of the *History* was perhaps the challenge that Pushkin assumed when in 1831 he decided to dedicate his *Boris Godunov* not to Zhukovsky, as originally intended, but to the historian. "Inspired by his genius," the playwright inscribed on the opening page, "Alexander Pushkin dedicates this work with reverence and gratitude to the memory of Nikolai Mikhailovich Karamzin, precious to all Russians." Some critics have since suspected that this dedication was itself ironic, belonging, through its very formulaic loftiness, to that category of parodic frames that Pushkin exploited so well in his other works of ambivalent genre.[116] We know in addition that Pushkin considered, among several options for opening and closing his play, a lengthy title that parodied chronicles and an ending on "Amen."[117] It will be my thesis, however, that this playfulness on Pushkin's part—while operative—in no way compromised Pushkin's respect for Karamzin's achievement or the sincerity of this dedication.[118] There are times when parody can in fact be a form of respect. It would become Pushkin's task to match Karamzin's genius in a very different mode.

The "chronicle truth" that Karamzin had ennobled into history Pushkin would dismantle, restore to the realm of rumor, and relocate as part of a world without divine guidance. In that special sense it would remain, as a judgment of history, "true." In a move prefiguring Tolstoy's ideas about history two generations later, Pushkin would demonstrate in his play that man might run history but this did not make him free—for man, in turn, is most often ruled by circumstance. And he might record history, but this did not make him truthful, for recording is itself a historical act. Pushkin's *Boris*—with its intense loneliness, its multiple points of view, its cruel command of the economies of blind self-interest—puts no faith in the larger principles that might govern the "shape of a past" or of a future. It is, as we shall see, that odd creation, a history play determined to transmit only a sense of the *present*.

In *Boris Godunov*, Karamzin's *History* is everywhere recalled and nowhere confirmed. In place of Karamzin's historical fabric, where a fixed past is woven into a fixed future, we have a series of glimpses at many different worlds—all poised for enormous changes at the last minute, and none forthcoming with anything like an explanation for events. *Boris Godunov* is, among much else, a play about the blindness of immediate experience. How Pushkin sustains that immediacy in a dramatically persuasive way until it ultimately becomes a philosophy of history will be the major concern of the next chapter.

III

Boris in Drama: *Pushkin*

Irony has entered all the languages of modern times. . . . Irony is everywhere, from the minimal and imperceptible to the loud that borders on laughter. Modern man does not proclaim, he speaks, which is to say he speaks with reservations. Proclamatory genres have been retained mainly as parodic and semi-parodic building blocks of the novel. The language of Pushkin is precisely of this kind, permeated with irony (to varying degrees), the equivocal language of modern times.[1]

KARAMZIN's *History* shaped the adventures of the past into a pattern, and one that presaged—for all the setbacks and sufferings—an ultimate triumph for the Romanov dynasty and the Russian state. Pushkin, on the contrary, was in principle suspicious of patterning. He delighted in breaking into and then reconstructing genres: *Eugene Onegin,* for all its metric rigor, is a catalogue of different language styles and genres, and "Poltava" achieves its powerful effect by shifting bluntly from intimate romantic narrative to national epic. Such bold play with boundaries has made Pushkin's work on historical themes difficult to classify, and gives us a clue to the paradox of Pushkin's historical fiction.

On the one hand historical figures are brought close, made intimate, shorn of rhetoric and regalia. Like the ordinary people they presumably "rule," the great often appear helpless to control, and even to modify, events. Yet on the other hand they remain, almost by default, the heroes. *Their* names—and not some social class or historical period—remain at the center of titles: Boris Godunov, The Black-amoor of Peter the Great, the History of Pugachev. The use of individual names as historical markers is of course quite compatible with a view of history as pattern. But in Pushkin a special irony attaches to the practice. His historical imagination presents epochs and social problems through the personality in such a way that historical figures are retained as central even as they are revealed as helpless. Pushkin combines a focus on individual psychology with a reluctance to grant the individual historical effectiveness, and this inevitably raises the most vexed historiographical questions: the relationship of character to event, the nature of power and change in history, and the very possibility of *any* individual recording a historically accurate narrative.

Given the scope of these issues, some critics have assigned to *Boris Godunov*—Pushkin's first sustained historical project—the status of a philosophical watershed in the poet's creative life. Pushkin, so this argument goes, did not promote any special moral, religious, or metaphysical system. He worked exclusively with actual events. In Boris Engelhardt's words, "the social environment almost exhausted the cosmos for him," because for Pushkin, a man of *this* world, a sense of history filled the space that in a more abstract thinker would have been occupied by religious or metaphysical problems.[2] What dominated in Pushkin's work before *Boris* were the epicurean early poems and the romantic individualism of Aleko, hero of "The Gypsies"; after *Boris*, Aleko's helplessness was, as it were, historicized, and the path was open for a new understanding and acceptance of the essential ineffectiveness of attempts to control and govern history.

To be sure, Pushkin had his own curious ideas about fate. But he had, it seems, little faith in divine providence—and, beyond a generalized commitment to Enlightenment ideas about human progress, little inclination to integrate or romanticize historical events. The "explanatory principles" of philosophically based histories appear to have been as unsatisfying to Pushkin as they were, for different reasons, to Karamzin. In his draft for a review of the second volume of Polevoi's *History of the Russian People* (1830), Pushkin criticized the French historian Guizot for his efforts to motivate a series of events by avoiding all that was "distanced, peripheral or *accidental*" in history. "Don't say *it could not have been otherwise*," Pushkin admonished:

> If that were true then the historian would be an astronomer, and the events of the life of mankind would be predicted in calendars like solar eclipses. But providence is not algebra. The human mind—as the folk expression goes—is not a prophet but a conjecturer, it sees the general course of things and can deduce from it profound suppositions, often justified by time, but it cannot foresee *chance*—that powerful, instantaneous tool of providence.[3]

Pushkin's dead seriousness about chance inevitably affected his reading of Karamzin's *History*—a narrative whose events were, if anything, overdetermined. But the actual moment of transposition is always complex. When an event is extracted from one context and reembedded in another, the move is governed by the generic constraints of both source and target. Just how easily Karamzin's *History* can be dismantled, thus making its events available to poets, depends on the sort of historian one presumes Karamzin to be.

Jurij Striedter, for example, has argued in an essay on Pushkin's uses of history[4] that generations of nineteenth-century writers could find their inspiration in the *History*—while disparaging its didactic framework—because Karamzin was not just a historian to his people; he was also their first, and perhaps greatest, mythographer. His *History* had turned the Russian past into a fund of accessible, richly poetic stories. The very process of reworking these stories, of circulating them in new form, fulfilled to some degree the unifying and symbolic function of myth in a culture. According to Striedter, Karamzin's unstable synthesis of moral narrative and scholarly apparatus did not detract from the *History*'s usefulness; on the contrary, it made the work an even richer source for later poets.

> . . . if Polevoi . . . complained that Karamzin lacked an interpretive idea in his historical writings, that his *History* was no more than a series of episodes and stories with an ahistorical moral tagged on, Pushkin states openly that what is a flaw for the historiographer is for the poet a grace. You can pick out single episodes, scrap the moral if you like, and have a ready-made literary subject.(297)

Striedter is right, certainly, in claiming that the episodic nature of Karamzin's *History* favored its selective appropriation. But he appears to underestimate the pervasiveness of the whole in each part, as Pushkin did not underestimate it. Pushkin seems to have drawn on the *History* with the understanding that each episode was suffused with the values and meanings of the whole—which in turn reflected the assumptions carried by the genre of didactic or moralistic history. There is in fact no way to read Karamzin and "scrap the moral"; Karamzin's voice is everywhere present in the selection and sequence of events, in the very coherence and inner logic of the narrative. Nowhere is this presence more noticeable than in the Boris Tale.

Both Karamzin and Pushkin approached history "poetically," and both were self-conscious experimenters with literary genre. Pushkin—as we know from his correspondence, drama reviews, and numerous drafts for a foreword to *Boris* dating from 1829–30—was as polemical about the needs of Russian drama as Karamzin had been about the prerequisites of a Russian history. But Pushkin abandoned his forewords unfinished and on several occasions expressed the conviction that his play would most definitely fail. "While writing my *Godunov* I reflected on tragedy," Pushkin wrote to Raevsky in 1829. "If I undertake to write a preface I will make a scandal; it is perhaps the most misunderstood genre."[5] The playwright's pessimistic reticence to explain stands in sharp contrast to the self-confidence of the historian, whose foreword to the *History* is so precise on the duties and benefits of his craft. As we have seen, Karamzin had integrated two established trends in Russian historiography through the medium of a popular prose style, one perfected over decades and almost guaranteed a good reception by the reading public. By contrast, Pushkin was setting out to create a sort of drama that had no real precedent, and he was writing it in a language that had not yet been heard on the tragic stage. He both drew on particular incidents in Karamzin's *History* and entered into a complex dialogue with the whole. For Pushkin, generic transposition was part of a complex generic debate.

From Romantic History to "Romantic Tragedy": The Triumph of the Part

"It was an exceptionally bad period for the drama throughout Europe," Michael Meyer writes in his biography of Ibsen. "During the half-century that had elapsed since the death of Schiller in 1805, a gap had opened between the theatre and the serious playwright. A number of interesting plays had been written, but most of them remained unperformed. . . ."[6] Among the interesting and unperformed playwrights of the period, Meyer mentions Büchner, Kleist, de Musset—and he might also have mentioned Pushkin.[7] Theatrical life in the Russian capitals during the 1820s was lively and diversified. Pushkin, however, was critical of the work being written for the theater. "The spirit of the age," he wrote in a draft preface to *Boris*, "requires important changes on the dramatic stage."[8] In particular Pushkin argued that the Russian history play—as developed in the Napoleonic period by the popular dramatists Ozerov, Kriukovskoy, and Ivanov—reflected neither Russian nor historical realities. It was a French form mechanically filled with Russian-language melodrama on national themes.[9]

The year *Boris* was cleared for publication Pushkin drafted a lengthy commentary on Pogodin's still unpublished drama *Marfa Posadnitsa* (1830). In that essay he lamented the absence of a native tradition of Russian drama and the consequent reliance of Russian playwrights on foreign models—especially Racinian tragedy. Following what he perceived to be the spirit of Shakespearean "popular drama," Pushkin wanted to infuse those tragic models with individual

psychology, psychology that would show how particular people be-
haved and thought in particular milieus at a particular time.[10] Just
how unusual a goal this was for the early nineteenth-century stage can
easily be lost on us today. Conventions of performance and the very
concept of tragedy precluded any real subtlety of characterization or
psychology, which were, in Meyer's words,

> not then regarded as necessary to a theatrical performance, any more
> than until very recently they were regarded as necessary in opera. Trag-
> edy was . . . a kind of grand opera without music, interesting only in so
> far as it afforded opportunities for sonorous declamations, spectacular
> outbursts and striking visual effects; comedy was merely an excuse for
> individual inventiveness. . . . There was no such thing as what we today
> would call a straight play; there was tragedy, comedy, farce and melo-
> drama, with or without music. (123–24)

What Pushkin was after, it could be argued, was a "straight play,"
something we would recognize today as a "problem play" or intellectual theater. He hoped to achieve it by evading the generic definitions
current at the time ("tragedy, comedy, farce and melodrama"), and
thus challenge his audience to examine the creation before labeling it.
But Pushkin did not only evade conventional labels; he also evaded
the very terms in which the struggle for new forms had been cast.[11]
He opposed French classicist norms in tragedy, but opposed equally a
Victor Hugo–style romantic drama. Rather than enter an established
fray and wedge out one existing form with another, Pushkin hoped to
redefine the categories altogether. He began with the choice of a term
that seems problematic from the start: "romantic tragedy."

In the summer of 1825 Pushkin wrote to Viazemsky that he had
undertaken "a literary task for which you will smother me in kisses—a
romantic tragedy!"[12] The term was not unknown to Pushkin's generation. The playwright Shakhovskoy, for instance, reworked Pushkin's
narrative poem "The Fountain of Bakhchisarai" for the stage, and it
was triumphantly hailed as a "romantic tragedy" at its premiere in
September 1825.[13] Dramatized romanticism in the 1820s was understood as spectacle, as something lofty and accompanied by music and
battles. That was its link with tragedy. Pushkin, however, clearly
meant something else by the term. His *Boris Godunov* had no music, no
mass battles, and its diction was anything but elevated. "I wrote a
tragedy and am very satisfied with it," Pushkin confessed to Bestuzhev
in November 1825, "but I'm terrified to publish it. Our timid taste
won't stand for true romanticism."[14]

What Pushkin meant by "true romanticism" and "romantic tragedy" cannot be easily resolved, for nowhere does he precisely define
the terms.[15] However, several documents from the *Boris* year (1825)

do touch upon the component parts of this odd hybrid genre. The first is a fragment, "On Classical and Romantic Poetry," in which Pushkin attempted to explain the essence of the romantic as he conceived it. He blamed the current mistaken notions about romanticism on French journalists, for whom "romantic" meant everything "bearing the stamp of dreaminess and German idealism, or based on superstitions or folk legends: a most imprecise definition."[16] As his formalist compatriots were to do a century later, Pushkin insisted on taking the form, and not the "spirit" or content, of the work as the classificatory unit. To the realm of the classical he relegated the "fixed genres" known to the Greeks and Romans—such forms as the epic, tragedy, ode, epistle, epigram, elegy. To the romantic he assigned all forms not known to the ancients and all forms that had either changed, were in the process of changing, or—most important of all—that reflected a consciousness that formal change was both inevitable and desirable. The romantic, in short, was the unexpected, that which Viktor Shklovsky a century later would call the "estranged" or "defamiliarized." By definition, a romantic cliché could not exist.

In 1825 Pushkin also discussed the nature of tragedy. In a critical fragment[17] and then more fully in a drafted letter to Nikolai Raevsky, Pushkin polemicized against simplistic concepts of verisimilitude on the stage. Drama was the least realistic of all genres, he insisted, and tragedy was the least realistic of all dramatic forms:

> Both the classicists and the romanticists have based their laws on *verisimilitude*, and that is precisely what the nature of a dramatic work excludes. Not to mention time, etc., what the hell sort of verisimilitude can there be in a hall divided into two halves, one of which is occupied by two thousand people who are supposed to be unseen by those on stage. . . .[18]

What mattered, Pushkin continued, was not an imitation of real life through the observation of arbitrary "unities" but "verisimilitude of situations and truth of dialogue—there is the real rule of tragedy."[19]

A further clue to Pushkin's generic intent came three years later, in 1828, in a letter drafted to *Moskovskii vestnik*.[20] That journal had published the monastery scene from *Boris* two years previously, and Pushkin was complaining of its reception. He had designed his play, he wrote, for a public "grown weary of the regularity and perfection of classical antiquity and the pale, monotonous copies of its imitators" (66). But in the existence of this public he had been cruelly disappointed. Readers were unwilling to accept any work of literature that did not obey familiar rules; "innovations are dangerous and, it seems, not necessary" (68). His calculated violations of action, time, place— and he added a fourth, unitary style—had not been understood as intended. This, Pushkin confessed, had shaken his authorial confidence. "I began to suspect that my tragedy was an anachronism."

This idea of anachronism is worth pursuing, for Pushkin might have meant it in several different senses. He could have been referring to the confusion that the play had generated among its own first audiences and readers, who could not place the work comfortably within the conventions of their own time. Or on a more internal level there was the mixing of times that had resulted from Pushkin's own incorporation of three very different source texts. As he wrote in 1830:

> I imitated Shakespeare in his broad and free depiction of characters, in his carefree and simple composition of types; Karamzin I followed in his clear unfolding of events, and in the chronicles I tried to guess the way of thinking and the language of the time. Rich sources![21]

There is evidence, however, of an even more self-conscious exploitation of anachronism in this play. In the politicized climate of post-Napoleonic—and post-Decembrist—Russia, drama on historical themes was routinely read as commentary on current events. Pushkin resisted this practice, considering it inherently anachronistic and a violence to the historical event. The public had found Pimen's political opinions "out of date." To this charge Pushkin responded obliquely:

> Do you want to know what else is keeping me from printing my tragedy? Those places in it which might be interpreted as allegories, hints, *allusions* . . . we do not understand how a dramatic author could completely renounce his own style of thought and relocate himself completely in the age he is depicting.[22]

Here we approach the central problem of historical drama, a problem that occupied Pushkin often in the post-*Boris* years. When dealing with historical themes, Pushkin wrote in his essay on *Marfa Posadnitsa*, the dramatic poet was obliged to be "as dispassionate as fate": "It is not his task to justify or accuse, to prompt speeches. His task is to resurrect a past age in all its truth" (181). But to "resurrect a past age in all its truth" and "relocate oneself completely in the age one is depicting" is no easy task. To portray the past honestly and to enter into history are in fact highly suspicious moves. Can the rewriting of an event ever faithfully represent the event? If we could truly enter the past we would not understand it; if the past could actually be re-created it would not, of course, know itself as past. "Allegories, hints, allusions" were impermissible, Pushkin suggests, because they were inherently anachronistic, past events exploited from the perspective of the playwright's present.[23]

This reluctance to indulge in a drama of allegories and allusions is well illustrated by the fate of one of Pushkin's projects just preceding *Boris*—his work on *Vadim*.[24] The story of this semilegendary Novgorodian patriot, who had supposedly led a revolt against the rule of Riurik in the ninth century, was popular in the Napoleonic period. Concerning this revolt the Nikon Chronicle states simply: "In 6371 (863), Riurik killed one Vadim the Brave and other Novgorodians." The very brevity of this account made it attractive for imaginative—and often allegorical—transposition. Karamzin, in keeping with his monarchical and centralizing imperative, was cautious in his reference to this rebellion, calling it "mere guesswork and fantasy";[25] Pushkin, on the other hand, was attracted by the tale. He developed it in three, all fragmentary forms. The first was a tragedy in iambic hexameter (the traditional Alexandrine line) begun in 1821 in Kishenev; of this, one scenic fragment has survived, three exchanges of dialogue between Vadim and a fellow conspirator. The tragedy was abandoned, and in 1822 Pushkin reembodied the story in a romantic narrative poem. Only the first canto is extant. In addition to these two fragments there are four brief plans for subsequent development; whether they refer to the tragedy or the poem has been impossible to establish.

Pushkin's reasons for abandoning his various *Vadim* projects have been debated. But from the perspective of *Boris Godunov*—Pushkin's second attempt at a historical drama on Russian themes—certain hypotheses suggest themselves. Judging from the form of the dramatic fragment and from the content of the plans, Pushkin appears to have projected, under the influence of Decembrist rhetoric absorbed in Kamenka and Kishenev, a typical allusion-based antityrant drama. The plot for such dramas was an established eighteenth-century convention. A tyrant with foreign troops conquers a people, who despise him; the tyrant is opposed by a popular hero at the head of a conspiracy, and this struggle for freedom is linked with a complex love interest often involving fused sexual and national betrayal. The playwright Iakov Kniazhnin, Sumarokov's son-in-law and a major tragedian of Catherine II's era, produced just such an antityrant drama out of the Vadim tale; his *Vadim Novgorodskii,* published posthumously in 1793 and then suppressed, had by Pushkin's time taken on contemporary, revolutionary resonances for the whole Decembrist generation.

But here, as so often elsewhere, Pushkin defined himself *against* the reigning trends. In light of the comments he made on tragedy (and on drama in general) three years later, one may assume that by 1822 he considered the neoclassical vehicle for historical drama already inadequate to transmit the historicity of an event—and unstageworthy as well. The narrative poem on Vadim that followed the

abandoned tragedy must have seemed similarly unsatisfactory, measured this time against Pushkin's maturing ideas on romanticism. In
its one surviving canto the poem never breaks free of its Byronic
model, and for Pushkin that model had always been more suitable for
depicting a single self-enclosed consciousness than an historical era.[26]
Pushkin, in short, seemed to have used Vadim of Novgorod to try his
talent in traditional forms of tragedy and romance—and found both
forms wanting as vehicles for history.[27] *Boris Godunov,* a "romantic
tragedy," would combine the two in an entirely new synthesis.

The definitions of "romantic" and "tragic" that had emerged in
Pushkin's theory and practice by 1825 were not yet explicit. But they
do suggest some generic features. "Romantic tragedy" is an original
form that not only is itself in the process of becoming but reflects the
spirit of becoming as well. In it, characters and their time are
"faithfully"—that is, not anachronistically—portrayed. These elements are not, to be sure, "faithful" or realistic in the brute sense:
theater is, and must remain, conventional. But what is real is the
credibility of dialogue and situation—that is, a sense that the future is
still open, that what we say depends on what others say to us, and that
the people on stage are transmitting only their *own* (not the playwright's) moral codes and experience.

Romantic tragedy, therefore, might be defined as a dramatic genre
"caught in its own [depicted] time." It is caught, first, without the
benefit of earlier fixed conventions for experiencing it. And it is also
caught in a cruel historical accuracy, because there are no set patterns
for extracting meaning from its events, no references—as in ceremonial drama—to future certainties, and no artificial closures. All
historical drama is written from a later present. But a playwright can
to various degrees exploit that later present within the drama itself.
Boris Godunov, I suggest, was Pushkin's experiment with minimal
exploitation of larger perspective.

This minimalism gives rise to a recognizable chronotope. The
time of romantic tragedy necessitates a certain sort of space. We might
now consider how the two are interwoven.

The Chronotope of Boris

Pushkin's twenty-three scenes stretch out over seven years, from 1598
to 1605, and no two adjacent scenes are set in the same place. Scenes
are only rarely labeled with a place or a time.[28] Events seem to be
linked not by sequence, not by confrontation or causality, but by
rumor. The two heroes, Boris and the Pretender, appear late, exit
early, and never meet; it is never clear exactly how their separate

biographies intersect or in what temporal framework. This license with the neoclassical unity of time was Pushkin's variation on the "dual time" of Elizabethan drama, that chronotope which made possible Shakespeare's compression of seventeen years into ten weeks in *Macbeth*. But Elizabethan dual time preserved a strict sequence and causality of events. Pushkin is more radical; events in one scene do not seem to depend directly on events in earlier scenes, and few references are made to "earlier" or "later." What is more, the relationship of one scene to another became increasingly abstract as Pushkin worked on the play. First he numbered the scenes, then he grouped them into *chasti* or parts, and finally he removed the numbers altogether. Time in this play is indeed concentrated, but it does not serve to bring people or events closer together in easily charted interaction. Thus the action of the play as a whole becomes not tighter but more diffuse.

Temporal discontinuity brings in its wake a certain kind of space. The setting changes with each scene, and the scenes are so short that sustained or intricate plots cannot develop. We merely glimpse the present as it appears to its participants. The important connectives seem to occur in the time and space that we do not see, between scenes. The last we see of the False Dmitri, he is sobbing next to his dying horse, his troops in utter disarray; the next we hear of him, he is triumphantly on the way to Moscow.

To note these features is not to suggest that Pushkin's short scenes are internally incoherent, open-ended, or unfinished. On the contrary, as several critics have remarked, many of Pushkin's individual scenes are "self-enclosed masterpieces which tend if anything to vie with each other, like excellently contrasted miniatures competing for attention, rather than to coalesce into a well-formed drama."[29] "What beauty the play has," Henry Gifford writes bluntly, "lies in the contrast of these finished parts."[30]

We might conclude that Pushkin's scenes were designed *not* to add up, at least not in ways traditional for the drama of his time. Among much else, Pushkin was taking to task the bias, as ancient as Plutarch, toward linear biography in historical drama. *Boris Godunov* shows us only the cataclysmic moments, when the fate of an individual interacts with the fate of a whole people. But even these biographical moments are not arranged in logical sequence and seem almost randomly selected. Instead of a series of interlocking and exemplary life situations, we are given an assemblage of glimpses drawn from different points of view—what one critic has called "poly-perspectival drama."[31]

So abrupt are these scenic juxtapositions that several critics have credited Pushkin with the discovery, in dramaturgy, of the principle of cinematic montage.[32] Sergei Eisenstein had this quality in mind when he spoke of Pushkin's *kinomyshlenie* or "thinking in film images";[33] more recently Sergei Bondarchuk, discussing his forthcoming television production of Pushkin's *Boris,* claimed that "Pushkin's genius had foreseen . . . the art of film."[34] Montage—which is in essence the creation of meaning through assemblage and juxtaposition—inevitably relies on a chronotope very different from that of the traditional history play or biographical narrative. In his survey of the fate of Pushkin's dramaturgy, Oleg Feldman sums up the challenge of such historical drama:

> Without tying history down to his own prejudices, Pushkin boldly, subtly, effortlessly revealed history's free multivoicedness [mnogogolos'e]. The voice of the poet became the voice of events, his art became the self-expression of history. . . . The self-sufficient, unenclosed episodes that make up the play encompass a segment of the *historical process,* preserving its natural open flow. These episodes cannot be fused into monolithic acts; they are not reducible to one place and are unthinkable without the temporal distance separating them. . . . Space and time in *Boris Godunov* are fully real forces that determine the growth of events.[35]

This radical approach to causality suggests an identity crisis for the play as a whole. Significantly, in the final draft Pushkin chose not to preface his play with a list of *dramatis personae*—as if the playwright himself declined to create any expectations about who must appear, or who would play what role. This tentativeness in identity at the most elementary level is reproduced thematically in the overall inability of characters in this play to believe, or to take, an oath. An oath is made on some value commonly acknowledged, on some shared identity. But in this play the identities, and even the events, are too scene-specific, too dependent on the particulars of each isolated time and space and on each self-serving restatement of "history." It is impossible to know who will survive a scene to reappear later, and what these survivors will present as true. Thus there can be no real oaths—only oaths staged or parodied.

Consider three examples. When Boris first hears of the Pretender and requests confirmation from Shuisky, that sly courtier swears that the Uglich death really happened. Boris, in this early scene, knows what an oath from Shuisky is worth. "No, Shuisky, don't swear," the tsar says impatiently. "Just answer. . . ." When Marina (in the garden by the fountain) scorns the False Dmitri for his rash honesty about his origins, he swears that no one but she had heard his confession. Marina mocks him:

> So you swear! and I'm to believe it—
> Oh, I believe. But by what, pray tell,

Are you swearing? Not by God's name,
As a pious convert of the Jesuits?
Or perhaps by your honor as a noble knight,
Or by your tsarist word alone,
As a tsar's son? Is that it? Speak up . . .

Marina is only too aware of the connection between oath-taking and identity, and since she insists on manipulating the latter she will discard the former.

In a final example, Boris, dying, asks the boyars to swear fidelity to his young son, Fyodor. This oath is arguably the most significant, for it alone is *public* and makes manifest what has been latently true throughout the play: that Boris's passion is not for his own life or reign but for his dynasty, for the rule of his son. Shuisky and Basmanov both swear immediate allegiance to Fyodor. So necessary to Boris is this oath that only after its uttering can he die, in his own words, "content." This mockery is the cruelest of all. Earlier in the play the tsar had a healthy suspicion of oaths. Now, to mark Pushkin's inversion of the usual progress of tragic heroes toward self-knowledge, Boris dies innocent of the most important political realities. Three short scenes later, Boris's wife and son are dead, and—for reasons no character can persuasively articulate—treason is universal.

Boris the Pretender

Samozvanstvo, pretendership, is the perfect container for the disjointed times and spaces in this play. No term better defines the distance separating the chronotope of Pushkin's *Boris* from its source material in Karamzin's *History*. Karamzin's plot is rife with "hints and allusions" because it presumes a consensus: the past comes together in a moral lesson that will be applied, with equal integrity, to the future. The biographies of important persons fit into history.

Thus Karamzin's Pretender is a fraud, a dreamer, but still of great historical importance as the instrument of Godunov's destruction.[36] Since the function of the Pretender in the *History* is largely negative and symbolic (a weapon *against* the guilty Boris), little attention is paid to the incompatible and "creative" aspects of his story. Grishka Otrepiev is simply a minor, closed personality, noteworthy only because of the name he had assumed and the resonance of that name in Boris's soul. Karamzin is careful to present the Pretender's problematic early biography as undisputed historical fact (XI, 74–76). The very matter-of-factness of his biography removes much of its mystery, and this helps Karamzin to sustain the progressive, coherent forward movement of the *History*.

For Pushkin, however, history did not necessarily progress or cohere. His pretender is therefore more elusive and autonomous. The measure of his success is always taken in the present—not, as in Karamzin, in some future retribution for past sins. Pushkin's Pretender succeeds because he *makes* history, or rather, he makes it up; he listens, absorbs, literally becomes the many personalities that others need to see in him. He assumes a different identity with almost every scene: he is a novice in the monastery, a townsman in the Tavern Scene, a Polish nobleman while courting Marina, a troop commander on the Russian border, a little boy mourning his horse after his first defeat. He can speak back whatever language is projected upon him. In the Cracow scene, for example, he answers the Pater in a syntax recalling Latin rhetoric; with Kurbsky and the Cossack later in the same scene he adopts a more heroic diction, and to the poet he praises, and imitates, Parnassian verse. This is the secret of his success. He is, as Afanasy Pushkin tells Shuisky, "po nravu vsem" (to everyone's liking), and each side perceives him as being on *its* side. Thus, of course, he can never come face to face with Boris, for then he would have to be himself. And the very lack of a self, the very absence of identity is, paradoxically, his identifying characteristic.

The written text of the play recognizes this multiplicity of identities for the Pretender by a bewildering list of labels for the "same" character: Dmitri, Grigori, *Lzhe*[False]dmitri, *Samozvanets,* even Grisha. Sometimes the labels on the lines change within a single scene, as in the confrontation with Marina at the fountain.[37] It is significant that in this fountain scene, the single one where the Pretender falters, everything is almost lost because he tries to tell the *truth.* No one, Marina included, wants his truth; his fate is to be what others want, and the truth, and strength, of his position is that he is only a pretext. Pushkin, characteristically, inserts this cruel lesson into a parodied love tryst, and has Marina herself demand of the Pretender an "honesty" about his past, which—once it fails to serve her interests—she rejects with disgust.[38] It is, we recall, the very move with which Prince Shuisky opens the play: he persuades the gullible Vorotynsky of the truth of Boris's crime at Uglich, and then, once Boris is crowned tsar, not only repudiates the story but tries to blackmail Vorotynsky for believing it. Nobody's biography can be taken for granted. Tsar Boris, in an agitated moment, realizes how this can affect his own fate after Shuisky announces the appearance of a pretender in Poland. "Kto na menia?" Boris asks himself incredulously. "Pustoe imia, ten' . . ." (Who's after me? An empty name, a shade . . .). Precisely this "empty name," which any passerby can fill with any desired content, is the continuity carrying the Pretender triumphantly from scene to scene. Characters with clear and steady personalities, straightforward about their desires like Marina Mniszech, Varlaam, Pimen, we see only once.

And we may perhaps conclude that history is also an "empty name," filled with meanings by those who interpret it, or want something from it.

That the very structure of Pushkin's play said something about history has not been lost on its best readers. When Meyerhold was rehearsing his production of Pushkin's *Boris* in 1936, he asked his company: "What was it in this subject that so frightened Nicholas I and the censors? Because a presentation of historical events was so much more terrifying from Pushkin than it would have been from any other writer of the period. . . ."[39] This terror that Meyerhold glimpsed—the subversion of history by the broadest possible concept of "identity crisis"—underlies one of the best recent readings of *Boris*.[40] What Pushkin attempted in his hybrid "romantic tragedy," Valentin Nepomniashchy claims, was to challenge the ideology of both neoclassicism and romanticism. The former made rational man the center of the universe; the latter merely reversed the hierarchy, opposing man to his world and condemning him, in Byronic fashion, to futile self-duplication. Both ideologies were equally monologic. And, Nepomniashchy argues, as dramatic principles they were equally unsatisfactory to Pushkin. Drama was dialogue—with others, with the environment—and it *develops,* it is not merely acted out or willed by heroes. Pushkin advocated neither Individuals nor the People as "subjects of history" or "heroes of drama"; they were the subjects and heroes only of their own personal fates. Thus this play, about a *Lzhe*dmitri challenging a *Lzhe*-tsar, is really about the larger problem of *Lzhe*-subjects. *Boris Godunov,* Nepomniashchy concludes, "is not a 'historical tragedy' in the usual sense of the term, but a tragedy about History."

In their different ways Meyerhold and Nepomniashchy arrive at the same conclusion. If there is any artistic unity to these dramatic scenes and personalities, it is in keeping with Pushkin's sense of history: a unity that does not explain but merely entraps.

In this play about pretendership, the fate of Boris is the reverse of Dmitri's. The Pretender has no need of psychological continuity; in fact, he celebrates his multiple identities. The locus for this multiplicity is Poland: the land of elected monarchs, independent nobles, the individual as a creator of destiny. In Pushkin's play the Poles are a colorful cultural alternative to Russia—free, selfish, foolish, invigorating. Poland is a place where ladies dance in public and poets flourish. Pushkin is ambivalent toward this world; on Polish soil his Pretender becomes a Western knight, and Pushkin seems to admire him for that.[41] His Dmitri is an opportunist pure and simple. His "cause" comes and goes; at any given moment he merely wishes to maximize his passion and his freedom, and Poland is that opportunity. The West is adventure space.

Tsar Boris, on the contrary, seeks a firm and singular identity. His station requires a voice resonant with authority and restraint. But such a voice is forever breaking down; in fact, it occurs only once, in the distanced and formulaic monologue of the coronation scene. The next time we see the tsar, three scenes and five years later, we are granted so sudden and intimate an access to his thoughts and complaints that tsarist dignity is completely undermined. The tone is wholly inappropriate for one ruling by divine authority and blessed by the Patriarch. Indeed, this compulsion to complain and to explain which marks the tsar throughout the play is precisely what defines Boris's power as so inevitably secular, the result of election and not succession. He is, in this metaphorical sense, a "Polish king," and soon will be cast off his throne by another sort of "elected" king—elected, that is, Polish style.

Thus the two heroes represent different solutions to the problem of personality and its historical (and dramatic) role. The Pretender can always find a voice, and a vision, proper to his many roles. He doesn't try to understand what's happening. Troops desert him too; disasters mount, military defeat is complete, but (as we see in scene 19) the False Dmitri simply falls asleep. It is the last we see of him in the play—returned, as it were, to the dream from which he woke in Pimen's cell. Afanasy Pushkin delivers the epitaph:

> Sweet dreams, Tsarevich.
> Ground to dust, saved only by flight,
> He's as carefree as a foolish child:
> And Providence, of course, will protect him . . .

Providence, in the ironic aside of Pushkin's own ancestor, somehow works hand in hand with those who let their plans go, who do not try to control events.

Tsar Boris, however, is increasingly denied the voice and the vision he requires. Caught in a web of informers and denunciations, he rarely has the information that he really needs. His deathbed monologue to his son while the enemy is at the gates is full of a pathetically misguided lyricism. The Pretender, following his own contrary course to self-realization, slips off into a dream. Neither protagonist seems to know what is happening outside the scene which at that moment contains him.

The play is designed to undermine just such links between scenes. As one critic of the work has suggested:

Pushkin structures his tragedy in such a way that there is none of that uninterrupted scenic action one finds in the multi-scened tragedies and chronicles of Shakespeare. None of the twenty-four scenes of *Godunov* furthers the development of the action in itself, but each moves forward the action of the tragedy as a whole. Each scene of *Godunov* is a dynamic result of the overflow of action that rages behind the scenes, that is, in life.[42]

The stage is where *ends*, not means, are displayed. Answers lie in life itself—and that will always be offstage because the means of history are hidden, obscure, unknowable. The engine of history is a black box. Thus it could be argued that Pushkin's plot, like the Boris Tale at its base, is itself a *samozvanets*, a pretender that invites and engenders response without identifying any source of authority within itself.

Tynianov once described Pushkin's innovation in tragedy as an "equating of major heroes with secondary ones"[43]—a way of saying that the play *has* no heroes. It was a sentiment frequently voiced as reproach in the 1830s. Heroes, by definition, have firm identities and heroic confrontations. In *Boris Godunov*, not only do the two major protagonists never meet but they seem to be living in different worlds.

Pushkin and Uglich

Confronted by this herolessness, critics have routinely searched the play for some other organizing structure. But such a structure would contradict every idea about history and drama that Pushkin embodies in this play: his suspicion of explanatory principles, his distrust of integrated heroic personalities on stage, his keen sense for the arbitrary and the accidental. Thus the search for a "hidden" unity in Pushkin's anomalous drama began. Soon after publication, Ivan Kireevsky suggested as unifying thematic thread Boris's guilt for the death of Dmitri.

> Boris's crime is not so much an action as an idea, a force which is slowly brought to light—first in the whisperings of a courtier, then in the quiet recollections of a monk, then in the solitary dreamings of Grigory, then in agitation at court, then in an uprising of the people, and finally in the massive toppling of a ruling house.[44]

That crime is indeed on the lips of literally every class and in every context: prince, hermit, adventurer, tsar, holy fool. But Kireevsky's most productive insight is not the ubiquity of Uglich as a fact of history. It is, rather, his realization that Boris's crime functions in the play less as an action than as an *idea*.

Kireevsky does not pursue this thought. But we might do so here,

in connection with that larger identity crisis which informs the genre
of romantic tragedy. Dmitri's death is present in *Boris Godunov* not as
fact but as rumor, and discredited rumor at that. The Uglich Affair
links the parts of this play together in the only way that self-sufficient
isolated worlds *can* be linked: not by direct knowledge but by subjective and secondhand accounts. Nowhere in Pushkin's play is Boris's
guilt documented. Uglich is the subject of hearsay, slander, delirium;
even the accounts of eyewitnesses like Shuisky and Pimen are self-
serving, packed with hypocrisy and faked miracles. The unifying
thread is not so much the fact of Boris's guilt at Uglich as the *rumor* of
it.

   This blurring of lines between the deed and the account of the
deed is paralleled in the play by another set of incompatibilities. As we
mentioned in chapter 1, Tsar Boris is victim of a most unfortunate
combination of fates. On the one hand, he is accused of engineering
Dmitri's murder, and on that account called a tsarecide and usurper;
on the other hand, the Pretender is being welcomed into Russia as the
True Tsarevich, and thus Boris could not have been his murderer.
Pushkin works this story in such a way that its very incompatibilities
serve to highlight the devices of romantic tragedy and motivate anew
this transposed version of the familiar plot. A guilty Boris can be
reconciled with a living Dmitri in only two ways. Either the Pretender's claim to be Dmitri is absurd, merely a pretext (as the Pretender himself confirms) for discord and war, or, on another and
more psychologized plane, the *fact* of murder must be seen as less
significant than the *intent* to murder—that is, Boris must be perceived
as guilty for merely desiring the death, as guilty as he would have been
had he actually executed it. The ambivalent, rumor-shrouded status
of the actual deed has led some students of Pushkin's play to suggest
that Boris was not in fact meant to be guilty of Dmitri's death. On the
basis of the evidence he is merely guilty of *wanting* it—and thus his
story, like Ivan Karamazov's, raises the Christian question of crime in
thought, of the desire as deed.[45]

   To keep his plot intact Pushkin draws liberally on both of these
explanatory strategies. Both the idea of the Pretender as pretext and
the possibility that Boris is only *presumed* guilty are allowed to stand
until the end of the play. This ambivalence calls into question the very
status of the historical event, and it does so on two levels: first, in the
outer social world, as the discrepancy between deed and rumor; then,
in the realm of the individual psyche, as the uncertain space separating deed and desire.

We might now sum up these component parts of the chronotope
governing romantic tragedy. Pushkin constricts time and space in the

play to the actual world available to any character at a given historical moment—and then saturates that world with chance, rumor, and the uttered (not the enacted) word. Such a chronotope propels the Pretender toward victory, for he epitomizes the flexibility and openness of the present. And it propels Boris toward defeat, for the entire burden of his reign has been *responsibility*—both for the past (for Dmitri of Uglich, for the famine and the fires), and for his own children in the future. Each protagonist is caught in his own time and space. And, in Pushkin's sense of the terms, the chronotope here is both romantic, because utterly unique to the character living it, and tragic, because that character cannot see above, around, or beyond his own situation. Without a doubt this ordinary intimate perspective, the sort that traps and intimidates, is a risk on the dramatic stage.

For and against a Playable Boris

It is hardly surprising that nineteenth-century critics by and large presumed that Pushkin's *Boris* could not be staged. Some, like Belinsky, went further, claiming that *Boris Godunov* was not drama at all. Belinsky's "Tenth Article" on Pushkin (1845), arguably the nineteenth century's most influential essay on *Boris Godunov,* simply dismisses the troublesome formal aspects of the work altogether. The play fails in art, Belinsky claims, for the same reasons that Boris failed in life. *Boris Godunov* is not really a drama at all. It is, rather, an "epic poem in conversational form"—but this lapse is not the fault of the dramatist. It is the fault of history. "Dramatism" requires personalities and ideas in conflict; sixteenth-century Russia, however, had no new political ideas and no concept of the individual. Thus Pushkin's play, by honestly reflecting its era, suffers from an inevitable epic wholeness that undercuts the dramatic principle.[46]

Pushkin, however, was convinced that the play could be performed. He even made preliminary inquiries in that direction in 1826.[47] But *Boris Godunov* was cleared for the stage only in 1866, and the few unsuccessful productions that were mounted in subsequent decades only served to make its "unstageworthiness" all the more canonical.[48] In the 1920s, Stanislavsky was doubting whether the play could be mounted at all without Musorgsky's musical support.[49] Since in his own time Musorgsky was roundly abused for violating, not realizing, Pushkin's verse, this is a curious statement—and an instructive lesson in the retroactive force of transpositions.

In the 1930s new stage productions were planned in connection with the centennial of Pushkin's death, and the mechanics of Pushkin's dramaturgy reexplored. Pushkin's "Shakespearism"—long an accepted part of *textual* studies on *Boris Godunov*—was extended to the

technical aspects of staging.[50] Theater historians began to suggest that
the tripartite stage of Elizabethan drama might indeed integrate
Pushkin's fast-paced and self-enclosed scenes into a more playable
whole.[51] For Pushkin's scenes *do* answer and echo one another—albeit
indirectly, whimsically, often in the style of absurdist dialogue. Pace
and proximity are all. A stage that could accommodate alternating or
almost simultaneous action on rear and front stages, without the
divisive formalities of acts, scenes, or curtains, would be most congenial to Pushkin's dramatic design. To be sure, there is no clear evidence that Pushkin was familiar with the layout of Elizabethan
theaters. But clearly such an Elizabethan-type stage could not be
found in the neoclassical theaters of the Russian capitals, and those
were the very theaters that according to Pushkin cried out for reform.[52]

One hundred years after Pushkin's death, then, a radical realization of the playwright's idea was becoming possible under the guidance of a series of innovative directors. But as Pushkin's chronotope
was reconstructed, the political unorthodoxy of the play became ever
more manifest. In the first chapter we mentioned Meyerhold's ill-
fated attempt to "return the play to Pushkin" in the 1920s and again in
the mid-thirties, as well as Liubimov's aborted production at the
Taganka Theater in 1982. Among those recent reconceptualizations
of *Boris* fortunate enough to be fully realized, one of the most interesting is by Anatoly Efros, who produced the play for Soviet television in
1971. Efros adapted the drama to the genre of "literary theater," with
a *chtets/avtor* (reciter-author) linking the scenes. The technical devices
of close-up camera shot and hidden microphone made possible normal everyday diction—that is, effective drama without dramatic gestures or intonation. There were no panoramas; for most scenes, a
single body filled the screen, and the "people" were one or two faces in
a slowly panning camera. Few characters moved, and most shots took
in only upper torso and face.

If Meyerhold's production had been all lightness and movement
to match the pace of Pushkin's verse, Efros on the contrary re-created
heavy ritualized Muscovy—richly costumed but visible only from the
waist up, almost riveted in place. But for all the differences in tempo,
Efros too aimed at a simpler, less operatic Boris. "In art, the theme of
the ordinary is a complex theme," he wrote of this production. "As
regards Godunov, something had to be minimized, made more modest, so that the *idea* might cease to be so modest and taken for granted
behind a general pomposity of style."[53] Boris leaning wearily against a
doorjamb speaking his famous monologues was more disturbing than
a declamation.

We are left with the intriguing thought that the chronotope of

Pushkin's "romantic tragedy" might resemble either that of Elizabethan drama or one from the age of television. The conventions of both allow for multiple points of view, swift shifts of scene, and a diminution of the distanced, declamatory hero. Television, in addition, promises an intimacy in isolation that no theater can match. A fragmented audience confronts a fragmented actor. The close-up of a face or torso can be heard and seen even when it speaks and moves with no dramatic authority at all.

Some Formal Considerations

This lack of "dramatic authority" in *Boris,* so clear on the level of characters and their confrontations, is ultimately an uncertainty as to how to deliver the lines. At the heart of the problem are two experiments Pushkin carried out simultaneously in this play, one on the verse line and the other on the concept of the spoken utterance in drama. Pushkin, we must not forget, was intent upon a radical reform of the Russian stage. It was to embrace not only the formal organization of scenes and plot but also the sound and intonation of the lines. None of the received models were "quite right," in romantic *or* tragic genres.[54]

Pushkin's dissatisfaction was due in part to the ambivalent status of stage language itself during the 1820s. As Vinokur points out in his essay on the language of Pushkin's *Boris,*[55] the reforms that Karamzin had brought about in the Russian literary language were not easily applicable to the reigning dramatic genres of the time. Drama lagged behind prose fiction; playwrights and critics attacked neoclassicism in the name of sentimentalism or romanticism but had not themselves worked out anything like a new language for the stage. A contemporary tragedian like Ozerov succeeded because he merely "enscened" narrative or lyric poetry. Both classical and sentimental tragedy remained genres of declamation, and thus essentially monologic.

It was in fact considered good tragic form (and a considerable artistic achievement) to create a cast of characters all of whom sounded more or less alike, regardless of age or social class. When these characters addressed one another, their dialogues tended to unfold in metrically regular rhymed lines, alternating "one-line monologues" (as Vinokur put it) in which two adjacent rejoinders did not have to answer one another. "Each rejoinder represented a sort of finished microcosm of speech" (129). Syntactically self-sufficient and intonationally neutral, these "dialogues" could be declaimed without much attention to the real nature of dialogic speech.

According to Vinokur, Pushkin's *Boris Godunov* was "the first Russian tragedy in which declamation ceased to be the basic and governing principle of dramatic language" (129). Exchanges in a dialogue were no longer "locked-in and static, but given in movement." At one level this movement was ensured by formal features: enjambments and frequent mid-line changes of voice, and word or sound repetition at the center (not the ends) of lines. But in a blunter sense, movement occurred because there were genuine boundaries to cross, that is, personality was differentiated. Different people spoke in different ways; the same person spoke differently at different times. This play, like the *Onegin* being composed alongside it, not only tolerated but relished its mixed languages and identities. As we know from his comments on Byron's drama, Pushkin considered this "multivoicedness" of primary importance for dramatic, as opposed to lyric, creativity.[56] Thus he strenuously sought difference—in intonation, tone, even inscription. In one scene of *Boris,* "On the Plain near Novgorod-Seversk," the tsar's mercenary troops converse in three languages; in the nineteenth century their conversation would have been typeset in three alphabets, Cyrillic, Latin, and German *Fraktur.*

No wonder, then, that the small circle of Pushkin's friends present at prepublication readings of the "tragedy" were somewhat disoriented. "The effect this reading had on us is impossible to describe," Pogodin wrote in his memoirs of a literary evening at the Venevitinovs in October 1826.

> We had gathered to hear Pushkin, we who had been raised on the verses of Lomonosov, Derzhavin, Kheraskov, Ozerov, whom we all knew by heart. . . . One must remember the mode of reciting verse that was dominant at the time. It was a singsong, bequeathed to us from French declamation. And instead of the highflown language of the gods we heard *simple, ordinary,* and nevertheless *poetic, engrossing speech!*[57]

In five scenes, and elsewhere in inserted segments, dialogue is directly represented as prose. But for the bulk of the play, speech is embedded in a poetic vehicle—and here Pushkin's solution has been criticized, even by Pushkin himself.

Pushkin had apparently considered using several different meters in *Boris.*[58] But ultimately the playwright settled for a unified poetic meter—the better, perhaps, to focus on his central task of juxtaposing poetry and prose. It was an easy decision to avoid the inflexible Alexandrine line, which up to then had been the accepted vehicle for serious drama in Russian. Pushkin replaced it with iambic pentameter, popular in English and German and much more appropriate than a syllabic line to the strong word-stress of Russian.[59] But for all his admiration of Shakespeare, it was not the loosely fitting Shakespearean pentameter that Pushkin imitated. Rather he created a Russian equivalent of the *French* pentametric line, omitting rhymes (except sporadic ones) but retaining a caesura (obligatory word boundary) after the fourth syllable. This meter, in the words of one theater historian, "gave the verse line a majestic and measured regularity, but deprived it of the inner movement characteristic of the iamb with movable caesurae."[60] Within the larger context of swiftly moving dialogue, then, the *inner* movement of each line was constricted. Pushkin might have been inspired by both Shakespearean precedent and "simple, ordinary speech," but in fact it is iambic tetrameter, not pentameter, that most realistically reflects the rhythms of spoken Russian.[61]

This situation creates a dilemma for performers. The text can neither be spoken naturally nor declaimed. So delicate a balance was required that Pushkin himself doubted the wisdom of his solution. He later admitted that this verse line "might have been a mistake," for he had thereby "voluntarily deprived his line of the variety peculiar to it."[62] In effect, the natural lightness and flexibility of the Pushkinian line was made to compete with a rather rigid meter, creating tensions and mixed expectations very much in keeping with the aesthetic of romantic tragedy—but quite unknown to both neoclassical and Shakespearean dramatic verse.

These tensions have fueled controversy about the playability of *Boris*, setting into motion debates over the relative weight of the play's "realistic" and "stylized" components. In Soviet scholarship much has been made of the play's realism. But even in the darker periods of party-mindedness, critics have confirmed the conventionality of Pushkin's stage language. One critic writing in the 1930s, in an essay intended for actors studying the dramatic pronunciation of *Boris,* defended the awkward French pentameter with the caveat that Pushkin, raised on strict forms, "sought limiting factors, even in blank verse."[63] And Nemirovich-Danchenko's 1907 production of the first nearly complete *Boris* at the Moscow Art Theater (twenty-two scenes) was later criticized for its excessive "naturalism," that is, for a striving after realistic effect that reduced the tragedy to an "archeological reconstruction of the past" and its verse lines to mere prose.[64] Clearly this uneasy hybrid of real-life dialogue and relatively fixed meter had no simple rules for delivery.

For all the intrusions of prose, then, Pushkin's unusual meter binds the verse portions together and has a stabilizing, slightly distancing effect on the play as a whole. Here we should recall Pushkin's own general attitude toward verisimilitude in tragedy. It was not, he believed, brought about through an observation of the classical unities. Nor was it achieved through a sort of elementary "realism," that is, by pretending that spectators did not exist or that the stage was a real room with four (not three) walls. In a stance similar to the position Meyerhold defended against Stanislavsky a century later,[65] Pushkin seemed to endorse language stylization as a means of setting off a higher, more compressed realism, a *simultaneous* sense that dialogue was both freely developing and yet the product of restricted circumstance. Pushkin insisted on an acknowledgment of convention and stylization as part of the honesty of staged art. The paradox of honest conventionality, of acknowledged artifice, is embodied in a verse line that conveys the particularities of everyday speech in a version of neoclassical poetics. This was "verisimilitude of situations and truth of dialogue" as the theater could best transmit them.

It should be pointed out that the lexicon and speech patterns of the characters in *Boris* are not "true" in any historical or linguistic sense. Like Karamzin before him, Pushkin interpreted history in words real for *his* generation. The tone of the whole is always dominated by Pushkin's own poetic language and ironic perspective. Pushkin does, however, insert Church Slavonicisms and folk expressions for local color—embedded in what Vinokur calls "language masks."[66] These insertions of dialect, prose, and archaism are part of another complexity in this play that must now be discussed, Pushkin's so-called mixing of styles. It is perhaps the most important of several dramatic innovations familiar to Pushkin's generation from Shakespeare.

The Shakespeare Connection

Pushkin's debt to the Bard is an established part of the canon, often and openly stressed by the poet himself.[67] But the romantics' discovery and use of Shakespeare in the early nineteenth century was, in Russia as elsewhere on the Continent, both highly specific and polemical. For Pushkin's generation the basic source was Letourneur's French prose translations, corrected by Guizot and Pichot, and especially the 1821 Paris edition, which included Guizot's "Life of Shakespeare" and a lengthy theoretical discussion of Shakespearean dramaturgy. Thus packaged, in prose translation and with a bulky apparatus, Shakespeare in Russia was less available as independent art, read for its own beauty and on its own terms, than as a tool to be used by progressive romantics against the conservatives. Pushkin himself made reference to Shakespeare most often in this way, as the positive term in a polemical comparison.[68]

This orientation is important. Shakespeare appealed in large part for what he was not; it was presumed that since he was not bound by the constraints of classicism he could express "real life" on the stage in a direct and unmediated way. Other constraints, different from those of classicism, often went unnoticed; prose translations, after all, did not much differ from plot summaries. The plays, in short, were perceived less as artistic structures than as antistructures, as celebrations of the right to violate rules.

Against this background, the question of Pushkin's "Shakespearism" becomes both richer and more ambiguous. Certainly one notes broad similarities in plot, character, and theme—even echoings of specific lines when *Boris* is read with Shakespeare's history or chronicle plays in mind.[69] Pushkin was clearly aware of the theoretical license Shakespeare provided for a "mixing of styles." In both playwrights' work, conspiratorial courtiers and kingly rhetoric share stage time with the bawdy humor of taverns and public squares. But what Pushkin did in his drama was stranger than anything his contemporaries had experienced in Shakespeare. As one Soviet historian of the Pushkin era put it, "Shakespeare was already known and comprehensible. But *Boris Godunov* was incomprehensible."[70]

The reasons for this "incomprehensibility" are of special interest today in the light of some recent Shakespeare scholarship. During the last three decades, revisionist critics[71] have argued that the received image of Shakespeare since the eighteenth century—Shakespeare as creator of character, and Shakespeare as propagandist for providential theories of history—is seriously flawed; the plays themselves, so these critics claim, do not display this integrity of personality and time, which was in fact anachronistically imposed on them. And this suggests an intriguing thesis: that Pushkin's "Shakespearism" might have been incomprehensible to his early nineteenth-century audiences because Pushkin, consciously or no, was reflecting in his play a *Renaissance* understanding of Shakespeare, one that contradicted the accepted received image of the Bard in the 1820s. Since that received image has been dominant in Western readings of Shakespeare up through Tillyard in the twentieth century, we might briefly summarize it here.

Shakespeare, as read in Pushkin's time and to a certain extent in our own, is indeed a mixer of styles—but this mixture has been seen as essentially mechanical. Drunken porters cavort obscenely after a king is murdered, but kings still sound like kings and porters like porters. That sort of mixing, of distinct styles attached to specific personalities, is immediately playable; each voice remains itself, even when in disguise. In this view, Shakespeare's audience might be expected to suspend belief and play with identity—but only for a short while and for fun. The audience is in on the joke, and eventually so are the players. "Real" personalities always emerge and are reconciled with one another in the end.

In this reading, Shakespearean monarchs do indeed mix the style of their speech at transitional moments. With his friend Poins, Prince Hal is both scapegrace and future king. But ultimately a monarch evolves in one direction, from child to man. There is nothing of Prince Hal in King Henry the Fifth; after the deathbed scene, his change of diction is abrupt and irreversible.[72]

Alongside this thesis of a one-way evolution of character is the analogous thesis of a relatively straightforward unfolding of Shakespearean historical time. As the Soviet Shakespeare scholar Leonid Pinsky has remarked, "chronicle time" is neither blind fate, nor indifferent fate, nor is it the "humorously subjective circular time" of the comedies. It is, rather, a force standing behind people and events, regulating them and protecting sequentiality; "time stands on guard, watching over the order of things."[73] For all the bloodletting and treason, the two tetralogies ultimately demonstrate a forward sweep of history, that fullness of Elizabethan national consciousness in which, reflecting the medieval chain of being, every event had its place and time.[74] In such an interpretation, *Henry VIII*—in effect more a dramatic romance than a chronicle—becomes a culminating statement on the nurturing effects of time. Like the royal infant Elizabeth, who in her cradle

> promises
> Upon this land a thousand thousand blessings
> Which time shall lead to ripeness,

the passage of days will lead to national glory, which is easy for the playwright to predict because it has already come to pass.

These twin theses, on the integrity of personality and on the cumulative nature of historical time, have been routinely attributed to Shakespeare—and were precisely the concepts Pushkin challenged in his romantic tragedy. *Boris Godunov* permits no such one-way evolution of character. This is because Pushkin does not *play* with identity; his identity crises are for real. Thus Pushkin's "mixing of styles" is a much more radical gesture than Shakespeare's was perceived to be; through it Pushkin manages to call into question the whole nature of biographical continuity in drama, and the integrity of the dramatic utterance. The utterance becomes complex, unpredictable, internally at odds with itself. The high sentiments of high personages are not always expressed in poetry; prose is not confined to comic scenes. Whereas the *meter* of the verse portions is remarkably stable, changes are continually worked upon the poetry-prose boundary. The very distinction between poetic and prose language is blurred as Pushkin shifts from rhymed poetry to unrhymed blank verse, from blank verse to rhythmic prose, from prose to *prostorechie* (popular speech).[75] Indeed, what often ends up as prose are precisely those parts where one would expect poetry: in the speech of exalted persons and in formal embedded genres. The Patriarch's complaint to the abbot, for example, is in prose, as is Ksenia's ritual lament on the death of her bridegroom.[76] The intent in these instances could be ironic—a sort of laying bare of convention—or, as in the case of the Patriarch, prose could actually work to increase the immediacy and authority of the utterance.[77] In either case this is clearly not the prose that Pushkin learned from Shakespeare's plays, in French translation or—later—in the original English. Shakespearean prose was seen largely as comic relief that relied on wordplay, puns, and dialect to reveal outspoken and lowborn characters for *what they were*. In Pushkin, prosaic intrusion more often reveals people for what they are *not* presumed to be, setting them against the discursive modes usually deemed appropriate for them.

Mismatching sentiment to genre was one way Pushkin seemed to exceed his Shakespearean model. Equally disorienting were the characters who changed diction from beginning to end of a single utterance. This Boris does, in a most unregal way, in his famous catalogue of complaints, "Dostig ia vysshei vlasti" (I have attained the highest power) (scene 7).

This scene-length speech shares honors with Pimen's as the best-known monologue in *Boris Godunov*. In our brief reference to this monologue above, we suggested that the "sudden and intimate access" it affords to Boris's inner life undoes the authority bestowed on the new tsar in the opening scenes. A closer look at this famous monologue is now in order, for it can be shown to interrogate authority on a much more profound level than is at first apparent.

As scene 7 opens, Boris emerges grim-lipped from a session with his sorcerers:

> I have attained the highest power;
> For six years now, I've reigned in peace.
> But there's no happiness for me. Is this not
> What happens when we're young?
> We fall in love, and thirst for
> Love's pleasures, but as soon as we've appeased
> The hunger of the heart with momentary possession
> We cool, grow bored, and languish . . .
> In vain the sorcerers have promised me
> Long life, and peaceful years in power—
> But neither power nor life delights me;
> I sense the coming wrath of heaven, and calamity.
> No happiness for me. I thought
> To make my people happy, glorious,
> To win their love by generosity—

But that vain hope I've put aside.
The mob despises living power.
They can love only the dead.
We are mad to let the popular applause
Or furious outcry move our hearts.
God sent a famine on our land,
The people howled, and perished in their agony;
I opened up the granaries, scattered gold,
Found work for them—and, raging,
They cursed *me*!
Then fire destroyed their homes.
I built new houses for them all—
I was the one, they said, who set the fires.
The judgment of the mob: find love in it!
I hoped for solace in my family.
I longed to treat my daughter to a wedding,
When death, like some black storm, took off
Her bridegroom; then the rumor spread
That I was guilty of my daughter's widowhood!
Me! The miserable father!
Whoever dies, I am the secret murderer:
I hurried Fyodor to his grave,
I poisoned my own sister, Fyodor's wife,
A holy nun . . . It's always me!
Ah! Now I know: there's nothing can
Console us mid the sorrows of the world
Except our conscience. Nothing else.
If healthy it can triumph
Over malice, evil slander.
But if there's a single spot,
One accidental stain,
Then woe! The soul flares up
With pestilential sores and pours
Its dreadful poison on the heart.
Reproaches hammer in my ears,
I'm nauseous, dizzy, and
The bloodstained boys before my eyes . . .
And I'd be glad to run, but where? It's awful!
Yes, he's pitiful whose conscience is unclean.[78]

   This monologue is usually considered a confession of guilt. But what in fact strikes us most forcefully in it is that it does not confess. Boris quite literally discards any authority that might console or absolve him. This process begins immediately after the scene opens, with the sorcerers and astrologers whom Boris had consulted. As a man of the sixteenth century Boris should, and by all accounts did, have a keen respect for soothsaying. But Pushkin, who had planned in an early draft to devote an entire scene to Boris with his magicians,[79] ultimately limits himself to a mere offstage reference to sorcerers, and then has Boris casually dismiss their testimony in the opening lines. Freed from the authority of prophecy ("They said I'd be happy—I'm not"), Boris then sets out to free himself from the authority of popular sentiment. It appears that the tsar has done everything right but gets no credit for it. The only reason offered is that the people "can love only the dead"—dark words that will take on new meaning when Dmitri literally rises from the grave.

It could be argued, of course, that there *is* a confession at the end: the stain on Boris's conscience can only refer to his role in (or at the very least his desire for) Dmitri's death. But this reference to guilt for Uglich comes only after a much more persuasive truth, the truth of rumor. It is this truth that transforms the monologue from a regal address into a bitter critique of the mechanisms of slander. Boris is absolutely correct: it doesn't matter what's true, but only what's believed. Innocence is indeed the best policy, not because of any moral absolutes but because only a healthy conscience can triumph over the "malice and evil slander" that will inevitably be heaped upon it by the mob, so resentful of any living power.

"Whoever dies, I am the secret murderer." This is the heart of the confession. Boris is *believed* to be the murderer of his son-in-law, of Tsar Fyodor, of Irina—and, quite possibly on the same plane of credibility, of Dmitri.

To be sure, Pushkin had no reason to disbelieve Karamzin's account of a historically guilty Boris. But his monologue is not the confession of a man crushed by guilt. Boris's bad luck is not the result of a crooked soul; that would be moral determinism of Karamzin's sort. Rather the opposite obtains: Boris, his soothsayers, and—perhaps—even the reader *presume* a crooked soul because there is no other way to explain the tsar's miserable bad luck.[80] When the monologue begins Boris is still bent on figuring out the world, pitting his intelligence against fate. Thus does he expend so much energy setting the record straight, posing as injured authority, resisting slander. Such tenacity will surface several more times in the play, usually after confrontations between Boris and his ambivalent allies Shuisky and Basmanov. By the end of the monologue and the end of the play, however, righteous irritation has given way to weariness, even to the cowardly urge to escape. The last five lines of the speech (with such phrases as: "I'd be glad to run, but where? It's awful!") caused a critical storm in the 1830s, because there was something so "unpleasantly comic" about the shift.[81]

All rulers, of course, inevitably bow to events beyond their control. But Boris, by the end of his monologue, has lost even the will to define himself against collective rumor. He *cannot understand* why he has been so victimized by fate, and his is a mentality that insists on understanding. As a result, his "unclean conscience" makes him not sinful but simply *zhalok,* "pitiable"—which is to say, unable to cope, powerless. Boris's predecessors, Ivan the Terrible and Tsar Fyodor, had been much less responsible in office. But as we shall see in Pimen's monologue, their "sins," of commission and omission, are absolved by the fact of their dynastic legitimacy. In the context of old Muscovy and according to its criteria for validating rulers, Boris the elected tsar is, with all his gifts, an anachronism—and this is transmitted by the incongruously modern, lyrical innerness of his monologue. The key to his illegitimacy is language. True tsars do not need to talk like that.

This is not, however, the whole of Pushkin's assault against verbal authority. Words themselves are asked to bear strange burdens, transmit forbidden information. In the above monologue, the breakdown of Tsar Boris's regal persona is signaled by the use of archaic words, with their connotations of Orthodoxy and pious dignity, to express very secular Western Romantic sentiment.

> Ne tak li
> My smolodu vliubliaemsia i *alchem*
> Utekh liubvi, no tol'ko utolim
> Serdechnyi *glad* mgnovennym obladaniem
> Uzh okhladev, skuchaem i tomimsia?

> Is this not
> What happens when we're young?
> We fall in love, and *thirst for*
> Love's pleasures, but as soon as we've appeased
> The *hunger* of the heart with momentary possession
> We cool, grow bored, and languish . . .

One expects a tsar to speak the lofty diction of *alchem* and *glad,* but to address God, not sexual desire. And one does not expect a tsar to compare the responsibilities of rule with the pleasures of carnal love. Boris's language is thus doubly inappropriate: the words to their subject matter, the subject matter to a tsar. Languages address one another even *within* the word.

This internal dialogism is part of what makes the role of Boris so difficult to pronounce, perhaps even to conceptualize, on stage. It is a problem that the supremely performable Shakespeare never had to face. There is a parallel here with the language of novels—and one reason why great novels are so rarely transposed into successful dramatic productions. Truly novelized language is also internally dialogic; no single voice can unfold it. As Bakhtin has written of that archnovelist Dostoevsky, such discourse

loses its composure and confidence, becomes agitated, internally un-
decided and two-faced. . . . It is difficult to speak it aloud, for loud and
living intonation excessively monologizes discourse and cannot do justice
to the other person's voice present in it.[82]

Critics have often commented on the oddness of Boris's language
in Pushkin's play—the insecurity, as it were, of the "I" at the center. It
has led some to suggest that Boris, motivated as he is by a guilty
conscience, speaks in the lyric mode.[83] But Boris's voice is not predominantly a lyrical "I." Far from celebrating the self, Boris cannot
even find a voice for the self. Like his rival the Pretender, Boris is in
search of an identity. But where Dmitri, with his abundance of successful lyrical masks, celebrates a noncoincidence of self and voice,
Boris is continually irritated, insecure, out of touch. These two alternatives are Pushkin's uncomfortable options in a play about the integrity of identity, and neither had any real precedent on the Russian
dramatic stage.

We see, therefore, that Pushkin's mixing of styles was no mere
mechanical exercise. He did not simply attach a given style to a given
character and then combine the characters—as the Shakespeare of his
time was reputed to do. Rather he refuted the very idea that individuals *had* a single style, and that language possessed clearly distinct
stylistic levels. As Vinokur has expressed it:

> An understanding of style [*slog*] as abstract principle, as independent and
> indisputable law, was organically alien to Pushkin. In general the division
> of language into various styles, in the sense of closed-off, hard-edged
> generic categories, is something completely incompatible with the contri-
> bution Pushkin made to Russian literary language. (135)

Pushkin's idea that "style is many men" and that "the man has
many styles"—none necessarily converging—implies a break with the
traditional image of Shakespearean historical time. Time does not
work to order events. Individuals who try to impose order, such as
Boris does in his opening monologue, discover that their generosity
and nobility of diction are denied, or unappreciated, everywhere else
in the play.[84] In *Boris,* the pose of nobility does not even survive the
Coronation Scene. After Boris and the boyars leave, those two unsavory courtiers Shuisky and Vorotynsky—the Brutus/Cassius element
in Boris's coronation—do not expand on their rights or their complaints. There is no high-minded conspiracy hatching the day their
Caesar takes the crown. Shuisky, in fact, is all too eager to enter the
pageantry and be lost in the crowd.

When, several years later, news reaches Shuisky's house in
Moscow that a Pretender has appeared in Poland (scene 9), Afanasy
Pushkin predicts "Such a storm, that Tsar Boris will hardly / Keep the

crown upon his clever head. . . ." Again we encounter the paradox of a play centering on historical individuals who do not, strictly speaking, invest any part of themselves to move history. Individuals need not risk their lives, defend a principle, or plot death to tyrants. *Time* works for the destruction of states.

Some critics have suggested that Pushkin's "Shakespearism" can be explained in part by the similarities between Elizabethan England and post-Napoleonic Russia: a growing national self-awareness, recent victories over a powerful enemy, the emergence of a vigorous young nation on the European scene.[85] But if Pushkin does allude to such parallels, surely the allusions are ironic. He was writing *about* an era contemporaneous with the era Shakespeare wrote *in*. For Russia, Pushkin's *Boris* is prelude to the Time of Troubles, and if there is any suggestion of a cycle at the end of *Boris* it is quite clearly a vicious one. In a letter to Raevsky Pushkin wrote that he planned to return to the Boris Tale with a sequel.[86] But what characters attracted him? Marina, Shuisky—hardly national heroes, of the nobility *or* the common people. Pushkin was attracted to people who reduced national interest to the level of personal ambition, and who met a violent, meaningless end. In Pushkin's projected sequence of historical figures, Tsar Boris would have easily won honors as the person most devoted to shaping the nation and answering its needs.

This peculiar dramatic signature of Pushkin's—an extreme polyphony of style, combined with a faith in the dismantling powers of time— should be kept in mind when considering the playwright's relationship to his major source, Karamzin. For although Karamzin, as we have seen, had intricate and inconsistent principles for investing his text with authority, his was ultimately a *fusing* enterprise. The perspective of chroniclers made common cause with the perspective of the historian, and Karamzin legitimately belonged (as Pushkin noted) to both categories at once. Karamzin's historicism, with its faith in the organic growth of the state, was for its time essentially "Shakespearean" as regards the relationship of hero to history. Pushkin's impulse, on the contrary, was always to cut back, partition authority, distribute language in such a way that no character ever sounded, for long, like himself. In Pushkin's rendering, even history did not "sound like itself," that is, did not sound as if it were being viewed from a secure future perspective.

As the better writers on Pushkin's "Shakespearism"[87] have noted, this consistent splintering of language and of time is one of the major differences between Pushkin and the English playwright as he was read in Pushkin's day. Time for Shakespeare was presumed to be merely a means; for Pushkin, it is very clearly a problem. And significantly, it is precisely this aspect of Shakespeare's received image that has recently come under review. "Futility sits deep in the bone of the histories," John Blanpied writes, "most poignantly when it seizes those figures who are most fiercely and complexly committed to the justi-fication of their lives in time."[88] Pushkin's dialogue with Shakespeare may yet turn out to be more true to Elizabethan, and twentieth-century, understandings of the workings of time than to the audiences of Pushkin's own era.

This sensitivity to time helps explain the provisional titles that Pushkin tried out for his play during the summer of 1825. One variant was "A Comedy about Tsar Boris and Grishka Otrepiev"; another, more elaborate, was "A Comedy about a Disaster Suffered by the Muscovite State, about Tsar Boris and Grishka Otrepiev, Written by God's Slave Aleks. son of Sergei Pushkin in the Year 7333 in the Village of Voronich."[89] The mocking self-reference of the title hints, perhaps, at Pushkin's acknowledgment that one could no more do away completely with anachronism than he himself could have actu-ally lived in 7333. But to the extent that retrospection can be elimi-nated in a history play, Pushkin does so. Part of the "comedy element" in this disaster is its very arbitrariness toward the future—designed, most likely, to dissuade the spectator from faith in frames. The larger perspective is precisely unreasonable, chaotic, without the redeeming morality of either chronicle or Karamzin.

Thus it could be argued that *Boris Godunov*, for all its potential classical resonances, is no Russian version of a Theban tragedy. No-where do we feel the heaviness of Greek fate. Events do not have the stamp of necessity. As one critic has shrewdly noted, the comic ele-ment "is by no means exhausted by one or two scenes in the Falstaff mode"; Pushkin's fate is embodied in an ironic freedom, and events develop absurdly, comically, anecdotally.[90] The play provides glimpses of everyday history as its participants might have lived it, caught in their own time. But there is one character in Pushkin who would stitch these fragments together into a providential whole—or so, at least, it seems at first glance. This is the chronicler Pimen.

Pimen

One of the major themes in *Boris Godunov* is the capacity of narrative to represent the past. It is a theme in continual dialogue with Ka-ramzin, although the issues it raises exceed any particular source text. In drama, a voice that speaks about the story must also be, to some extent, a fictive character *in* the story. And historical drama commonly highlights, through a character or a recurrent theme, the dilemma inherent in portraying the past in a present-tense form. But rarely, it would seem, can an entire scene be read as a discussion of drama's relationship to history—and at the same time be an integral, even central, part of the drama's ongoing plot. Pushkin's "Night. A Cell in Chudovo Monastery" is such a scene.

The scene opens with the old monk Pimen reflecting on his labors as a chronicler. His monologue contains some of the best-known lines in Pushkin's play:

> Yet one final story—yet one more—
> And then I end my chronicle.
> My task will be accomplished, a task
> That God had set me. It was His purpose
> To make me his witness all these years,
> To train me in the writer's careful art.
> Someday another monk will come and find
> My work, my ardent, nameless labor;
> Then he will light his lamp as I have done
> And blow the dust of centuries from my pages
> To copy over all my true accounts
> So that the Russian land will know,
> In years to come, what went before.
> Our tsars in this will be remembered—
> For their glorious deeds, for golden benefactions,
> And for their sins, their secret midnight deeds,
> On which we beg our Savior's holy mercy.
>   My old age seems to me another life:
> The fleeting world now eddies past
> . As once it pounded madly, full of action,
> Turbulent as some overpowering ocean.
> The world seems silent to me now, and still.
> Some faces linger dimly in my memory,
> And some few phrases echo in my ears,
> But all the rest is gone, irrevocably
> Gone. . . . it's almost day. My lamp is dim. . . .
> And yet one final story—yet one more.[91]

The novice Grigory, asleep in the same cell, awakes from a troubled dream and sees Pimen writing. He is struck by the old man's piety and industry and says, in a stage aside:

> His brow is clear, his eyes reveal no trace
> Of veiled thoughts, of hidden speculations.
> The same calm face, the same composure always.
> Like a clerk who sits all day at statutes
> So he looks alike at innocent and guilty,
> On good and bad, dispassionately sifting
> Without anger, without pity, without sorrow.

Novice and elder fall into conversation. Grigory tells Pimen his nightmare, and to calm the young man Pimen recommends fasting, prayer, and the wisdom of the lives of Muscovy's most recent rulers. Tsars Ivan the Terrible and his son Fyodor receive respectful homilies. But as Pimen approaches his own present he becomes increasingly passionate, even prophetic:

> Oh frightful, unforeseen calamity!
> Our sins are punished for offending God—
> A regicide now reigns as Russia's tsar!

Grigory, aroused by the story, encourages Pimen to tell him about the murder of Dmitri twelve years earlier in Uglich. Pimen, it turns out, was an eyewitness to that event:

> Oh, I remember!
> God made me witness to that evil deed,
> That foul and bloody crime. I had been sent
> To Uglich, on vague suspicion,
> In the middle of the night. Next day
> At matin prayers we heard a tolling bell,
> The beating of alarms, and noise and cries.
> The people ran to the tsarina's house.
> I ran there too. All Uglich was assembled.
> Upon the ground the young tsarevich lay:
> His royal mother swooned beside his corpse,
> His wet nurse wept in piteous anguish—
> And there the angry people dragged the godless
> Nurse that had betrayed him.
> Among them Bitiagovsky then appeared
> Like wretched Judas, pale with his crime.
> "Assassin" was the furious general cry,
> And in an instant he was torn to pieces.
> His three accomplices next tried to flee;
> The cowardly villains all were bound and brought
> Before the child's warm corpse—
> Which—wondrous to relate!—began to tremble.
> "Confess!" the people shouted, and beneath
> The axe the wicked men confessed—
> And swore it was Boris that set them on.

Pimen closes the scene with a comment that the tsarevich "would have been Grigory's age, and reigning now." With this mournful story of Dmitri's murder and Boris's usurpation, Pimen will end his chronicle.

My son, Grigory—
I have taught you how to read and write.
I pass along my task to you.

But it is too late. Stirred by Pimen's stories, by their miracles and coincidences, Grigory is no longer content to *copy.* Cursing Boris, he swears that the "terrible denunciation" (*uzhasnyi donos*) of the chronicler will be carried into life, and that the usurper-tsar will not escape the judgment of this world nor of God.

This scene has been frequently cited as proof of Pushkin's "closet drama" intent. Nothing happens, after all, but talk, and Pimen's monologues are excruciatingly long. But in fact the scene is profoundly active: pretendership, *samozvanstvo,* is born here, and born directly out of a chronicler's account. Pimen is grooming Grigory as his successor, but Grigory wants nothing of that life for himself. He is attracted by precisely the opposite approach to life, Tsar Boris's approach. Ironically, this entire scene—so apparently static, yet so full of decisions in the making, action on the threshold—teaches Grigory one lesson: when fate denies you what you desire or deserve, wrest it from her. If Boris can seize the throne, so can Grigory Otrepiev. The novice does not want to record history, he wants to make it, and in this sense Pimen's chronicle is midwife to the event.

In earlier versions it was not always Pimen who played this role. Pushkin wrote two scenes in 1825 that he subsequently omitted from the published version of the play in 1831; in one of them, "At the Monastery Wall" (based on an episode in Karamzin), Grigory is motivated in a very different way.[92] The scene was to follow the action in Pimen's cell. In this omitted scene, Grigory complains about the tedium of monastic life to a fellow resident, the so-called evil monk (*zloi chernets*). If only, Grigory says, the khan would attack Muscovy, if only Lithuania would invade, if only the tsarevich Dmitri would rise from the dead and lead us into battle against Boris! Don't talk nonsense, the *chernets* answers, it is not for us to resurrect the dead. But if you were to play a trick on our "stupid and superstitious people. . . ." It takes Grigory some time to grasp the import of these words; when he does, he announces: "It's settled. I am Dmitri, I am the Tsarevich." The evil monk then has the last word: "Give me your hand, you will be Tsar."

This disappointing scene so clearly resembles a pact with the devil that some critics have linked Grigory with Faust.[93] We know that Pushkin had begun reading Goethe during his southern exile, and that the idea for his own "Faust" fragment dates from 1825. But ultimately that scene, along with similarly melodramatic passages in other scenes, was eliminated. Motivation for Grigory's act was to come not from the demonic but from the godly monk, not from the devil but from Pimen. And the actual moment of decision was moved offstage, as were so many other crucial moments in the play. We are given the preconditions of an event only.

Pimen, then, is a highly polemical and energetic figure in the drama. His way of telling stories provides the impetus to pretend. Meyerhold, in his 1936 rehearsals for *Boris,* seems to have projected just such a Pimen—restless, childlike, cunning, a professional writer who knew well the power of words.[94] Yet Pushkin himself was disarmingly "orthodox" in defense of his chronicler. In October 1826 he submitted this scene to *Moskovskii vestnik,* where it appeared the following year—making it the first (and, along with the Inn Scene, for five years the only) published portion of the play. Dissatisfied with its reception, Pushkin drafted an angry letter to the journal in 1828. The scene, Pushkin said, had not been understood. He had intended Pimen, an image "both new and familiar to the Russian heart," to "embellish the simplicity" of his verse. But Pimen's "naïveté, humility, and total lack of frivolity or prejudice" had apparently offended the public instead of charming it. People considered his political ideas "out of date." Such a complaint was unjust, Pushkin claimed, because Pimen was not his invention; he was a composite of everything that had captivated the poet about the ancient chronicles.[95]

What captivated Pushkin about chronicles in general might also have been what he found so congenial in that "last chronicler," Karamzin. Characteristic of both was a sort of innocence, but it was neither careless nor naïve; it was innocence as a literary construct, stylized and rhetorically sophisticated. "Chronicle style" raises two questions in this scene. The first concerns Pushkin's use of Karamzin's *History;* the second, the possibility that Pimen, as realized here, might in fact transmit a sense of history appropriate to that dramatic form of another age, romantic tragedy.

Pimen's role in Pushkin, as kindly mentor to a restless young novice, appears to be a composite of three historical figures in Karamzin. The first is Grigory Otrepiev's own elder kinsman, Zamiatni-Otrepiev, "who had long lived as a monk in the Chudovo Cloisters" (XI, 74). Grigory settled in his kinsman's cell after much wandering about Russia, and there purportedly first conceived the idea of becoming tsar in Moscow. That idea was not well received by the other monks ("some laughed at him, others spat in his eyes"); the Patriarch heard of the scheme, and Grigory fled the monastery with two other Chudovo residents, Varlaam and Misail. These three men, under the guise of wandering monks, were finally taken in by the kindly Archmandrite of Spassky Cloister—and this Archmandrite becomes the second source for Pushkin's Pimen. Grigory had now become bolder. Before fleeing this second haven, he left a note for the old man saying that he was the tsarevich Dmitri and would not forget this kindness when he returned to the throne of his fathers. "The Archmandrite was terrified," Karamzin writes, "but not knowing what to do, he decided to keep silent" (XI, 76).

In Karamzin, then, there are multiple monasteries and various degrees of deception before the bold act is launched. Grigory's actual escape is described this way:

> And so it was that the Pretender first revealed himself when he was still within the boundaries of Russia: so it was that a runaway priest took it into his head to overturn a great monarch and ascend the throne through a crude falsehood, in a realm where the Wearer of the Crown was considered God on Earth—where the people had never yet betrayed their tsars, and where an oath given to an *elected* tsar was no less sacred for faithful subjects! Except for the actions of implacable Fate, except for the will of Providence, how could one explain not only the success but even the very idea of such an enterprise? It seemed like madness; but the madman chose the most reliable path to this goal, Lithuania.
>
> In that country an ancient and natural hatred for Russia had always been of great help to our traitors . . . and there the Pretender also hurried, not by a direct route but via Starodub, toward the Luevy Hills, through dark forests and wilds, where a new companion served as his guide, a hermit of the Dneprov Monastery, Pimen; and where, having finally passed out of Russian territory near the village of Slobodka, he offered a heartfelt thanks to Heaven for his fortunate escape from all dangers. (XI, 76)

This third Pimen is only a name. He plays the role, say, of the Innkeeper in Pushkin, or perhaps the boy she recommends for a guide (". . . go straight across the swamp to Khlopino, and from there to Zakharievo, and from there any child can take you to the Luevy Hills . . ."). The historical Pimen is not the psychological goad but an actual physical guide, an accomplice in the Pretender's treachery and escape. Pushkin takes the name of this episodic character[96]—a less-than-heroic minor figure, later interrogated by Shuisky as an accomplice in Grigory's escape from Russia[97]—for his ideal chronicler, an impartial witness to history.

In both *History* and drama, of course, Pimen is crucial to the Pretender's success. But pretendership born out of a story proves much more powerful than the mere act of showing the way to the border. Karamzin's Pimen is necessary only as a mechanical aid to guarantee the success of Grishka Otrepiev. Pushkin's Pimen, however, makes possible the growth of history out of chronicle—that is, his "final story" on the regicide Tsar Boris becomes the first step in Grigory's self-made story.

Of the many critics who have offered readings of Grigory's transformation into Dmitri, the most persuasive remains Ilya Serman.[98] Pimen is an accomplice in Grigory's rise to power, Serman suggests, not because one led the other across the Lithuanian border but because Grigory read Pimen as a *poet* (not a monk) would read a chronicle.

In the context of his age, the historical Grigory was a young man with unusual literary talents. When the Patriarch Iov heard of him, Karamzin writes, "he made him a deacon and took him into his own service for his booklearning skills: for Grigory not only knew how to copy texts ably but even composed sacred canons, better than many of the scholars of that time" (XI, 75). On the basis of these historical data, Serman develops the idea that Pushkin created his Pretender as a poet—in an era when poetry did not exist as a social or aesthetic value.

Support for this reading, and some insight into Pushkin's own fondness for the False Dmitri, can be found in an earlier variant of scene 11 ("Cracow. Wisniowiecki's House"). There the Pretender is offered verses by a Latin poet. The Russian defector Khrushchov leans over and asks Gavrila Pushkin "who that man is." "*Piit* [A poet]," Pushkin answers. "And what is that?" asks Khrushchov. "How can I explain it?" Pushkin says. "In Russian there's only *vershepisets* [a scribbler of ditties] or *skomorokh* [a wandering minstrel-jester]. . . ."[99] Most likely this gratuitous exchange from the mouth of Pushkin's own ancestor reflected the poet's own irritation at the obstacles (both social and bureaucratic) that prevented a Russian poet of the 1820s from becoming a professional writer. Perhaps because this allusion was so strong, and thus out of place in romantic tragedy, Pushkin decided to eliminate the lines. But the larger point was made through the Pretender's whole receptivity to poetry and to the open life. A poet was a *creator* of roles in a society where all roles were supposed to be fixed.

That the Pretender should issue from Chudovo Monastery—the Monastery of the Miracle—is no accident. As he himself later admits to Marina, he had "prepared a miracle for the world" (*gotovil miru chudo*), and such a Dmitri needs neither external agent nor evil monk to spur him on. Purely political confrontations cannot really seduce a poet. As Serman interprets Grigory, he is a pretender from internal necessity. His poetic nature is struck by repetition and coincidence: the "miraculous" threefold repetition of his dream, the "miraculous" coincidence of his age with the tsarevich's. And he will create another *chudo,* the resurrection of Dmitri from the dead. Pimen's failure to pass on his copier's task to Grigory is in large part due, then, to a poetic nature confronted with a certain sort of provocative text—a text that was open to the *creative* miracle.[100]

In support of Serman's reading, we might now look more closely at the chronicle-monologues that Pimen delivers in his cell. Earlier drafts indicate that as Pushkin worked on the play he made Pimen's language in the opening lines successively more calm, distanced, and archaic.[101] The famous "final story" (*poslednee skazanie*) that opens and closes the first monologue had at one time been a "terrible legend" (*uzhasnoe predanie*).[102] But ultimately the initial image of Pimen is shorn of such partisan language. The quality of *uzhas* (terror) is transferred, in Grigory's final theatrical curse of Boris, to Grigory's *perception* of Pimen:[103] "Meanwhile a hermit in a dark cell / Writes a terrible denunciation [*uzhasnyi donos*] of you. . . ." By the end of the scene, Grigory is quite aware of Pimen's polemical stance. But this awareness develops gradually, in, as it were, a listening act.

In the opening lines Pimen presents himself as an evenhanded transmitter of "true accounts," a reproducer of texts to be copied over later by others. And in his waking remarks Grigory reinforces this image: here is a writer who "looks alike at innocent and guilty, on good and bad, dispassionately. . . ." But Grigory, and the reader or spectator of the scene as well, quickly learns that Pimen is *not* dispassionate. To be sure, Pimen does manage to speak with a certain pious distance about earlier tsars—because those "legitimate" rulers preceding Boris, despite their terrible sins requiring immense penance, never provoked the wrath of heaven. Pimen thus grants them a rhetorical framework that absolves their shortcomings. But whenever the current reign comes up, that is, the times or deeds of Boris Godunov, Pimen's language is both aggressive and condemnatory.

Pimen, in short, is not the later objective compiler, lending form and a distanced authority to received texts. He is the present recorder of the chronicle accounts he recites to Grigory, a man with strong political convictions as well as considerable personal experience in the events he describes. He "fought beneath the ramparts of Kazan," "served Shuisky in the Lithuanian wars," "saw the orgies of Tsar Ivan's court." And most important, in 1591 he was eyewitness to events in Uglich.

Pimen's account of the Uglich murder closely follows the account in Karamzin (X, 75–80). We, of course, can now detect an anachronism here; Pimen could not have told his story the way he did. He relates a post-1606 story, full of the formulas of a Saint's Life— "bezbozhnaia predatel'nitsa-mamka" (the godless traitor-nurse), "Iuda Bitiagovsky" (the Judas Bitiagovsky)—in 1603. But it is unlikely that Pushkin was aware of this inconsistency. Pushkin wrote at a time when the textology of chronicles was in its infancy, and when, we recall, he was sufficiently persuaded by Karamzin's methodology to defend the historian in print: "He told his story with all the truthfulness of a historian, he everywhere referred to the sources—what more can be demanded of him?"[104]

We should assume, therefore, that Pushkin intended Pimen's "simple and naïve" narrative of Uglich—based in fact on a much later, thoroughly hagiographical rendering of events—to be something that Pimen could have indeed delivered. As Pushkin himself allowed, Pimen was a *composite* of everything that had captivated him about the chronicles, and as such was more a synchronic image than a historical figure.[105] This play, with its *Lzhe*dmitri and its *Lzhe*-tsar Boris, cannot really be said to contain a *Lzhe-letopisets* (false chronicler). But one detail in Pimen's account gives us pause, because it is so clearly a departure from Karamzin. It concerns the moment when the "murderers" of Dmitri name Boris as the guilty party, and here Pimen creates out of Karamzin's material an additional miracle.

Karamzin, we recall, gave the following closure to his account of Dmitri's martyrdom:

> The nine-year-old Holy Martyr lay bloody in the arms of the woman who had raised him and who had wanted to protect him with her own breast; he *trembled like a dove*, expiring, and died, never hearing the shriek of his desperate mother. . . . (X, 79; emphasis in original)

Karamzin's tone is hagiographic, but there is no element of the supernatural in his account. In fact, after the mob fatally wounds the three alleged murderers, Karamzin, while relying on chronicle sources, motivates their last-minute confession in a modern and "sentimental" way: ". . . the villains, expiring, lightened their conscience, or so it is written, by a sincere confession: they named the main party guilty in Dmitri's death: Boris Godunov" (X, 80).

When Pushkin puts this story in Pimen's mouth, however, the motifs of the death and the deathside confession are rearranged.

> The cowardly villains all were bound and brought
> Before the child's warm corpse—
> A miracle [*chudo*]! Suddenly the dead body trembled.
> "Confess!" the people shouted, and beneath
> The axe the wicked men confessed—
> And swore it was Boris that set them on.

The "trembling" of Dmitri now comes *after* death, not before, and it is the resultant miracle (rather than any pangs of conscience) that persuades the murderers to repent and betray Boris's name.

One should note here that the miracles Pimen relates in this scene are of two types. There is first the "unheard-of miracle" (*neslyshannoe chudo*) that occurred at Tsar Fyodor's deathbed: a predeath vision followed by the "holy fragrance" and "radiant visage" of the corpse. These details are standard equipment in the death of saints, and Pimen retells them with the confidence of a compiler embellishing on the biography of an anointed monarch. The Uglich "miracle," however, purports to be an eyewitness account. Pimen does not only retell that story, he has *seen it happen;* it is thus both an eyewitness account and a chronicle, a testimony and a denunciation, a primary and a secondary source.

These two activities are separate. But Pimen, with his chronicle view of the world, perceives within the realm of "primary source" both the natural and the supernatural; both are part of testimony.[106] Pimen's final commission to Grigory, to "describe, without any cunning or cleverness, everything that you have been witness to in life," includes in equal part the profane ("war and peace, the reign of monarchs") and the sacred ("holy miracles, prophecies, and heavenly signs"). From the perspective of Pimen as storyteller—and here we should recall the narrator of Karamzin's mature chronotope—both aspects constitute a seamless whole. But the actual *audience* for Pimen's story, Grigory, everywhere sees rents in the fabric, potential for precisely cunning and cleverness, for personal initiative. Again Ilya Serman has caught the essence of this intersection of fictions, where Pimen's poetry of spiritual integration meets Grigory's poetry of active entry into life:

> The poetic nature of Grigory is won over by that very same element of the poetic in Pimen's story: that element of the miraculous without which, in the understanding of a person of the late sixteenth century, scarcely a single earthly event could be accomplished. It convinces Grigory decisively of Boris's guilt and prompts him to create a miracle himself. . . .[107]

The Chudovo Monastery Scene can thus be viewed as a conversation between two poetic mentalities. One is the medieval chronicler, interpolating miracles into the past on behalf of a providential history. The other is a new type of secular poet, who with joyful cynicism exploits self-made miracles in an open future. Pimen, in Pushkin's words both "childlike and wise," represents a traditional way of validating historical process; Grigory, soon to be Dmitri, both emerges from Pimen and superannuates him.

"One way to study the historical consciousness of an era, a writer, a literary text," Thomas Greene has written, "is to look at the role of the character or voice perceived as superannuated."

Superannuation invites irony; by presenting the superannuated figure ironically (even when this figure is the poetic speaker), the text ostensibly detaches itself from that figure's archaic perspective and asserts its own relative modernity, points to the greater width of its own horizon. The text refuses to subject itself to this figure's limitations of understanding; it takes a step into an emergent present which the superannuated are incapable of taking.

In *Boris Godunov,* the figure of Pimen functions both as archaic voice and as generative force, as a true *author* of action in the play. Greene acknowledges the duality of such characters:

> . . . the outmoded character will incarnate to some degree the past that has nourished the writer and his work, and that he repudiates at his peril. The superannuated character will typically attract ambivalence, the ambivalence of all historical change, and this divided awareness will affect the posture of the text toward its own historicity.[108]

Pushkin's Pimen embodies just this sort of ambiguity. He is a narrator craftier than Karamzin himself in the matter of creating miracles, and yet somehow he retains the naïveté and simplicity of a recorder of true events. Pimen's ability to combine craft and innocence surely has its analogue in the ambivalence that Pushkin brought to any scheme purporting to explain historical process. In the Monastery Scene Pimen is indeed the "voice of history"—in the sense that he makes the past sensible for himself and his contemporaries in terms of his *own* laws for ascribing meaning. Like his debased counterpart in the secular sphere, Prince Shuisky, Pimen makes Uglich *work for him.*

For we must not forget that both Pimen and Shuisky, both the sacred and the profane investigator, were eyewitnesses at Uglich. Both were fabricators of accounts that seem, in the contexts of their telling, either implausible or too conveniently and partially accurate. In the play's crucial opening scene, where the dominant morality is established, Shuisky makes it quite clear that to witness something is not necessarily to perceive the truth about it. In his own later retelling of Uglich to Tsar Boris—a scene, in fact, that uncomfortably parallels Pimen's recitation to Grigory—Shuisky makes liberal use of his own interpolated miracles to unnerve the superstitious tsar. Storytellers are opportunists, and as we watch history in the making we are reminded that history is not only made from, but also made *by,* stories. We recall how Pushkin had chastised Pogodin for isolating the "historical facts" about Uglich and then submitting them to a court "governed by *today's* laws." Pimen, and Pimen's account of Uglich, are precisely embodiments of *yesterday's* laws—which are, according to Pushkin, the only court of history.

Thus the Monastery Scene stands as the master appropriation of reality that all other characters will follow. After that "terrible denunciation" in the lonely cell, it becomes Boris's peculiar misery that he must confront Uglich in conversation with every social class of his world: the nobility through Shuisky, the church through the Patriarch, the common people through the holy fool, and, on his deathbed, his own family through Tsarevich Fyodor. What Boris knows, and his reasons for acting as he does, must always be measured against what others find it expedient to believe. As one perceptive critic has observed:

> Boris's rationalistic confidence that he could achieve, through the force of his own intellect and will, happiness and glory for his people, win their love, is destroyed by the objective force of things. . . . The destruction of rationalism inevitably occurs simultaneously with the destruction of individualism.[109]

This shrinking of Boris's ability to assert his own story is a perfect prelude to death—both physical and, in the larger sense, historiographical. Boris's attempt to make sense of events comes to an end, opening the way for an expropriation of his biography by the forces of rumor and political expediency. This shift, too, is part of Pushkin's dialogue with Karamzin. For the duration of the play Boris has struggled hard against Karamzin's verdict on him. In fact the "Dostig" monologue—Boris's first statement in his own voice—bitterly recites, and attempts to refute, the slander that Karamzin is at such pains to document.[110] Karamzin, we recall, opens his account of Boris Godunov's role in history with this judgment: "Had he been born to the throne, he would have deserved to be called one of the best monarchs in the world; but born a subject, with an unbridled passion to rule, he could not resist temptation when evil seemed to his advantage . . ." (X, 7).

At the end of Pushkin's play, Tsar Boris literally collapses into phrases taken directly from Karamzin's description of him. In a startling transfer of Karamzin's voice to the hero, Pushkin puts these words into the mouth of the dying tsar:

> I was born a subject, and to die
> A subject, in obscurity, should have been my lot.
> But I attained the highest power . . . how?
> Don't ask.

This line is a significant variation on its celebrated Shakespearean model in *King Henry IV, 2,* the deathbed dialogue with Prince Hal.

> . . . God knows, my son,
> By what bypaths and indirect crooked ways

I met this crown, and I myself know well
How troublesome it sat upon my head.

Prince Hal, in confident response, can tell his father: "You won it, wore it, kept it, gave it me." His future is secure. Fyodor, however, has only two lines to utter, chillingly prophetic:

No, no—live and reign a long time yet,
The people, and we, will perish without you.

As Pimen properly divines, this is the *final story*. Pushkin could not have followed his *Boris* with a version of *Henry V*. The heir is dead, and the play ends on silence.

Endings

Romantic tragedy has few options for strong closure. This is due, in part, to the conflicting demands of the two parent genres. Romantic (open) forms of closure are incompatible with the traditionally reso- lute closing-down of tragedy, and the paradox for Pushkin was to bring the two together. How does a "romantic tragedian" deal with the expectations of wholeness and historical perspective that inevita- bly burden the final lines of a play? All endings impose a meaning on the middle and the beginning. To *end* is to assign fixed value. But the radical instability of assigned value is one of the play's central themes.

Thus Pushkin could not make use of the familiar models for closure commonly met with in more traditional historical drama. Several such models are in evidence in other versions of the Boris Tale, both pre- and postdating Pushkin. There can be, for example, an acknowledged distortion of known history to fit dramatic canon. This was Sumarokov's solution in his *Dmitrii Samozvanets*. In the com- pletely fanciful fifth act, Dmitri raises a dagger over the tsarevna Ksenia, only to stab himself when she is rescued by her lover at the final moment. Virtue triumphs, fidelity is rewarded, chastity is pre- served, and evil is tricked into punishing itself: here is an ending appropriate to the stage villain that Dmitri has been throughout the play, and a dramatic climax that an eighteenth-century audience would have expected from tragedy. Dramatic closure coincides with moral closure.

Other solutions, more historically faithful, are also possible. A playwright might seek to emphasize some larger principle, or unity, in a given sequence of historical events that would make less arbitrary the beginning and ending points of a dramatic whole. "Murder of a tsarevich" is one such motif, and to a certain extent Pushkin makes use of it. His *Boris* opens on a reminiscence of Uglich, and ends on its reenactment in the death of young Fyodor—another tsarevich, or rather former tsarevich, dead by the hand of another usurper-tsar.[111] Aleksei K. Tolstoy, rewriting the Boris Tale as epic drama in the 1860s, exploits this motif triply by opening his *Dramatic Trilogy* on a reference to the death of Ivan the Terrible's eldest son and heir, the "original" murdered tsarevich.[112] German versions of the tale, in particular Friedrich Hebbel's 1864 drama *Demetrius,* have made extensive use of the *Vorspiel* or *Vorgeschichte,* in which a narrator provides historical context and unifying themes. Any given drama, of course, can cover only one interlocking series of episodes from the ongoing historical process. But techniques of framing and closure can make those episodes resonant with larger meaning, and perhaps even reveal in them a key to more general historical truths.

For reasons that should by now be clear, none of these options were congenial to Pushkin. Neither an appeal to dramatic convention nor an attempt to fit the dramatic sequence into a larger and meaningful historical framework could answer the needs of romantic tragedy. Pushkin ultimately devised a third alternative: he ended his *Boris* on silence.

The context of the final (twenty-third) scene is chilling. Young Tsar Fyodor Borisovich is at the window of his Kremlin residence when a beggar approaches, asking alms. We learn the politics of the situation only when a guard drives the beggar away, saying it is not permitted to speak with prisoners. The rest of the scene is dialogue, indirect and loosely constructed, between the royal children and the common people on the Kremlin square. The people argue about the fate awaiting the surviving Godunovs:

"Poor children, like birds in a cage."
"There's nothing to feel sorry for, it's a cursed clan!"
"The father was a scoundrel, but the children are innocent . . ."
"No apple falls far from the tree . . ."

Through the window the tsarevna Ksenia sees boyars arriving. The crowd, too, comments on their arrival and makes way. Here as in the opening scenes with the *narod,* Pushkin is careful to keep his vision and the words he apportions within the restricted limits of his characters' world. There are no asides to the audience to broaden perspective, no rhetorical statements of intent. We hear and see only what the participants themselves can hear and see—and in a sequence that makes sense only from *within* the event.

The royal children back away from the window. "Oh, they must be asking Fyodor Godunov to take the oath [to Dmitri]," one voice from the crowd suggests. But others doubt it: they hear noise and unnatural shrieking from inside the house. Mosalsky appears on the porch and announces, in the prose Pushkin reserves for those terrible, authoritative moments that cannot be made rhetorical by poetic diction:

Maria Godunova and her son Fyodor have poisoned themselves; we have seen their dead bodies. (The people are silent [*molchit*] in horror.) Why are you silent? Shout: Long live Tsar Dmitri Ivanovich!

Narod bezmolvstvuet.
[The people are silent.]

This final line of text, the stage direction *narod bezmolvstvuet* (the people are silent, the people do not respond) has been the subject of much controversy. Debate has centered on both the form and content of the line.

On the formal plane, it has been argued that *narod bezmolvstvuet* proves Belinsky's point: Pushkin's text is not drama at all. The two words are not formally a stage direction, so this argument goes, for Pushkin did not enclose them in brackets—thus signaling his intent to have them *read* rather than performed.[113] There is further trouble in the final lines with the two verbs for "being silent." Qualities of silence, that is, subtleties of the verb *molchat'* (to be silent) as against *bezmolvstvovat'* (to not respond, to be silent where a response is expected) are ingenious, critics admit, but they can hardly be acted; these distinctions are a matter for the printed page. Thus Pushkin tried to write a drama for the stage but the details of the apparatus give him away.

The status of the stage direction is indeed an interesting theoretical problem—especially in eras when the study of play texts is institutionalized independently from performance.[114] This "autonomous" aspect of play texts, operative even under the most congenial conditions, could only have been reinforced in the case of Pushkin's *Boris*—which was cleared for the stage only in 1866, forty years after its writing. Pushkin, to be sure, had little hope that his play would pass the theatrical censorship and openly expressed a distaste for submitting it.[115] But to acknowledge this reluctance on the part of the poet is quite different from insisting, as some have done, that Pushkin never intended his play to be a performable thing—or that qualities of silence are not dramatically realizable. The shocked silence of recognition at the end of a play was to become famous on the comic stage with the premiere of Gogol's *Inspector General* in 1836. But perhaps not until the very end of the nineteenth century did the question of pauses and silences on the dramatic stage become crucial, when acting companies confronted the drama of Anton Chekhov.

Serious attention to Pushkin's silence in performance came only in the twentieth century, arguably with Meyerhold's productions of the play. "Pushkin posed a most interesting and difficult problem for the Russian theater of the future," Meyerhold jotted in his notebooks. "How does one play silence so that it comes out louder than a scream?"[116] A solution was reached with the help of Prokofiev's musical score—or, perhaps better, soundtrack—for the 1936 production. Throughout the *narod* scenes, eerie "people's choruses" on and off stage were to moan wordlessly with open mouths.[117] The sudden withdrawal of this sound at the end would create the force of the word *bezmolvstvuet,* a falling away of the background sounds of speech.

In addition to the problem of dramatic silence, the ending of *Boris* has been complicated by the fact of censorship—or, rather, by the reconstitution of possible censorship. In the 1825 completed manuscript the play ends on the cheer: "Long live Tsar Dmitri Ivanovich!" When the published text appeared in 1831, that cheer had been removed and replaced with the *narod bezmolvstvuet.* Which ending reflected Pushkin's true intent? The divided authority of two "original" texts, one in manuscript and the other in print, has generated a whole history of end-dominated readings of the play, which the Pushkin scholar M. P. Alekseev has chronicled.[118] Behind each successive interpretation of the ending phrase there grew up a philosophy of history—and of drama—which was then attributed to Pushkin.

The ending was at first ignored in the more general incomprehension surrounding *Boris.* Discussion of the issue was launched in 1839 in an anonymous review in the journal *Galateia,* where the silence at the end was interpreted as shock, horror, submission to fate—the silence of a Niobe turned to stone at the death of her innocent children. Only with Belinsky's celebrated 1845 essay on the play was the ending moved beyond the realm of pathos. Belinsky read the people's silence as a positive act, a curse; "In this silence of the people can be heard the terrible, tragic voice of a new Nemesis proclaiming its judgment over the new victim. . . ."[119] The people thus rose in stature. Their nonresponse was now resistance, not mute compliance. Annenkov, in his 1855 edition of Pushkin's works, first noted that Pushkin's own autographed manuscript ended differently from the published text—with the cheer and not the silence. Additional archival material on the play became available in the 1880s, including various censors' reports. Consequently, the 1887 Morozov edition of Pushkin's works provided *narod bezmolvstvuet* with its first marginal gloss. The silence was there, Morozov intimated, not by Pushkin's choice but at the insistence of the censor—who considered the original cheer, addressed to a pretender, "politically reprehensible." In fifty years the line had moved from its central position as key to the work, to a footnote.

Closer investigation revealed, however, that the censor's report on which Morozov based his analysis did not mention the ending among the objectionable passages. The precise reasons for the original ban were never revealed to the poet, and he did not discuss the matter in his correspondence. Morozov himself, in his later 1916 edition of Pushkin's works, modified his earlier conclusions, admitting that there was no decisive evidence either way: the people's silence at the end might have been inserted by the censor or might have been entered by Pushkin voluntarily.

To this day, the form and status of the line continue to accumulate new interpretations.[120] But even more intense than the debate over status has been speculation over the *content* of this two-word ending. Critical attention appears to be equally divided between the two words, the people and their silence. Both issues will be considered here, and in terms of two questions. What, first, might Pushkin have intended by giving the final word—or opportunity for a final word—not to the regal hero but to the common people? And second, what are the implications of ending a play on the *absence* of response?

The Narod *as Hero*

In the Soviet period, critical readings of *Boris Godunov*—however sophisticated—have invariably endorsed to some degree the *narod*, or common people, as hero. The ideological advantages of such a "progressive" reading are obvious. But in spite of this choral support, Pushkin's critical essays—and the text of the play itself—do give some ground for such an interpretation. On several occasions Pushkin polemicized on behalf of *narodnaia* (folk) drama and in defense of dramatists willing to deal seriously with *sud'ba narodnaia* (the people's fate). *Boris Godunov* opens and closes on mass scenes, where the people are overtly cynical about authority and disrespectful toward representatives of the crown. Tsar Boris himself admits their power, and not only in his self-serving monologue early in the play. When, in scene 20, Basmanov downplays popular rebellion ("The people are always secretly inclined to revolt . . . but a rider guides his horse firmly, the father controls the child"), Boris answers darkly: "The horse sometimes unseats its rider, the son is not forever in his father's power." One scene later, this prophecy seems to have come true: Gavrila Pushkin persuades Basmanov to defect with the comment that the Pretender has simply become too strong to resist—strong not in military support, which is mere drunken rabble, but strong in "popular opinion" (*mneniem narodnym*).

The centerpiece of the argument is always the crucial ideological position of the people at the end. By refusing to cheer the Pretender, the people reserve the initiative; the play closes, as it were, on "their turn." As Stanislav Rassadin has reworked this idea, "The people could not yet talk of something, but they *could* be silent about something. . . ."[121] Their silence was a necessary stage in their historical development. In the future, so this argument goes, the people would talk; at the very least this particular silence meant that they had rejected the meager options offered them by a tsarist bureaucrat in 1605, and this was an important step forward. The people's consciousness matured during the play, from passively cynical in the first scenes to passively defiant in the end. The *narod* had achieved potentially heroic status.

In this reading, the people are perceived as powerful not in their present incarnation—as "rabble," as silence—but in their *future*, in their ultimate historical role. This line of interpretation has been enormously important in the domestication of Pushkin's play for Soviet audiences, and in attempts to locate *Boris* in more traditional hero-based drama. Serious critics can now confront, and resolve, a difficult node in Pushkin's political thought: the fact that the playwright clearly gave the people a prominent role yet at the same time denied them a positive image. For however generously one approaches the *narod* in this play, it is simply not heroic. Neither here, nor in Pushkin's several poems where a "crowd" (*tolpa*) or "mob" (*chern'*) plays a role, is there anything but despair of and contempt for the people's response. Indeed, if the people are perceived solely in the plane of the present, then *Boris Godunov* can be read—and has been read—as a mature statement of Pushkin's conservative world view.[122] A displacement of the "true" people from present to future, however, recaptures the play for progressive history. Boris Engelhardt, to cite only one practitioner of this move, makes a reassuring distinction between the *tolpa* we see on stage and the authentic *narod*, a historical force behind the wings. The crowd, Engelhardt admits, is irrational, ambiguous, inconsistent. Pushkin could never have put his faith in such a "senseless wild herd." But the *narod* was a concept dear to Pushkin; it was this force, dignified by silence, that we were meant to remember in the final lines of the play.[123]

This separation of an ideal platonic *narod* from its actual historical embodiment in the play is, as Ilya Serman has argued, a rather recent phenomenon.[124] The now canonical *narod*-as-hero platitude had its beginnings in the 1905 Revolution. That exhilarating experience of popular uprising set off in the intellectual community a search for historical precedents—although antiautocratic feeling among the common people was, as far as we know, a twentieth-century development. Critics began to read both Pushkin's play and the folk consciousness of the early seventeenth century in a profoundly anachronistic way. Nineteenth-century sociological and political interpretations of the play, Belinsky's in particular, were unearthed and publicized. But, Serman argues, Pushkin had very little interest in the *political* content of the people's mind. What intrigued him was a way of thinking, and especially that contradictory unity of folk beliefs at the basis of the *Boris* plot that made possible the simultaneous presumption that Boris was a murderer and that the returning tsarevich was authentic. In this reading, the people's silence at the end was neither passive nor active as a political force; the *narod* did not understand, and did not desire, that sort of power. As Serman reads Pushkin's intent, *narod bezmolvstvuet* is the silence of shocked expectation. The Russian people of the seventeenth century lived not by political consciousness but by a faith in miracles, and by continual expectation of a miracle.

This did not mean, however, that the people expected the actual course of history to benefit them. And since it did not, the people were forever ungrateful and suspicious. Tsar Boris himself notes bitterly, and with full understanding, that "living power is always hateful to the mob." The people—inert, hostile to any dynamic force—would not take active or conscious steps toward change. Such was the meaning of their silence. "This waiting for a miracle," Serman concludes, "was regarded by Pushkin as a general feature of the Russian folk mind."

To expand on Serman's provocative reading, we might conclude that quite possibly the final line *narod bezmolvstvuet* was intended neither to ennoble nor to debase the people. It simply traps them, as do so many lines in this play, in their own time. To give the people energy and visibility, as Pushkin does, is not to give them a progressive direction or a sense of history. The ending is simply open, unknown. In a formal sense this could be Pushkin's parodic comment on endings. But it is also a sign of the paralysis and contradiction at the center of the *Boris* plot, and perhaps also in the popular consciousness as Pushkin portrayed it. Only the Pretender, a *creator* and not an awaiter of miracles, could break out with his poetry into a new age.

Karamzin and Pushkin: Closing Down the Tale

This curious *narod bezmolvstvuet*, equally portending openness and paralysis, has its own dialogue with Karamzin. In the *History*, nowhere is the historian's voice more clearly heard than at the endings of chapters, where deeds are summed up in exhortatory maxims. Karamzin's events always have their frame, and in the Boris Tale especially no detail is without its place in the larger progression. Pushkin's borrowing from Karamzin for his final scene might at first seem compromised by the existence of two "authoritative" endings for the play, the cheer of the manuscript and the silence of the printed text. But in fact both of Pushkin's endings have explicit parallels in the *History.*

The phrase *bezmolvie naroda,* the silence (or better the non-response) of the people, is a fixed expression in Karamzin. It is often paired with its opposite, the shout, and both can express various degrees of active censure, servility, and genuine enthusiasm. Karamzin does not seem to invest either alternative with any moral superiority, and neither has a measurable effect on events. When we first meet Boris (X, 8) after Belsky's revolt, both options (shouting and silence) occur together: "The people were either silent, or hailed the justice of the tsar." At the peak of Boris's power under Fyodor the people are again reduced to these two modes of response:

> At that time Boris Godunov, in the eyes of Russia and of all powers having relations with Moscow, stood at the pinnacle of greatness, in full control of the Tsardom, and saw around himself nothing but speechless [*bezmolvnyi*] slaves, or loudly praising [*gromko-slavosloviashchii*] slaves hailing his high achievements. . . . (X, 69)

When Boris is elected tsar the same two options are mentioned, but now only one is safe: "No one dared contradict, or be silent: all shouted: 'Long live our father, Boris Fyodorovich!'" (X, 134). After Boris's death, the ascension of young Fyodor, and during the successful drive of the Pretender toward Moscow, both of Pushkin's endings are repeatedly laid out side by side:

> Thousands shouted, and the Riazan folk first: "Long live our Father, *Gosudar'* Dmitri Ioannovich!" Still others were silent [*bezmolvstvovali*] in astonishment. (XI, 115)

Karamzin understands the necessity for the Fall of the House of Godunov. But he is nevertheless stern toward defectors, both among generals and civilians. The people are presented as almost universally unreliable:

> Only in Orel did a handful of brave men not wish to betray the law: these worthy Russians, unfortunately unknown to history, were cast in prison. All others eagerly fell to their knees, praising God and Dmitri. . . . All were agitated—not from horror, but from joy. Gone was that stronghold of shame and fear that keeps men from treason. . . . (XI, 117)

Meanwhile, in the capital, young Tsar Fyodor

> calmly awaited his fate on an impoverished throne, already seeing around himself no more than a few trusted friends, despair, confusion,

pretense, and from the people silence, although a threatening one: a readiness for great change, which all hearts secretly desired. (117)

Karamzin is cautious, as we have seen, in his treatment of popular rebellion. The people's silence in the above passage is moral hesitation. Tsar Fyodor Borisovich had come to the throne, after all, through the right of succession; he ruled by dynastic legitimacy. As Karamzin was surely aware, the claims of legitimacy for Boris's *son* Fyodor and for Filaret Romanov's son Mikhail were the same: related as nephews by marriage to the previous dynasty.[125] Thus Fyodor Borisovich is seen by Karamzin, and by the Russian people in Karamzin's image of them, as an innocent, attractive figure, a victim of fate. In a passage glossed "Tsarecide"—which became the source for Pushkin's final scene—Karamzin explains the brutal murders of the Godunovs this way:

> Young Fyodor, Maria and Ksenia, sitting under guard in the house whence Boris's ambition had driven them into an arena of destructive grandeur, guessed their fate. The people still respected in them the sanctity of Tsarist rank—and perhaps the sanctity of innocence as well. Perhaps, in the very frenzy of rebellion, the people hoped that the alleged Dmitri would prove generous, and once having seized the crown would grant these unfortunates their lives—if only in isolation in some distant monastery. But in this instance generosity seemed to the Defrocked Priest incompatible with politics: the more attractive the personal qualities of the deposed and legitimate tsar, the more was he to be feared by this *Lzhe*tsar who had reached the throne through the evildoing of several and the delusions of many. The success of one treason always prepares the way for the next, and no distant wasteland could keep the royal youth from the compassion of Russians. (XI, 122)

Karamzin's orientation toward the Godunovs has undergone a major shift. So great is the power of legitimacy, albeit only several months in effect, that even the Pretender—knowing his own pretense—is afraid of it. While alive and on the throne Boris had been the usurper, and the rumor of the True Tsarevich had threatened his reign. Now that Boris's son is reigning by dynastic succession, *he* is the "legitimate tsar," and the Pretender, in hideous repetition of the theme, becomes False Tsar and tsarecide.

The people are caught in this delicate play between competing legitimacies. Whether they cheer or remain silent has no effect on historical events, because they too are trapped in the cycle of murder and deceit that Boris Godunov had begun. Karamzin thus presents the people kindly in the final scene: they are endlessly compassionate, thoroughly deluded.

It was announced to Moscow that Fyodor and Maria had committed suicide by poison; but their corpses, boldly put on display, bore unmistakable signs of strangling. The people crowded round the poor coffins where these two royal victims lay, the wife and son of the power-monger who had both adored and destroyed them—after having passed on to them the throne, for horror and a most violent death. "The sacred blood of Dmitri," say the chroniclers, "demanded untainted blood, and the innocent have fallen for the guilty—so, criminals, fear for your nearest ones!" Many looked on with simple curiosity, but many also with compassion; they pitied Maria, who, although the daughter of Ioann's most despicable hangman and the wife of a saint-killer, nevertheless lived by good deeds alone; never had Boris dared to reveal his evil intentions to her. And they pitied Fyodor even more, he who bloomed with virtue and promise: he was so gifted, he promised such wonderful things for the happiness of Russia, if only that had pleased Providence! . . . Thus was God's punishment brought to bear on the murderer of the True Dmitri, and a new punishment began for Russia under the scepter of a False one! (XI, 123)

To end his chapter, then, Karamzin uses the people and their compassion to isolate and distance the *sviatoubiitsa* (saint-killer) Boris from his own, newly legitimate family.

Pushkin, of course, challenges throughout his play just such an easy understanding of "bestowed" legitimacy. Therefore Pushkin structures his ending so that the people respond before, but not after, the announcement of the deaths. The horror that Karamzin felt toward tsarecide, a horror permeating the final pages of this chapter in the *History,* is transferred by Pushkin to the people's silence. In the context of a play where the people have provided, up to the very end, almost exclusively comic relief, this silence has the same *force* as the solemn voice of providence in the *History.* Here are Karamzin's gullible people, turned into comic figures and then denied the content and direction of Karamzin's providence. As Tynianov noted, if parody of a tragedy can produce comedy, then surely the reverse can also be true.[126]

One recent interesting reading of *Boris* has suggested that Pushkin's play is really about the evolution of a secret.[127] It is first withheld by Shuisky, then manipulated, nurtured, partially revealed, and eventually (in that final silence) passed on to the future. This image of history as a sequence of manipulated secrets is a good one for *Boris,* where events matter less than rumors about events and everyone with a story to tell is aware of the power of storytelling. Pushkin chose the only ending strategy that did not pretend to sum up a story or reveal a secret: he withheld response altogether. And by embedding this silence in an irregularly inscribed stage direction, Pushkin very possibly intended to play with the very idea of a frame for his drama. Stage directions are aids to actors and directors: audiences do not read them but *sense* them by their results. Pushkin's directive of silence, both an onstage direction and an offstage comment about history, breaks down the boundary between play and extra-play reality. Thus romantic tragedy achieves a tragic, "open" closure.

Here too we detect a hidden dialogue with Karamzin. In 1815 the historian had dedicated the first volumes of his *History* to Emperor Alexander I with the inscription: "The history of a people belongs to the Tsar" (I, xvi). In 1825, several months before beginning work on *Boris Godunov*, Pushkin wrote to Gnedich: "The history of a people belongs to the poet."[128] And indeed, the two "poets" in Pushkin's play—the Pretender and Pimen—do make history. Nowhere does Pushkin suggest, despite all later hopeful readings of *narod bezmolvstvuet*, that the history of a people belongs to the people. That move in the Boris Tale would not be made until the 1860s, in an era that witnessed an explosion of interest in the newly emancipated peasant and the potential of the Russian folk. During just those years Modest Musorgsky set to work on his opera *Boris Godunov*, and to his libretto he brought a radically new reading of both Pushkin and Karamzin.

IV

Boris in Opera: *Musorgsky*

In his historical music drama Mr. Musorgsky makes partial use of the text of Pushkin's *Boris;* but, without slavishly subordinating himself to that greatest of Russian poets, he supplements the text with scenes from Karamzin's narrative, with other scenes which he freely invents, and, finally, with folk songs. Even in those places where he follows Pushkin, he rearranges the verses with the confidence of a man who is above prejudice. . . . The realism with which Mr. Musorgsky is permeated forced him to perform a merciless operation on Pushkin's verses. . . . He has torn large strips from the living body of Pushkin's poetry and applied medicinal plasters from his own home apothecary over the gaping wounds. . . . This is far from being Pushkin, but we can console ourselves with the fact that this is life itself.
—Hermann Laroche, music critic for *Golos,* after the 1874 premiere of *Boris Godunov*[1]

CRITICAL COMMENT, in this century and the last, has not been kind to the libretto of *Boris Godunov.* The premiere of the opera made a strong impression on the Petersburg public, but music critics were harsh on the literary aspects of the work. One reviewer referred to a "cacophony in five acts and seven scenes" in which the composer-librettist had seen fit to "correct" Pushkin—in verse that was just as "free and shocking" as the music.[2] In a series of letters to the journal *Grazhdanin,* Nikolai Strakhov wrote with heavy irony that the composer had evidently "found everything in Pushkin insipid, weak, unclear—so he attempted to heighten the color, enhance the tone, provide stronger emphases. . . . This is not poetry, not even prose, but some sort of misshapen collection of words."[3] Even Cesar Cui, spokesman for the Balakirev Circle and Musorgsky's close personal

142

friend, regretted that "Mr. Musorgsky did not adhere to Pushkin more strictly: he melodramatized Boris . . . and replaced many of Pushkin's most marvelous verses with others that are quite mediocre and at times tasteless." In general, Cui assured his readers, "the libretto is beneath criticism."[4]

Musorgsky was stung by these comments, especially those coming from within his own musical camp. Such reservations about the verbal text—which was, as we shall see, Musorgsky's *second* transposition of Pushkin's *Boris*—were indicative of the theoretical differences that had developed between other musician-innovators in the Balakirev Circle and Musorgsky, who was at that circle's most radical fringe.

Criticism of the *Boris* libretto must be viewed, however, as part of a larger issue. Disrespect for libretti and accusations against librettists have a long and respectable history, rooted in what is essentially a generic problem. By what standards, it has been asked, should a libretto be judged? What is its appropriate relationship to its source text, its music, and the system of dramatic and musical norms in which it participates?

These questions have recently received sophisticated treatment in a number of intercultural studies by American scholars.[5] None of them, however, deals in careful detail with the libretti of Russian opera.[6] The relative impenetrability of Russian as compared with French, Italian, or German prompts a certain modesty in the conscientious opera theorist concerned with words; one recent excellent historical study of the opera libretto omits Slavic libretti altogether because of the language barrier.[7] Soviet scholarship, for its part, has not devoted much attention to theoretical frameworks for studying the verbal texts in its own rich Russian operatic tradition. "The history of the Russian opera libretto," writes one prominent Soviet musicologist, "has been very poorly researched."[8]

We might open our discussion, then, with a generic question. A libretto extracted from a drama, an epic, or a novel clearly ceases to be drama, epic, novel. Libretti almost inevitably leave behind the literary genre of their source texts. But what do the libretti themselves become?

Transposition into Opera

The transposition of widely differing genres into sung texts for opera is so complex a process, and so variously approached by its practitioners, that it is difficult to see how libretti can be classified as a single and undifferentiated genre. Among the elementary distinctions that must be made is, first, who actually creates the verbal text. If composers are their own librettists (as Musorgsky and Wagner were on principle), do they compose the words themselves or adapt another's text to their own needs? If librettist and composer are two separate creating personalities, what is the nature of the interaction? Here the generic traditions and constraints of different sorts of opera come into play.

At one pole there is what might be called the "preexisting" libretto. Here the model is the eighteenth-century Italian poet Metastasio, whose libretti were so compelling as poetry that generations of composers vied with one another in setting them to music. Whereas composers did, of course, adapt libretti to their needs, the inspiration for the musical whole remained the words. In the early years of opera, in fact, libretti survived much more reliably than musical scores—to the point where the very memory of the genre was often kept alive by the verbal text.[9]

In periods when the musical component is both more individualized and better preserved, interaction between musician and poet can vary widely. At one extreme there is the famous case of Hugo von Hofmannsthal and Richard Strauss, who lived in the same city but were so temperamentally incompatible that they rarely met, communicated almost entirely through letters, argued ceaselessly on aesthetic matters—and yet created operatic masterpieces. At the other extreme there can be a highly personal, perhaps even obsessive compatibility between musician and poet. Musorgsky began to room with the young poet Arseny Golenishchev-Kutuzov soon after undertaking to set the latter's best poems in two song cycles, "Without Sun" and "Songs and Dances of Death." Musorgsky suggested the themes, organized the poetic sequence, and—if one compares Kutuzov's published versions of the poems to Musorgsky's song texts—greatly improved the poems *as poems* in the process of revising them for music.[10] One might be tempted to argue, in fact, that the closer the cooperation between poet and composer (and ideally their coexistence in a single consciousness), the closer to an integral artwork the opera libretto becomes, and the more legitimate an object of aesthetic analysis.

Russian music scholars have considered this union, in one person, of composer and librettist to be particularly characteristic of Russian (as opposed to West European) opera in the nineteenth century.[11] This is, in fact, one of the reasons advanced why the Russian opera libretto has not more often been the object of independent study. The professional librettists of the past (Metastasio in Italian, Scribe in French) achieved their high status by essentially perfecting a formula. Because the operas written to these texts were also rigidly codified, the libretti could become in a sense independent artworks and preexist their music. In Russia, however, a class of professional librettists in the Western sense never really emerged.

The reasons for this situation are familiar from the history of other genres in post-Petrine Russia: the relative youth of Russian-language opera, and the ever-present competition from better established West European models.

Nineteenth-century Russian libretti were produced by two categories of author. The 1830s and forties were the era of the amateur librettist, literary figures who also dabbled in music and whose contributions were usually collective (such as the four-man team that helped Glinka achieve a libretto for his *Ruslan and Liudmila*). The second half of the century, in contrast, was dominated by composers who were their own librettists (Dargomyzhsky, Musorgsky, Borodin), or by librettists who, for all their ultimate operatic fame, began predominantly as experts in spoken rather than operatic dramaturgy (Modest Tchaikovsky, Vladimir Belsky). This absence, in the Russian tradition, of a clear "discipline" of librettology has worked against serious theoretical consideration of the genre.[12]

One good index of our reluctance to "take libretti seriously" is the genre's extreme vulnerability to parody. It is frequently remarked that the libretto has all the features of poetry—except poetic merit. The potential for parody in any genre is increased, of course, when conventions for realizing the genre are both multiple and rigid. Thus the operatic work, with its highly stylized blend of verbal, musical, and dramatic art, is an inevitable place to experiment with departures from convention—precisely because opera has always been so full of it. Experimentation is inevitably felt to be more radical in opera than it would be, say, in a novel, where anticonventionality is almost a trademark of the genre. In transpositions from spoken to sung texts, furthermore, certain literary source texts have been traditionally linked with particular target genres in music: fairy tale or epic drama with grand opera, for instance, and lyric poem with song cycle. Powerful effects can be achieved when these conventional pairings are violated.

In the second half of the twentieth century, when literally *any* text can be sung, the very concept of incompatibility between verbal and musical genres has eroded. Thus we have some difficulty appreciating the force of certain innovations felt to be very radical in Musorgsky's time. When Musorgsky set some beggar's cries, the love song of a village idiot, and two hauntingly realistic Nekrasov poems to music as art songs, the critic Hermann Laroche denounced them as "for the most part just rows of non-melodious exclamations, clever for the ear and inappropriate for intonation, accompanied by chords of some sort, or by chord-like figures, the cacophony of which—sometimes naïve, sometimes malicious and intentional—exceeds all description."[13]

Laroche admired much in *Boris* but he fourid it, too, generically unsettling—and therefore difficult to analyze for authorial intention. Nowhere, he said, was the listener "given rest with a broad, refined, rounded melody; [the opera] consists entirely (not unlike the libretto, but to a much greater degree) of separate scraps, haphazardly inter-mingled and, as it were, thrown by chance into a single common vessel."[14] Measured against the well-regulated norms of French and Italian opera, Musorgsky's failure to "round off" melody and poetic form did indeed seem like carelessness, or perhaps like unconscious self-parody—and any deeper principles underlying this new operatic and librettistic structure could easily be overlooked.

The charge of "haphazard mingling" and "separate scraps" is familiar to us from the polemics surrounding Pushkin's play. In fact, Cesar Cui's comments on the *Boris* libretto in his review of the opera's premiere almost read like the early reviews of Pushkin's *Boris*. As Cui wrote:

> There is no plot, no character development conditioned by a course of events, no sustained dramatic interest. This is a series of scenes—having, to be sure, some connection with known fact, but still stitched together, fragmented, in no way organically linked. You watch each scene with interest, but each constitutes a separate entity without connection to those that precede or follow, so that you are not concerned with what comes next. The scenes can be transferred around or rearranged; any of them can be discarded or new ones inserted and the opera will not be changed, because *Boris Godunov* is not an opera but only a series of scenes. . . .[15]

Thus Musorgsky's 1874 libretto, and indeed the whole structure of his opera, was faulted for two quite incompatible flaws. In the large, the libretto appeared to repeat the sins of its source text, carrying over into opera the absence of "organic links" and "sustained dramatic interest" that had so struck the early critics of Pushkin's play. This was, as it were, an excessive fidelity to the source. But on the small scale the libretto was denounced for being unfaithful to Pushkin's actual verse line—however problematic that verse had proved for the stage. "Weren't you ashamed," one operagoer wrote Musorgsky, "to defile the immortal verses of Pushkin with your illiterate, incompetent, tasteless, crude cadet doggerel?"[16] Clearly the derived libretto, in this case and in general, deserves some framework of analysis that does not rely primarily on fidelity.

One such framework might be the familiar translator's spectrum, with its "literal" or interlinear equivalent at one pole and its free adaptation or "poetic imitation" at the other. We noted in chapter 1 that transposition has certain parallels with translation. And just as interlinear translations serve one purpose and free adaptations another, so libretti too can establish various successful relationships with their source material. In order to understand the theoretical issues raised by Musorgsky's libretto, it might be helpful here to consider three operas from the Russian experience, each of which confronts a different principle of transposition and draws on a different genre as source text.

Three Principles for Adapting Texts

At the "literal" end of the spectrum we find the musical setting of a verbal text word for word. Here the very concept of libretto disappears, for the text is not "adapted" for music—it is, rather, realized with the help of music. The dominant value remains the communicative potential of the verbal message. Whatever organizing principles the music itself might offer in structure or development are reduced to a minimum. This was the aesthetic Alexander Dargomyzhsky applied to his setting of Pushkin's *Stone Guest* (1867–68), which in turn inspired Musorgsky's attempt to realize musically Gogol's farce *Marriage*. Dargomyzhsky's studied avoidance of key signatures and his reluctance to repeat musical material (unless accompanied by repetitions in the text) seemed to his disciples an enviable honesty to the Russian word and to literary expression. As Richard Taruskin has remarked:

> The sole yardstick by which the success or failure of such music could be measured was the degree to which the composer had been able to "perform" the text as the author intended it. . . . Truth of expression in such music utterly replaces all other criteria and functions of the art: music need no longer be "beautiful," but it must at all costs be accurate.[17]

The extreme literalism of this "word-for-word" pole in text adaptation has tended to restrict its products to pedagogical exercises. Musorgsky himself absorbed the lessons of *Stone Guest*, carried them in another direction in his work on *Marriage*, but then abandoned that project after the necessary skills had been learned. As we shall see, musical accuracy in reproducing a received text was only part of Musorgsky's aesthetic, albeit an essential one for *Boris*.

At the other extreme from word-for-word settings is the free adaptation, of which Borodin's *Prince Igor* might serve as a model. The libretto of this opera—or, rather, the complex eighteen-year evolution of its libretto—is testimony to the intricate mechanics of moving a twelfth-century epic, "The Lay of the Host of Igor," into nineteenth-century romantic opera.[18] Beyond a basic plot outline and cast of characters, almost nothing of the Igor Tale survives the transposition. Igor himself quickly disappears into captivity and his wife, Yaroslavna, carries the "heroic" role for half the opera. Yaroslavna's enemy is her own brother, Galitsky, romantic villain and troublemaker at court. The enemy Khan Konchak becomes a congenial host—and Konchakovna, his beautiful daughter, is so smitten by Igor's son Vladimir that she risks his life to keep him with her in camp. In a move that recalls Karamzin's ahistoric presentation of chronicle material two generations earlier, Borodin thoroughly updates the psychology and behavior of the participants in the tale. He recasts personal motivation around the idea of romantic love—so foreign to Russian medieval epic in general—and around the plight of lovers' separation. The central plot of the epic, a patriotic appeal to the Kievan princes for national unity, is reworked to highlight the exoticism and sensuousness of the *enemy* side. At the time of Borodin's writing, such romanticizing of the Orient had long been a popular European project.[19] *Prince Igor* is a document in this tradition—with the difference, of course, that Russia was *both* West and Orient at once, and therefore a search for the exotic was also, in a special way, a search for the self.[20]

This inclusive embracing of both East and West fit perfectly with Borodin's opera aesthetic. Not one to trace the subtle shift of a mood or a word through a narrative text, Borodin valued above all pageantry and song. "A purely recitative style would go against the grain," the composer wrote in 1876, "and in any case I am not given to this kind of writing. . . . Details and minutiae of any sort are completely out of place in opera; everything should be written with bold strokes. . . ."[21] This boldness was realized not through words but through quick changes in rhythm and color. As attested by the success of the Polovtsian Dances from Act II—by far the most popular of the *Igor* music—effective contrast was best achieved when it was brilliant and abrupt, within the music and between cultures. In historical opera of this sort the fate of nations is a secondary factor.

Extracting a romantic core from the Igor Tale meant discarding its stateliness and restraint, and reapportioning within it elements of lament and political homily. The enormous distance between epic poem and opera is nicely summarized in Borodin's Act IV. There the lofty central portion of the Lay (Prince Sviatoslav's lament and the "Golden Word" mourning Igor's defeat) is reflected only in passing and from the mouths of fools: Eroshka and Skula, two drunken rogues and draft-dodgers, dance, call for drink, and sing incoherently of Igor's shame.

The Igor Tale describes a celebrated military defeat. But Borodin replaces the Lay's refrain—"the grass bends low with grief"—with joyful choruses of setting off and returning home. *Prince Igor* ends on a hymn of joy, "Vremia krasnoe nastalo nam!" (Wonderful times have come!). This buoyant closure is possible because in romantic opera of

Borodin's type the reunion of the hero with the heroine, of Igor with his faithful Yaroslavna, *is* a "happy ending." That Igor's defeat prefigured an invasion from the East of calamitous consequence does not register in the music. Happiness for the hero is happiness for the opera.

Borodin's exceedingly free adaptation of the original text is highly successful on its own terms. But it is not a necessary adjustment to the requirements of music or staged drama. Musorgsky, several years earlier, had made his own national opera out of national defeat: *Boris Godunov* narrates another failure of leadership that led to invasion (this time from the West) and to political collapse. But Musorgsky, as we shall see, used his tale of defeat to challenge certain conventions of romantic opera, not to embody them. The original "Lay of the Host of Igor" is in fact much more Musorgsky's than it is Borodin's text. By altering that text so radically in the libretto, Borodin drew attention to the boundary between medieval epic and romantic opera—and, as in all successful transpositions, created a sort of dialogue between the two genres.

Between these two extremes of word-for-word setting and free adaptation lie the infamous examples of Tchaikovsky's *Eugene Onegin* and Prokofiev's *War and Peace*. This category of opera, perhaps the most vulnerable to charges of betraying its original, is organized around the principle of "scenes from classic works." The transposer follows the source text closely in some areas and appears to violate it flagrantly in others. In "scenes-from" operas the audience is expected to know the *from*, so evaluation always takes place against the active background of a source text that is familiar. This text is not reproduced word for word, not wholly reconceptualized, but is to varying degrees "reemphasized." The dialogue between literary source and libretto is always paramount—even, one could say, a part of the work itself.

Because the composer of a "scenes-from" opera expects this dual awareness from the audience, the opera suffers most when moved from native to foreign cultures—unless, of course, the source text is itself a document of world culture, as, say, Shakespeare has become. Classics in a culture are common denominators. And therefore libretti on the "scenes-from" principle presume the sort of audience implied for epic performances: the story is known, suspense and the specifics of start and finish are not at issue. One can begin, or end, anywhere, and the charge of "leaving something out" rarely applies since precisely the variation of a known text under different circumstances constitutes the appeal and strength of the transposition.

Let us briefly consider, as an example, the operatic *War and Peace*. The opera has been much maligned by admirers of the novel, who point out that Tolstoy despised opera; to recast, then, his baggy-monster novel in the most conventional and unlifelike of genres could only be parody, and disrespect for Tolstoy's creative aesthetic. But when Prokofiev set the work for a Soviet audience during World War II—organizing its thirteen scenes around the idea of treason, personal and national—he never pretended that this setting *replaced* Tolstoy. As with all "scenes-from" libretti, organizing principles originate within the opera but the larger background of the source text must always be firmly in place, in dialogue with what has been omitted. Here a clear thematic parallelism emerges between the two parts of the opera.

Part I, "Peace," is limited to one dramatic episode: the seduction of Natasha Rostova and its subsequent effects on three men—Andrei Bolkonsky, Anatol Kuragin, and Pierre Bezukhov.[22] Embedded in the midst of the Peace scenes, but not chosen for musical treatment, is the famous incident of Natasha at the Opera. In Natasha's life that opera experience represents a mistake, an illusion, the breaking of a vow, and then seduction: planned, thwarted, punished. This sequence determines the structure of the seven Peace scenes. And on a much vaster scale, the same sequence is suffered by Russia as a nation in Part II of the opera, "War." There has been a betrothal, a seduction by Napoleon, an invasion of territory. The result in both parts is the soiling of Natasha, of Moscow, of Russia (all feminine entities in Russian)[23]—but in each case a greater and purer woman would arise from the ruins. Such a message was timely indeed for the Soviet 1940s. In the choral epigraph that opens the opera (a free setting of the first paragraph of Book III, Three, 2) Prokofiev pointedly removes all of Tolstoy's specific mentions of Smolensk and Borodino. The unison chorus sings only of a "sense of insult" and of "disaster awaiting the enemy." All are generalized sentiments appropriate to the Second, as well as to the First, Fatherland War.

It is helpful to recall here that Tolstoy, in his many trial starts for *War and Peace*, also considered a military scene and a historical discussion as openings for his work. He rejected both in favor of Anna Scherer's salon—and nothing, in fact, could be more novelistic than this elegant, ironic babble in several languages that constitutes Tolstoy's first chapter. Prokofiev returned in his opening scene to the idea of a military overview. And in this emphatically single-voiced epigraph, opera speaks to novel from its own special ground.

This transposition of Tolstoy's masterpiece alters and omits a great deal. But distortions of "plot"—a plot that in any case the audience is expected to know—matter much less than Prokofiev's very real cooperation with Tolstoy in other areas of the novelist's world. The composer worked on this opera for ten years, resisting throughout the advice of his colleagues to recast Tolstoy's prose into more conventional aria form.[24] Whole segments, even paragraphs, of Tolstoyan prose are set to music almost unaltered. Prokofiev thus managed to keep the *language* of a Tolstoyan novel intact inside an opera. This is both violence to, and collusion with, Tolstoy. And the prose-based opera that results is an authentically coauthored work, dependent on a dialogue between the two authors for much of its richness, and for an appreciation of the type of realistic lyrical opera Prokofiev was striving to create.

Musorgsky's *Boris* clearly belongs to this last category of opera transposition, "scenes from classic works." The composer assumed that he did not have to tell Boris's tale in "organically linked" scenes, any more than Pushkin, with Karamzin as *his* backdrop, had to fill the Russian public in on all the details of the story. "Here is my tragedy," Pushkin had written to Nikolai Raevsky in 1829, "but I request that before you read it you skim through the final volume of Karamzin. . . ."[25] This category of transposition always requires that the source text be fresh in mind, for such transposers do not reproduce a text; rather, they *remind* their audience of it.

Thus three very different principles for libretto adaptation are linked, at their base, with the issue of authority of the source text. The text can be considered sacred, as in word-for-word settings. Or the text, after serving as general source for characters and plot situations, can be more or less discarded—the case with free adaptations. Or the two texts, literary source and derived libretto, can be equally authoritative. This final category of libretto, based on national classics, is best perceived as an active dialogue between literature and opera. Prokofiev's *War and Peace* preserves Tolstoy's prose but sings it; Tchaikovsky's *Eugene Onegin* transforms Pushkin's novel by lyricizing it; and Musorgsky's two versions of *Boris Godunov,* as we shall see, draw on both Pushkin and Karamzin to make their own statements about the place of opera in transmitting themes of history and personality.

To appreciate this last category, we must presume that the librettist or librettist/composer is aware of the genre of his source text, and that the changes effected on it are not arbitrary. It has been a general presumption of this study that stories or themes do not float as formless matter; they appeal to potential transposers for reasons that have as much to do with the manner of their telling, and the specific historical contexts in which they are told, as with particular characters and situations. Thus the composer-librettist who selects from literature does not part company with all literary considerations. But a difficult and much-disputed question still remains—upon which rests, it could be argued, the very inclusion of Musorgsky's libretto in a study of this sort.[26] Does a verbal text, adapted for opera from a literary source, have any artistic merit separated from its music?

Is the Libretto Literature?

When Igor Stravinsky set *Oedipus Rex* in Latin in 1927, he rejoiced at "composing music to a language of convention," where "one no longer feels dominated by the phrase, the literal meaning of the words. . . . The text thus becomes purely phonetic material for the composer."[27] Wherever the verbal text of a musical work functions in this way, as "purely phonetic material," it would indeed be difficult to defend the libretto as an integral work of literary art. But the libretto is not unique in this dependent status.

The same charge of "incompleteness" and lack of autonomy can be brought, although perhaps less urgently, against any art form in which *performance* is a crucial component. Certain genres of poetry— Russian trans-sense verse, for example—are just as devoid of "semantic meaning" and just as dependent on a sort of musical rendering as any libretto written in a language of convention. Stage drama, too, cannot be realized without the extraverbal considerations of intonation, body language, placement and movement through scenes. Yet poems and dramatic works are readily gathered into books to be studied on their own and read to oneself. The dramatic script has long since achieved the status of a privately experienced, self-sufficient text. As we noted earlier, there have been periods in operatic history where the libretto, too, approached such status.

This would seem to suggest that libretti are not beyond literature but rather at one end of it, where literature shares territory with other performance-oriented arts. Music itself, of course, has known periods where minimal notation in the bass line was "realized" anew by each performer. Realizing a libretto is a more comprehensive and radical task than realizing a figured bass, a stage play, or a recitation set to dance. But in common with them, notation is incomplete on the printed page. And appreciation of the art depends upon a knowledge of the conventions within which the notation operates.

What is required, then, is a poetics of the libretto—beginning with a catalogue of effects that a libretto can hope to achieve. Toward this end the opera scholar Ulrich Weisstein has laid out a basic grammar.[28] The libretto *is* a literary form, he argues, but as with every other genre we must learn the conventions for reading it. Foremost among these conventions is the presence, in most libretti, of two modes of time. One mode (recitative time) is horizontally progressive and dialogic; the other (aria time) is vertical, introspective, "timeless."

Since music slows down speech, libretto words are fewer and more slowly paced than their counterparts in drama. Character is usually heightened and simplified. But this simplification in character profile is compensated for by complexities elsewhere. Unlike spoken drama, where verbal complexity is linear and as a rule developed by one voice at a time, a libretto can exhibit *simultaneous* complexity: many voices, including the "voice" of a musical motif, can sound at once. Even if one discounts the strictly musical component, to comprehend the superimposed words of, say, a vocal trio where each part sings a different text requires some effort from a reader unpracticed in deciphering "libretto time."

Reading a libretto in the context of its own conventions, as Weisstein urges, is clearly the first step toward any literary appreciation of it. But the sense of a libretto as integral art is eroded by more than the mere absence of rules for reading it. In the contemporary experience of opera, both musical integrity and the dimension of the stage have become fragmented and detachable. Recordings eliminate the visual component, concert performances the acting. "Opera excerpts" are performed as a genre in their own right—as "dramatic excerpts," particularly from works by various playwrights in a single evening, rarely are. Set pieces are performed out of context as if they were independently composed songs; particular arias are often identified more with certain virtuoso vocal interpretations than with their place in any narrative plot.

At the root of the problem, of course, are those two modes of operatic time which invest the words of recitative and the words of aria with such different qualities. Recitative tells the story, and therefore has narrative integrity and forward movement. Aria, already of another temporal order, almost begs to be set free from the plot. The more rounded musical structure of aria and arioso reflects this detachability from the dramatic situation; such pieces can be sung on stage as elaborate "asides" that no one else in the cast hears and that conventionally mark no passing of time. The opera libretto, in short, seems to come apart all too easily even on its own terms. And as a consequence, the libretti of many well-known operas come to resemble pastiches of already autonomous material, somehow less than the sum of their parts.

Even where the operatic work is fully realized as staged spectacle, there is the additional complicating question of cuts in performance. Opera has proved enormously more vulnerable in this regard than drama or more modest vocal literature. Cuts are variously motivated, of course, for reasons of time, politics, personal taste, and theatrical convention. Among the more spectacular "abridgements" experienced by Musorgsky's *Boris* in its early theater history we might note the loss of the entire Chudovo Monastery scene from the 1874 premiere, probably for time considerations,[29] and the elimination of the Inn Scene from Diaghilev's 1908 production of the second Rimsky version—on grounds that such "low style" was unacceptable for French Grand Opera.[30] Cuts become canonized in performance; conflations and recombinations of canonized performances breed ever new operas, and ever more garbled libretti.

A final category of problem is encountered with libretti adapted from recognized literary masterpieces. Musorgsky's *Boris* is inevitably compared with Pushkin's, just as Verdi's *Otello* is always experienced in the shadow of Shakespeare. But a certain irony obtains in the case of *Boris Godunov*. Verdi has not *replaced* the dramatic *Othello*—nor, for that matter, has Tchaikovsky replaced Pushkin's *Eugene Onegin* or *Queen of Spades*. Those source texts were already fully successful on their own terms, and the success of the operatic transpositions has not had a prejudicial effect on the originals.

With the *Boris* transposition we experience more ambivalence, perhaps even bad conscience. And the reason, most likely, is that Pushkin's play has been considered by most of its critics to be a *failed* masterpiece. It failed precisely where Pushkin most hoped it would succeed and prove exemplary: the dramatic stage. Ever since Musorgsky reworked the text into a libretto, therefore, he has been simultaneously accused of "violating Pushkin" and of "resurrecting Pushkin"—that is, by destroying Pushkin's actual verse he realized the text dramatically for the first time and made it truly stageworthy. As Musorgsky gained in stature in the twentieth century, his statement of the Boris Tale became the familiar and canonic one. But it is, and was, regarded as a betrayal of Pushkin through the very spectacular nature of its success. Everything about romanticism that Pushkin disliked was, loosely speaking, "operatic."

Thus Pushkin and Musorgsky, two giants of nineteenth-century culture, have done each other complicated services. And this is because a transposer can be powerfully attracted to a text yet not scruple to change it. Part of the initial attraction for Musorgsky lay in the very hybrid nature of Pushkin's play, which seemed to afford the same possibility for disappointing expectations in opera that Pushkin had carried off with such (perhaps regrettable) success in drama. Just as Pushkin had played with the label on his work, settling on "romantic tragedy," so Musorgsky toyed with names for his: on the title page of an early *Boris* scenario he wrote "musical presentation," effaced it and wrote "opera," and eventually settled on "people's musical drama" as the genre of his later operas on Russian historical themes.[31] Both playwright and composer understood that innovation must name itself anew if it was to be free of old generic responsibilities. And just as Pushkin's artistic evolution reflected the literary debates of his decade, so Musorgsky's development as a composer encompassed the musical debates of the 1860s. A word about those here.

Russian Music in the Reform Decade: Two Schools

In their striving to free Russian culture from uncritical dependence on Western models, Karamzin and Pushkin had pointed the way toward a Russian history and a Russian drama. But neither historian nor poet perceived his task as "anti-Western." Both were eclectic and cosmopolitan, with an aristocratic sense of their place in society and their role as cultural professionals. When we turn to music, however, we find the reforming impulse more complex, and embedded in a different ideological hierarchy. The era of Karamzin and Pushkin had witnessed the emergence of a mature, flexible literary language for Russian. But a *musically* distinct language for Russia, in the sense of an ideology and an institutional base, did not really come into being until the 1860s.[32] That decade, so tumultuous socially and politically, also saw the emergence of rival camps in music. Thus Musorgsky could find himself in a position analogous to Pushkin's four decades earlier: that of spokesman for a specifically Russian aesthetic.

The rivalry between these musical camps had some surface resemblance to a Westernizer-Slavophile rift. When the piano virtuoso Anton Rubinstein founded the St. Petersburg Conservatory in 1862, he openly modeled it on German music schools and staffed it largely with foreigners. Its basic texts, for teaching and performance, were the eighteenth-century European musical classics. As its patron the conservatory boasted the Grand Duchess Elena Pavlovna, German by birth, who represented in her person that alliance between the court and Western music which had been characteristic of musical culture in the capital since the early eighteenth century.[33] In opposition to this conservative standard, a small group of musical "nationalists" (Balakirev, Borodin, Cui, Rimsky-Korsakov and Musorgsky) sought to incorporate into their compositions more of Russia's native cultural heritage. The group's adviser and ideologue, Vladimir Stasov, referred to these five as a *Moguchaia kuchka* (Mighty Handful); its members, who have come to be called *kuchkisty*, did share certain Slavophile sentiments.

Familiar as such labels are, however, Westernizer versus Slavophile is not an adequate framework for viewing Russian music in the 1860s. For reasons involving church bans on polyphony and musical instrumentation, Russia lacked a well-developed native tradition of secular art music. Thus even the so-called nationalist composers were dependent on Western forms. The conservatory taught counterpoint, fugue, and the classical forms of a symphony; the Balakirev Circle analyzed Schumann, Lizst, and the irregularities of a Berlioz symphonic poem. It was one sort of Western heritage against another. For many of the *kuchkisty* the issue was less West versus East than it was classicism versus romanticism.[34]

But the ideological implications of the rivalry are larger than this. When the St. Petersburg Conservatory opened in 1862 the faculty roster indeed included very few Russian names. Musorgsky referred derisively to its parent institution, the Russian Musical Society, as the "local German Ministry of Music,"[35] and there were elements of antisemitism at work here as well.[36] Rubinstein never dignified his critics with a reply, and during his tenure as director of the conservatory he forbade students and colleagues to write for the papers. Thus the press belonged to his opponents, and to a certain extent documented history has as well.[37] But Rubinstein never claimed to serve *Russian* music with his conservatory. He wished to serve the cause of music in Russia, and to create a legal status for Russian musicians.

This final point is crucial. The conservatory's efforts on behalf of musicians coincided, in time and spirit, with the Emancipation Proclamation, which was focusing national attention on the legal rights of a vast new class of citizens. In the late eighteenth century Catherine the Great had awarded painters, sculptors, and actors the rank of Free Artist, which exempted them from poll tax and military service as well as granted them the right to move legally about the empire. These privileges were not, however, extended to musicians.[38] The new conservatory was the first institution officially enabled to bestow "Free Artist" status upon musical artists, and thus its standards were high and very carefully regulated. A conservatory diploma not only certified a graduate as a professional; it granted him or her the rights of citizenship as a full-time musician. Students of music would no longer have to go abroad or study with foreigners in the capitals. It is certainly true that Rubinstein had staffed his conservatory with foreigners in its early years, for there were not enough qualified Russians. To remedy that situation was one of the main reasons why the conservatory had been established.[39]

The conservatory approach to music was organically alien to many of the amateur musicians of the Balakirev Circle, and to the "Free Music School" that grew out of that circle in 1862. This distinction between amateur and professional is perhaps the most fundamental of the various dichotomies at work (West versus East, classicism versus romanticism) in the rivalry between Free School and conservatory. In many ways the competition was artificial, for the two institutions performed very different services. The conservatory trained professional performers and music pedagogues. The Free School offered lessons in elementary music theory, notation, sight-singing, and vocal training—rudimentary skills to the population at large. There was even some overlap in patronage and personnel, and relations in the early 1860s were often quite cordial. But for much of the decade rivalry between the two groups was very real.

This was in part due to competition for the limited slots of musical leadership in the capital. It was also due to a genuine sense of wounded national pride on the part of the *kuchkisty,* who readily understood that the conservatory's "professionalism" did not only mean high standards and corporate identity. It also meant a prolongation of the transplanting ethos in Russian music: the domination of bel-canto style, the vogue of Italian singers and German instrumentalists, the low legal limits for royalties paid to native composers and musicians. Some *kuchkisty* resented as well the second-class funding of the Russian Opera Company, which paled beside its brilliant Italian counterpart in Petersburg. But these nationalistic and economic feuds, while intense for certain members of the *kuchka,* were not at the center of the dispute for Musorgsky. When he referred in his correspondence to Rubinstein as *Dubinstein* or *Tupinstein*—oakhead or dull-wit[40]—it was not out of personal malice. It was indicative, rather, of Musorgsky's very different view of the creative process and how to nurture it.

Musorgsky's Musical Aesthetic

"I rejoice in your successful concerts and I wish health to the newborn school!" Musorgsky wrote to Balakirev in April 1862.

> . . . The natural, free development of natures . . . is considerably more pleasant than scholastic or academic training. . . . In Piter [Petersburg], two schools have been organized, only an insignificant distance apart but totally contrasting in character. One is a professoria; the other, a free association of those who seek an intimate relationship with art. In one, Zaremba and Tupinstein, in their professional anti-musical togas, stuff the heads of their students with various abominations and infect them in advance. The poor pupils see before them not human beings but two fixed pillars to which are nailed some silly scrawls purporting to be musical laws.[41]

In this letter Musorgsky is advocating, albeit crudely, the tradition of Rousseau in music.[42] The opposition of emotional spontaneity to mere technical training was almost a cliché among populists of the 1860s.[43] One treatise in this tradition that influenced all members of the Balakirev Circle was Chernyshevsky's 1855 essay "The Aesthetic Relations of Art to Reality"—reputed to be Vladimir Stasov's favorite among Russian books on aesthetics.[44] That relation, simply put, is this: beauty is life, and the most lifelike in art is therefore the most beautiful. The wellspring of all music is the human voice. But, Chernyshevsky argued, even singing is no longer pure. It exists in both an artificial mode—deliberate, calculated, and ornamented, like "an aria from an Italian opera"—and a natural mode, embodied in folk song and in other musical expression governed by emotion rather than structure. Chernyshevsky even insisted that feeling and form are opposites:

> The difference between natural and artificial singing is the difference between an actor playing the role of a cheerful or sad person, and a person who is in fact cheerful or sad about something; it is the difference between the original and a copy, between reality and imitation.[45]

The most famous illustration of this musical primitivism in the literature of the period probably occurs in Tolstoy's *War and Peace:* Natasha Rostova's "natural" folk song at Uncle's versus her "artificial" (and disastrous) experience at the opera.

But Musorgsky was not satisfied for long with this dichotomy. As Richard Taruskin has argued in his magisterial study of Russian opera in the 1860s, Musorgsky aimed to extend the idea of "natural singing" far beyond the sentimental and romantic implications of Chernyshevsky's polemic.[46] The dichotomy that Chernyshevsky—and Tolstoy—drew between form and feeling was clearly inadequate. Folk songs, after all, could be highly formal things, and arias were not by definition devoid of feeling. For a musical realist the productive distinction was not only between form and feeling but also between acting and living—or, put another way, between the singing of a past emotion and the "speaking" of a present one. What excited Musorgsky was not the folk song as a "natural" form but the more general possibilities of sung prose and naturalistic melodic declamation.

Here we must consider Musorgsky's musical aesthetic in the context of his fellow *kuchkisty,* who were appreciative of his talent but often mystified by his excesses.[47] In company with them Musorgsky valued native Russian folk rhythms, modalities, popular song, and church chant, and was opposed to teaching (or creating) music by authoritative "laws" imported from Europe. He too was fascinated by the fusion of words and music—but felt that Wagner's solution was inadequate, as it gave too much prominence to the symphonic element and pressed words into the service of a mythic, unnatural text.[48] Where Musorgsky parted company with his fellow innovators in the late 1860s, however, was in his radical ideas about the proper musical setting of language.

From Pushkin to Gogol: Setting the Prose Word

By 1868 several of the *kuchkisty* had begun work on operas. One major inspiration was Dargomyzhsky's experiment in setting Pushkin's *Stone Guest*. What so impressed the younger composers was Dargomyzhsky's determination to respect every one of Pushkin's words, that is, his attempt to embody musically a received text in such a way that each line was given individualized expression. This words-first aesthetic seemed to satisfy perfectly Chernyshevsky's criteria for honest art: *The Stone Guest* was technically formless, there was no arbitrary division into aria and recitative, and the music did not distort the emotional impact of the text. The very extravagance of this task, together with Dargomyzhsky's disdain of sceptics, was taken as proof of its radical honesty. As Dargomyzhsky wrote to one of his pupils in 1857:

> The majority of our music-lovers and journalistic hacks do not acknowledge any inspiration in me. . . . [But] I do not intend to lower music to an idle pastime for their sakes. I want the sound to express the word directly. I want truth. They are not able to understand that.[49]

In sympathy with Dargomyzhsky's detractors, however, one must admit that it is not self-evident how sound can directly express the word.[50] And this is because the word itself has several components, each of which demands its own mode of musical realization. A musician might, for example, attempt to imitate the actual *sound* of the word, its phonetic aspect (that is, through a timbre suggest certain vowels or consonants). Or in some way he might portray the *meaning* of the word (its semantic aspect), either narratively, as in program music, or through isolated onomatopoeic effects—musical equivalents of chirping birds or a rap on the door. The word might also be realized through the associative power of certain musical genres: the lullaby, the dance, the triumphal march. And then the musical setting itself could attempt to mirror the intonation of words uttered in context.

The musical realization of spoken intonation is complex. On one overtly mimetic level, musical pitch can reproduce and heighten the intonation curve of a given utterance; thus a musician striving to follow the pronunciation norms of a language would set, say, a question differently from a declarative statement or a command. But intonation is not merely a matter of a single voice. In a musically expressed question the setting could also reflect (through a tentativeness and instability in melody or harmony) that larger context in which all questions occur—namely, the expectation of an answer, the uncertainty of resolution, an avoidance of cadence. Such an approach would be sensitive not so much to the individual word as to the "speech genre," or relatively stable *type* of utterance, of which the word is a part.[51] And there is, finally, one additional complexity present in almost all oral conversation: indirect discourse. The musical expression of one voice quoting another requires the most subtle interlayering of intonations, whose precise notation is dependent upon the degree of stylization or parody implied in the quotation.

Dargomyzhsky was attentive to some of these aspects of the word, but not all. Intonational and programmatic detail is certainly present in *The Stone Guest.* But its most successful episodes are built around a key musical phrase, one conditioned in its original instance by a portion of the verbal text but then permitted to develop according to the laws of musical combination and development.[52] Thus *The Stone Guest* remains, in its basic impulse and in the framing techniques for each phrase, essentially a lyric work, what Taruskin has called a "gargantuan through-composed romance."[53] When Musorgsky, under influence of Dargomyzhsky's aesthetic, began to set Gogol's *Marriage,* he emphasized another aspect of the word altogether: how it sounded in conversation.

Musorgsky's very choice of source text already held the key to his departure from Dargomyzhsky's model. Pushkin's *Stone Guest* was an elegant, compact poetic text. To realize it honestly in music meant to reflect the text's own lyricism and, as it were, its already librettistic quality. *Marriage,* on the other hand, was aggressively antilyrical, written in a colloquial prose that lacked dignity either of diction or of theme. What *Marriage* did have in abundance was highly personalized, everyday talk.

"Art is a means of conversing with people and not an end in itself," Musorgsky was to write in an autobiographical sketch near the end of his life. "The task of the art of music is to reproduce in musical sounds not merely the mood of a feeling, but primarily the mood of human speech."[54] During the summer of his work on *Marriage,* Musorgsky's letters are full of his "listening acts." To Rimsky-Korsakov he wrote in July 1868: "Whatever speech I hear, no matter who speaks it (and no matter what is said), my brain is already working on a musical exposition of that speech."[55] Later that month he speculated in a letter to Rimsky whether the unusual genre of his *Marriage* would be understood. "If you dismiss operatic tradition altogether," he wrote, "and can imagine musically a conversation on stage, conversation without a twinge of bad conscience, then *Marriage* is an opera."[56]

Musorgsky was certainly right in cautioning Rimsky to dismiss operatic tradition. For Gogol's text had appealed to him on grounds quite different from the usual librettistic criteria of heightened emotion, romance, lyricism, and pathos. Musorgsky prized *Marriage* as a treasure-house of intonation. As he wrote to Cesar Cui in the summer of 1868, the strength of Gogol's humor lay in "those changes in intonation which occur in the characters during dialogue, apparently for the most trivial reasons and on the most insignificant words."[57] The difference between Dargomyzhsky and Musorgsky is contained in this shift of emphasis from the word as a semantic unit to the word as *spoken in dialogue,* the word as utterance.

According to Musorgsky's own testimony, an important influence on these "intonation exercises" was the German aesthetician Gervinus, whose monograph detailing the relations between *Musik* and *Betonung* (accent or stress) appeared in 1868.[58] What speech and music had in common, Gervinus pointed out, was the primacy of the *accent* in communicating emotion. And what is peculiar about spoken accent is that it never occurs twice in quite the same context.

This was Musorgsky's path to the Dargomyzhskian credo of the "unrepeatability" of the sung word. It decrees the dishonesty of repetition and internal development—not because the word itself has some inherent individuality but because speech situations are always specific, and always changing. Other musical realists of Musorgsky's circle worshiped the word; Musorgsky had no such fetish for the word as a lexical unit. He readily changed the words of a received text if the communicative potential could be enhanced in the new medium. Minor adjustments were made on Gogol's *Marriage,* and, as we shall see, very major ones in the second version of *Boris.* Musorgsky would change words, but he would not distort accent. And this was because, in Musorgsky's aesthetic, the word took on meaning only while being uttered in context.

Since speech is forever changing in response to new contexts, it followed for Musorgsky in this early radical period that any music written to speech would have to forego autonomous, purely musical development. Thus did Musorgsky so readily discount the creative potential of preexisting systems and "musical laws." The idea of a law or a norm was not in itself offensive. Human speech also had its laws, Musorgsky admitted, and the laws that governed speech were in fact musical ones. But the difference between these regenerative laws of speech and the laws of fugue and counterpoint was all important: "these laws are not immutable; they grow and progress, like all of man's spiritual world."[59]

Musorgsky's commitment to the unsystemic and open-ended element in musical speech acts thus went far beyond his own personal distaste for conservatory-style music theory and technique. He hoped to liberate Russian speech from its incarceration in non-Russian forms. Russian speech, he believed, had been crippled by borrowings and dilution; as a result, its intonation—and thus communicative potential—had been distorted. This failure to embody speech properly had more than aesthetic implications. As Musorgsky wrote to the literary historian Vladimir Nikolsky, "to capture artistically the intonations of the human voice" would be "a deification of the human gift of speech"—and this would lead, perhaps, to "the capture of our thinking processes as well."[60] Musorgsky too was a product of the utopian ideologies of his time.

Such an extravagant conception of what the music-speech continuum could reveal set Musorgsky apart from his fellow composers in the circle, as well he knew.[61] In an obituary written one month after Musorgsky's death, Cesar Cui included the following among the late composer's deficiencies: ". . . a tendency to exaggerate, to take correctness of declamation to the point of reproducing the voice's real intonation, to reduce scenic portrayal to onomatopoeic effects and musical truth to realism. . . ."[62] In this formative *Marriage* period, Musorgsky did indeed equate such realism with musical truth.

From Gogol Back to Pushkin: Sung Speech into Historical Opera

Musorgsky's musical comrades were enthusiastic about the *Marriage* project—more, perhaps, for its theoretical daring than for its musical achievement. But the composer himself, in the autumn of 1868, abandoned *Marriage* after the first act to take up work on *Boris*. Musorgsky rarely documented the reasons for his creative shifts. In this instance, however, he was quite explicit about his change of task. As he wrote to Liudmila Shestakova: "If God grants me life and strength, I shall speak on a grand scale. After *Marriage,* the Rubicon will have been crossed. But *Marriage* is a cage in which I have been locked until I am tamed; then I can be free."[63]

What this freedom was to mean is suggested in a letter to Golenishchev-Kutuzov nine years later, when Musorgsky remarked on this crucial watershed between *Marriage* and *Boris*. There he admitted both the correctness and the limitations of the *Marriage* model:

> . . . *Marriage* was only the humble exercise of a musician, or better a non-musician, who wished to study and grasp the twistings of human speech in that unmediated, truthful exposition given them by that unsurpassed genius Gogol. *Marriage* is an etude, a trial for the chamber. From the grand stage one must convey to the audience in bold relief the speech of

characters, each true to his own nature, to his habits and "dramatic inevitability."[64]

In that same letter, Musorgsky mentioned in passing that Pushkin "had written *Boris* in dramatic form [but] not for the stage." In so doing the composer echoed the conventional wisdom of both drama and opera critics—even those who greatly admired the play. But then Musorgsky cautioned against any mechanical transference of a written text into a sung one, and offered thoughtful advice on the transposition of literary work to libretto. "Woe to them whose whim it is to use Pushkin or Gogol merely as a text," he continued to his letter:

> Just as only the genuine, sensitive nature of the artist can create in the realm of the word, so the musician must maintain a very "polite" attitude toward the [other's] creation, in order to penetrate its very substance, the very essence of that which the musician intends to embody in musical form. The genuine and truly artistic cannot be anything but capricious, because independently it cannot easily be embodied in another artistic form. . . .

In his search for the musical "essence" of Pushkin's *Boris*, Musorgsky created two quite different operatic transpositions. Both versions give evidence of a reverence for the word, but on quite another plane from the word-for-word setting of *Stone Guest*. The 1869 *Boris*, Musorgsky's original submission to the Theater Directorate, is conceptually quite close to *Marriage;* the 1874 revised version, a step back from this extreme position, adopts another and more flexible creative methodology.[65] As we shall see, this second *Boris* fuses two principles—one innovative and the other more conventionally operatic. For the "grand stage" Musorgsky provided highly dramatic musical portraiture, of the sort that communicated not only words but also heightened feelings and events. This he combined, however, with a recasting of much of the text so that it could be sung as amplified spoken dialogue.

One might ask what Musorgsky initially saw, and admired, as the essence of Pushkin's *Boris*. The composer himself scarcely mentions his work on the first version of the opera in his correspondence; for that period (1869) we have almost no letters from Musorgsky at all. But one might speculate. Here was a powerful story of inner torment, a broad historical canvas, comic scenes already cast in colloquial prose, and the absence of lyrical love interest—which was never Musorgsky's special strength. At a deeper level, however, one suspects that Musorgsky as dramatist was attracted by certain similarities in aesthetic position between himself and the poet.

Embarking on their *Boris* projects, both Pushkin and Musorgsky had written to friends that their spiritual resources had matured, and "now they could truly create."[66] Both chose to embed the historical theme in contemporary language—language whose very incorporation into art was itself a polemical event. In this project both men bypassed romantic forms in favor of a more mimetic mode of representation—mimetic, to be sure, only if judged by the conventions of their respective staged arts. The charge of "excessive realism," brought against Musorgsky even by his musical allies, was perhaps inevitable because of the highly conventional nature of opera. But Pushkin too, working in the more flexible medium of drama, had chosen to enhance the oddness of his *Boris* by calling it a "tragedy," thereby inviting comparison with all the fixed features that *Boris* specifically violated. "Artistic truth cannot endure preconceived forms," Musorgsky wrote in 1875,[67] in much the same spirit that Pushkin had complained about the classicists (and many of the romanticists) of his day. Throughout their creative lives, both poet and composer welcomed the chance to confound audience expectations and recombine or parody solemn genres.[68]

Because of the highly formal nature of the genre, opera reform tends to be a dialogue with *past* exemplars. Musorgsky, however, began his investigations into the genre with a focus on the present context of Russian speech. Unlike Pushkin—who never lost sight of artifice on the stage—Musorgsky, in his *Marriage* period, actually spoke of clothing live conversation in music "without a twinge of bad conscience." And this insistence on current context was reflected in his attitude toward history as well. He tuned his ear above all to the present. History, for him, was never silent or dead: it was everything that had survived into the present, that had left its traces on the present and was empowered to *change* the present. Indeed, the dramatic core of the operatic *Boris*—those repeated hallucinations of the slain Dmitri—is an embodiment of this very principle. The task of the artist, as Musorgsky wrote Vladimir Stasov in 1872, was to portray this "past within the present."[69]

It is now easier to understand Musorgsky's scepticism toward the "German School" in Petersburg. In his opinion the formalism of the conservatories could only lead to a reliance on received models and a repetition of closed forms. A composer's duty, as Musorgsky later wrote to Kutuzov, was to listen to a literary source text with great "politeness" but then to *respond* to it from a new present and in a new medium—not merely to reproduce it. Musorgsky did not feel that either of his transpositions did violence to Pushkin's text. In keeping with his new medium and with an aesthetic at least partially shared by the author of his source text, Musorgsky in his initial version recreated Pushkin's *Boris* as dramatically heightened sung prose.

The Chronotope of a Libretto in Prose

"If poetry and music have seemed to people since ancient times to be sisters (and even twin sisters, born from the once unified art of song), then the kinship of music and prose seems considerably more distant." Thus does one specialist on the Russian romance open her discussion of the link between music and prose in Musorgsky's vocal writing.[70] Only in the twentieth century, she points out, did prose texts become the norm in Russian opera. Before this time most vocal music was set to verse texts, and prose itself—especially in the latter half of the last century—had a particular polemical orientation. Prose had become stylistically flexible, colloquial, and was perceived as categorically opposed to the conventional abstractions of poetic speech. As we have seen, Musorgsky embraced to the full this general conception of prose as something spoken, as something with a voice and therefore with a point of view. Setting prose to music was not just an aesthetic task; it was a whole world view, a means by which art could pay tribute to real experience.

A prose libretto, which for Musorgsky meant a *spoken* text, confronts several problems unknown to more conventional "numbers" opera. Of these problems the most crucial to resolve is that of opera's dual time and space. We have already mentioned dual time, the two poles of recitative and aria. Traditionally, recitative is the dynamic "spoken" message, taking place in real time and moving action forward. Aria, in contrast, is a song, and tends to function as a static element in the drama. Each of these opera times has its appropriate space. Recitative is social: it usually occurs in dialogue, and people on stage are supposed to hear and respond to it. Aria, however, can stop action. Often it is sung not to other characters in the opera but to oneself or to the audience, as a sort of private confession. People onstage may not be expected to listen in, and therefore the aria's act of expression need not serve to motivate the actions of other participants in the opera. These categories, of course, can overlap. When a recitative is cast as a stage aside for the audience alone, it must be played in "aria time and space." Conversely, under certain circumstances an aria can become part of the dramatic action.

The relatively distinct boundary between these two operatic chronotopes makes them excellent targets for parody. And indeed, "realistic" opera often parodies this boundary—as Prokofiev does in *War and Peace*, when he permits an onstage character to "hear" a private aria and then surprise the singer with the illicit information thus gleaned.[71] More common than laying bare the convention, however, is the attempt by opera reformers to fuse these two chronotopes into one. Many radically prose-based operas are in essence sung plays, composed entirely in "recitative time and space." What the audience sees and hears is what the participants on stage see and hear—and no more. Time cannot be stopped; the libretto must be lived through (albeit at a slowed pace), in imitation of everyday life.

Fused-time libretti are difficult to sustain. A grand opera built exclusively on through-composed recitative is likely to appear diminished both dramatically and musically. Here several mediating structures are possible, and by way of example we might note the devices perfected by Musorgsky in his realistic chamber songs of the late 1860s. The prose he selected, or created, for musical treatment was not altogether unworked. He rhythmicized it and then set it to various speech genres—or, better, musical-speech genres—that had affinities with the appropriate communicative situation: lament, children's ditty or taunt, beggar's cry, prayer.[72]

Musorgsky constructed his original version of *Boris* (1869) somewhat along these lines. Musical-speech genres organized both intonational patterns and a dense fabric of identifying motifs. But this version was returned to the composer for revision, and during his ensuing work on the opera Musorgsky introduced a number of inserted choruses and songs—for monks, for the innkeeper, and for the tsarevich. The challenge for Musorgsky in most of the scenes was to keep these musical insertions from reverting to "aria time and space."

The solution—not, of course, without precedent in Musorgsky's time—was to ensure that each song or chorus made sense *as a song* within the logic of the dramatic action, and that the surrounding recitative responded to it. Internal reasons for a character to be singing were to be found wherever possible inside the drama. Thus "inserted songs" would protrude in the opera just as they protrude in everyday spoken life, and would be heard as songs by the other characters onstage. In a backdrop to Pimen's monologue, monks sing on the way to mass—and Pimen hears them and comments on them. The innkeeper sings to herself out of boredom, interrupting her own song when she thinks she hears guests arriving and then resuming it when they pass on. The tsarevich Fyodor sings because he is a young child (of the operatic Fyodor's infantilization we will speak later), and his foolish songs and pranks profoundly impress his father the tsar—who opposes the "truthful tales" of his son to the lies and treachery that are sung to him elsewhere in the opera.

Aria time and space do indeed dominate certain scenes in the revised *Boris,* as we shall see. But a "recitative chronotope" succeeds in governing many unexpected places in the opera—places full of separate songs functioning as self-enclosed melodic entities. In the words of one Musorgsky scholar: "*Boris* is no stranger to closed musical forms. But both the duration and the structural logic are permeated with a feeling of the scene, with a feeling for real scenic time and space."[73]

Here we note an interesting variation on a theoretical issue much debated several decades later by the Russian formalists. In their theory of plot, the formalists distinguished between action that was "motivated" (or explicable in terms of earlier events) and action that was "defamiliarized" (that is, unmotivated and therefore defiant of tradition). By inserting "motivation" where operatic tradition often omitted it, Musorgsky managed to defamiliarize plot by in fact *motivating* it. The possibility of doing so, of course, derives from the difference between plot conventions in opera and in narrative fiction.

A second challenge for the prose librettist (in addition to fused operatic time) comes in the inevitable tension between a spoken text, preeminently a unit of communication, and a text set to music—which is always to some extent stylized. What must be avoided is any sense that in singing the lines the singer is "citing" them, that is, performing someone else's words. Music must amplify speech, but not distort it or separate it from the act of direct communication. Both Dargomyzhsky and Musorgsky had shown, on a simple mimetic level, that a musical setting could imitate rather successfully the intonational and rhythmic patterns of Russian speech.[74] But—as Musorgsky doubtless realized of his initial *Boris*—this "primitive correctness" in reflecting individual intonations made no real provision for the dramatic integrity of the hero, and little for the integrity of the opera as a whole. Indeed, it could be argued that any aesthetic that insists on art reflecting life, on verbal texts echoing free conversation, would have to dispute the very concept of a well-made integrated artwork.

Musicologists have offered various schemes for understanding dramatic wholeness in the two *Boris* versions, identifying musicodramatic periods, melodic motifs, and musical keys associated with certain characters or recurring ideas.[75] Work has also been done on Musorgsky's concept of recitative. Soviet specialists on Musorgsky's vocal dramaturgy have investigated this latter concept within the framework of a "grammar" for recitative forms.[76]

The first step toward such a grammar entails the establishment of a norm. In his opening stages of work on the opera, Musorgsky apparently achieved this objective by laying out his recitative initially as calm, relatively expressionless speech.[77] Both rhythm and duration of tones were distributed to reflect the natural contours of conversation: long spoken syllables or accents received longer metric pulse, and intonation and phrasing were modeled on breathing patterns. The end of an utterance coincided with the end of a musical phrase. Lesser degrees of pause—what would be commas or semicolons in transcribed speech—were registered in the degree of cadence allotted to the vocal line.

In his initial version of the opera Musorgsky retained this speech-worthy norm for secondary characters, and for main characters at rest. But in the heightened portions of the narrative, in those passages which in this fused chronotope function as aria does in dual-time operas, departures from the norm were both necessary and desirable. Musorgsky's operating rule was this: departures from the norm were dictated by emotional and dramatic considerations only, never by melody or musical structure. In the initial *Boris* these adjustments were multilayered and subtle. Untransformed norms remained in effect for primitive or superficial characters—the Innkeeper, for example, and Varlaam. But in the main characters at their great moments—Boris during his hallucinations, Shuisky in his fawnings before the tsar—the spoken norm was deliberately distorted, as indeed it would be in normal speech. Sometimes Musorgsky worked mockingly with genre, causing a character to break out of recitative into lyrical song or arioso; in a major noncomic adult character, this usually signified delusion.[78] At other times Musorgsky bent or amplified the speech line with the help of musical motifs. Since Musorgsky associated certain musical keys with certain characters or moods, keys could be superimposed on motifs to indicate a "subtext" of mixed emotion, guilt, or struggle for power.[79]

Through these creative distortions of the speech norm, Musorgsky achieved flexibility and subtlety for his major characters. His point of departure in the initial *Boris* was the assumption that norms have meaning only in context; consequently, words and sentences have meaning only as utterances. Musorgsky set no recitative in isolation. So when complex, emotionally charged characters occasionally *reproduce* a norm—as Grigory does in front of the police in the Inn, and the holy fool does in front of Tsar Boris—the dramatic effect of such self-discipline is enormous. Musical utterance takes on the cunning of our everyday verbal acts of masking and manipulation.

Musorgsky's Prose Line

Committed to setting a speaking line, Musorgsky had little trouble in his initial version with those scenes in Pushkin's *Boris* that were already written in prose. The operatic text of the Inn Scene is in fact almost identical with Pushkin's. But the bulk of Pushkin's play, and the great majority of the material Musorgsky chose to set, is cast not in prose but in a poetic meter. As we noted in the previous chapter, this meter accommodates neither a normal speech pattern in Russian nor a strictly declamatory mode. Adjustments were necessary to make Pushkin's line more prosaic.

Soviet musicologists have offered various typologies of the transformations Musorgsky effected on Pushkin's verse line. The most comprehensive of these typologies, drawn up by Aleksei Ogolevets, posits four basic patterns for adjusting Pushkin's norm.[80] Two entail direct changes in the rhythmic weight of the normative line, and two involve an altogether arrhythmic displacement of the beat.

The first, "verselike" manner *(stikhotvorcheskaia manera)* merely intensifies what is already there: strong elements in the rhythm are made stronger, weak elements weaker. This elevated iambic beat is used during moments of heightened emotion or rhetorical flourish. Although its base is lyrical, the verselike manner is essentially dialogic; whatever stylization it displays is a deliberate departure from the speech norm for communicative effect. A second dialogic pattern that Ogolevets detects is the so-called prosaicized *(prozaizirovannaia)* manner, which utilizes real spoken accent and therefore often calls for a significant rearrangement of verbal material. A third manner, "monologic" or "archaicized" *(arkhaizirovannaia),* produces an emotional, highly pulsating prose—prose that is so heavily and regularly accented that it seems to be sung in a trance. This is prose on the far side of the prose of life, and, not surprising, its mix of prosaic and monologic elements constitutes the special cunning of Pimen's vocal line. Finally there is the "singing" *(raspevnaia)* line, which became increasingly conspicuous in Musorgsky's work in the early 1870s as he moved away from strict *kuchkist* realism.[81] *Raspevnost'* is absent in *Marriage,* scant in the initial version of *Boris,* more prominent in the revised version, and dominant in *Khovanshchina.*

We will return to some of these modes of adjustment later in the chapter, when considering specific sections of the two libretti. The point to stress here is that Musorgsky, in both his versions, was in no way "careless" with Pushkin's text. Where it suited his dramatic purpose he painstakingly made prose out of Pushkin, disrupting the regular pulse of the lines, even occasionally reconstituting verselike rhythm against the dialogizing background of the prose norm. This activity sometimes involved the most minuscule alterations. Musorgsky would replace, for example, Pushkin's particle *zhe* with a nonsyllabic *zh* of his own, or reverse the order of words to change stress, or alter a punctuation mark.[82]

In the 1850s even unrhymed verse in a libretto was considered a novelty by Russian opera composers. We can therefore see why Musorgsky's achievement, one mere decade later, in the area of melodic prose seemed to his contemporaries so extraordinary. On the strength of these dramatic realizations, D. S. Mirsky has called Musorgsky "the greatest Russian tragic poet of the period."[83] Far more common in Musorgsky's own era, however, was the opinion voiced by Nikolai Strakhov:

> [Musorgsky] redid Pushkin's drama: he changed scenes, changed the speech of the characters, remade the verses and added many of his own. And it is clear that he not only has no idea of dramatic art but also of a good line of verse; in fact, he has no idea of what verse is in general, and what is meant by poetic meter.[84]

But Musorgsky was interested in *prose*, not poetry, as the grounds for a norm. He did not arbitrarily distort Pushkin's verse line but deliberately restructured it, as attentive as any poet to the small sounds of vowels and consonants and to the speech rhythm of the sentences. Even in the Inn Scene, set from Pushkin's text essentially unchanged, Varlaam's lines are subtly abridged so that words with the *o* vowel predominate—making it possible to display Varlaam's comic *okanie* or unstressed *o*.[85] And Stasov recalls in his biographical sketch of Musorgsky how the composer had charged him with finding, for the final act, "Latin calls for Jesuits with an abundance of the letter *i* and *u*, to express their cowardly fear."[86] But the strongest testimony to Musorgsky's passion for the proper word comes from the composer's close friend and collaborator, the poet Arseny Golenishchev-Kutuzov. Kutuzov wrote in his *Reminiscences of Musorgsky*:

> At the time I was a fervent admirer of Pushkin, and considered any distortion of his work to be an impermissible sacrilege. . . . But it was a strange thing. Musorgsky could not endure any comments about [verbal] texts he had composed. About the music he would talk very willingly and often agreed with the comments. But any criticism on a [verbal] text he had written irritated him, and he always stayed with his own opinion.[87]

The Boris Tale as Libretto: Musorgsky's Two Versions

Locating an authoritative libretto for *Boris Godunov* is a complicated process, dependent in large part on one's definition of authenticity. The troubled history of *Boris* opera versions cannot be considered here in any detail.[88] The basic shape of the problem, however, is of general interest for libretto studies.

There are at least four—and arguably as many as nine—distinct versions of *Boris*.[89] Two are by Musorgsky himself (1869 and 1874); two are by Rimsky-Korsakov (1896 and 1908). Rimsky, lamenting the fact that *Boris* had been removed from repertory a year after its composer's death and fearing for its complete extinction,[90] reworked the 1874 version of the opera so radically that only fifteen percent of its bars were left unchanged.[91] He has since come under much hostile attack for his cosmeticizing of Musorgsky's original.[92] But it should be noted that some of the changes Rimsky inflicted—such as reversing the order of the final two scenes so that the opera ended conventionally on the hero's death—could be justified as a return to Musorgsky's *initial* (1869) version. So successful did the Rimsky adaptations become that Musorgsky's own published texts went out of print.

In the 1920s interest began to grow in the "original," that is the pre-Rimsky, *Boris*. A major landmark was the publication, in 1928, of a scholarly edition of Musorgsky's original by the Soviet musicologist Pavel Lamm. But Lamm's methodology raised questions. Confronted with two authorial versions and presuming the major differences to be the result of censorship, Lamm proceeded by conflation: he presented every scene (music, text, and stage directions) in its maximally full form. Thus this composite "original" represented neither of the versions Musorgsky actually wrote.

Lamm's conflation gave new authority to further reworkings and "restorations." In 1926 Ippolitov-Ivanov orchestrated, in the Rimsky style, the St. Basil's Scene from Musorgsky's 1869 version—a scene that Musorgsky himself eliminated in 1874 but that was reinstated by Lamm. In 1940 Dmitri Shostakovich reorchestrated the opera;[93] in the 1950s Karol Rathaus reworked a conflation of Musorgsky's texts that aimed to preserve the composer's own meter, rhythm, melody, and harmony. Almost every decade, so it seems, "retextures" *Boris* in a different ratio of original score to creative—or corrective—logic.

Musorgsky's opera has thus been compromised, and perhaps also enriched, by a history of peculiar and incompatible charges. On the one hand, Musorgsky himself is considered musically inept, a "savage genius," and therefore in need of creative reshaping.[94] On the other hand, the Imperial Theaters and contemporary critics are castigated for their reluctance to appreciate this genius, and censorship or other external pressure is presumed to have dictated most of the changes that Musorgsky made in his own libretto and score.[95] These issues will emerge in our discussion only as they relate to Musorgsky's own two versions.

The chronology of work on *Boris* is briefly as follows. Musorgsky completed *Boris* in orchestral score in December 1869. This initial version contained seven scenes, all taken from Pushkin and following the poet's text in those scenes quite closely.[96] Excepting the low comedy of the Inn Scene, the opera in this form was a severe monodrama on Boris's conscience—and, not surprisingly, it ended conventionally with the death of the hero. But little else in the libretto was conventional or expected. There was no Polish Act. And thus there was almost nothing for the female voice, no love interest, no arias or vocal ensembles, no set pieces or dances, "nothing [as one biographer put it] but grimness and gloom except for one scene of comedy at the Inn."[97] This early profile of the opera in fact reflects the two poles of Musorgsky's songwriting at this time. At one end we find a tragic, and at the other end a comic, realism—bypassing the more conventional romantic lyricism of the chamber art song in between. In this, incidentally, Musorgsky was being true to the spirit of his source. Pushkin too, we recall, had been intrigued by the idea of a tragedy without true love in it, and so portrayed his Marina as a cynical parody of the traditional romantic heroine.[98]

The Mariinsky Theater Directorate rejected this version in February 1871. Musorgsky immediately set himself to the revision, but in what mood has been a matter of conjecture. The standard Soviet biography, Georgy Khubov's *Musorgsky*, dismisses the issue rather lightly, claiming that the rejection was "not altogether unexpected, and did not cast him into despair."[99] Vladimir Stasov, on the other hand, claims that he had tried (even before the directorate's verdict) to convince Musorgsky of the need for changes, but the composer had stubbornly resisted.[100] In any case, Musorgsky reworked the opera throughout 1871 in the direction recommended by the directorate and by his friends—much more radically, in fact, than appears to have been necessary to assure its acceptance.[101]

On the large scale, Musorgsky drew closer to Pushkin by incorporating more of his scenes. But on the small scale, the revised libretto departed much more drastically from Pushkin's actual verse line, and from the characters that verse line engendered. Musorgsky shortened considerably the unwieldy monologues in the Monastery Scene, cutting out entirely Pimen's account of the Uglich murder.[102] He returned to Pushkin and finished a Polish Act based on scenes 12 and 13, plus a scene in Marina's boudoir—inspired by one of the two scenes Pushkin had written in 1825 but had not included in his published edition of the play in 1831.[103] Pushkin's Marina, however, was too thinly drawn and too deficient romantically for a conventional operatic role. Musorgsky apparently turned for details to Faddei Bulgarin's emotional chronicle on the Mniszech family,[104] and to strengthen the Polish presence still further he created out of Karamzin and later nineteenth-century sources a new character not present in Pushkin at all, the Jesuit Rangoni.

In addition to the Polish element (and its concomitant romantic and political intrigue) Musorgsky inserted into the revised version a number of set pieces and songs: two choruses of monks, the Innkeeper's "Song of the Drake," the tsarevich's parrot song and chiming-clock duet with Ksenia,[105] the Song of the Gnat and hand-clapping sequence with nurse. The most important structural change in the new version comes, however, at the end. There Musorgsky added an entirely new scene after the death of Boris, in which the Pretender appears amid popular rebellion in a forest near Kromy. This final scene—which occurs neither in Pushkin nor in Karamzin—will be considered separately, but here we should note that the new scene was balanced by the cutting of an entire earlier scene, the confrontation between Boris and the holy fool in front of St. Basil's. One episode from that scene (the band of boys stealing the fool's kopek) was, however, recycled in the Kromy finale.

The existence of two authorial versions of *Boris Godunov*, each in fact separate and complete but appearing to rework much of the same material, has encouraged a license with extant texts that is notorious even in opera's spotted history. Motivated, perhaps, by a desire to keep as much of Musorgsky's music (and libretto) as possible, scenes and segments are freely spliced and recombined. The Kromy Forest Scene—and especially its final fool's lament—is praised as a grim musical equivalent of the popular horror behind Pushkin's *narod bezmolvstvuet*. But while respecting Musorgsky's "revised" intent as regards the ending, scholarly editors—and performances—have been loath to part with the powerful St. Basil's Scene, so central to Pushkin and to a full image of the conscience-stricken tsar. Thus its exclusion from the 1874 revision is attributed to external (or "internal") censorship—even though the Kromy Scene, considerably more subversive, passed the censor in the 1873 libretto. St. Basil's is reinserted into the revised opera, and, to make the overall text cohere without excessive repetitions, the fool's first appearance is excised from the final scene.

This sort of free play with extant versions is only possible, of course, because Musorgsky's character, reputation, and position as creator in a closed society combine to reassure the later interpreter that Musorgsky did not himself know his best intentions. To complicate matters still further, "revised" versions of the opera stabilized at various points. There are extant several vocal scores and libretti in manuscript, a holograph full score of 1872, the Bessel libretto of 1873, and the published piano-vocal and full scores of 1874. Each differs from the others in details of vocal line, text, performance markings, and stage directions. As Lamm himself points out in defense of his conflation methodology, Musorgsky's peculiar composition habits make reconstruction and dating hazardous. The composer did most of his work in his head; even early drafts were written in a neat calligraphy, on small sheets of music paper, which were then clipped and repasted in the process of revision. Rough ideas, first drafts, and final copy all look much the same.[106]

At the heart of the problem, however, lies the more general question of authorial intention, especially as later researchers reinvest it in drafts and versions. As Gary Saul Morson has pointed out:

> Most textologists adopt one of two approaches to canceled and reworked drafts. The first assumes that the earliest material represents the writer's basic ideas and is therefore most authoritative concerning his intentions; the second, by contrast, assumes that the latest draft is more "mature" and therefore most authoritative . . . . On logical grounds, however, it would seem to be equally possible to defend the authority of either the first or last draft—or, for that matter, any other . . . . Which edition is to be preferred, the first, the last, or the "best"? Or perhaps some composite of all?
>
> It seems to me that the only possible answer to this question is that the edition to be chosen depends on why one is doing the choosing . . . . No edition and no draft is *intrinsically* preferable or more authoritative *per se*.[107]

In the polemics surrounding *Boris,* these two poles (privileging "first" and "last" versions) were represented in the late 1920s and early thirties by two eminent Soviet musicologists, Boris Asafiev and Pavel Lamm. In a series of influential essays beginning in 1928, Asafiev argued that the initial 1869 version was the authoritative text, more faithful both to Pushkin's drama and to Musorgsky's original inspiration.[108] The initial *Boris* is indeed closer to the *Marriage* aesthetic, both in its fidelity to the source text and in its endeavor to replace the conventional opera "scene" with something like localized, unmediated "chunks of life."[109] But of course authentication need not be a backward-looking process. Lamm projected forward, presuming that every new item written had its newly valid place in the whole; conflation, therefore, would in his opinion most closely approximate the composer's ultimate intention.[110] To cement this methodology in place, Lamm labeled the initial 1869 version "preliminary" *(pred-varitel'naia)* and the 1874 version "basic" *(osnovnaia)*—as if the former were not a finished work but a mere sketch for the latter.[111] In fact, both are finished works. And one can only conclude that in the process of revising the opera a new concept of the work emerged, which Musorgsky then developed along the lines of a new creative logic. At different stages in his own evolution, the composer approved of *both* versions.

The coexistence of several "approved" versions of a single work is in fact something of a trademark for Musorgsky. "Both his operas and his romances (and especially the latter) exist in a multitude of versions," Asafiev writes,

> and all are approximations . . . . It is sometimes hard to say which variant is more perfect, just as is often the case with variants of folk songs . . . . In Musorgsky we are dealing with someone groping for the dynamic nature of musical form, someone who privileges "variants in formative stages" over those forms which, once achieved and fixed in place, are finished forever, closed off.[112]

In the readings of the libretto that follow, I will draw on both of Musorgsky's versions,[113] In doing so I risk somewhat to participate in the policy of conflation and intersplicing of texts that has already done such injustice to Musorgsky's reputation as a musical craftsman. This risk can be minimized, however, by keeping in mind not only the coexistence of multiple versions but also the "finishedness" of each version as a conceptualized whole.

As Richard Taruskin demonstrates in his recent analysis of the two authorial versions,[114] the 1869 opera was still quite "Pushkinian," a product of orthodox *kuchkist* principles of transposition. Musorgsky set the source text in an almost unrelieved declamatory style, a strategy that worked well in the "bouffe" scenes but inevitably resulted in a musically, and dramatically, diminished hero. In the years between the rejection of that first version and the resubmitted score, Musorgsky reconceptualized the opera and his own goals. The second version—to invoke the terms of this present study—involved a genuine chronotopic shift, a retreat from Pushkin and a return to static psychological tragedy reminiscent of Karamzin. In this new version Musorgsky made the climactic moments more theatrical, the identifying leitmotifs more restrained, and the orchestral support more continuous. He added an entirely new ending scene composed in what amounted to an "oratorio style." The evidence suggests, in short, that Musorgsky did not compose one opera and then reluctantly adjust it piecemeal; he made, rather, two separate transpositions of Pushkin's text. Pushkin glints through the first, Karamzin through the second.

Romantic Tragedy into Realistic Opera: General Principles of Transposition

Any act of transposition restates some features of the source text, freely interprets others, and subjects still a third group to the relatively nonnegotiable constraints of a new medium or genre. In his two moves from spoken to musical theater, Musorgsky brought all these categories of adaptation to Pushkin's play. We might briefly note some general factors that appear to have governed the transpositions.

There were, first, constraints imposed by the musicoliterary genre of the libretto itself. To accommodate a musical setting within reasonable time limits, scenes had to be omitted and the chosen scenes compressed. In considering the choices Musorgsky made from among Pushkin's twenty-three scenes, we should keep in mind the status of the source text in the 1860s. Pushkin's play had passed the theatrical censorship only in 1866. Although the 1870 premiere performance of the play (sixteen out of twenty-three scenes) was not a success, Musorgsky drew his libretto almost entirely from scenes that had been performed in 1870. The 1874 premiere of the opera at Mariinsky Theater even recycled the sets and costumes from the Pushkin production—and these externals, incidentally, were among the most highly praised aspects of the opera's first run.[115] The close interaction between the two productions inevitably intensified comparison between dramatic text and revised libretto, and doubtless accounted for some of the harsh accusations of "infidelity" as well.

Once his selection of scenes had been made, Musorgsky had several options. With the constraints and liberties of the "scenes-from" opera in mind—which, to repeat, did not require "completeness" in the telling since the story was already known—Musorgsky could either set segments of Pushkin's text essentially unaltered or he could rework, heighten, and compress the text, thereby opening up a dialogue between spoken and musical theater. As we have seen, the initial version follows the first approach and the revised version the second. But both versions, significantly, succeed at restating in a musical setting two basic (and somewhat incompatible) aspects of Pushkin's *Boris:* its "Shakespearism" and its laconicism.[116]

Pushkin's tragedy, we recall, achieved a delicate balance between formal convention (the French pentametric line) and a "mixing of styles." This we interpreted as Pushkin's comment on the necessity of acknowledging, as well as challenging, aesthetic norms. The libretto of *Boris* likewise works stylistic multiplicity against the inevitably stylized conventions of opera. The libretto even intensifies the "Shakespearean" element in Pushkin, increasing the individuation of spoken (or musically declaimed) lines. In the 1820s Pushkin had stunned neoclassical sensibilities by casting the common people in neutral, literary speech; in the 1860s Musorgsky reworked that vocal line into cruder and even more colloquial popular expression. Consider, for example, Pushkin's dialogic exchange among the common people in his scene 3:

"O chom tam plachut?"
"A kak nam znat' . . ."

"What are they crying about over there?"
"How are we to know? . . ."

In their time, such lines were remarkable for their ability to transmit natural conversation within regular meter. No less remarkable, then, is Musorgsky's lowering and coloring of the diction to a level altogether unexpected in grand opera:

"Mitiukh, chevo oryom?"
"Vona! Pochom ia znaiu!"

"Mitiukh, what're we howling about?"
"Huh! The hell if *I* know . . ."

(Bessel, 5/*BG74*, 59)

Even in those extended sections—such as the Inn Scene—set almost verbatim from Pushkin, Musorgsky added expletives, exclamations, and word repetition to reflect more accurately the irregularity and intonational variety of everyday speech.

Musorgsky's "Shakespearism," however, was more than just the mixing of high and (very) low speech. As the Soviet musicologist Ivan Sollertinsky shrewdly noted, "there was something from Shakespeare in Musorgsky's very creative *method*."[117] In the relatively impoverished verbal world of a prose libretto—where real action must occur, yet where there is time for so few words—each word must carry more than its weight and be instantly convertible into palpable images and dramatic action. Whereas Pushkin's drama is enormously dependent upon *talk* (and its social debasements, slander and rumor), Musorgsky's opera—especially in its second version—has little of this radical scepticism toward the word. For Musorgsky, words represent the real; they can reach into the conscience and speak truth. Words cannot conceal identity forever but must inevitably and ultimately reveal it. Musorgsky's creative designs are in fact based on the conviction that every voice "has its own special point of view, its own artistic mark, its aesthetic base," and that these factors are musically realizable.[118]

Thus in Musorgsky, words can, and do, open out into action—and sometimes into very threatening action. A word can literally take on time, space, and flesh, as happens with Boris's hallucinations of Dmitri. Here is a dramatic intensity linked directly with *Hamlet* and *Macbeth*, and quite absent in Pushkin's more restrained, ironic mode.

But Pushkin's restraint is also very present in Musorgsky. This restraint must be measured, of course, not against the norms of spoken drama but against those of performed opera, especially the Meyerbeerian and Wagnerian norms of Musorgsky's era. And the quality cannot be sought in the operatic heroes—who are, perhaps of necessity, larger than life. Restraint comes in the overall musical texture of the opera, its orchestration.[119]

The asceticism and sparseness of Musorgsky's orchestration, even in the 1874 version, was a major factor in Rimsky-Korsakov's decision to overhaul the opera.[120] By the time Rimsky undertook his revision in the 1890s, he had become a thoroughly professional musician: conservatory professor, bandmaster of the Imperial Navy, master of the bright, vigorous sound that promised a reliable product under all conditions and therefore tolerated a certain redundancy and overlap. Musorgsky's often thin, discordant, hollow sound could not have impressed Rimsky as reliable; even with all musicians singing and playing their hardest, there was no guarantee of dramatic climax. It is likely that Musorgsky saw "professionalism," by its very reliability, as tending toward the mechanical; to this Musorgsky seemed to oppose the ideal amateur, who had to listen, strain, commit everything, and stun the listener with unexpected results.[121] Thus Musorgsky's goal, one might say, was an outgrowth of his peculiar understanding of the honesty of amateur art: minimal orchestration, maximal expectations.[122]

With this minimalism in mind, how much Asafiev's description of Musorgsky's dominant musical texture recalls Pushkin:

> Laconicism and a precision of intonation in the dialogues, against a background of measured regularity and steadiness in tempi and rhythm—here speaks the fine sense of the opera dramatist, as opposed to those cantata-like or oratorio-like elements so frequent in Glinka and Borodin . . . .[123]

What Pushkin and Musorgsky share is a general commitment to an economy—and even an asceticism—of means. This economy shows up in different ways, of course, against the different generic norms of the tradition in which each artist worked. Such a combination, of an exuberant mixed style with an overall restraint of means, links the opera with the drama in a way not immediately clear from the libretto alone.

The balance of this chapter is devoted to those three portions of the Boris Tale which have organized our discussion in the earlier chapters: Boris's monologues, the image of Pimen, and the ending scene. Although Musorgsky's two versions differ substantially in these scenes, certain general features calibrate the distance of both libretti from their dramatic source.

First, where Pushkin is careful to emphasize the separate and episodic nature of his scenes (forever provoking interest in characters

who then never reappear), Musorgsky in his revised version just as
deliberately forges links within and between scenes—through recurring characters, themes, and events. In the 1874 opera, Varlaam
appears first in the Inn and then again in the final scene, inciting a
mob of tramps against Boris on behalf of the resurrected Tsarevich
Dmitri.[124] Pimen not only controls his own scene in Chudovo Monastery but also (to be sure, for reasons more political than literary) takes
over the role of Pushkin's Patriarch. The holy fool, too, has multiple
appearances: in the revised version he appears twice in the final scene
to lament the fate of Russia.

In addition to the linkage provided by recurring characters,
Musorgsky binds the whole together through the crime at Uglich. But
the binding process is different in the two versions. In his initial
version Musorgsky makes generous use of identifying motifs, the
most prominent of which belongs to Dmitri. Originally, in fact, the
idea of Dmitri commanded two themes, one for Grigory in Pimen's
cell and another for the murdered tsarevich. When Grigory "becomes" Dmitri, the murdered tsarevich theme begins to dominate and
proliferate. It is heard whenever the Pretender appears, or dreams of
power, or whenever Boris remembers Uglich. This theme is variously
orchestrated and framed. When first heard during Pimen's monologue, it is bright, lyrical, songlike—the hope of a miracle. It then
becomes the Pretender's theme, self-confident and majestic. When
sung by Shuisky to Boris, the theme becomes agitated and threatening. Some critics have suggested, after tracing various incarnations of
the theme, that the murdered tsarevich motif does not belong personally to anyone; it represents not an event but an *attitude* toward an
event.[125] Thus from the start Musorgsky musically embodied
Kireevsky's thesis that the unifying idea of Pushkin's drama is the
murder at Uglich.

One of the major differences, however, between drama and
opera—and, more subtly, between the two versions of the opera—is
the degree to which Musorgsky's Boris believes in the fatal centrality
of this guilt to his life and his rule. In the revised version Boris is
raised to tragic stature and transformed into a thoroughly pathetic
figure.[126] His internal torment is so great that it erases distinctions
between past and present, public and private. His hallucinations come
to him in the Duma chamber as well as alone; his very first words in
the opera, purporting to celebrate a coronation in a formal public
setting, are "My soul grieves." Boris literally does not know what time
and space he is in, and this peculiar dazed chronotope is his special
marker.

The almost solipsistic centrality of Boris in the second version is
given additional weight, as Richard Taruskin points out, by Mus-

orgsky's new and much more restrained use of the musical motif. Boris's own motives are reduced. Dmitri's theme, however, is expanded, while at the same time limited in its scope. In the minds of all characters but one it refers exclusively to the Pretender, to the *False Dmitri*. That one exception is Tsar Boris himself: when he sings (or thinks, or hears) the motif, it means Uglich. The tsar is, as it were, drained of his own identifying motif and literally filled with Dmitri's, now signifying for him alone both the slain and the resurrected tsarevich.[127] And thus there is forged musical, as well as psychological, proof of Boris's disintegration and death through guilt—a guilt that other and more sober characters in the opera might have dismissed had the tsar been more in control of it.

Even when Boris gazes at his own son he recalls Uglich. This, surely, is the logic behind Musorgsky's consistent infantilization of both Fyodor and Dmitri. The boys are portrayed or referred to as "little children," infants scarcely out of the cradle who prattle and play with toys.[128] Their innocence and purity make all the more terrible the fact of Boris's guilt, and the repetition of Dmitri's fate in young Fyodor underscores the timelessness of Boris's world.

The tsar's guilt introduces a final area where Musorgsky reinterprets Pushkin in a major way: the interaction between tsar and people.

The Narod *as Operatic Hero*

We have seen how the opening and closing "people's scenes" in Pushkin's play gave rise to the idea of the *narod* as hero. This notion has been applied with even more fervor to the second version of the opera—which also opens and closes on the people, and whose author was considerably more populist in temperament than Pushkin. "I imagine the people as a great personality, animated by a unified idea," Musorgsky wrote as a dedication on the title page of *Boris* in January 1874. "This is my task. I have tried to resolve it in opera."[129] Whereas Pushkin's *narod* were select voices from the crowd, Musorgsky scored for large groups: in the opening scenes ragged masses are herded together in support of Boris, and at the end the masses are already in open revolt. That final scene, Kromy Forest, will receive its own discussion below. Here we will touch upon two general areas in the 1874 libretto where the operatic *narod* differs from its dramatic counterpart: in its presence as *chorus,* and in its power over the mind of Tsar Boris.

Musorgsky employed a variety of choral writing techniques in his revised *Boris.* They range from solo scenes with sonic choral backdrop to scenes where the people are themselves the prime movers of action, either in compact ensemble choruses or in "dialogue" choruses based, as is melodic recitative, on natural speech intonations.[130] The type of choral setting chosen can be seen to reflect, or ironically refract, the degree of cohesion and historical effectiveness of the people. In the cynical opening scenes, for example, "speech sketches" of individual personalities dominate; in the more enthusiastic (although also more deluded) choruses of Kromy, unison settings imply some sense of collective purpose.[131]

Here we must note an important qualification. Musorgsky was committed to portraying the folk collective, but this was, at all important moments, a *differentiated* collective. The goal, in Asafiev's words, was not so much a "chorus of the people" *(khor naroda)* as it was "the people as a living person" *(khor—zhivoe litso),* a *multi*voiced entity.[132] This was surely one of the reasons why Musorgsky provided such lengthy stage directions before his *narod* scenes, designating which groups were whispering, which scratching the backs of their heads or wandering listlessly across the stage.

Masses on the Russian operatic stage were not new. Mikhail Glinka had provided a large onstage role for the *narod* in his *Life for the Tsar* (also based on events from the Time of Troubles) back in 1836. But Glinka's crowd scenes in that opera function as the traditional antiphon chorus, a sort of vocal backdrop that glorifies the heroes and literally repeats their words.[133] Musorgsky's choral writing deliberately opposes itself to this echoing practice. The choruses in both versions of *Boris* are parodic, individualized, and double-voiced. The people quarrel, beg, torture, and sing constantly (and indifferently) of violence; rather than reinforce the heroes or the solo parts, the people as chorus routinely distort, threaten, and ridicule the leading roles.[134] Musorgsky's crowds are much more abused, and much more cynically aggressive, than anything in Glinka—or, for that matter, in Pushkin. The first scene of the prologue of *Boris* opens on a police officer (absent in Pushkin) threatening the people down to their knees with a cudgel. Those *Slava* (Glory!) choruses are all extracted under the whip.

In fact a peculiar feature of the libretto is the extraordinary amount of violence, both discussed and mimed, whenever choruses sing. This is true not only of the final "revolutionary" scene, where the boyar Khrushchov is bound, baited, "mated" to a hundred-year-old crone and then prepared for hanging, all to a mock *slava* chorus; it is characteristic of most choruses in the opera, even in reasonably civilized settings. The Boyar Duma, for example, opens Act IV, scene 1, quarreling about the fate of the Pretender. The second bassos want to execute, then hang the body so that ravens can peck at the corpse; the first bassos want to burn the body and thrice curse the ashes; the tenors recommend scattering the ashes to the winds *(BG74,* 99–100). In Act III, 2, the Polish chorus circles the fountain in all its finery while singing about smashing Boris.[135] This latent or explicit violence is present in most group voices, and it is especially strong when the organizing principle of the chorus is political: electing a tsar, fighting the enemy, dealing with *this* world. But there is another type of chorus in the libretto, completely absent in Pushkin. This is a heavenly chorus, and we first hear it in the opening scene.

Editorial cuts, authorial reconsiderations, and possible censorship pressure have blurred the outlines of this initial choral scene. The fullest version is to be found in the 1869 manuscript; in the revised 1874 version Musorgsky himself omitted the final episodes and Rimsky confirmed this cut in his definitive editions.[136] But it is instructive in this instance to consider the fullest version of the people's initial appearance, for here is a complex portrait still quite close to Pushkin's cynical handling of the *narod.* The scene opens on a crowd that is in equal parts obedient, resentful, and indifferent. It is coerced into glorifying Boris. Mitiukh, a voice from the crowd, does not even know what the shouting is about until a group of peasants tell him that "we want to place a Tsar over Russia." At the end of the scene Mitiukh, and others, are still in the dark—for chorus scenes in the 1869 opera are opportunities not for confirmation but for dissension and further confusion. "Go meet the Tsar with icons," a portion of the crowd prompts Mitiukh. "Tsar, what Tsar?" another portion asks faintly. "What do you mean, *what* Tsar?" the other group retorts; "Boris . . ." At that point the police officer reappears. "You herd of sheep," he shouts, "turn up tomorrow in the Kremlin." "It's all the same to us," the people mutter, as they drift away. "If they order us to howl, we'll howl in the Kremlin too . . ."[137]

This powerful ending to the scene—the image of Mitiukh's dull confusion and the total indifference of the populace—exists in the 1869 manuscript only. The published libretto and score of 1873–74 end on the preceding episode, the arrival of a chorus of crippled *bozh'i liudi* (God's folk or pilgrims), who sing of Russia's suffering, the coming of a time of darkness, and eventual deliverance (Bessel, 8/*BG74,* 61–62). Hearing them, the people sink to their knees—this time of their own accord. This otherworldly reverence will intrude at other, similarly politicized moments in the second version of the opera: the monks' chorus that accompanies Grigory's cursing of Tsar Boris, and the monks who move slowly onstage for Boris's tonsure and death. In the form of a holy fool the same prophetic voice will supplant the torture of the boyar in the closing scene. This overlap-

ping of government violence with orthodox piety is subtle and ambivalent—much as it is in Pushkin, with his ambiguous Pimen and his
matter-of-fact Patriarch.

In the fullest version of this opening scene, then, a police officer
and two forced political acts frame the heavenly chorus. And frame is
precisely the point. Mitiukh, the voice from the crowd, does not know
why the police are forcing people to their knees, and likewise does not
know what the pilgrims are singing about—or why. At the end of the
scene the crowd tests him and he cannot remember, except for something about the Donskoy and Vladimirskoy icons. "That's bad,
brother," a part of the crowd murmurs. But it is Mitiukh whom we
remember as an embodiment of the people's voice. He understands
neither government violence nor religious processions, and appears
indifferent to both.

This is indeed a complex picture of the people, who are shown as
instinctively able to shift from a political to a pious register but who
ultimately parody both. The contrasts set up in the 1869 opening
scene will be echoed, as we shall see, in the 1874 final scene at Kromy,
where the people move from random carnivalized violence to parody
of another church—this time the Catholic. In his people's choruses
Musorgsky goes beyond both Karamzin and Pushkin, amplifying
through music all that is anarchic, servile, and incongruous in his two
source texts. And yet this morally ambiguous, multivoiced crowd does
retain some of the functions of the ancient Greek chorus. It comments on the sins of the heroes and passes its own sort of twisted,
limited judgment. This judgment is all the more terrible because—as
in Pushkin—it is *historical;* here, too, the people have no transcendent
perspective or point of view.

Commenting on the American premiere of *Boris Godunov* in 1913
(which was, of course, the revised opera in a Rimsky redaction), one
contemporary critic sympathized with the plight of the opera's first
audiences:

> To them it had much strangeness of style, a style which was not easily
> reconciled to anything with which the modern stage had made them
> familiar. They saw and heard the chorus enter into action, not for the
> purpose of spectacular pageantry, nor as hymners of the achievements of
> the principal actors in the story, but as participants.[138]

The chorus in Musorgsky's opera does not merely witness. It is as
implicated, and as compromised, as any of the solo roles. How this
sort of *narod* can nevertheless achieve a sort of heroic status will be the
burden of our discussion of the Kromy Scene.

The popular chorus is one area where the operatic *narod* breaks new ground in the Boris Tale. Equally significant is the image of the *narod* that reigns in the mind of the opera's hero, Tsar Boris. Here, not surprisingly, the 1874 version is the more instructive. The musical motif of the laughing crowd in the Pretender's nightmare literally grows into the theme of Boris's hallucination.[139] Gone from the revised opera are the hostility and self-righteous irritation toward the people that had so marked Pushkin's tsar. Musorgsky's Boris is guilty before the people literally from his first word. And here we see clearly the spirit of Musorgsky's time, its determination to portray the people realistically while at the same time romanticizing the guilt of the landowning classes.

The 1860s demanded moral seriousness from its art, and especially from historical drama. An edict prohibiting the depiction of the Romanov dynasty on stage worked to direct playwrights to the Time of Troubles, and several gifted writers—Lev Mey, Nikolai Ostrovsky, Aleksei K. Tolstoy—produced plays on this period. The *Smuta*, along with the Petrine reforms, became a touchstone for the discussion of contemporary issues.[140] The year of the *Boris* premiere, 1874, was also the year of the *khozhdenie v narod*, the "Going to the People" movement that began so idealistically and ended in such disillusionment. In a sense, the guilty Boris was the biggest and most colorful repentant nobleman of the post-Emancipation years. But to understand Boris's role in this "romanticized realism"[141] of the period, we must look at his three major monologues.

Tsar Boris's Great Monologues: The Return to Karamzin

The operatic image of Boris depends, of course, upon which version of the opera is analyzed. In our discussion we will favor the revised version—which exemplifies Musorgsky the librettist in his most active mode, and the opera in its most mature form.

The primary change Musorgsky works on Pushkin is to lift Boris *out* of dialogue.[142] Whereas Pushkin's tsar is earnestly negotiating, maneuvering in changing political situations, Musorgsky's Boris is isolated and self-absorbed. To be sure, he does address others—his son, his daughter, Shuisky. But he does not so much speak to them as allow them to eavesdrop on him. He stage-whispers, not to the audience but to the other characters. Others rarely tell him anything new, and even "news"—such as the appearance of a pretender in Poland—merely reminds him of what he already knows. Thus the core of his role is contained in a chain of declamatory monologues, in which the addressee is not any single living person but rather the awful event at Uglich. Even with others, the operatic Boris is essentially alone.

Consider the Coronation monologue, Boris's first appearance (prologue, scene 2). Pushkin's tsar, we recall, addresses the Patriarch, the boyars, his predecessor, Tsar Fyodor, and then ends with an invitation "to all, from grand noble to blind beggar" to attend his coronation feast. This is the very image of the iconic tsar, at the one moment in the play when he most coincides with his office. Musorgsky, who by the time of his revision understood and valued pageantry, used much of Pushkin's material—condensing somewhat, adjusting for rhythmic reasons, but presenting basically the same Boris with many identical lines.[143] Two changes, however, are significant.

Pushkin's Boris opens the monologue (scene 4) with a straightforward address to his audience:

> You, Father Patriarch, and all of you boyars,
> My soul is bared before you . . .

This baring of the soul is a mere rhetorical device, however. It is appropriate to a formal public display of consolidated power—and is perceived, in the play, against the background of those sly courtiers and slandermongers of the opening scene, Shuisky and Vorotynsky. Whatever "confessions" come our way in the first half of Pushkin's drama, we can be sure that Boris is in control of them. And indeed, what the newly crowned tsar "lays bare" before his people are his piety, his sense of duty, and his generosity—even maneuvering his rhetoric so that the two times he utters that dangerous word "power" (*vlast'*, lines 3 and 12), it falls on an unaccented beat surrounded by sentiments of humility and sanctitude.

Musorgsky's Boris, on the contrary, opens directly with a confession of bad conscience. His speech is cast in a diction that no one present at a coronation should hear:

> My soul grieves!
> Some involuntary terror
> Has fettered my heart
> With evil foreboding.

(Bessel, 10/BG74, 65)

In Pushkin, Boris ritualistically humbles himself before the dynasty he had superseded: "mighty Ioann," and then his brother-in-law Fyodor, the "Angel-Tsar." In the opera, however, these predecessors are omitted. "Evil foreboding" leads directly into Pushkin's line 8:

O righteous one! O my powerful father!
Look down from heaven on the tears of your faithful servants . . .

"Father," in Pushkin's context, refers to the Angel-Tsar Fyodor; in Musorgsky's context it clearly suggests God. Pushkin's Boris lives in a historical chronotope, Musorgsky's in a timeless one; his lines are spoken within history but outside it. The operatic Boris—as is clear from his first uttered lines—is not addressing his contemporaries, and not even the immediate past of his regal forebears. He is addressing his own conscience and divine judgment against it, and thus he hastens to connect the responsibilities of his new office with his guilt.

The second difference between Pushkin's and Musorgsky's treatment of this scene concerns the placement of the monologue within it. Pushkin's Coronation monologue follows the double-voiced machinations of both Shuisky and the *narod*—thus preparing us, to a certain extent, for the smooth, well-modulated image of the tsar that then emerges. We are set up to expect a crafty and triumphant politician on the throne. In the opera Boris's first monologue is wedged between two enforced *slava* choruses. But the threat of the knout and the indifference of the people do not diminish the grandeur or pathos of the operatic Boris. Rather the contrary is true: Boris plays, in scene 2 of the prologue, the role that the *bozh'i liudi* or God's folk played in scene 1: a pious interlude between two manipulated cheering sessions. And just as we took the chorus of crippled pilgrims seriously in relation to its frame, so here Boris sounds an immediate and genuinely suffering note.

In both drama and libretto, this first regal address ends on lines inviting the public to a feast. But where Pushkin's tsar begins and ends a public figure, Musorgsky's tsar is first presented to us from the inside. In 1598 he is already grieving, as it were, in 1604 terms. Because his chronotope is essentially timeless, his actions at particular historical moments are bound to appear anachronistic.

The second and most celebrated Boris monologue in Pushkin, "Dostig ia vysshei vlasti" (I have attained the highest power), becomes the most famous of Boris's arias in the opera. But the fame accrues to very different texts. Pushkin's monologue, we recall, is remarkable for the extent to which its speaker does *not* sound like a tsar: Boris speaks about young love, about his personal unhappiness, about grudges against the mob, and only at the end does he mention his trouble with that single stain on his conscience. Here the operatic equivalent is worth considering in both its 1869 and 1874 versions, for this particular scene in Act II was almost entirely recomposed, words as well as music. Both versions alter Pushkin—one slightly, the other greatly—but in opposite directions.[144] Thus one can trace, in the process of the revision, Musorgsky's emerging conceptualization of the tsar's timeless and tragic stance.

Following Pushkin, the 1869 Boris recriminates bitterly against the people and their ingratitude. But the final lines of the monologue depart from Pushkin to suggest the image of a slandered, perhaps even an innocent, tsar. Instead of an immediate transition from that list of falsely attributed murders (of Tsar Fyodor, of Irina) to the "single stain" on his conscience, the operatic Boris in this first redaction sings:

> Whoever dies, I am the secret murderer:
> I poisoned my sister the Tsaritsa,
> I hastened Fyodor's end.
> I [did away with] that unfortunate child,
>   the young tsarevich . . .

The line about the tsarevich is not Pushkin's but Musorgsky's; through it, the death of Dmitri of Uglich is entered in the same plane of rumor as the other absurd slander circulating at court.

All the irritation that Pushkin had written into the monologue is present here in full force, and fully justified. But the libretto, as we see, goes even further than Pushkin's text in equivocating on the question of actual guilt. That the operatic Boris *feels* guilty cannot be doubted—and even presumed guilt can give rise to hallucinations, which plague both the initial and revised Boris.[145] But is he indeed responsible, did the event really occur at his command? Or does Boris feel guilty, rather, because he entertained the thought of murder, or because others blamed him for it? The issue of actual historical guilt is even more problematic at this point in the initial libretto than it is in the play. Musorgsky, unlike Pushkin, was writing in the Age of Dostoevsky.

Thus the image of Boris in the initial version is a complex structure. All scenes in the opera but one deal directly with Boris's crime, and five out of the seven scenes feature the tsar himself on stage. But the actual deed underlying the guilt is softened, dispersed, equated with rumor—very much in Pushkin's spirit. As we noted above, the music of the opera contains no single murder motif per se, only variations on the Dmitri theme that reflect multiple opinions about the murder. Through ingenious manipulation of Dmitri's signature motif, we "hear" the crime first from others' points of view and then from inside Boris's own soul—in what Richard Taruskin has called the "magnificent ambiguity . . . of a musical psychologist of genius."[146]

The 1874 version of the monologue retains the centrality of the guilt but expresses it in a more externalized and unambivalent way.

The key to the shift is contained in the first adjustment Musorgsky makes in Pushkin's text—an adjustment, to be sure, that was also present in the 1869 text but whose potential was not there developed. The word *izmuchennoi* (tormented) is inserted into Pushkin's third line:

> I have attained the highest power;
> For six years now, I've reigned in peace.
> But there's no happiness for my tormented soul.

In Russian the addition functions as a "prosifier" of the sort frequently met in slightly adjusted lines of the libretto.[147] But it is also a cue that this is the same thoroughly guilty Boris of the Coronation monologue, unchanged after six years in power. Unlike Pushkin's Boris—who recalls the crime and then angrily resolves to ignore its consequences—Musorgsky's Boris is from one monologue to the next a man of intimidating continuity. In his revised version Musorgsky omits the entire midportion of the monologue (where Boris complains about the ingratitude of the mob) and replaces it with text of his own. This new text is less narrative than impressionistic. A perfunctory mention of personal unhappiness and his daughter's widowhood opens directly into a catalogue of horrors for the guilty:

> How heavy is the hand of the threatening judge,
> How terrible the sentence over a criminal soul . . .
> All around, only darkness and impenetrable gloom!
> If only there were a ray of comfort . . .
> My heart is filled with sorrow,
> My weary spirit grieves and languishes.

> (Bessel, 31/*BG*74, 82)

In Pushkin, we remember, the *narod* are presented as ungrateful tormentors of a maligned tsar—and the audience, therefore, is always aware that Tsar Boris is telling the story *his* way. In the Musorgsky of version II, the word is not placed under such suspicion. When the operatic Boris confesses, he does so in short nonnarrative outbursts straight from the heart. As the monologue continues, the *narod* moves to the status of victim—and Boris, because he acknowledges their new status and laments their suffering, is sympathetically granted the status of victim as well.

> I, the ruler of Rus,
> Begged for tears of consolation . . .
> And then, denunciations:
> A boyars' plot, intrigue in Lithuania,
> Secret machinations.

Famine, plague, fear, devastation,
As if an enraged beast were ransacking
A plague-infested people, and
Poor, hungry Russia groans . . .
And the people name me the cause of all these evil things,
And on the public squares they curse the name Boris.

In the revised version, then, Boris's relationship to the *narod* takes on an entirely different tone. Musorgsky transforms the bitter cynicism of Pushkin's tsar into a *Seelendrama* where both tsar and people trace national tragedy back to its source in Boris's bad conscience. This is, we recall, the very move that Karamzin makes in those chapters of the *History* which follow Boris's death, where Russia's coming tragedy is repeatedly linked with the "ruins of Uglich" howling to heaven for vengeance. The second version of the opera restores Karamzin's sense of Divine Providence to Pushkin's text. And Musorgsky creates for the libretto a truly static Karamzinian hero—with the difference, of course, that this new Boris combines in a single body both guilty narrated object and stern narrative voice, and can thus know why and how his story must end. After his "Dostig" monologue—and arguably even after his Coronation monologue—Boris has nothing to learn from any outside source. From now on, external events will not shape him for the future but only remind him of his past self. For this static conception of character, the monologue-arioso is the perfect vehicle, a "prism of the thoughts and feelings of the tsar."[148]

Musorgsky somewhat distances and estranges this image of the tsar—the better, perhaps, to foreground its conventionality and thus reaffirm the realist aesthetic governing other aspects of the opera. Quite possibly the inserted songs in Act II, those pointedly frivolous ditties with the tsarevich and the domestics, work toward this end. "I concocted the words for this [criminal] arioso myself," Musorgsky wrote Stasov of his revised second act. "It is somewhat disgusting and tiresome to see and hear the grinding of the criminal's teeth, so, after *this*, a little mob of nursemaids bursts in, howling and wailing . . . ."[149] The audience is diverted by these antics—but Tsar Boris never is. He cannot really hear them. And in this lies the significance of the overtly comical and high-spirited frame for that most devastating confession; the horror of the people's fate becomes all the more grim for the childish prattle that attempts to interrupt it.

The hallucination scene that closes down the revised Act II gives us one more clue to the new status of the *narod* in the opera. At Boris's request Shuisky has just retold the Uglich story, which is to confirm the death of the tsarevich and thus the fraudulence of the Pretender. But since Tsar Boris lives in a present that serves only one purpose—to restimulate his past—this retelling brings no consolation, as that consummate psychologist Shuisky was quite certain it would not. Instead, the story triggers the actual physical "return" of the bloody child. In his horror Boris wails:

> Chur, chur ditia!
> Narod . . . Ne ia!
> Volia naroda . . .
>
> Back, back, child!
> It was the people, not I!
> The will of the people!

(Bessel, 38/BG74, 88)

In the context of the "Dostig" monologue earlier in the same scene, the people have now become both victim and ultimate court of absolvement.

With the exception of one small abridgement, initial and revised versions of Boris's death monologue are the same. Musorgsky preserves only thirteen words from Pushkin's text. This is no surprise, because the contexts of the death in drama and opera are so different. Where the dramatic Boris dies suddenly and for no apparent reason—thus reinforcing the radical critique of causality that underlies the entire play—the operatic death is much more traditionally motivated. As we shall presently see, it is Pimen who delivers the Uglich story that sends Boris to his spectacular onstage death. The move that Shuisky had so slyly calculated to bring on the tsar's hallucination in Act II (a retelling of Uglich) is repeated in Act IV, to even greater—which is to say, to fatal—effect. The Death Scene itself will be discussed in connection with Pimen, but here one aspect of the deathside monologue should be noted.

By the time of his final scene the tsar has developed two types of dialogue.[150] The first governs conversations with himself (the hallucinations) and is almost always cast in irregular, prosified speech. The second applies when Boris addresses others: Shuisky or Pimen. Then he switches to a slower, more metrically versified musical line. Prose, it is clear, indicates a willingness to embrace guilt and tell the truth; verse rhythms, on the contrary, signify that Boris is still trying to play a role, to "recite" the lines of someone he has no right to be. And significantly, after his collapse, Boris's first words to Fyodor are uttered in a conversational prose recitative. The final lines before death alternate between a verselike (*stikhotvorcheskaia*) and a proselike (*prozaizirovannaia*) setting, as the tsar tries to maintain the dignity of his office while at the same time confronting the truth of his illegitimacy. His collapse into prose at the final moment is complete:

I'm still Tsar! . . .
I'm still Tsar! . . .
Oh God! Death!
Forgive me . . .

(Bessel, 60/*BG74*, 106)

For Musorgsky, it is the ordinary that purifies—and so, ironically, as Boris descends to prose his status is elevated in the opera. Pushkin's Boris, we recall, approached death with increasing lyricism. This could well have been the poet's own double-edged comment on the seductions, both sublime and disabling, of the lyric. Musorgsky's Boris, self-critical and more suspicious, dies in possession of more truth. Dying, the operatic Boris understands the gravity of his legacy and the fact that his death alone will not redeem anything; it is merely the prelude to more death. Several years later Musorgsky was to bring this same utterly unsentimental understanding of mortality to the final song in his cycle "The Songs and Dances of Death." There Death, mounted on a white steed under the moonlight, surveys the battlefield and promises the dying of both sides that they will be totally forgotten—and that he, Death, will so thoroughly trample their bones into the damp earth that they will never be raised.[151]

The operatic Boris has no illusions, in short, and insists on his regal responsibilities to the last. Not for him are the cramped spaces of romantic tragedy, where authority drains away and disastrous advice goes unchallenged. The operatic Boris trusts nobody. "Listen, Fyodor," he sings. "Don't believe the promises of the scheming boyars, be alert to their secret relations with Lithuania, punish treason mercilessly, punish without charity, attend strictly to the people's judgment, for that alone is not hypocritical."[152] He dies every inch the alert, obsessed, prose-wise tsar.

This final gesture, linking the wisdom of a strong, merciless, and yet guilt-ridden tsar with the voice of the people, conforms well to both statist and populist ideologies of Musorgsky's time. It profoundly distinguishes his libretto from Pushkin's text.

But an even more abrupt departure from Pushkin takes place, as we have seen, in the character of the tsar in the revised version of the opera. We suggested in chapter 1 that Pushkin's *Boris* is a "realistic hero trapped in a sentimental plot." He is a man of hard work and bad luck, whose most dramatic acts are to wipe the sweat off his brow and gesture loudly by gasping for air. With the fate of a tragic hero but none of the significance, Boris lives out that fate with no heroics at all. He is forced to bear the burden of his traditional guilt without the traditional means to release it—means of the sort that Karamzin provided so eloquently in his providential history and Musorgsky was to provide through music. Because Pushkin's tsar is always "seen from

the side, through the eyes of those present,"[153] the audience gets to
know him as the characters on stage do. Boris remains a riddle—and
as the play develops, so does he.

The operatic Boris of the revised version is constructed differently. He has ample, perhaps too ample, opportunity to discharge
his guilt, and his guilt is all he knows—from his first *skorbit dusha* (my
soul grieves) to his final *prostite* (forgive). He accepts suffering for
Uglich, and for national calamity as well. He is, in fact, willing to
assume *every* responsibility—and yet this obsession, paradoxically, prevents him from being simply responsive. Answerable to eternity, he
cannot answer in the present. He is literally "locked into a system of
monologic utterances, . . . lifted above everything that surrounds
him."[154]

This operatic equivalent to Karamzin's Boris cannot recombine
or reevaluate his past in the light of his present; he cannot develop at
all. For Karamzin and ultimately for Musorgsky, characters and events
serve to *reveal,* but not to change or to create anew, the potential of
Boris's inner self. The character most active in this revelation of the
operatic tsar's closed personality is the chronicler Pimen.

Pimen

Pushkin's chronicler creates people. The monologues of Pushkin's
Pimen—and especially the story of Uglich—literally give Grigory an
identity, and Pimen's mode of appropriating stories becomes a model
in the play for all the self-serving stories that follow. Less complex, less
self-conscious as a narrator, Musorgsky's Pimen nevertheless plays an
equally crafty role, and among the stories he appropriates in the
opera is Pushkin's story of him. Two major differences between the
dramatic and the operatic Pimen must be noted at the outset.

The first concerns Uglich. The initial 1869 libretto reproduces
the Monastery Scene essentially without change, and Pimen's account
of the Uglich murder remains intact with a few additions, inversions,
and prosifiers.[155] The death of the tsarevich occupies eighty-four bars
of music at the end of an already very lengthy melodic recitative.
When this version of the opera was returned to Musorgsky for revision, among the changes he effected was (in the composer's own
words) "a shortening of Pimen," possibly as part of his refinement and
curtailment of the Dmitri motif.[156] In the 1874 version of this scene,
events of Uglich are reduced to a single mention in an exchange of
eight bars. Musorgsky transferred details of the Uglich murder to
Shuisky, who thus delivers a considerably longer and enriched eyewitness account of the event to Tsar Boris in Act II.

To complicate matters further, the 1874 premiere of the opera—

and subsequent performances in the 1870s—omitted the Monastery Scene altogether. Not until 1879 did the public first hear the scene, and even then only as an isolated entry in a concert setting. Not surprisingly the scene was unfavorably received, compared by one humorless reviewer to an "emaciated and slightly rotten oyster, on which a few drops of lemon juice have been sprinkled . . . to make it easier to swallow."[157]

In a curious inversion, then, the opera reverses the impression produced by Pushkin's text. *His* Monastery Scene first appeared as a separate excerpt in 1827, four years before the play as a whole was cleared for publication. Thus anticipating in print its larger context, Pushkin's Pimen rapidly became an object of interest and the center of polemics. The operatic counterpart of the scene, however, lagged behind its larger whole by as many years as Pushkin's scene had preceded it. Few critics of the opera saw the Monastery Scene as central, and one who did comment on it, Cesar Cui, remarked that "it was a very good thing this long and boring scene was omitted" from the opera's premiere performances.[158] The scene was never performed in its proper operatic sequence during Musorgsky's lifetime. As a result, the interaction between Pimen and Grigory either appeared dispensable to its earliest audiences or was not noticed at all.

The excision of Uglich from the score, and the Monastery Scene from performance, was probably not due to censorship pressure. Pushkin's text on the same scene had been approved for the stage back in 1866. But censorship considerations did indeed prompt the second adjustment in Pimen's role. Long-standing prohibitions against the representation of ecclesiastics on the dramatic stage obliged Musorgsky to label Pimen a hermit (*otshel'nik*) rather than a monk, and to eliminate altogether the part of the Patriarch—who could not be thus disguised. The Patriarch's account (in Pushkin's scene 15) of a miracle at Dmitri's graveside was, however, still central to Musorgsky's design, in both initial and revised versions. That story was to motivate the death of Boris, fuse Pushkin's scenes 15 ("Tsarskaia duma") and 20 ("Tsarskie palaty"), and remove the casual, inexplicable element in the tsar's sudden collapse. Musorgsky's solution in the opera was to give the Patriarch's crucial monologue to Pimen.

The Death Scene in the opera (Act IV, i, *BG74*, 99–106) exemplifies well Musorgsky's externalization and enfleshment of the word. It opens on boyars debating various means of death by torture for the Pretender. Shuisky enters, and to an undercurrent of dissatisfaction at his treacherous ways (here as elsewhere, choruses undermine soloists) he recounts how he has glimpsed through a crack in the door the tsar himself gripped by hallucination. No one believes Shuisky until the actual appearance of the tsar in delirium interrupts Shuisky's description. The tsar repeats the very words that Shuisky had cited ("Chur! Chur!" / Away! Away!). In a marvelous reversal of Pushkin—for whom the more times a story is told, the *less* likely it is to be true—the cited word in the opera calls up and verifies the authenticity of its source, literally becomes reality.

The presence of the boyars brings the tsar to himself. Before he can convene a session of the Duma, however, Shuisky—that master storyteller and coordinator of others' stories—begs to present a "humble hermit" who will tell a tale confirming the tsarevich Dmitri's death. Pimen's reappearance in the tsar's chambers creates the only direct link between the Grigory-Dmitri scenes and the Boris scenes, a link quite absent in Pushkin. This second tale of Pimen's—originally the Patriarch's—consists almost entirely of a single embedded story, that of a blind shepherd who miraculously regains his sight at Dmitri's grave. Musorgsky compresses Pushkin's text somewhat but otherwise sets the story almost without change.

In the drama, we recall, Boris is so distressed by the Patriarch's story that Shuisky must step in and close the scene. But then the dramatic Boris rallies; his ability to rally is in fact one of his determining "open" characteristics in the play. Five scenes later he is bargaining toughly with Basmanov, mere minutes before his fatal and totally unexpected collapse. He exits, and suddenly we hear from some anonymous boyars that the tsar has fallen from his throne and is bleeding from the mouth and ears. The tsar is carried in, and then takes leave of his son. The dynamics of this scene underscore the privileging of offstage space and unnamed messengers that marks Pushkin's reluctance to assign visible cause to historical events.

In Karamzin, we should note, the death of Boris is also mysterious and "offstage" (XI, 107–109). But in the providential framework of the *History*, absence of historical cause merely offers an opportunity for the author to supply moral or psychological cause—and Karamzin indeed supplies it. It is this Karamzinian context that Musorgsky fleshes out as dramatic event in the opera: offstage death becomes center-stage action, with no ambivalence about cause at all.

Boris is seated on his throne as Pimen enters. Exactly as Shuisky hopes, reassurance from Pimen on the matter of Uglich is no reassurance at all, but rather a prelude to death. It reminds Boris that his position is hopeless: he is a murderer if Dmitri is dead, a usurper if Dmitri is alive. In a significant stage direction, the old chronicler, upon entering the royal chambers, "looks intently at Boris" (Bessel, 57/*BG74*, 103). The "anonymous labor" of his chronicle, that denunciation of Boris which some monk was supposed to dust off many years hence, is now about to take on flesh and become a very real confrontation. Pimen no longer records history; like his erstwhile disciple Grigory, he too is now *making* it.

Eighteen bars after the point in Pimen's narrative where the blind shepherd hears the angel's voice in his dream ("I am Dmitri the Tsarevich!") Boris gasps for air and tumbles unconscious from his throne. Thus does Musorgsky create a psychological, onstage equivalent to the blood—in truth Dmitri's blood—that "poured from the nose and throat" of both Karamzin's and Pushkin's Boris in their final hour. The tsar revives only long enough to call for tonsure and for his son.

Musorgsky's Pimen, like Pushkin's, is a highly polemical and dangerous character. His skillful manipulation of miracles triggers both the Pretender's rise and Boris's death. But the function of miracles in the opera and in the play could not be more different. In Pushkin, Pimen embroiders his Uglich Tale with a trembling corpse and Grigory, inspired by the creative possibilities of storytelling, goes forth into the world and creates a miracle. Miracles are possible because stories lie—or at least are always provisional—and words can cover up or create new truth.

The operatic Pimen, in contrast, tells miracles that *reveal* the truth. The right word can undo a tsar, catch the conscience of a king. A sinister detail in the final death scene, deliberately masked in one of those "heavenly choruses," verifies Pimen's eternal truth. When Boris calls for tonsure, a choir of monks (here called *pevchie*, choristers) enters and sings a hymn reminiscent of the monks' chorus in the Monastery Scene (*BG*74, 105–106). But *what* they sing is no longer a formulaic background prayer. The words—more intelligible, to be sure, in the printed libretto than during performance—chill. The tsar has just been tonsured. But instead of the relief such ceremony should bring, the refrain of guilt continues to resound. Even Boris's death will not silence it. In muted couplets widely separated by dialogue between the dying tsar and his son, the *pevchie* sing:

> I see a dying child
> I weep, I cry . . .
> He twists, he trembles
> He calls for help
> And for him there is no salvation . . .

These dark words apply equally to past and future, to Dmitri's murder at Uglich many years earlier and to the fate in store for young Fyodor on stage. Pimen's chorus of monks has reemerged as the Furies. And through Pimen the tsarevich Dmitri claims his victim, punishing Boris with a timeless replay of his guilt.

Stasis thus characterizes both Boris and his avenger Pimen. Unforgettable crime meets its implacable judge. To better set off the timeless confrontation of the two major protagonists—and in the opera, Pimen is a major protagonist—Musorgsky develops, in the very different time and space of the new Polish scenes, another ecclesiastic: the Jesuit Rangoni.

Rangoni represents the wrong sort of storyteller. Papal nuncio for the Polish Church and consummate Jesuit, he manipulates, makes and extracts false promises, eavesdrops, lies. He appears everywhere in the Polish scenes, stealing into Marina's boudoir, urging her to prostitute herself for the church, offering to act as go-between for the inexperienced Pretender, and—always the procurer—persuading Marina to procure Russia for Rome. During the love duel-and-duet by the fountain Rangoni is hiding away in a bush, listening. Musorgsky's romantic handling of the scene must of necessity exclude Pushkin's cynical closing lines, spoken by the Pretender, about the snakelike untrustworthiness of women. Rangoni, however, absorbs that sentiment. The Polish Act ends on a prolonged kiss, during which Rangoni emerges to gloat over his prey.

This sinister figure is a considerable historical liberty,[159] and the changes Musorgsky works on the real Rangoni are all in the direction of melodramatic villain. Pushkin, we remember, had one such crafty cleric—the *zloi chernets* (evil monk) of the omitted scene—in his 1825 version. Pushkin ultimately eliminated him and embedded the craft more subtly in Pimen; Musorgsky resurrects him on the other side of the border.

Pimen, we should note, is just as politically astute as Rangoni and just as aware of the power of his analogous position. But Pimen's craftiness is presented on an entirely other plane. He does not need to negotiate, nor must he rely on the powers of *this* world. All he must do is tell his stories—his *truthful* stories, as we know from his opening monologue—and through his chronicler's voice and the force of miracle the judgment of history can literally kill.

Musically, the role of Pimen presents a special challenge to Musorgsky's realism. As we noted above, Musorgsky (especially in his initial version) sought to create melody out of the intonation patterns of actual utterances—and thereby avoid the sense that a singer was citing someone else's words. But Pimen's is precisely a recited, remembered text. His passion is the passion of the narrated life. As both participant in the action and carrier of his own remembered story, Pimen must therefore command a repertoire of discourses. His vocal line must distinguish between chronicle account and direct dialogue with Grigory, and must register those points where Pimen stops speaking personally to the novice and starts speaking impersonally to history.

Musorgsky initially cast the basic "chronicle line" in a melodic recitative recalling Dargomyzhsky's *Stone Guest*. As in that earlier work, the model was not the intonation curve of normal Russian speech but a more verselike line, often a lyrically rounded phrase. But Pimen, as we have seen, is not only a chronicler of the past; he is also a creator of the present. Thus he has two musical motifs, and they link his first (Monastery) and second (Kremlin) appearances in a subtle musical interplay.[160]

The first motif, a repeated figure of undulating seconds accompanied solely by chords at the open fifth, is the celebrated "writing theme" denoting Pimen's present, his secluded life in Chudovo Monastery. A second, more agitated theme suggests Pimen's tumultuous past in Tsar Ivan's court. The writing theme, of course, dominates the early part of Pimen's opening monologue in the Monastery Scene ("Yet one final story . . ."). Its thin, measured quality reinforces the slightly archaic coloration of Pushkin's lines and highlights the asceticism of the monastery, the lofty profession of chronicling, and the recited character of Pimen's speech. For most of the monologue the vocal part remains relatively steady in tempo, with an occasional stylized echo of church music. Passion is reflected through intermittent agitation in the instrumental line, as if the task of the voice were to impose discipline on some inner and more anarchic force.

When Grigory awakes, a more prosaicized line intrudes—and the second motif dominates. What had been a "past" theme now takes on future potential. Significantly, it is this second motif that structures Pimen's recitative of the blind shepherd's miraculous cure in Act IV. For Pimen's past has come to represent not just the court of Ivan the Terrible but the general phenomenon of legitimate power—as invested both in Ivan and in Ivan's son, the tsarevich Dmitri. Thus the motif mortally threatens Boris.

The writing theme also threatens, however, for it is the vehicle of denunciation. Its musical contours resemble the theme of Boris's troubled conscience, and so writing penetrates thought. The chronicler *poses* as isolated and detached. But the pen is not innocent, just as telling stories to the novice Grigory was not innocent. In the revised version of the opera Pimen's moral force is further amplified, for there his expanded role joins forces with the expanded, heightened texts of Boris's monologues. Pimen in fact functions as another sort of hallucination of guilt, Boris's bad dream that everyone can see.

Neither drama nor revised version of the opera, however, ends on a confrontation between Boris and an externalized embodiment of his conscience. Both Pushkin and Musorgsky turn instead to the *narod,* the common people, for the closing image. Pushkin gives us a few bewildered voices on Red Square; Musorgsky ends his tale several months earlier, on a scene of noisy popular rebellion. This final scene, "A Forest near Kromy," has been the centerpiece for those many readings of the opera positing the *narod* as hero. It has stimulated in this century a debate among musicologists almost as intense as the debate among Pushkinists over the famous final stage direction of the play, *narod bezmolvstvuet.*

Endings: Transcending Karamzin, Rethinking Pushkin

A mass "people's scene" to end the opera was suggested to Musorgsky by Vladimir Nikolsky, close friend and literary historian, in the summer of 1871. Musorgsky was then deep into his revisions. Rimsky-Korsakov, his roommate at the time, was experimenting with crowd scenes for his *Pskovitianka,* and the Kromy scene in *Boris* owes much to the Pskovian *veche* in Rimsky's Act II.[161] But for all its timeliness and the friendly support that accompanied its creation, this final scene has been criticized for carelessness, faulty structure, and incomplete integration into the whole. A quick survey of the scene's chronology will indicate why.

The sequence of events (*BG74,* 107–112) is an eerie and disjunct variation on the opera's opening scenes. Again ragged masses crowd the stage, but this time deep in the forest rather than on Red Square, and the people themselves are the police. A band of tramps has caught and bound boyar Khrushchov, supporter of Boris. He is ridiculed with a "Glory to Boris's boyar" chorus and then forced, with much obscene jeering, into a mock "marriage" with an old woman. This grim prelude to torture is interrupted by the arrival of a holy fool, followed (somewhat incongruously) by a group of young boys. The fool sings a lament; the boys tease him, twang his metal cap, and steal his kopek. This episode, in turn, is interrupted by the arrival of Misail and Varlaam, the vagrant monks who had accompanied Grigory across the border and are now in the advance guard for the tsarevich Dmitri.

As the monks chant about Boris's sins, the tramps break into a spirited song celebrating their own Russian boldness and calling for Boris's death. But their tune is broken into by a Latin chant offstage, sung by arriving Jesuits. The tramps do not take kindly to these "wolves howling," and Misail and Varlaam—ever the opportunists—suggest to the people that they hang the "heathen crows." The Jesuits are hauled off into the woods. But this action, too, is interrupted, this time by the arrival of the Pretender himself on horseback. All the disgraced parties of past and present—the boyar Khrushchov, the tramps, the Jesuits—gather round and glorify Dmitri, each in his own language, and triumphantly usher him off. The holy fool hops back onto an empty stage. As the alarm sounds and the surrounding landscape burns, the fool sings his lament on the coming destruction of Russia.

This scene of false starts, abrupt changes of mood, and conflict-ing ideologies has provoked accusations of formlessness. It seems too easily to disintegrate into unconnected parts. Immediately recogniz-able, of course, is a fragment of the discarded St. Basil's Scene from the 1869 version, based on the famous scene 17 in Pushkin, where a jeering crowd of boys steals the holy fool's kopek. Musorgsky had in fact pasted several pages of that discarded scene directly into the revised score. But the climax of the scene—the confrontation between holy fool and tsar, and the startling punishment the fool suggests to avenge his stolen coin ("Slit their throats like you slit the throat of the young tsarevich")—has entirely disappeared. In the opera there is no such confrontation, nor can there be, because by this time in the opera Boris is already dead.

The final scene of the opera is in fact a historical anachronism. Kromy, southwest of Moscow, was headquarters for the rebellious Don Cossacks in 1604 and under allegiance to the Pretender. It took six months of fighting, in the bitter winter of 1604–1605, for Boris's troops to capture the fortress. This pyrrhic victory so exhausted government troops that widespread defection followed. Karamzin describes the siege largely in terms of military strategy (XI, 105–106); Pushkin refers to its events only obliquely, in a discussion between Gavrila Pushkin and Basmanov (scene 21). Musorgsky, however, ul-timately ends his opera on it—sensing, perhaps, the central impor-tance of this struggle for the Godunov dynasty. But in history, Kromy was beseiged while Boris was still alive and on the throne. To be sure, the anachronistic distribution of scenes (in this case, Kromy *after* Boris's death) is a common enough move for oft-transposed historical themes, whose very familiarity releases them from the obligation to reproduce any exact linear sequence of events. Critics of the Kromy Scene have nevertheless invoked this anachronism as proof of the scene's "irregularity," and perhaps even its dispensability, to the oper-atic whole.[162]

The uncertain integration of this final scene was made even more tenuous by its early performance history. *Boris Godunov* was per-formed, complete except for the Monastery Scene, four times in the 1873–74 season and eight times in 1874–75. When the opera was revived in 1876–77, the Kromy Scene was omitted as well. In a celebrated passage from his memoirs of Musorgsky, Golenishchev-

Kutuzov insisted that the composer approved of, and even welcomed, this omission. Musorgsky, according to Kutuzov, confessed in the mid-seventies that the Kromy Scene "slandered the Russian character." "An infuriated crowd kills and punishes," Musorgsky purportedly said, "but it does not ridicule its victim."[163] Not only, then, is the scene absent from Pushkin and from Musorgsky's initial version. It soon disappeared from the stage altogether, and—some would argue—with Musorgsky's blessing. When Rimsky-Korsakov reworked the opera he doubtless felt he was being generous to the Kromy Scene by reinstating it at all—although he did tuck it into the middle of the work, thereby removing its anachronistic aspect along with its special status as ending. Rimsky could easily justify the change as faithful to Musorgsky's original (1869) inspiration to end the opera on Boris's death.

This is not, however, the end of the textual problems raised in this scene. The 1873 Bessel libretto was printed with Musorgsky's own footnotes noting sources for various material. Most of these notations are scant (nothing more than the phrase "from Pushkin") and seemingly arbitrary. But the Kromy Scene differs from preceding scenes in the large number of specific page references it contains—in this case, to Karamzin's *History*. Working with the edition of Karamzin most likely used by Musorgsky (the sixth, 1851–53), researchers on the *Boris* libretto have made the intriguing discovery that these specific page references are *false;* that is, apart from some indirect comment, these pages do not describe a popular revolt of the sort Musorgsky depicts at Kromy.[164] Could this have been a ploy, they ask, to placate the censor—who would overlook the revolutionary implications of the libretto if the scene appeared to be grounded so concretely in Karamzin's officially approved *History?* Others have argued persuasively that Musorgsky's inspiration for Kromy was neither Pushkin nor Karamzin but Nikolai Kostomarov—friend of the composer, *narodnik* historian, and author of an immensely popular account of the Time of Troubles (1866).[165]

The above readings are a part (albeit a revisionist part) of a long history of interpretations that make the people's rebellious inclinations central to the scene. We might look briefly at this tradition, for not surprisingly the final scene of *Boris*—with its textological ambiguities and its revolutionary, democratic motifs—has proved extraordinarily attractive to Soviet Musorgsky scholars. Several issues of the leading music journal, *Sovetskaia muzyka,* have featured forums debating the status and ideological significance of the Kromy Scene.[166] Two general lines of interpretation have emerged.

Both have their origin in the late 1920s–early thirties, when Musorgsky's own versions of the opera and Kutuzov's memoirs on the composer first became available. The first line argues for the elimination—or at least the relocation—of the scene, on grounds that it was absent from the first version, anachronistic in the second, viewed with reservations by Musorgsky himself, and full of ambivalent traits unflattering to the Russian people.[167] The second line, by far the more influential, argues for the retention of Kromy as the final scene, and even for its centrality to the ideology of the opera. This majority opinion is in turn divided into an orthodox-Stalinist and a revisionist wing.

During the 1930s and forties it was not uncommon for Kromy to be evoked as proof of Musorgsky's faith in the "blacksoil strength" of the masses, and as such it was incorporated into campaigns against "Westernized bureaucracy" and "obscurantism."[168] In this interpretation, the Kromy Scene constituted "a natural development of that hidden condition of popular protest" which had been embedded in the final scene of Pushkin's drama.[169] Much was made of the composer's sympathy for the lower classes, of his many songs featuring orphans, beggars, and idiots, and of his increasing tendency to make the *narod* the hero of his operas. *Boris* was indeed followed by *Khovanshchina* (rebellion under Peter the Great), and Musorgsky even projected a *Pugachevshchina*, an opera inspired by Pushkin's short novel *The Captain's Daughter*.[170] The very replacement of an individual name, like Godunov, with the collective suffix -*shchina* (signifying societal disorder brought about by the excesses of the proper noun, i.e., Khovansky and Pugachev) seemed to indicate a shift in gravity from traditional hero-based opera to "people's musical drama." When individual personality gives way to collective movements, so this argument runs, the result is always ennobling.

The other wing of interpretation, more interesting and flexible, holds that Kromy is indeed central to the opera—but not necessarily in any optimistic or progressive sense. One of the earliest and most subtle of these readings[171] compares the smoothed-over Rimsky version of Kromy with the abrupt unmodulated tonalities of Musorgsky's original, and concludes that precisely these unmediated shifts and shocks in the music carry the political message: one of endless, meaningless, mindless struggle. In this reading, Kromy does not portray the masses in conscious rebellion. Nor does it portray chaos. What Musorgsky gives us, rather, is a set of calculated dead ends, a series of musical and political ideas that do not develop or modulate but break off, start afresh, and then collapse.

This approach to Kromy permits the patriotic researcher to classify Musorgsky much as Lenin classified Leo Tolstoy, as a "mirror" of the contradictions of the epoch.[172] A vacillating, opportunistic, basically monarchist *narod* was absolutely real to the Time of Troubles, and to Musorgsky's time as well. Following this line, Yuri Keldysh sees the final act (containing the Death Scene and Kromy) as a standoff between *two* paralyzed wills, that of Boris and that of the people; such paralysis was the historically correct prelude to the end of a dynasty and wholesale invasion of the nation.[173] And Emilia Frid, in a variant on this "realistic" view, notes that while choruses onstage to end an opera were certainly not new, Kromy was remarkable for the presence of a chorus that was then, at the last moment, taken away.[174] Choruses of people, even people in delusion, evoke a solidity and provide robust sonic closure. Instead the opera ends essentially on empty space. This absence of the people at the end is almost confirmation of their nonexistent historical direction and absent political consciousness.

Both "positivist" and "realistic" readings of Kromy are, as we have seen, fundamentally *political*. They hold in common an obsession with power—that is, with the people's gain or lack of it—and a historical perspective on the people that favors contexts intelligible to *our* time. Yet another recent interpretation of the scene[175] adopts a different, and less politicized, strategy, drawing on aspects of medieval culture given wide currency in recent years by Bakhtin and Likhachev.[176] Such a reading attempts, as it were, to provide for Musorgsky a framework similar to that which Ilya Serman provided for Pushkin— that is, one in which the *narod* is motivated on its own seventeenth-century terms and not on terms laid down by the intelligentsia of the author's, or the critic's, present.

Such an interpretation presumes that the structure of the Kromy Scene is governed by the logic (or antilogic) of carnivalization and medieval parody. It can only be valid, of course, to the extent that Musorgsky intuitively sensed in popular culture what Likhachev later described. That he did so seems at least possible, for we know from the fantastic masks of his correspondence as well as the accounts of contemporaries just how intimately Musorgsky identified with jesters, and how irrepressible were his own impulses to parody.[177] There are, I hasten to add, serious drawbacks to such a reading. But a "carnivalized" Kromy is so provocative an extension of the ideological ambivalence of Musorgsky's ending scene that it merits some further speculation here.

In the carnival laughter of medieval parody, Likhachev explains, "laughter is directed not at others but at oneself and at the situation created within the work itself."[178] The target of parody is not the style or content of a given work, not the style of a given author, but rather the presumption of stability itself, the very idea of generic and semantic fixedness. This sort of parody cannot be reduced to a politics because it is, in a real sense, an alternative to politics.

Likhachev points out that medieval Russian parody divided the universe into two worlds, one "the real, organized world of culture" and the other the "unreal, not organized, negative world of 'anti-culture' . . . a complete confusion of all meanings."[179] This concept of a second, so-called *kromeshnyi mir*—an antiworld outside or apart from everyday reality—began to erode, Likhachev claims, in the early seventeenth century, around the time of Boris Godunov. The devastating enfleshment and politicization of the concept in Ivan the Terrible's *oprichnina* had degraded the antiworld from a model of carnival reversibility (for the *kromeshnyi mir* was always temporary) to a widespread and stable reality.[180] But traces of its logic remained in folk culture up through the nineteenth century.

This logic might have been part of "the past in the present" that so appealed to Musorgsky. The breakdown of the folkloric world and its interpenetration by random elements of politics was a cultural reality for Russia of the early seventeenth century, and it is also the reality we see in the Kromy Scene. From this perspective the incoherence of that scene begins to make another sort of sense. The tramps in Kromy respond to each new political threat by carnivalizing it. The mock coronation and mock wedding ceremony for the boyar Khrushchov—not to mention the very real threat of his torture unto death—are not consummated. Targets are forever changing, old victims are abandoned for new, and *all* victims (boyars, Jesuits, tramps) come together in the great hope represented by the Returning Tsarevich. Here is the one chorus that does not undermine its hero. Dmitri is the embodiment of everyone's unrealizable dream, a genuine miracle that looks different to each witness and thus tolerates easily the most impossible political alliances. The cheering crowd of former enemies that usher Dmitri offstage are not political allies; they are a carnivalized collective. This is indeed Pushkin's Pretender, "po nravu vsem," everything in potential.

It is therefore appropriate that this Pretender be introduced to the Russian forest by Varlaam and Misail, carnivalized clowns who had assisted Grigory's transformation into Dmitri during the Inn Scene with traditional carnival tools: wine, rhythmic puns, buffoonery, obscenity, and parody of the verbal formulas of both church and state. The violence in the Kromy Scene is different from the violence sung and acted elsewhere in the opera. There, in scenes where Boris is featured, we meet the policeman with the cudgel and quarreling boyars who sing darkly of torture. That is *state* violence, institutionalized and predictable. The tramps do not defeat that; they laugh at it. Kromy takes place in a time and space different from the other scenes: popular protest, perpetual decrowning, and ridicule all come together.[181] As Likhachev reminds us, this is not so much laughter at the carrier as it is laughter at the *form*, the pretense to permanent authority.

If such a reading is entertained, this fine balance of factors makes staging the final scene extraordinarily difficult. Certainly the number of failed Kromy performances is legion. Often its activity strikes audiences as simply aimless; more often its duality is collapsed into simple viciousness. Exemplary of the latter approach is Stanislavsky's 1928 production of *Boris*. As his lengthy notes on the final scene indicate, Stanislavsky spent a good deal of time teaching his opera company the concept "riot." Here is how he coached singers on torturing the boyar Khrushchov: "The tenors harass him cheerily, the bassos are glum. They pull him out as they would a dead cat. They set him up. They wipe their noses in a dark mood. They evidently intend to keep the game up for some time. . . ."[182] But surely this is not the spirit of the scene. Musorgsky was right in experiencing—as Kutuzov claimed he did—some bad conscience over Kromy if the people on stage performed their parts as a *politics*. In this "carnivalized" reading, the point of the scene is more apolitical, perhaps even antipolitical. Such a reading also suggests a new perspective on the closing image of the *yurodivy*, the holy fool.

The fool emerges twice out of the mocking, roving laughter of the scene. We should recall here the role played by the *yurodivy* in the St. Basil's Scene—which, although omitted from the revised version of the opera, is unavoidably present from Pushkin and constitutes a subtext to this interpolated fragment. In that earlier scene the *yurodivy* clearly functions as a carnival double of the tsar. The people in the square mistake his entrance for Boris ("Is it the Tsar?" "No—it's the *yurodivy*"); the boys knock at his iron cap as if it were a crown, and— most importantly—the fool not only confronts Boris with the crime of Uglich but even asks that the crime be repeated. Confrontation between tsar and fool embodies the tsar's guilty conscience, re-created and externalized by his mocking double.

When the fool is detached from the tsar and inserted into the Kromy Scene, however, the whole logic of his lament and his double appearance takes on new meaning. He is no longer a carnival double exposing the conscience of a regal sinner in the shadow of the Kremlin. Now he is part of a much more diffuse force, already carnivalized, in the heart of the forest—and there, he announces the "exit out of culture" that a true *yurodivy* represents to his people.[183]

The final dialogue in Kromy has left Boris far behind. It is now a dialogue between holy fool and the people's fate. If the fool is viewed politically, as part of the "real" world, then his lament is indeed a straightforward reference to the coming national disaster. But if he is viewed as a carnivalized figure, from *within* the carnival world, his image changes. One false tsar is dead, and a second false tsar has just departed the stage. In this context the fool is not merely an avenging conscience and prophet of doom, not merely a singer of failure in *this* world, but a spokesman for the "inside-out" world that rejects success and authenticity altogether, that is disgusted by success and so relativizes all standards by which good and evil are judged. This startling summation, through folk psychology, of Musorgsky's suspicion of formal system could constitute one possible reading of the Kromy Scene. It would be quite in keeping with the radical interrogation of established genres that so marks the Boris Tales of Pushkin and Karamzin.

Such a carnivalized reading of Kromy should be pursued with caution, however. For here we confront the elusiveness of Musorgsky's own testimony, and the long tradition of recombination and conflation that has plagued the two authorial versions of *Boris*. Elements of carnivalization are quite possibly present in the Kromy Scene. But if they are operative at all, then they coexist with two other better-documented realities in Musorgsky's work, one ideological and the other formal. First, Musorgsky's art always reflected a high-mindedness about the people and their heroic suffering that must not be compromised by any suggestion of a playful attitude toward the people's fate. Medieval parody need not, of course, be "playful" in that sense. Its relativizing of all value and its placement of the people *beyond* politics can in fact be seen to elevate the people in both complexity and stature.

Second, evidence indicates that by the 1870s Musorgsky had left behind his *kuchkist* disdain for a well-structured, formally balanced work of art.[184] The revised opera exhibits surprising formal symmetry. Two crowd scenes open and close the work, and the intervening scenes alternate neatly between Boris and the Pretender. The precise emotional and architectural center of the opera is Boris's great hallucination, where his guilt and the people's fate are fused. If Musorgsky, in short, was laughing at formal system, he was doing so as an ideology *within* the work, not through any arbitrariness in the form of the opera.

As regards its internal structure, the Kromy Scene is also a step back from the realist aesthetic of the 1860s. As Richard Taruskin has convincingly demonstrated, Musorgsky's ending scene seems calculated to supplant the "bouffe"-like declamatory strategies of the initial version with more conventionally operatic numbers.[185] The scene's seven self-contained musical numbers are not cast as choruses in recitative time, which had been the pattern for most of the inserted songs in earlier scenes. They resemble, rather, pageant or oratorio

pieces in which spoken interludes—and binding, narrative material—
are rare or altogether absent. Thus a paradoxical tension is achieved
in Kromy. The narrative action itself is continually and awkwardly
interrupted while the musical embodiment of the action is composi-
tionally rounded and conventional in its musical structure. What
Taruskin has called the "frieze-like monumentality"[186] of this final
scene is also compatible, we should note, with the reversibility inherent in both carnival and anachronism.

One might ask, from under this wealth of coexisting readings,
what sort of a sense for history emerges from Musorgsky's second
Boris transposition. The mocking laughter of the final scene, together
with the fool's desperate lament, suggests several lines of interpretation. First, there is the suggestion that history—like the successive
interrupted events in Kromy Forest—is a dead end and leads nowhere; when everything is mocked, history *has* no meaning. If we
perceive in Kromy a more open and carnivalistic structure, however,
then we could say that, on the contrary, history goes everywhere; what
appears from one perspective to be political indecisiveness is from
another and more folkloric perspective a rich multiplicity of meanings, a world whose actors can be brought together only through a
pretender. And finally, there is a reading that focuses on the holy fool
himself. In Kromy, it could be argued, the fool incorporates real
ambiguity—as fools so often do. His lament on the coming disaster for
Russia does indeed emerge out of mockery, and in that sense embodies the meaninglessness of history. But this gesture is itself full of
moral meaning. The recognition of a void—so common in nihilist
views of history—is completely compatible with earnestness in art.
The holy fool, alone at the end, literally clears the stage of falseness.
The Boris Tale, in fact, has always been concerned with the clearing
away of falsity, with the absent center in scenarios of legitimacy.

Through these various readings of Kromy we glimpse anew the
interplay of Musorgsky's sources in the final version of his text. From
Pushkin he seems to have absorbed a pervasive scepticism about
historical events, and about our ability to know or control them. The
actual incidents in Kromy are probably inspired by Kostomarov's
compassionate rendering of the Time of Troubles. And in the larger
perspective of Musorgsky's two *Boris* transpositions, the presence of
this curiously static finale in the second version reinforces the composer's shift back toward Karamzinian time and space, that chronotope which had for so long and so successfully governed the Boris
Tale.

Concluding Remarks

IN THE MID-1930s, when the Soviet literary establishment was busy creating guidelines for the proper
image of man and of history in the new socialist-
realist novel, Bakhtin, just released from exile, wrote
a lengthy essay on the *Bildungsroman*.[1] The essay
deals with literature's assimilation of historical time.
Ancient adventure novels of ordeal, Bakhtin argued, were structured with no true variables: a
static, unchanging image of human personality confronted a static and unchanging world, and interaction between the two—while real—was inevitably
mechanical. The Enlightenment witnessed the
emergence of differentiated historical time. This
new time, Bakhtin claimed, left its mark on both world and character:
personality began to emerge not only against a static world (a context
with one variable) but against a changing world as well (a context with
two variables). This rough schema of options for human emergence is
illustrated, interestingly enough, in our four transpositions of the
Boris Tale.

Karamzin's plot for Boris is cast essentially as a "novel of ordeal."
Boris Godunov, a finished image at his first appearance, is not free to
develop or to refashion the terms by which he is judged; he is tested,
revealed, and found wanting. Pushkin's play, in contrast, is a genuine
"novel of emergence." The old plot, Karamzin's plot, continually tests
Boris. And until the very end Boris fights against that plot, insisting
on his right to speak *his* version of events—that is, his right to emerge
as a personality. But the traditional burdens of tsarist rank sit awkwardly on an elected tsar. Without dynastic security Boris must still
assume responsibility, even for chance events; he cannot presume, but
can only seek, a unity of image. Here the elected tsar must fail. Only

207

the Pretender Dmitri can truly live in a world of two variables—that is, in a world where a flexible, emerging personality can respond to, and take advantage of, an emerging and ever-evolving present. If Tsar Boris is obsessed with imitating tradition and the signs of legitimacy, then the Pretender, in contrast, has literally no memory at all. He looks ever forward, toward a world of changing values and changing foundations, where the very standards of validation differ from one day to the next.

Characteristically, Pushkin parodies the struggles of both his heroes. Boris collapses back into Karamzin's nondevelopmental chronotope at the moment before death, and Dmitri—for all his flexibility and freedom—does not really emerge as an integrated personality. This is the price of his survival and success. He responds *in* time, but the passage of time leaves no mark on him; he does not accumulate personhood.

Musorgsky's first version of the opera is a finished, but transitional, work. It "realizes" Pushkin musically within essentially chamber limits. The second version, a bolder transposition for the "grand stage," intensifies the potential in both of the inherited heroes. Boris is returned to Karamzin, thereby reminding us of the price extracted by stable, morally insistent concepts of history and of the word. The final Kromy Scene, while reflecting Karamzin's stasis, moves into an ideological realm that Karamzin never entertained and Pushkin only hinted at. The people literally absorb the Pretender, removing him to the realm of fantasy. And the people's fate—not Boris's or Dmitri's—has the final word. The opera, thus experienced, is a catalogue of generic models for individual and national emergence—composed at a time when both Russian people and Russian state were debating anew questions of identity.

Generic distinctions have traditionally served to invoke, in a given text, the appropriate conventions for arriving at meaning. In studying transpositions, however, more than one genre must always be kept in mind; the conventions invoked are always multiple, and their interactions complex. The Boris Tale—the four major transpositions discussed in this volume, and many minor ones as well—evolves not only from work to work and from author to author but is continually deflected, and redirected, by traditions of performance and commentary. When two transpositions are produced by a single author, as in the case of Musorgsky, the dialogue between works becomes part of the creative evolution of a single transposer.

In the closing paragraphs of his 1935 essay "Discourse in the Novel," Bakhtin discusses two transformational processes to which all products of language are subject: canonization and reaccentuation.[2]

The first, he warns, we should be wary of, for canonization hardens literary images in place and prevents free growth. The second, however, we should welcome; reaccentuation loosens up literary images and guarantees them a long life by embedding them in new contexts. Near the end of this discussion, Bakhtin adds the afterthought: "Of great importance as well is the re-accentuation of images during their translation out of literature and into other art forms—into drama, opera, painting" (421). The example he gives is Tchaikovsky's "rather considerable re-accentuation" of Pushkin's *Eugene Onegin*. A footnote then directs us to the "extremely interesting problem" of double-voiced parodic and ironic discourse in opera, music, and choreography. On that suggestive note the essay ends. Although Bakhtin makes only the preliminary moves, his ideas almost inevitably suggest a poetics of transposed themes.

What might such a poetics hope to accomplish? Just as a theory of translation does not, and should not, provide formulas for extracting meaning, so a theory of transposition cannot guarantee that a particular shift will be meaningful, or to what extent. What it can do, however, is suggest a perspective on cultural history, a way of selecting, combining, and—as it were—interrogating texts. As transpositions of a theme accumulate and comment on one another, the sequence of events becomes shared knowledge, almost invisible. The story itself becomes a sort of "norm," a neutral and expected background, and is retold in genres that have their own normative hierarchies of convention and deviance. These retelling processes thus become motivated by deviations *from* (as well as fidelity to) a norm. To read transpositions is to link together specific norms, and specific violations of a norm, in a coherent way.[3]

Transposition can do more, however, than merely provide a focus for viewing generic innovation. It can serve as indication of changes in cultural sensitivity from one era to the next. Within the same culture, different elements emerge and expand at different times to carry the weight of the story. Ksenia was merely an ornament in Karamzin but is a vehicle of salvation in later Boris plays. Pimen scarcely existed in history, but gives voice to Pushkin's ideas about historiography and to Musorgsky's ideas about the Russian conscience. Boris himself was portrayed as a usurper in post-Napoleonic Russia, as a heroic Westernizer at midcentury, and as a damned soul at the century's end—and indeed, he is all these things. The longer a story circulates the more difficult it becomes to assign a fixed significance or morality to its parts. Thus does the literary rewrite of a historical theme tend to be so sensitive a reflector of its author's present, and tend so often to become allegorical.

Lastly, a poetics of transposition should provide some insight into genre and chronotope that goes beyond the private intent of the transposers themselves. Sequences more complex than the three genres dealt with here are certainly possible, and might include, for example, the completely nonverbal narrative (a story expressed through mime or dance). But even the relatively kindred genres of history, historical drama, and dramatic libretto—linked as they are through the word—present an interesting and rather complex spectrum. At one end, historiography, we have a relative privileging of objective factors (if not "facts"); of the three genres, historiography is the most dependent upon verifiable texts in the nonaesthetic world. When deviations from prevailing historiographical criteria of validation become too severe, the text is felt to be not history but fiction. At the other end there is the libretto, also privileging objective factors but very different ones—the requirements of musical structure and the dynamics of setting voice. Too much music and the words disappear; too slavish a respect for words and the opera becomes what Musorgsky probably felt his first version of *Boris* had been, deficient dramatically and musically. Both historical and operatic statements of a theme thus appear to have nonnegotiable components: some kind of fidelity to the documented event on the one hand, some conformity to laws of effective musical theater on the other. In between these two is the much more fluid genre of historical drama, where "authority" is up to the playwright to define. Karamzin and Musorgsky have had their detractors, but it is not doubted that Karamzin is a historian and Musorgsky a musician. Many do doubt that Pushkin is a dramatist. One can be, it seems, a closet playwright but not a closet historian or musician—and this tells us something about the play inherent in our own generic definitions.

A reaccentuation, like any other work of art, must of course cohere as a whole on its own terms; it too is the product of creative "combustion" in the mind of a single artist. But reaccentuations are also inevitably, inherently pluralistic. Musorgsky's two *Boris*es neither destroy nor realize the earlier versions of the tale by Karamzin and Pushkin; they reconceptualize and comment on them. The sorts of dialogues discussed in these chapters can be assumed to exist among all transpositions that together constitute one strand of a cultural tradition. And precisely the fitting and misfitting of one work to its predecessors is what creates an awareness of the boundaries separating them, along which a culture becomes aware of itself. This, surely, is one of the implications of Bakhtin's moving testimony to cultural transposition in an early essay:

> One must not imagine the realm of culture as some sort of spatial whole, with boundaries but also with internal territory. The realm of culture has no internal territory. It is distributed entirely along the boundaries: boundaries pass everywhere, through its every aspect, the systematic

unity of a culture extends into the very atoms of cultural life, it reflects like the sun in each drop of that life. Every cultural act lives essentially on the boundaries: in this is its seriousness and its significance; abstracted from boundaries, it loses its native soil, it becomes empty, arrogant, it degenerates and dies.[4]

Notes

Chapter 1: *Boris Godunov* and a Poetics of Transposition

1. L. N. Tolstoi, "Neskol'ko slov po povodu knigi *Voina i mir*," in *L. N. Tolstoi: Polnoe sobranie sochinenii* in 90 vols., vol. 16 (Moscow: GIKhL, 1955), 9–11. Tolstoy argues that the duty of historians is to isolate and rank events, to create singleminded heroes, while the artist's task is to enflesh and complicate a hero so thoroughly that no single idea can be extracted from him.

2. See Leo Tolstoy's comment, as recorded by Goldenweizer: "I think that every great artist must create his own forms. If the content of fictional literature can be endlessly varied, so then can their form." A. B. Gol'denveizer, *Vblizi Tolstogo* (Moscow: GIKhL, 1959), 116. Exemplary of this position is the "generic definition" Tolstoy provides ("Neskol'ko slov po povodu knigi *Voina i mir*," 7) for his *War and Peace*: "What is *War and Peace*? *War and Peace* is what the author wanted and was able to express in that form in which it was expressed."

3. See Ilse N. Bulhof, "Imagination and Interpretation in History," in *Literature and History,* ed. Leonard Schulze and Walter Wetzels (University Press of America, 1983), 3–25; also Hayden White, "The Historical Text as Literary Artifact," *Tropics of Discourse* (Baltimore: Johns Hopkins University Press, 1978), 81–100.

4. See, for example, Herbert Lindenberger, *Historical Drama* (1975); Joseph Kerman, *Opera as Drama* (1952); Gary Schmidgall, *Literature as Opera* (1977); Peter Conrad, *Romantic Opera and Literary Form* (1977); and Seymour Chatman, *Story and Discourse: Narrative Structure in Fiction and Film* (1978).

5. See, for example, Yu. Tynianov, "Dostoevsky and Gogol: Toward a Theory of Parody," in *Dostoevsky and Gogol: Texts and Criticism,* ed. Priscilla Meyer and Stephen Rudy (Ann Arbor: Ardis, 1979); for a typology of discourse relations, see Mikhail Bakhtin, *Problems of Dostoevsky's Poetics*, ed. and trans. Caryl Emerson (Minneapolis: University of Minnesota Press, 1984), ch. 5.

6. Yu. Tynianov, "Illiustratsii," in *Arkhaisty i novatory* (Leningrad, 1929; repr. Slavische Propylaen, Band 31, Munich: Wilhelm Fink Verlag, 1967), 500–509. All intergeneric illustration is caricature, Tynianov claims: pictures are never quite right in a novel; program music explicated is inevitably comical.

7. For a lucid discussion, see Barbara Herrnstein Smith, "Narrative Versions, Narrative Theories," in *On Narrative*, ed. W. J. T. Mitchell (Chicago: University of Chicago Press, 1981), 218–19.

8. See, for example, Seymour Chatman, "What Novels Can Do That Films Can't (and Vice Versa)," in *On Narrative*, 117–36. Although Chatman does mention the medium-genre distinction, the focus of his attention is on the "double time structuring" of narrative quite independent of medium.

212

9. P. N. Medvedev/M. M. Bakhtin, *The Formal Method in Literary Scholarship*, trans. Albert J. Wehrle (Baltimore: Johns Hopkins University Press, 1978), 130, 134. The volume first appeared under Medvedev's name in 1928.

10. See Hayden White's Preface to his *Metahistory: The Historical Imagination in Nineteenth-Century Europe* (Baltimore: Johns Hopkins University Press, 1973), x: "I have been forced to postulate a deep level of consciousness on which a historical thinker chooses conceptual strategies by which to explain or represent his data. On this level, I believe, the historian performs an essentially *poetic* act. . . ."

11. M. M. Bakhtin, "Forms of Time and of the Chronotope in the Novel," in *The Dialogic Imagination: Four Essays by M. M. Bakhtin*, trans. Caryl Emerson and Michael Holquist (Austin: University of Texas Press, 1981), 250. Bakhtin discusses Greek romances on 86–110.

12. See Bakhtin's essay on Goethe, "Roman vospitaniia i ego znachenie v istorii realizma," in M. M. Bakhtin, *Estetika slovesnogo tvorchestva* (Moscow: Iskusstvo, 1979), 223–24. A translation of this essay, and others in *Estetika*, is forthcoming from University of Texas Press (1986–87).

13. Consider Tchaikovsky's letter to Sergei Taneev, 2 January 1878: "I composed this opera because I was moved to express in music all that seems to cry out for such expression in *Eugene Onegin* . . . The opera *Onegin* will never have a success [at the major houses]: I feel already assured of that. . . . I would much prefer to confide it to the theatre of the Conservatoire. . . . This is much more suitable to my modest work, which I shall not describe as an opera, if it is published. I should like to call it 'lyrical scenes,' or something of that kind. This opera has no future!" Modeste Tchaikovsky, *The Life and Letters of Peter Ilich Tchaikovsky*, ed. and trans. Rosa Newmarch (New York: John Lane, 1906), 255–57.

14. See Bakhtin's discussion of the "posthumous life" of Shakespeare in his "Otvet na vopros redaktsii 'Novogo mira,'" in *Estetika*, 328–35. Neither Shakespeare nor his contemporaries knew the great playwright that we celebrate today, Bakhtin claims; in no way could we squeeze *our* Shakespeare back into the Elizabethan epoch. Are we then ascribing to his works something that was "not in them," are we distorting them? There will always be distortion, Bakhtin argues, but that is not why Shakespeare has grown. He has grown because certain aspects of his work, certain sides of his language and implications in his world view, could only be revealed posthumously. "An author is captive to his epoch, to his own present," Bakhtin writes. "Subsequent times liberate him from this captivity, and literary scholarship is called upon to assist in this liberation" (332).

15. Consider, for example, Andrei Amalrik's expulsion from Moscow State University in 1960 for his nonconformist thesis on the Normans, and the political scandal surrounding Olzhas Suleimenov's *Az i Ya* (1975), with its suggestion that a Polovtsian might be the author of the Igor Tale.

16. Roman Jakobson, "On Linguistic Aspects of Translation," in Reuben Brower, *On Translation* (Cambridge: Harvard University Press, 1959), 233.

17. For a survey of the problem, see Itamar Even-Zohar, "Translation Theory Today: A Call for Transfer Theory," *Poetics Today* 2, no. 4 (Summer/Autumn 1981): 1–7.

18. For a brief survey of the works in English, see Ervin Brody, *The Demetrius Legend and its Literary Treatment in the Age of the Baroque* (Rutherford, N.J.: Fairleigh Dickenson Press, 1972); and E. Salgaller, "The Demetrius-Godunof Theme in the German and Russian Drama of the Twentieth Century" (Ph.D. diss., New York University, 1956). In Russian, see M. P. Alekseev,

"Boris Godunov i Dmitrii Samozvanets v zapadnoevropeiskoi drame," in *Boris Godunov A. S. Pushkina*, ed. K. N. Derzhavin (Leningrad: Gos. akad. teatr dramy, 1936), 73–124.

19. Noteworthy German Demetrius dramas were written by Schiller (1805), Bodenstedt (1856), Hebbel (1864), and, in the twentieth century, Paul Ernst (1905), Lernet-Holenia (1926), and a grotesque version by Wilhelm von Spaun (1936), infused with Nazi ideology and anti-Semitism. Ervin Brody discusses these works in *The Demetrius Legend*, 221–28, 230–36, 287–89.

20. Rainer Maria Rilke, *The Notebooks of Malte Laurids Brigge*, trans. M. D. Herter Norton (New York: Norton, 1949), 162–63.

21. Aleksei Khomiakov, *Dimitrii Samozvanets* (1833); Aleksandr Ostrovskii, *Dimitrii Samozvanets i Vasilii Shuiskii* (1867); and Aleksei Suvorin, *Tsar' Dmitrii Samozvanets i Tsarevna Ksenia* (1904).

22. See K. F. Ryleev, *Polnoe sobranie stikhotvorenii* (Leningrad: Sovetskii pisatel', 1971), 146–52.

23. The early seventeenth century experienced a number of new genres, including such threshold categories as secularized history *(Novaia povest')* and saints' lives told by family members. For the breakdown of literary "etiquette" and medieval canon during this period, see Dmitri Likhachev, *Poetika drevnerusskoi literatury* (Moscow: Nauka, 1979), 95–102.

24. *Tsar Boris*, Act IV, scene ii. In A. K. Tolstoi, *Dramaticheskaia trilogiia* (Leningrad: Sovetskii pisatel', 1939), 407.

25. See D. S. Likhachev, *Chelovek v literature Drevnei Rusi* (Moscow, 1970), 12–25. Only after Ivan the Terrible and Boris Godunov, he claims, does it become possible to distinguish the personality of Russian rulers in historical sources.

26. N. M. Karamzin, *Istoriia Gosudarstva Rossiiskogo*, vol. XI (St. Petersburg: Evdokimov, 1892; reprint ed. Slavistic Printings and Reprintings 189/11, The Hague: Mouton, 1969), 123.

27. V. N. Turbin, "Kharaktery samozvantsev v tvorchestve A. S. Pushkina," *Filologicheskie nauki* (Moscow: Vysshaia shkola) 6 (48) (1968): 92–94. Boris Uspensky addresses the folk-religious roots of Russian pretendership (in the sacralization of the monarch and the concomitant linking of pretenders with carnival and the Devil) in B. A. Uspenskij, "Tsar and Pretender: Samozvančestvo or Royal Imposture in Russia as a Cultural-Historical Phenomenon," trans. David Budgen, in Ju. M. Lotman and B. A. Uspenskij, *The Semiotics of Russian Culture*, ed. Ann Shukman (Ann Arbor: Michigan Slavic Contributions, no. 11, 1984), 259–92.

28. See, for a brief discussion, Michael Cherniavsky, *Tsar and People: Studies in Russian Myths*, esp. ch. 1, 16–17. See also Alain Besançon, *Le Tsarevitch Immolé* (Paris: Plon, 1967), ch. 2, for an imaginative discussion of the political and religious implications of sacrificial royalty. Besançon traces the Tsar-as-Christ motif (a father who permits or orders a son to be killed) through Russian history, from its religious origins in Boris and Gleb to the more secularized variant in Peter the Great's execution of his son Alexis (77–128). Martyred tsareviches haunt the nineteenth century, Besançon points out, both as avengers and as saviors.

29. See Part I of K. V. Chistov, *Russkie narodnye sotsial'no-utopicheskie legendy* (Moscow: Nauka, 1967). Chistov divides his data into three categories of tales: those about a Golden Age (ideals projected temporally into the past), those about "distant lands" (ideals projected spatially beyond the limits of the known feudal world), and those about True Deliverers (the ideal not yet achieved but present in the promise of a returning savior) (16–17). The

Deliverer manifests himself in eleven stages (30–32)—all of which, incidentally, have points of contact with the Dmitri Legend.

30. The legend of the saintly pilgrim Feodor Kuzmich, who died in 1864
and was presumed by many (both low- and high-born) to be Alexander I in
disguise, is indication of the vitality of this faith in the magic survival and
resurrection of tsars well into the nineteenth century.

31. Yu. M. Lotman, "O Khlestakove," *Trudy po russkoi i slavianskoi filologii*
(Tartuskii universitet) XXVI (1975): 19–53. An excellent translation of this
essay under the title "Concerning Khlestakov" can be found in Alexander D.
Nakhimovsky and Alice Stone Nakhimovsky, eds., *The Semiotics of Russian
Cultural History: Essays by Iurii M. Lotman, Lidiia Iu. Ginzburg, Boris A. Uspenskii*
(Ithaca: Cornell University Press, 1985), 150–87.

32. See his "Obozrenie russkoi slovesnosti za 1831 god," *Evropeets*, 1832,
no. 1:106–15.

33. For more on the mythical and classical bases of Pushkin's *Boris*, see
O. P. Aranovskaia [Olga Arans], "O vine Borisa Godunova v tragedii Pushkina," *Vestnik russkogo khristianskogo dvizheniia*, no. 143 (IV, 1984): 128–56, a
longer version of "An Interpretation of Pushkin's Tragedy *Boris Godunov*,"
delivered at the Midwest Slavic Conference, Chicago, 7 May 1982.

34. Paul Ernst, *Demetrios* (Leipzig: Insel-Verlag, 1905). In this retelling,
Nabis is weary, fatalistic, and only too willing to relinquish his throne to the
Pretender. His famous monologue is not, as in Pushkin, a catalogue of
complaints but rather a prelude to suicide. Before revealing his self-inflicted
wound to Demetrios, Nabis cautions his rival against the seductiveness of
power and the unreliability of the people. Demetrios begs Nabis to stay on
and help him rule. The play presents the odd spectacle of two kings fated to
govern in ungovernable times, each dissuading the other from the task.

The Soviet critic Mikhail Alekseev ("Boris Godunov i Dmitrii
Samozvanets v zapadnoevropeiskoi drame," 120–122) has given a most interesting Russian reading of this German reading of a Russian theme. Of all the
major German versions of the tale, Alekseev claims, Ernst's Nabis most
resembles Boris as Pushkin drew him. "But why did the author find it necessary to 'antiquate' the plot in this way? Did a Russian setting cramp his
archeological exoticism?" (121). Alekseev suggests that the full force of
Schopenhauerian pessimism, characteristic of Ernst and of prewar Western
Europe in general, could better find its expression "in Sparta during the time
of its most complete national degeneration" than in Russia, suffering from
mere "court revolutions and temporary chaos, sicknesses of a still young
Russian state organism. . . ."

35. See N. Barsukov, *Zhizn' i trudy M. P. Pogodina*, 22 vols. (St. Petersburg:
Stasiulevich, 1888; reprint ed., Slavistic Printings and Reprintings 162, The
Hague: Mouton, 1969), vol. I, 19–20; for a fuller account, see vol. II, 393–94.

36. Barsukov, vol. IV, 111.

37. The entire work was not published until 1868, but an excerpt appeared in *Sovremennik* in 1837; see N. Pogodin, "Smert' tsaria Borisa
Feodorovicha Godunova. Istoricheskiia stseny 1605 g. aprelia 13," *Sovremennik* (St. Petersburg) 5 (1837): 247–78. Pogodin's Boris is a vigorous, proud,
humane tsar—guilty of pride, but not of Uglich—with a realistic (and thus
pessimistic) outlook; on his deathbed he comes to believe, as Pushkin's Boris
never does, in the treason of his generals. The fragment ends not on the
people's silence but on Pushkin's *first* variant: "Long live our tsar Dmitri
Ivanovich!"

38. A. S. Suvorin, "O Dmitrii Samozvantse," first published in *Novoe*

Vremia in 1894, reprinted in *O Dmitrii Samozvantse* (St. Petersburg: Izd. A. S. Suvorina, 1906). Page references in the text are to this 1906 edition. Suvorin's conviction that Dmitri was the true son of Ivan IV had some support among historians of the period, all of whom drew upon the influential testimony of Jacques Margeret, French mercenary in Russian service under both Boris and Dmitri. His *Estat de l'Empire de Russie et Grand Duché de Moscovie* was published in 1607, and culminates with the case for an authentic Dmitri. See the excellent annotated translation by Chester S. L. Dunning, *The Russian Empire and Grand Duchy of Muscovy: A 17th Century French Account by Jacques Margeret* (Pittsburgh: University of Pittsburgh Press, 1983), 80–91.

39. For a more thorough discussion of these four Boris plays, see my "Pretenders to History: Four Plays for Undoing Pushkin's *Boris Godunov*," *Slavic Review* 44, no. 2 (Summer 1985): 257–79.

40. For a good introduction to Heiseler's life and works, see André von Gronicka, *Henry von Heiseler: A Russo-German Writer* (New York: King's Crown Press, 1944). Born in Petersburg of German parentage, Heiseler left Russia for Munich in 1898 at the age of twenty-three and stayed sixteen years. The outbreak of World War I found him in Petersburg, where he was impressed into service for the tsarist and later revolutionary governments of Russia. In 1922 he made a daring escape on a German freighter. Trilingual since childhood, Heiseler had at one time hoped to write in Russian as well as German. But he came to believe that a poet had only one voice-center, and his was German. That was the language of his art; Russian was the language of his service.

41. See Itamar Even-Zohar, "The Position of Translated Literature within the Literary Polysystem," in his *Papers in Historical Poetics* (Tel Aviv: The Porter Institute for Poetics and Semiotics), pp. 21–27. Even-Zohar claims that translated literature forms a "system" of its own in a given target culture, and interacts in a structured way with native literature. In those cultures where translated texts are received as privileged or primary, the culture readily adapts and absorbs foreign models—often to the detriment of native tradition. In other cultures, translations occupy a secondary position, and translators are required to find native models in order to render foreign texts accessible to their audience. In those situations "non-equivalent" translations would be the norm.

42. Sumarokov's Demetrius-drama is essentially a retelling of his *Hamlet* with the same cast of characters: a vicious usurper-king (Dmitri/Claudius), a virtuous maiden whom the usurper wishes to wed (Ksenia/Ophelia), the maiden's unscrupulous or seemingly unscrupulous father willing to sell his daughter to the king (Shuisky/Polonius; in Sumarokov, Ksenia is *Shuisky's* daughter, not Godunov's), a distraught lover (Georgy/Hamlet) who intervenes just in time to save the beloved from death. Both dramas are available in English in *Selected Tragedies of A. P. Sumarokov*, trans. Richard and Raymond Fortune (Evanston: Northwestern University Press, 1970).

43. See E. G. Etkind, "Poeticheskii perevod v istorii russkoi literatury," in *Mastera russkogo stikhotvornogo perevoda*, I (Leningrad, 1968), 17–18.

44. Sumarokov in fact prefaced his *Dmitrii Samozvanets* with a foreword protesting the practice of mixing genres and lamenting the popularity of the *Comedie larmoyante* in Russia. For a fine discussion of Sumarokov's understanding of translation, and the function of his *Hamlet* as an eighteenth-century carrier of Shakespeare, see Joyce S. Toomre, "Sumarokov's Adaptation of *Hamlet* and the 'To Be or Not To Be' Soliloquy," in *Study Group on Eighteenth*

Russia Newsletter 9 (1981). Her approach to the play is exactly the one I recommend for studying transpositions:

> In the English-speaking world, each generation has reinterpreted *Hamlet* according to its own needs and values. For us, the variables are limited: the directors, actors and stage sets may change, but we retain, with qualifications, the bedrock of Shakespeare's text. For non-English speakers, the language changes with each translation; for them, the continuum is at some other level. Just as there are fashions in acting, there are styles of translation. Both are transitory. Unlike the original text, a translation, with rare exceptions, barely survives its own generation. Fixed in time, it functions as a photograph, capturing and revealing many details of that society's aesthetic, political and moral values. Seen in succession, a series of translations traces the change in those values and thus can serve as a cultural history in miniature. (6)

45. For a discussion of the Pushkin/Bulgarin relationship, see A. A. Gozenpud, "Iz istorii literaturno-obshchestvennoi bor'by 20-kh—30-kh godov XIX v. ('Boris Godunov' i 'Dimitrii Samozvanets')," in *Pushkin: Issledovaniia i materialy,* 6 (Leningrad: Nauka, 1969), 252–75.

46. See B. P. Gorodetskii, *Tragediia A. S. Pushkina 'Boris Godunov'* (Leningrad: Prosveshchenie, 1969), 69–71, 82–83.

47. For a brief account of this debacle, see S. N. Durylin, *Pushkin na stsene* (Moscow: AN SSSR, 1951), 76–79.

48. So argues the Soviet musicologist Boris Asafiev in his "'Boris Godunov' Musorgskogo kak muzykal'nyi spektakl' iz Pushkina," in B. V. Asafiev, *Izbrannye Trudy,* vol. III (Moscow: Izd. AN SSSR 1954), 105–107.

49. In addition to Musorgsky's famous versions, there is the 1884 opera *Dimitrij* by Antonín Dvořak, grand French opera in the style of Meyerbeer. Dvořak began work on his *Dimitrij* in 1881, the year of Musorgsky's death, apparently with no knowledge of the Russian composer's work. The libretto, by Marie Červinková-Riegrová, was a hybrid work inspired by Schiller's fragment, Khomiakov's and Ostrovsky's Dmitri plays, and a recent drama on the theme by the Czech playwright Ferdinand Mikovec. Its plot is solidly in the German tradition, adjusted to fit the structural components of romantic opera. See John Clapham, *Antonin Dvořak* (London: Faber and Faber, 1966), 275–76; and Paul Stefan, *Anton Dvořak* (New York: Greystone Press, 1941), 112–18. The American concert premiere of *Dimitrij* took place at Carnegie Hall on March 28, 1984.

50. For commentary and a superb translation of Meyerhold's own notes to the production, see Paul Schmidt, ed., *Meyerhold at Work* (Austin: University of Texas Press, 1980), ch. IV ("Meyerhold and Pushkin").

51. See the account of the 1925 production by Meyerhold's assistant, Boris Zakhava: "Dva sezona," in Schmidt, 98–99.

52. As Meyerhold told his actors, Prokofiev was to provide the "seething background" to the Time of Troubles. Percussive instruments would realize a sort of "peculiar jazz" appropriate to the sixteenth century, and to the cacophony of soothsaying and battle. See A. V. Fevral'skii, "Prokofiev i Meierkhol'd," in *Sergei Prokofiev: Stat'i i materialy,* 2d ed. (Moscow: Muzyka, 1965), 108–16.

53. I. Martynov, *Sergei Prokofiev* (Moscow: Muzyka, 1974), 338.

54. For details by eyewitnesses of this production, see Paul Debreczeny, "Boris Godunov at the Taganka: A Note on a Non-Performance," *SEEJ* 28, no. 1 (1984): 99–101, and Nicholas Rzhevsky, "Adapting Drama to the Stage: Liubimov's *Boris Godunov,*" *Slavic and East European Arts* (Special Issue on Recent Polish and Soviet Theatre and Drama) 3, no. 1 (Winter/Spring 1985): 171–76.

55. See "Lyubimov's Fall," *The New York Times*, Thursday, March 15, 1984; and "Yurii Liubimov uvolen s posta glavnogo rezhissera teatra na Taganke," *Novoe Russkoe Slovo*, 8 March 1984. Rzhevsky suggests ("Adapting Drama," p. 175) that the banning of *Boris* was due to the direct parallels some government officials saw between Liubimov's portrait of Boris and Andropov's rise to power.

56. A. S. Khomiakov, *Dimitrii Samozvanets*, in *A. S. Khomiakov: Stikhotvoreniia i dramy* (Leningrad: Sovetskii pisatel', 1969), Act II, vi, 365: "Mne pamiatny sadov zelyonyi sumrak / Alleia lip i pleshchushchii fontan . . ." (I remember the green twilight of the gardens / The avenue of limetrees and the splashing fountain . . .). The couple must have lived through Pushkin's play to remember it, but Khomiakov then proceeds as if another text, not Pushkin's, had been experienced by his hero and heroine.

57. Pushkin to N. N. Raevsky *(fils)*, July (after the 19th), 1825. *A. S. Pushkin: Polnoe sobranie sochinenii*, vol. XIII (AN SSSR, 1937), 197. Henceforth referred to as *P:Pss*.

58. Viazemsky passed on this advice in a letter to Pushkin, 6 September 1825, when by Pushkin's own admission half the tragedy was completed. *P:Pss* XIII, 224 (Viazemsky) and 226–27 (Pushkin's response).

59. See his drafts of an introduction to *War and Peace*, and his 1868 article "Some Words about *War and Peace*" (fn. 1). "In the recent period of Russian literature," Tolstoy writes, "there is not a single artistic prose work rising at all above mediocrity which quite fits into the form of a novel, epic, or story."

60. See the argument in "What Language Should a Future Pillar of the Motherland Speak?" in F. M. Dostoevsky, *The Diary of a Writer*, trans. Boris Brasol (Santa Barbara: Peregrine Smith, 1979), 1886, III, 2, 399–400.

Chapter 2: Boris in History

1. N. M. Karamzin, *Istoriia Gosudarstva Rossiiskogo*, vol. XI (St. Petersburg: Evdokimov, 1892; reprint ed. Slavistic Printings and Reprintings 189/11, The Hague, Mouton, 1969), 72. All references are made to this twelve-volume edition. Translations are my own.

2. Ya. Eidel'man, *Poslednii letopisets* (Moscow: "Kniga," 1983), 95. The first eight volumes of the *History* were published in 1818 (although vols. I–III are inscribed 1816, and vols. IV–VIII, 1817); volume IX appeared in 1821, volumes X and XI in 1824, and the twelfth volume, left incomplete at the author's death, was published in 1829.

3. Zhukovsky to I. I. Dmitriev, 18 Feb. 1816. In V. A. Zhukovskii, *Sochineniia v trekh tomakh*, vol. 3 (Moscow: Khudozhestvennaia literatura, 1980), 483.

4. P. A. Viazemsky, as cited in N. L. Rubinshtein, *Russkaia istoriografiia* (Moscow: OGIZ/Gospolitizdat, 1941), 186. Efforts to verify this quotation in Viazemsky's own writings have been unsuccessful. I thank William Mills Todd, however, for referring me to various echoes of this sentiment, especially in Viazemsky's *Staria zapisnaia knizhka* (Leningrad: Izdatel'stvo pisatelei, 1929), 71.

5. A. S. Pushkin, "[Iz avtobiograficheskikh zapisok]," Nov. 1824. *P:Pss* XII, 305.

6. See the discussion in Henry M. Nebel, Jr., *N. M. Karamzin, A Russian Sentimentalist* (The Hague: Mouton, 1967), 88–90.

7. For the discussion that follows, I am indebted to Sidney Monas, whose provocative commentary on a late draft of this chapter is everywhere reflected and especially in this paragraph.

8. L. N. Tolstoi, *Sobranie sochinenii*, vol. 19 (Moscow: Khudozhestvennaia literatura, 1965), 120.

9. For an excellent analysis of the *primechaniia*, but one that nevertheless does not attempt to resolve their ambivalent authority, see J. L. Black, "The Primečanija: Karamzin as a 'Scientific' Historian of Russia," in *Essays on Karamzin: Russian Man-of-Letters, Political Thinker, Historian, 1766–1826*, ed. J. L. Black (The Hague: Mouton, 1975), 127–47.

10. See N. Polevoi, "Spor v nemetskikh zhurnalakh ob *Istorii gosudarstva Rossiiskogo*," *Moskovskii telegraf* XVIII (1827): 216–17: "Without a doubt Schlözer, creator of a critical survey of northern history, would have read with lofty envy the first chapters of the *History of the Russian State;* they are written with the help of his far-sighted criticism, but perfected to an extent that Schlözer could not have expected from his own indirect researches."

11. Karamzin to A. I. Turgenev, 21 January 1813: "My library had the honor of turning into ashes together with the Palace of Facets; my manuscripts, however, are safe and sound in Ostafievo. It's a great pity about the Pushkin manuscripts: they all burned, except those that were with me. An irretrievable loss for our History! The University also lost everything: the library, the study." "Pis'ma N. M. Karamzina k A. I. Turgenevu," *Russkaia starina* 97 (January–March 1899): 237.

12. For an excellent discussion of the potential of the gloss, see Lawrence Lipking, "The Marginal gloss," *Critical Inquiry* 3, no. 4 (Summer 1977): 609–55. In Lipking's view (612), the gloss serves to reaffirm the relation of part to whole in an environment where parts cohere: the world is a book, and glosses help to understand what is already there, "an unfolding of parallel, equally authoritative meanings into infinity" (622). By the end of the seventeenth century the gloss had lost its authority; authors had become self-conscious. The gloss began to suggest not the fulfillment of One Text but the disintegration of texts into many infinitely valid readings. Facts, so-called, were relegated to footnotes.

See also the opening comments in Shari Benstock, "At the Margin of Discourse: Footnotes in the Fictional Text," *PMLA* (March 1983): 204:

> By definition, footnotes are physically more constrained than the primary text . . . their purpose being to elaborate on the text without engulfing it; at the same time, they are freer to adopt a new line of rhetoric. Again, this split capability invites a shift in perspective and function, and the notations adjust the limits of the textual universe in which they participate. . . . Finally, footnotes appear to be (and often are) afterwords, appended to a text that is not in itself fully accessible to readers. . . . They allow the writer to step outside the critical discourse and comment on it from a perspective that may be different from (and in a voice that may be separate from) that established in the text.

The *primechaniia* seem to lie somewhere between footnote and gloss. Karamzin awards both parts of his *History* equal but different authority: his *primechanie* is not (as is a footnote) a true gesture of submission to a largely scholarly truth upon which the text is dependent.

13. J. L. Black, "The Primečanija," 137–38.

14. J. Luria (Ya. S. Lur'e), "Problems of Source Criticism (with Reference to Medieval Russian Documents)," trans. Michael Cherniavsky, *Slavic Review* XXVII, 1 (1968): 21.

15. See M. O. Koialovich, *Istoriia russkogo samosoznaniia* (St. Petersburg, 1884), 172–75. Nikita Muraviev devoted an entire lengthy essay to refuting the foreword, insisting that "not peace but eternal battle should exist between evil and good," and that the role of history was not to "reconcile us with imperfection" but to "urge us on to perfection." See "Zapiska Nikity Murav'eva 'Mysli ob Istorii Gosudarstva Rossiiskogo' N. M. Karamzina," in "Dekabristy-kritiki 'Istorii Gosudarstva Rossiiskogo' N. M. Karamzina," *Literaturnoe nasledstvo* I (Dekabristy-literatory) (Moscow: Izd. Akademii nauk SSSR, 1954), 585.

16. *P:Pss* XVII, 16. In Pushkin's defense, however, it should be noted that this epigram—however cruel—was not wrong. It is precisely the *necessity* of autocracy that Karamzin was defending, in keeping with his understanding of human nature and the lessons of Russian history. I thank Sidney Monas for this observation.

Several anti-Karamzin epigrams of the period were attributed to Pushkin, but he ultimately acknowledged authorship of only one. For an extended discussion of Pushkin's motivations behind this and later statements on Karamzin, which includes good background on the aesthetic and political reception of the *History* in the teens and twenties (the odd alliances it fostered, the parodies it spawned, and the surprise of its "archaicized" sentimental style), see V. Vatsuro, " 'Podvig chestnogo cheloveka,' " *Prometei* (Moscow) 5 (1968): 8–51.

17. K. F. Ryleev to F. Bulgarin, 20 July 1821. In *Sochineniia i perepiska Kondratiia Fyodorovicha Ryleeva* (St. Petersburg: tip. Glazunova, 1874), 215.

18. A. S. Pushkin, "[Iz avtobiograficheskikh zapisok]," *P:Pss* XII, 306. Pushkin wrote the passage in 1824–25 and published it in *Severnye Tsvety* in 1828. The poet himself had just been released from institutional censorship into the personal censorship of the tsar; he was not yet fully aware of what that entailed. For an excellent discussion of Pushkin's defense of Karamzin in terms of the institutions of literature in the 1820s (patronage, the salon, and commercial publishing), see William Mills Todd III, "Institutions of Literature in Early-Nineteenth-Century Russia: Boundaries and Transgressions," in *Literature and History: Theoretical Problems and Russian Case Studies*, ed. Gary Saul Morson (Stanford: Stanford University Press, 1986), 79–85.

19. See, for example, Rubinshtein, *Russkaia istoriografiia*, 176–77; V. I. Astakhov, *Kurs lektsii po russkoi istoriografii*, Part One (Kharkov: Izd. Kharkovskogo univ-ta, 1959), 144–45; B. P. Gorodetskii, *Dramaturgiia Pushkina* (Moscow: Akademia nauk, 1953), 142–44.

20. M. Pogodin, *Nikolai Mikhailovich Karamzin po ego sochineniiam, pis'mam i otzyvam sovremennikov*, II (Moscow: tip. Mamontova, 1866), 24–25. It should be pointed out, however, that Pogodin's "picture of pre-Karamzinian chaos" was subjected to severe criticism by Paul Miliukov in the 1890s. See *Glavnyia techeniia*, 129, in note 22 below.

21. Rubinshtein, *Russkaia istoriografiia*, 153.

22. P. Miliukov, *Glavnyia techeniia russkoi istoricheskoi mysli*, 3d. (St. Petersburg: Averianov, 1913), 143. The work, first published in 1897, was quickly recognized as the first radical reconsideration of Karamzin in the context of the nineteenth century.

23. For an excellent brief survey of Karamzin's contributions to language in the context of the eighteenth century, see Hans Rogger, *National Consciousness in Eighteenth-Century Russia* (Cambridge: Harvard University Press, 1960), ch. III ("Towards a National Language"), especially 120–25.

24. For a good discussion of Karamzin's positive (and negative) models, see K. N. Bestuzhev-Riumin, "Karamzin kak istorik," *Zhurnal ministerstva narodnogo proveshcheniia*, pt. 83 (St. Petersburg: Golovin, 1867): 1–20, especially 9–12.

25. Cited in J. L. Black, *Nicholas Karamzin and Russian Society in the Nineteenth Century: A Study in Russian Political and Historical Thought* (Toronto: University of Toronto Press, 1975), 38.

26. Karamzin to A. I. Turgenev, 3 April 1810. "Pis'ma N. M. Karamzina k A. I. Turgenevu, 1806–1826," *Russkaia starina* 97 (February 1899): 231.

27. Eidel'man, *Poslednii letopisets*, 57.

28. In a brief essay on his sources (included in the early printings of the *History* but omitted in later editions), Karamzin listed fourteen categories of historical material he had utilized as evidence. Among the expected chronicles, state papers, and church documents one finds (for example) "rituals," and then an entry on "ancient coins, medals, inscriptions, folktales, songs, proverbs." See "Ob istochnikakh rossiiskoi istorii do XVII veka," in N. M. Karamzin, *Istoriia Gosudarstva Rossiiskogo*, vol. I (St. Petersburg, 1818), xxvii–xxxv.

29. See Lomonosov's introduction to his *Ancient Russian History* (1766): "Anyone who sees in Russian legends deeds and heroes equal and similar to the Greeks and Romans has no reason to denigrate us in the face of them but should lay the blame on the heretofore insufficiency of our art. It was through art that Greek and Latin writers transmitted their heroes to eternal posterity, in full glory." "Vstuplenie" to *Drevniaia rossiiskaia istoriia ot nachala rossiiskogo naroda do konchiny velikogo kniazia Yaroslava pervogo* (St. Petersburg: Akademiia nauk, 1766); reprinted in M. V. Lomonosov, *Polnoe sobranie sochinenii* VI (Moscow-Leningrad: Akademiia nauk, 1952), 170.

Lomonosov's 1764 essay, "Idei dlia zhivopisnykh kartin iz rossiiskoi istorii" (Ideas for vivid pictures from Russian history) is a forerunner of Karamzin's 1802 essay, "On Events and Characters in Russian History that Can Be the Subject of the Arts." See also the discussion by T. S. Karlova, "Esteticheskii smysl istorii v tvorcheskom vospriiatii Karamzina," in *XVIII Vek*, sb. 8 (Derzhavin i Karamzin v literaturnom dvizhenii XVIII–nachala XIX veka) (Nauka, Leningrad, 1969), 282–83.

30. Lomonosov himself is subject to numerous "corrections" in Karamzin's notes. For a brief discussion, see J. L. Black, "The Primečanija," 146.

31. N. M. Karamzin, "O sluchaiakh i kharakterakh v rossiiskoi istorii, kotorye mogut byt' predmetom khudozhestv" (On events and characters in Russian history that can be the subject of the arts), originally published in *Vestnik Evropy*, 1802, no. 24. Cited here from *Sochineniia Karamzina*, 4th ed., vol. 7 (St. Petersburg: tip. Smirdina, 1834), 223, 222.

32. Miliukov credits this formulation to Srednii-Kamashev, whose article "Istoriia, kak nauka" appeared in *Vestnik Evropy* in 1827 (*Glavnye techeniia*, 5).

33. Hayden White, "The Burden of History" (1966), in *Tropics of Discourse* (Baltimore: Johns Hopkins University Press, 1978), 28, 43.

34. For reasons both political and physical (his connection with Novikov and the Masons, the later Moscow Fire), Karamzin either destroyed, or witnessed the destruction of, many of his personal papers. Letters addressed to him have not survived. Since his family was not subject to the official postmortem search (as was, say, Pushkin's widow), personal materials were dispersed in private hands. See Eidel'man, *Poslednii letopisets*, 60, 148.

Even under the best circumstances, however, Karamzin's archive might well have provided no "keys" to his development. As one recent scholar has remarked, "[His] letters are not a very reliable source. The Historiographer never entrusted himself fully to paper. Privy to state service for decades, he was accustomed to being cautious. . . . His favorite form was the hint, his favorite trope, the figure of passing over in silence. In general he was a man of few words." Vatsuro, "'Podvig chestnogo cheloveka,'" 31.

35. N. Polevoi, "Spor v nemetskikh zhurnalakh ob *Istoriia Gosudarstva Rossiiskogo*," *Moskovskii telegraf* XVIII (1827): 208.

36. See N. Apostolov, "Karamzin, kak romanist-istorik," in *Zhurnal ministerstva narodnogo prosveshcheniia* (Petrograd: Senatskaia), Part 62 (April 1916): 190–98.

37. For a detailed analysis of the various narrative voices developed by Karamzin in his prose, see Roger B. Anderson, *N. M. Karamzin's Prose: The Teller in the Tale* (Houston: Cordovan Press, 1974), especially 86–100, 190–208, 264–70.

38. "More than one old man has assured me of the truth of this," Karamzin's narrator informs the reader in a footnote to his assertion that Natalia's father, Matvei, was a good host. "Natalia, boiarskaia doch'," in N. M. Karamzin, *Izbrannye sochineniia*, vol. I (Moscow-Leningrad: Khudozhestvennaia literatura, 1964), 624.

39. I am grateful to Judith Vowles of Yale University for sharing with me her thoughts on this topic, which draw on her own research into Karamzin's vexed relationship with eighteenth-century literary models. See also the discussion in Henry M. Nebel, Jr., *N. M. Karamzin, A Russian Sentimentalist* (The Hague: Mouton, 1967), ch. VIII ("Prose: Historical, Moral, and Romantic Tales"), especially 151.

40. "Istoricheskiia vospominaniia i zamechaniia na puti k Troitse," in N. M. Karamzin, *Sochineniia Karamzina*, vol. 8 (Moscow: tip. Selivanskogo, 1804), 377.

41. See G. Makogonenko, "Literaturnaia pozitsiia Karamzina v XIX veke," *Russkaia literatura*, no. 1 (1962): 68–106, especially 103–104.

42. Karamzin criticized, for example, the fragmentation and failure to synthesize events that marked some contemporary historians. Commenting on Fesler's *History of Hungary* in a letter to A. I. Turgenev, he allowed that the man "wrote intelligently and well," but his work was all "copied from others without discrimination, without criticism . . . it is a compilation, but not a creation, there is no unity, no character, no soul." (Karamzin to A. I. Turgenev, 20 October 1815, in "Pis'ma N. M. Karamzina k A. I. Turgenevu, 1806–1826," *Russkaia starina* 97 [February 1899]: 469.) The improper unity was no improvement, however. Karamzin was exasperated with the new "philosophical" schools of history. When he received from S. S. Uvarov one of Schlegel's recent books, he retorted, "Isn't he just chasing after the specter of new ideas? He makes secondary causes primary, it's a sort of historical mysticism. . . ." (Cited in Eidel'man, *Poslednii letopisets*, 74.)

43. "The skeptical school," one recent scholar has noted, "understood the critique of a source basically as a confrontation of its testimony with some general system of historical development established *a priori*." See J. Luria (Ia. S. Lur'e), "Problems of Source Criticism (with Reference to Medieval Russian Documents)," 2.

44. See Bestuzhev-Riumin, "Karamzin kak istorik," 11: "Everything foggy [*tumannoe*] was repellent to Karamzin." Also consider Pogodin's comment on Karamzin's naïve methodology: "While telling his tale, Karamzin did

not think about system; he presumed, apparently, that system should emerge naturally from the narration; he wanted only the truth, which would itself instruct, and every predetermined direction of history was harmful to it." M. Pogodin, *Nikolai Mikhailovich Karamzin*, II, 194.

45. N. Polevoi, "*Istoriia Gosudarstva Rossiiskago* (Sochinenie N. M. Karamzina)," *Moskovskii telegraf* (1829, Part 27): 467–500.

46. An instructive, if extreme, example might be found in Mikhail Pokrovsky, whose *History of Russia from Earliest Times* (1910–14) was a work as fraught with controversy as Karamzin's own. Pokrovsky represented a mode of social and materialist historiography wedged, as it were, between the nineteenth-century historians (still organized around the reigns of tsars) and the *re*-glorification of heroes and great national leaders under Stalin. An admirer of Lenin, Pokrovsky was not blind to the force of great men in history. But he opposed portraying Russia's past as a series of tsars, and just as strenuously opposed a past composed of Pugachevs. A history of monarchs, *and* one of revolutionaries, were both histories of individual personality, and equally un-Marxist.

Pokrovsky's chapters on the *Smuta* could not be more different from Karamzin's. Issues of murder and guilt are dismissed as slander, and the emphasis is on the social classes supporting Boris's candidacy. See M. N. Pokrovskii, *Izbrannye proizvedeniia, Book I: Russkaia istoriia s drevneishikh vremen* (vols. I and II) (Moscow: Mysl', 1966), 335–60; also Roman Szporluk, ed., *Introduction to Russia in World History: Selected Essays by M. N. Pokrovskii* (Ann Arbor: University of Michigan Press, 1970), 12–42.

47. As V. I. Astakhov wrote in his standard textbook on Russian historiography: "Karamzin often utterly departs from his sources in the interests of giving logical grace to the pragmatic narrative and a rhetorical beauty to the style. In those places where he must document his monarchical point of view, he simply distorts these sources." V. I. Astakhov, *Kurs lektsii po russkoi istoriografii*, Pt. I, 145.

48. A. Gulyga, "Podvig Karamzina," *Voprosy literatury* 10 (October 1979): 211–30. Vatsuro's " 'Podvig chestnogo cheloveka' " (1968) discusses the *History* in much the same open-minded spirit (see n. 16), stressing Karamzin's distinction between autocracy and despotism, and the legitimacy of Pushkin's defense of Karamzin against the Decembrists.

49. Eidel'man, *Poslednii letopisets*, 158–59.

50. See L. N. Luzianina, "Problemy istorii v russkoi literature pervoi chetverti XIX veka (Ot 'Istorii Gosudarstva Rossiiskogo' N. M. Karamzina do tragedii A. S. Pushkina 'Boris Godunov')," Diss. for Candidate of Philological Sciences, Leningrad State University, 1972, chapters 1–3. A concise summary of her approach can be found in her sixteen-page *Avtoreferat*, 9–13. For further discussion, see L. N. Luzianina, "*Istoriia gosudarstva rossiiskogo* N. M. Karamzina i tragediia Pushkina *Boris Godunov* (k probleme kharaktera letopistsa)," *Russkaia literatura*, no. 1 (1971): 48–55.

51. Pogodin, *Nikolai Mikhailovich Karamzin*, II, 190.

52. Eidel'man, *Poslednii letopisets*, 61–62; see also Makogonenko, "Literaturnaia pozitsiia Karamzina," 105.

53. The discussion that follows on pp. 43–45 is condensed and adapted from Luzianina, "*Istoriia gosudarstva*," 49–51.

54. See Luzianina, *Avtoreferat*, 11: "Karamzin attempts, in his own attitude toward what he depicts, to achieve that 'moral freedom to judge deeds and characters' which, in the historian's opinion, was characteristic of the

chroniclers' position. In the final volumes of the *History* we have a type of narration no longer determined by a two-pronged elucidation of the fact [i.e., both as chronicle and as historian's frame.]"

55. Cited in Eidel'man, *Poslednii letopisets,* 150.

56. See Luzianina, *"Istoriia gosudarstva,"* 51.

57. Luzianina, *Avtoreferat,* 11.

58. See, for example, M. B. Rabinovich, *"Boris Godunov* Pushkina, *Istoriia Karamzina* i letopisi," in *Pushkin v shkole: sbornik statei* (Moscow: Izd. Akademii pedagogicheskikh nauk RSFSR, 1951), 311–12.

59. N. M. Karamzin, "O taine kantseliarii" (1803), in *Sochineniia Karamzina,* vol. 8 (St. Petersburg: tip. Smirdina, 1835), 130: "Our chroniclers are not Tacituses, they did not judge monarchs, did not relate all their deeds but only the brilliant ones. . . ."

60. N. M. Karamzin, "Ob istochnikakh rossiskoi istorii do XVII veka," in *Istoriia Gosudarstva Rossiiskogo* (1818), vol. 1, xxix–xxx.

61. J. Luria (Ia. S. Lur'e), "Problems of Source Criticism (with Reference to Medieval Russian Documents)," 1.

62. For a good summary of the history of internal source criticism and the art of decoding chronicles, see A. G. Kuz'min, *Nachal'nye etapy drevnerusskogo letopisaniia* (The nature of the chronicles and methods for studying them) (Moscow: Izd. Moskovskogo universiteta, 1977), 25–54.

63. Edward L. Keenan, Jr., "The Trouble with Muscovy: Some Observations upon Problems of the Comparative Study of Form and Genre in Historical Writing," *Medievalia et Humanistica,* n.s. no. 5 (1974): 110.

64. For a brief account in English of Shakhmatov's career and his pathbreaking *Razyskaniia o drevneishikh russkikh letopisnykh svodakh* (Findings regarding the ancient Russian Chronicle compilations, 1908), see George Vernadsky, *Russian Historiography: A History* (Belmont, Mass.: Nordland, 1978), 335–40.

65. "The chronicle was intended first and foremost not for posterity, but for contemporaries, and chronicle compilations were put to use in political struggles," Ia. S. Lur'e writes in *Obshcherusskie letopisi XIV–XV vv.* (Leningrad: Nauka, 1976), 15. See also the Introduction to M. D. Priselkov, *Istoriia russkogo letopisaniia XI–XV vv.* (Leningrad: Leningradskii gos. universitet, 1940), 5–15; and V. A. Rybakov, *Drevniaia Rus': Skazaniia, byliny, letopsis* (Moscow: Akademiia nauk, 1963), 158: "The time has passed forever when historians could dip into the wealth of chronicle material and, ignoring the differences [among them], cite without discrimination such individual phrases as 'the chronicle says . . .' or 'the chronicler said. . . .' In fact no such common stock of chronicle information existed. . . ."

66. D. S. Likhachev, *Poetika drevnerusskoi literatury* (Moscow: Nauka, 1979), 262–63.

67. A. S. Pushkin, *"Istoriia Russkogo naroda,* sochinenie Nikolaia Polevogo," originally published in *Literaturnaia gazeta,* 1830, no. 4. *P:pss* XI, 120.

68. For a good discussion, see I. Toibin, *"Istoriia gosudarstva Rossiiskogo* N. M. Karamzina v tvorcheskoi zhizni Pushkina," *Russkaia literatura,* no. 4 (1966), 41–44.

69. R. G. Skrynnikov, *Boris Godunov* (Moscow: Nauka, 1978). A very readable, if occasionally imprecise, translation has been published as Ruslan G. Skrynnikov, *Boris Godunov,* ed. and trans. Hugh F. Graham (Gulf Breeze, Fla.: Academic International Press, 1982). Page references are made to this translation; quotations adjusted where necessary for accuracy or tone.

Skrynnikov has published a great deal on Godunov and the Time of

Troubles. For additional details on the events under discussion here (the death in Uglich and the election of Boris), see his "Boris Godunov i Tsarevich Dmitrii," in *Issledovaniia po sotsial'no-politicheskoi istorii Rossii* (Sbornik statei pamiati B. A. Romanova) (Leningrad: Nauka, 1971), 182–97, and "Boris Godunov's Struggle for the Throne," *Canadian-American Slavic Studies* 11, no. 3 (Fall 1977): 325–53.

70. For a convenient summary of his findings, see S. F. Platonov, *Boris Godunov* (Petrograd, 1921), trans. by L. Rex Pyles as *Boris Godunov, Tsar of Russia* (Gulf Breeze, Fla.: Academic International Press, 1973). Page references in the text are made to this translation.

Popular biographies are distributed along the pro- and anti-Boris spectrum. Stephen Graham's *Boris Godunov* (New Haven: Yale University Press, 1933), based on Karamzin and Kostomarov, represents the most negative secular portrait in English; Ian Grey's more recent *Boris Godunov: The Tragic Tsar* (New York: Scribner's, 1973) is an open apology, substantially adopting Platonov's conclusions and thus obliged to defend itself against the canonical artistic treatments.

71. See Platonov, *Boris Godunov*, 148–52. An even more fervent exoneration of Boris, and in a wider social context, can be found in Platonov's *Smutnoe vremia* (Prague, 1924; reprint ed., Russian Reprint Series X, The Hague: Europe Printing, 1965), 67–85. Platonov stresses the fact that the princely nobility considered *both* the Godunovs and the Romanovs—allies during the early years of Fyodor's reign—upstart "newcomers through marriage to the throne" (69). The Romanovs most likely broke with the Godunovs out of petty jealousy. Platonov refers to the Uglich Affair simply as "an event in Muscovite life that could be used against Boris." It could never have triggered a political crisis unless powerful nobles chose to exploit it. In this reading Boris is very much a victim of the Romanovs, and not the other way around.

72. V. O. Kliuchevskii, "Sostav predstavitel'stva na zemskikh soborakh drevnei Rusi," in *Opyty i issledovaniia, pervyi sbornik statei* (Petrograd, 1981), 358–472; on the 1598 *sobor*, 408–27. It should be noted, however, that Skrynnikov takes issue with Kliuchevsky on the legitimacy of Boris's election, relying on evidence of two forgeries in Boris's electoral documents. See "Boris Godunov's Struggle for the Throne," 325–33.

73. Two eminent historians of the period, A. A. Rudakov and K. V. Chistov, differ on this point. According to Rudakov, the rumors about a "tsarevich murdered on order of Boris" began in 1598 and were then incorporated into documents starting with Shuisky's *gramota* of 1606. Chistov, who has studied the death of Dmitri as oral legend, insists that rumors of evil intent long predated Boris's election, in fact, predated even the death itself. See n. 78 below.

74. A good English-language summary of the research can be found in George Vernadsky, "The Death of the Tsarevich Dimitry: a Reconsideration of the Case," *Oxford Slavonic Papers*, vol. V (Oxford: Clarendon Press, 1954), 1–19.

75. I. I. Polosin, "Uglichskoe sledstvennoe delo 1591 g.," in I. I. Polosin, *Sotsial'no-politicheskaia istoriia Rossii XVI-nachala XVII v.* (Moscow: Akademiia nauk, 1963), 218–45. Of course, Polosin admits, Boris isolated the Uglich court and kept the Nagoi family under surveillance during the first part of Fyodor's reign. But the political scandal of Dmitri's death would have harmed Godunov far more than it could have helped him; indeed, it could be argued that Dmitri's death was arranged by Boris's *enemies*. In this Skrynnikov concurs; see his "Boris Godunov i Tsarevich Dmitrii," 191.

76. Polosin insists that Pushkin knew the *Sledstvennoe delo* perfectly well, and yet accepted all the same the version of murder by Godunov. Relying on indirect evidence in the "Dostig ia vysshei vlasti" monologue, Polosin suggests that Pushkin could *not* have held Boris responsible for the murder, "for that would not have been a [mere] stain on his conscience but moral degeneration, a crime" (244). Thus the tragedy of Boris is that he *desired* the death, not that he caused it; his guilt was the result of a coincidence between the accidental death in Uglich and his "thoughts about a potential crime." The concept of "crime in desiring the deed," weakly developed here by Polosin, is a very productive avenue into Pushkin's *Boris* and will be explored more fully in chapter 3.

77. See S. F. Platonov, *Drevnerusskiia skazaniia i povesti o smutnom vremeni XVII veka, kak istoricheskii istochnik*, 2d ed. (St. Petersburg: tip. Aleksandrova, 1913). Platonov divides his material into three parts: eyewitness accounts written during the *Smuta*, accounts dating from Tsar Michael's reign (1613–45), and later secondary material (chronicles, manuscripts, and tales).

78. A. A. Rudakov, "Razvitie legendy o smerti Tsarevicha Dimitriia v Ugliche," in *Istoricheskie zapiski* (Akademia nauk) 12 (1941): 254–83; K. V. Chistov, *Russkie narodnye sotsial'no-utopicheskie legendy XVII–XIX vv.* (Moscow: Nauka, 1967), 33–60. In English, a good survey (and excellent bibliography) can be found in A. H. Thompson, "The Legend of Tsarevich Dimitriy: Some Evidence of an Oral Tradition," *The Slavonic and East European Review* XLVI, no. 106 (January 1968): 48–59. My brief account in the text (pp. 54–57) is a composite of information from the above essays, supplemented by material in Platonov and Skrynnikov.

79. See D. S. Likhachev, *Poetika drevnerusskoi literatury*, 80–101. For a brief survey in English of the concept of "literary etiquette," see William Edward Brown, *A History of Seventeeth Century Literature* (Ardis, 1980), 26–28.

80. For a vivid account of the pretenders and their social role, see Chistov, 40–49, 60.

81. Rudakov, 283; Platonov, "Skazaniia i povesti. . . ," 417.

82. "Istoricheskiia vospominaniia i zamechaniia na puti k Troitse," in N. M. Karamzin, *Sochineniia Karamzina*, vol. 8 (Moscow: tip. Selivanskago, 1804), 300–77. The essay was first serialized in *Vestnik Evropy*, 1802, part 4, nos. 15–17.

83. See M. Pogodin, "Ob uchastii Godunova v ubienii Tsarevicha Dimitriia," first published in *Moskovskii vestnik* 1829, no. 3, repr. in M. Pogodin, *Istoriko-kriticheskie otryvki* (Moscow: tip. Avgusta Semena, 1846), the footnote on p. 305: "In closing I note that the Historiographer himself previously (in his observations on the road to Troitse) was inclined to defend Boris, and he was the *first*, to his great glory, who commented on the injustice of the chronicles: it is remarkable that later in the *History* he changed his mind, without providing any reasons which might have prompted him to do so."

See also Kiukhelbeker's diary entry for 2 July 1832: "I read through Karamzin's little article which I hadn't read for ten years, 'Historical Reminiscences on the Road to Troitse . . .' An entirely different man is writing and judging here than the one who wrote the *History of the Russian State*, and I don't know, aren't Karamzin's thoughts more just in 1802 than in 1820 and the subsequent years? At least they are more sincere." V. K. Kiukhel'beker, *Puteshestvie, Dnevnik, Stat'i* (Leningrad: Nauka, 1979), 153.

84. For a good discussion of Karamzin on usurpers, see K. V. Bazilevich, "Boris Godunov v izobrazhenii Pushkina," in *Istoricheskie zapiski*, I (Moscow: AN SSSR, 1937), 33–35.

85. The text here is translated by Richard Pipes, *Karamzin's Memoir on Ancient and Modern Russia: A Translation and Analysis* (New York: Atheneum, 1959), 110. Pipes's prefatory essay is still the most lucid introduction to Karamzin's political views as a historian. Further page references provided in the text.

86. For a discussion of various types of "nondevelopmental" biographical chronotopes, see "Forms of Time and Chronotope in the Novel," *The Dialogic Imagination: Four Essays by M. M. Bakhtin*, 140–42.

87. ". . . [Boris] est' tiran, khotia eschche i robkii." This opens up a rich new epithet, "Robkost' Godunova" (Godunov's timidity), which glosses an entire later episode in Karamzin (XI, 94) and is parodically reworked by Pushkin in Shuisky's cynical lines: "He'll overstep the line; Boris is not so timid" (Pereshagnyot: Boris ne tak-to robok).

88. *Prim.* #223 cites one of the most famous character portraits in Fletcher's *Of the Russe Commonwealth:*

> That hee is a naturall sonne to Joan Vasilowich, the Russe people warrant it, by the fathers qualitie that beginneth to appeare already in his tender years. He is delighted (they say) to see sheepe and other cattel killed, and to looke on their throtes while they are bleeding (which commonly children are afraid to beholde), and to beate geese and hennes with a staffe till he sees them lie dead.

Cited here according to the text in Edward A. Bond, ed., *Russia at the Close of the Sixteenth Century* (London: Hakluyt Society, 1856), 22.

89. See J. L. Black, "The Primečanija," 140.

90. A. I. Mankiev (Mankievich) was a Pole serving as secretary to Prince Andrei Khilkov, under whose name the *Iadro* was published. Mankiev wrote the book while in Sweden as a prisoner of war and admitted that the conditions of its composition precluded any scholarly verification; he included whatever details struck his fancy as being "worthy of note or remembrance." Throughout the eighteenth century the *Iadro* was attributed to Prince Khilkov; Karamzin was the first to credit it to Mankiev. For a brief discussion of the *Iadro*, see A. S. Lappo-Danilevskii, "Ocherk razvitiia russkoi istoriografii," in *Russkii istoricheskii zhurnal*, book 6 (1920), repr. Slavistic Printings and Reprintings 259/4 (The Hague: Mouton, 1971): 24–29.

See also the foreword to the *Iadro* itself, by the Russian historian G. F. Müller. Müller is at pains to acknowledge the many errors in the manuscript, most of which he had put right, and notes that the book "was composed under dim and chaotic conditions [*temno i ne skladno*]." ("Predislovie" to Andrei Yakovlevich Khilkov, *Iadro Rossiiskoi Istorii* [Moscow: Pechat' pri imperatorskom Moskovskom universitete, 1770], 3–5.)

91. Andrei Yakovlevich Khilkov, *Iadro Rossiiskoi Istorii*, 213–14.

92. This observation is made by Rudakov at the end of his essay "Razvitie legendy" (283), but Rudakov does not discuss its significance.

93. Consider the discussion of this event in Constantin de Grunwald, *Saints of Russia* (London: Hutchinson, 1960), 36–37: "At first sight there is something paradoxical in this canonization. Neither Boris nor Gleb, the victims of a dynastic quarrel, were killed for their attachment to the Christian religion; they had neither sought nor desired their death, like the ancient martyrs. Until the moment when the tragedy occurred during their short lives they had not risen to the lofty pinnacles of holiness."

94. Skrynnikov, *Boris Godunov*, 52.

95. *Lektsii po russkoi istorii professora S. F. Platonova*, ed. Iv. Blinov, 10th ed. (Petrograd: Senatskaia tipografiia, 1917), repr. Russian Reprint Series 64 (The Hague: Mouton, 1967), 231.

96. Karamzin's citation of the *Delo* appears to be complete. Compare *prim.* ##230, 231, 238, 240, and 243 of volume X with the edition of the *Delo* most likely to have been at Karamzin's disposal (*Sobranie gosudarstvennykh gramot i dogovorov,* vol. 2, 1819), 103–23. The original of the *Delo,* a scroll with its first sheets missing and showing clear evidence of cutting and pasting, was not responsibly examined by scholars until the twentieth century (V. I. Kleyn in 1913). It is still a disputed document. See Vernadsky, "The Death of the Tsarevich Dmitry: A Reconstruction of the Case," 4–5.

97. See L. N. Luzianina, "Ob osobennostiakh izobrazheniia naroda v *Istorii Gosudarstva Rossiiskogo* N. M. Karamzina," in *Russkaia literatura XIX–XX vekov* (Uchenye zapiski Leningradskogo universita, 1971, seriia filologicheskikh nauk), 6–17. My analysis, however, differs somewhat from hers.

98. For a good discussion of these contradictions, see I. Z. Serman, "Paradoksy narodnogo soznaniia v tragedii A. S. Pushkina *Boris Godunov,*" trans. by Caryl Emerson and Nathan Rosen as "Paradoxes of the Folk Mind in Pushkin's *Boris Godunov,*" unpublished essay.

99. N. M. Karamzin, "Vospominaniia i zamechaniia na puti k Troitse," 353.

100. Boris might have spilled innocent blood, writes Karamzin, but "almost all his other imaginary crimes seem to me absurd, worthy of the coarse ignoramuses who through slander wished to flatter the reigning Romanov name" (365–66).

101. See Alexander Herzen, "The Russian People and Socialism, An Open Letter to Jules Michelet," in his *From the Other Shore,* trans. Moura Budberg (London: Weidenfeld and Nicolson, 1956), especially 178–80.

102. In an interesting English parallel to the Russian story, recent historiography has tended to exonerate Richard III from guilt in the matter of the young princes' death. The party responsible in the English instance for the "continued historical misunderstanding" is Shakespeare, whose power to canonize plots in his own country's history easily equals Pushkin's power in the Russian context.

103. See James H. Billington's expansion of these two terms in his *The Icon and the Axe: An Interpretive History of Russian Culture* (New York: Vintage, 1970), Pt. III, 1, "The Split Within," 121–24.

104. Rudolf Bachtold, "Karamzins Weg zur Geschichte," in *Basler Beitrage zur Geschichtswissenschaft,* Band 23 (Basel, 1946).

105. "What a miracle these last two volumes of Karamzin are!" Pushkin wrote to Zhukovsky in August 1825. "What life! C'est palpitant comme la gazette d'hier." Pushkin to Vasily Zhukovsky, 17 August 1825. *P:Pss* XIII, 211.

106. See the discussion in A. L. Slonimskii, "*Boris Godunov* i dramaturgiia 20-kh godov," in "*Boris Godunov*" *A. S. Pushkina,* ed. K. N. Derzhavin (Leningrad: Gosudarstvennyi akademicheskii teatr dramy, 1936), 67–68. Karamzin made the request in January 1826. To be sure, the refusal was not made solely for personal reasons. For months Pushkin's friends had been agitating for the poet's release from house arrest in Mikhailovskoe, and Pushkin wryly remarked that his new play—already notorious through several unauthorized public readings—should not circulate, especially not in the august company kept by Karamzin. Apropos of *Godunov*'s inaccessibility, Pavel Katenin wrote Pushkin (11 May 1826): "Not long ago I had a good laugh at your (such as it was) response to the desire of a certain well-known person to read your tragedy: *Godunov*—it's not for ladies, and I won't give it to you [the

pun in Russian is: "Tragediia eta ne dlia dam, i ya ee ne dam"]. Tell me, did you really say that?" *P:Pss* XIII, 277. For another thoughtful account of the relationship between Historiographer and Poet quite free of the cult of Pushkin, see E. F. Shmurlo, "Etiudy o Pushkine. 1. Rol' Karamzina v sozdanii pushkinskogo *Borisa Godunova*," in *Pushkinskii sbornik*, Russkii institut v Prage (Prague: tip. Politika, 1929), 27–40.

107. Pushkin to Viazemsky, 10 July 1826, *P:Pss* XIII, 286. "Is it possible," Pushkin continues in this letter, "that not a single Russian can produce a worthy tribute to his memory?" One month earlier Viazemsky, in Petersburg for Karamzin's funeral, had written to Pushkin (12 June 1826): "You're a naughty boy and have sinned often with your epigrams against Karamzin, just to grab a smile from some scapegraces and scoundrels. . . ." To this Pushkin responded (10 July): "I am grieved by your letter . . . and what are you calling my epigrams against Karamzin? There was only one, written by me when Karamzin had withdrawn himself and wounded my vanity and my sincere affection for him . . ." *P:Pss* XIII, 284–85. See the extended discussion in Boris Tomashevskii, "Epigrammy Pushkina na Karamzina," in *Pushkin: Issledovanie i materialy*, vol. I (Moscow-Leningrad: Akademiia nauk, 1956), 208–15.

108. Pushkin considered reworking the several pages on Karamzin in his memoirs—that small portion which he had not burned in 1825—but, as he wrote to Viazemsky five months after the funeral: "I reread my pages on Karamzin, nothing there is fit to print" (*P:Pss* XIII, 304; 9 November 1826). Four months passed, and Pushkin wrote Delvig from Mikhailovskoe: "Our silence on Karamzin is indecent enough; it's not for Bulgarin to interrupt it. That would be even more indecent . . ." (*P:Pss* XIII, 334; 31 July 1826). This inability, among Karamzin's closest friends and successors, to formulate an appropriate eulogy is yet further testimony to Karamzin's ambivalent legacy.

For a good discussion of the government's posthumous "canonization" of Karamzin and the cautious moves by Pushkin and others to articulate a "counter-eulogy," see Vatsuro, " 'Podvig chestnogo cheloveka,' " 38–51.

109. M. Pogodin, "Ob uchastii Godunova v ubienii Tsarevicha Dimitriia," *Moskovskii vestnik* 1829, no. 3. Cited here from M. Pogodin, *Istoriko-kriticheskie otryvki* (Moscow: tip. Avgusta Semena, 1846), 273–305. Page references in the text are to this later volume.

110. See Pogodin's letter to S. P. Shevyrev, 26 Sept. 1829: "From Pushkin I've heard nothing at all, because for a whole two hours running he did nothing but go on about my article in defense of Boris, and then we were interrupted." ("Pis'ma M. P. Pogodina k S. P. Shevyrevu," *Russkii arkhiv* 1882, Bk. III, 112.) See also the entries in Pogodin's diary, 19 September–7 October 1829: "Several conversations with Pushkin about Boris . . ." and 30 April 1831: "I went to Pushkin's and argued with him for four hours about Boris. He is the *Procureur du Roi*, and I'm the defense lawyer. I cannot get all the answers out of him, but I begged him to write an article, for which I already have a ready-made rebuttal. . . ." (In "Pushkin po dokumentam Pogodinskogo arkhiva," *Pushkin i ego sovremenniki*, vyp. XXIII–XXIV [Petrograd: tip. Akademii nauk, 1916], 102, 113.)

111. "Zametki na poliakh M. P. Pogodina, 'Ob uchastii Godunova v ubienii Tsarevicha Dimitriia,' " *P:Pss* XII, 243–56. The comments were made on a copy of *Moskovskii vestnik*, 1829, no. 3, and first published in 1913.

112. Pushkin did not share the sceptical view toward chronicles as historical source that had begun to gain adherents in the 1830s. "Look how Schlözer began his critical investigations!" Pushkin wrote in his "Comments on Reading

Schlözer's *Nestor.*" "He copied out the chronicles word for word, letter for letter . . . but *our* [historians]!" *P:Pss* XII, 207.

113. B. M. Eikhenbaum, "Cherty letopisnogo stilia v literature, XIX v.," in *Trudy AN SSSR,* Institut russkoi literatury, otdel drevnerusskoi literatury, XIV (Moscow-Leningrad, 1958), 545–46.

114. A. S. Pushkin, *"Istoriia russkogo naroda,* sochineniia Nikolaiia Polevogo," *P:Pss* XI, 120.

115. See, for example, the discussion in V. A. Bochkarev, *Russkaia istoricheskaia dramaturgiia perioda podgotovki vostaniia dekabristov (1816–1825 gg.),* Uchenye zapiski, vypusk 56 (Kuibyshev: Kuibyshevskii gos. pedagogicheskii institut, 1968), 347–49. For a more aggressive (if less persuasive) excerpting of the evidence to prove that Pushkin appreciated Karamzin the poet but was cool, or even hostile, to Karamzin the historian because of the latter's lack of a "specific theory," see B. D. Grekov, "Istoricheskie vozzreniia Pushkina," in *Istoricheskie zapiski,* I (Moscow: AN SSSR, 1937), 6–9.

116. See B. P. Gorodetskii, *"Boris Godunov* v tvorchestve Pushkina," in Derzhavin, ed., *Boris Godunov A. S. Pushkina,* 30. Gorodetsky classifies the dedication with the "no less familiar" parodic foreword to *The Bronze Horseman,* in which Pushkin insists on the historical veracity of his data and provides his readers with a factual reference.

117. For variants on the title, see *P:Pss* VII, 290. For a variant on the ending, see *P:Pss* VII, 302: "End of the comedy, in which the main personage was Tsar Boris Godunov. Glory to the Father and the Son and the Holy Ghost, Amen."

118. This presumption also makes genuine the sentiment expressed by Pushkin in one of his draft prefaces for *Boris:* "My tragedy is already known to almost everyone whose opinion I value. Among my listeners only one has been missing, the one to whom I am indebted for the idea of my tragedy, whose genius inspired and supported me; whose approval I imagined as the sweetest reward and which was the only thing that distracted me during my solitary labor." Dated September 1829. *P:Pss,* XI, 140.

Chapter 3: Boris in Drama

1. M. M. Bakhtin, "Iz zapisei 1970–1971 godov," in *Estetika slovesnogo tvorchestva* (Moscow: Iskusstvo, 1979), 336. For a translation of these notes, see Mikhail Bakhtin, *Speech Genres and Other Late Essays,* trans. Vern McGee, ed. Caryl Emerson and Michael Holquist (Austin: University of Texas Press, 1986).

2. See B. Engel'gardt, "Istorizm Pushkina," in *Pushkinist: Istoriko-literaturnyi sbornik,* II, ed. S. Vengerov (Petrograd: 1916), 2.

3. A. S. Pushkin, "[O vtorom tome *Istorii russkogo naroda* Polevogo]" (1830), *P:Pss* XI, 127. These notes, left unpublished at the time of Pushkin's death, were first entered into a Collected Works in 1855 (Annenkov's edition).

4. Jurij Striedter, "Poetic Genre and the Sense of History in Pushkin," *New Literary History* 8, no. 2 (Winter 1977): 295–309. Karamzin's *History* as mythologizing agent is discussed in the opening paragraphs, 295.

5. Pushkin to N. N. Raevsky *(fils),* 30 January/June 1829. *P:Pss* XIV, 48.

6. Michael Meyer, *Henrik Ibsen: The Making of a Dramatist 1828–1864* (London: Rupert Hart-Davis, 1967), 122. I thank Paul Schmidt for his reminder that a bad period for drama is not necessarily a bad period for theater or for stage performance. Historical grand opera, romantic ballet, and melo-

drama all flourished during the 1820s and thirties; it was precisely their success, in fact, that had made Pushkin so ardently desire a reform of the theater. Comedy, farce, and melodrama were *popular* forms. It was only much later in the nineteenth century that theater underwent the "intellectualization" that was to reduce it to a relatively minor cultural phenomenon.

7. One recent study does develop this parallel. Mark Pomar devotes ch. 11 of his "Russian Historical Drama of the Early Nineteenth Century" (Ph.D. diss., Columbia University, 1978) to a comparison of *Boris Godunov* and *Dantons Tod*.

8. "[Nabroski predisloviia k *Borisu Godunovu*]," *P:Pss* XI, 141.

9. For a good discussion of these early Russian history plays and a reading of Pushkin's *Boris* as an inversion of their traditional techniques, see Pomar, especially ch. 7.

10. "[O narodnoi drame i drame *Marfa Posadnitsa*]," *P:Pss* XI, 181: "[The dramatic poet] must refrain from being too clever or from favoring one side and sacrificing another. The people of past days, their minds, their prejudices should speak in the tragedy—and not the poet, not his political opinions or his secret or open bias."

11. As many critics have pointed out, "the battle with classicism under the banner of romanticism was an already traveled path," and Pushkin rarely repeated earlier polemical moves. See the good discussion in V. A. Bochkarev, *Russkaia istoricheskaia dramaturgiia perioda podgotovki vosstaniia dekabristov (1816–1825)*, 368–72; also, the succinct account by I. V. Kartashova, "Romantizm i formirovanie dramaturgicheskoi sistemy A. S. Pushkina," in *Romantizm v khudozhestvennoi literature* (Kazan': Izd. Kazanskogo universiteta, 1972), 23–38.

12. Pushkin to Viazemsky, 13 July 1825, *P:Pss* XIII, 188.

13. For a discussion of other concurrent "romantic tragedies," see A. L. Slonimskii, "*Boris Godunov* i dramaturgiia 20-kh godov," in *"Boris Godunov" A. S. Pushkina*, ed. K. N. Derzhavin, 58–59. Early nineteenth-century dramatic theory made a distinction between "old" and "new" tragedy: the old was governed by fate, the new (also called romantic or Christian tragedy) by free will and moral conscience. But here as well, Pushkin's *Boris* did not fit easily into the given categories. See Bochkarev, 444–47.

14. Pushkin to A. A. Bestuzhev, 30 November 1825. The letter continues: "By romanticism we understand Lamartine . . . no matter how much I read about romanticism, none of it is quite right." *P:Pss* XIII, 244–45.

15. The capricious evolution of Pushkin's use of the term "romantic" has been carefully traced. See John Mersereau, Jr., "Pushkin's Concept of Romanticism," in *Studies in Romanticism* III, 1 (1963): 24–41, and in Russian, V. Sipovskii, "Pushkin i romantizm," in *Pushkin i ego sovremenniki: materialy i izsledovaniia*, vypusk XXIII–XXIV (Petrograd, 1916; repr. ed. Slavistic Printings and Reprintings, 123/8, The Hague: Mouton, 1970), 223–80.

Sipovsky's essay deals first with romanticism in general and then with Pushkin's use of it. In his view, romanticism's most enduring characteristic is its individualizing impulse—of persons, nature, nations, and epochs (233–35). In the young Pushkin this impulse was centered on the psychological "I"; later it was expanded to include the fates of nations and peoples. Regrettably, Sipovsky devotes only a paragraph to romantic tragedy, calling it, in essence, realism (279). But his general thesis merits attention, with the cautionary note that "individualization" as a key to the romantic impulse should be used with care. The romantics were certainly more interested in "the individual" as such than were, say, their neoclassical predecessors. But of equal importance to many romantic writers were the supra- and subpersonal strata: the nation, and unifying archetypes in the unconscious.

16. "O poezii klassicheskoi i romanticheskoi," *P:Pss* XI, 36. The essay is in the tradition of August Wilhelm Schlegel's *Lectures on Dramatic Art and Literature* (1808), whose lectures #1 and #22 deal with the classical-romantic dichotomy. But Pushkin refutes this definition. Nothing, in fact, could be further from Pushkin's understanding of romantic tragedy than Friedrich Schlegel's famous definition of the romantic: that which "presents a sentimental theme in a fantastic form." See Friedrich Schlegel, "Letter About the Novel," in *Dialogue on Poetry and Literary Aphorisms,* ed. and trans. Ernst Behler and Roman Struc (University Park: The Pennsylvania State University Press, 1968), 98.

17. "O tragedii," *P:Pss* XI, 39.

18. Pushkin to N. N. Raevsky *(fils),* second half of July (after the 19th), 1825. *P:Pss* XIII, 197.

19. Ibid.

20. "Pis'mo k izdateliu *Moskovskogo vestnika," P:Pss* XI, 66–69.

21. "[Nabroski predisloviia k *Borisu Godunovu]," P:Pss* XI, 140.

22. "Pis'mo k izdateliu *Moskovskogo vestnika," P:Pss* XI, 68. For a level-headed discussion of the discrepancy between this letter, so polemical against allusions in tragedy, and other comments by Pushkin that suggest a subtext in contemporary events, see S. Bondi, "Dramaturgiia Pushkina," in his *O Push-kine: Stat'i i issledovaniia* (Moscow: Khudozhestvennaia literatura, 1978), 198–200.

23. For an excellent discussion of Pushkin's attitude toward literary and historical allusion, see G. A. Gukovskii, *Pushkin i problemy realisticheskogo stilia* (Moscow: GIKhL, 1957), 9–13. In his commentary on Pushkin's letter to *Moskovskii vestnik,* Gukovsky speculates on the factors that "kept Pushkin from publishing his tragedy." If it was a fear of allusions—in this case, to the Uprising of December 1825—then it was surely no allusion embedded there by the playwright; *Boris Godunov* was completed *before* the uprising took place. What Pushkin feared, rather, were allusions supplied by the reader of 1827.

24. For a good discussion of the Vadim project, see Bochkarev, 381–83.

25. Applying his usual criteria, Karamzin distrusts the account in the Nikon Chronicle because it is a relatively late version, not confirmed in Nestor. See *Istoriia gosudarstva Rossiiskogo* I, 77:

> We do not know any other trustworthy details [on Riurik's reception in Novgorod]: we do not know whether the people blessed the change in their civil statutes; did they revel in happy peace and quiet, so rarely known to societies run by the people? Or did they lament the loss of their ancient freedom? Although the most recent chroniclers do say that the Slavs became indignant at their slavery, and a certain Vadim, called the Brave, fell by the hand of the powerful Riurik together with many of his accomplices in Novgorod—and indeed it is a possible event; people accustomed to freedom might wish for rulers to protect them from the horrors of anarchy, but they might also have regretted [the invitation] *if* the Varangians, compatriots and friends of Riurik, oppressed them—nevertheless this piece of information, since it is not based in the ancient tales of Nestor, seems to be mere guesswork and fantasy.

26. Pushkin was a great admirer of Byron's narrative verse but a critic of the dramas. In an unpublished note dating from 1827, Pushkin explained why:

Byron cast a one-sided glance at the world and at the nature of humanity, then turned away from them and sank into his own self. . . . Ultimately he achieved, created and described a single character (namely his own). . . . When he began to compose his tragedy *[Cain]*, he distributed to each character one of the component parts of this gloomy and powerful character, and thus splintered his majestic creation into several petty and insignificant characters.

"[O dramakh Bairona]," *P:Pss* XI, 51.

27. For an excellent discussion of the *Vadim* variants and *Boris Godunov* perceived in the framework of "open and closed forms of drama," see Mark Ia. Poliakov, *Voprosy poetiki i khudozhestvennoi semantiki* (Moscow: Sovetskii pisatel', 1978), 103–13 ("Otkrytaia i zakrytaia forma dramy. *Vadim Novgorodskii i Boris Godunov*").

28. One recent reading of the play, by Stanislav Rassadin, ingeniously argues that there *is* a unifying framework for these diffuse scenes, and it is derived from a seemingly minor detail: the placement of the four specific historical dates in the text. They mark three "temporal turning points," each governed by a new voice, idea, ideology, and understanding about history. The first period (20 Feb. 1598 → 1603, scenes 1 through 5) is Shuisky's zone. Its mode is irony, its genre farce, and no words here can be believed. The middle period (1603 → 16 Oct. 1604, scenes 5 through 14) is the zone of *samozvanstvo*, pretendership, with the concomitant heroic and Faustian possibility of asserting one's own dreams. The final period (16 Oct. 1604 → 21 Dec. 1604, scenes 14 through 16) is the zone of the chronicle; here voices from the crowd take over from the monologue, and historical event is separated from individual personality. In the end both Boris and Dmitri prove to be pretenders—thus the title of Rassadin's chapter, "Dva samozvantsa"—and both are dispensable to history. See Stanislav Rassadin, *Dramaturg Pushkin* (Moscow: Iskusstvo, 1977), 12–35.

29. A. D. P. Briggs, *Alexander Pushkin: A Critical Study* (London: Croom Helm, 1983), 163.

30. Henry Gifford, "Shakespearean Elements in *Boris Godunov*," *The Slavonic (and East European) Review* 26 (1947–48): 158.

31. For a discussion of these perspectival shifts, see Poliakov, 106–107.

32. See, for example, V. Frolov, "Khronotop v *Borise Godunove* A. S. Pushkina i printsipy kinomontazha," in *Kino i literatura: sbornik nauchnykh trudov*, vyp. 16 (Moscow: Vsesoiuznyi gos. institut kinematografii, 1977): 3–18. Also, Poliakov, 109, and Iu. L. Freidin, "O nekotorykh osobennostiakh kompozitsii tragedii Pushkina *Boris Godunov*," *Russian Literature* VII (1979): 27–29.

33. For a discussion of montage and audio-visual relations as they pertain to film techniques embedded in Pushkin, see Sergei Eisenstein, *The Film Sense*, trans. and ed. Jay Leyda (New York: Harvest/Harcourt, Brace & World, 1975), 46–55.

Pushkin's works are a recurring inspiration and example throughout Eisenstein's theoretical writings. In an essay written to mark thirty years of Soviet cinematography, Eisenstein wrote: "On Pushkin's resources of montage-like and plastic expressiveness, and on the importance of this most laconic of all masters of the word for film culture, one could write dissertations." "Tridtsat' let sovetskogo kinematografa i traditsii russkoi kul'tury," in S. M. Eizenshtein, *Izbrannye proizvedeniia v 6-i tomakh*, vol. 5 (Moscow: Iskusstvo, 1968), 196.

34. For this interview with Sergei Bondarchuk on his new *Boris*, see Pavel Sirkes, "Avtor stsenariia—Pushkin," *Sovetskaia kul'tura*, 24 November 1984, 8.

Bondarchuk (who cast himself in the role of Boris) stresses that Pushkin had designated as hero of his play not a character, not (although this point is tacitly made) the *narod,* but rather the *event* as a historical whole. This, Bondarchuk claims, was the montage principle that had been so indispensable to him in his film adaptation of *War and Peace.* Bondarchuk sees Tolstoy as the most direct continuator of Pushkin's work. "The method of coupling and linking-together, so very productively developed in *War and Peace,* is taken from *Boris Godunov."*

35. O. Fel'dman, *Sud'ba dramaturgii Pushkina* (Moscow: Iskusstvo, 1975), 59, 60–61. Although Feldman does not make explicit reference here to Bakhtin, use of such Bakhtinian terms as "multivoicedness" was much in vogue among Soviet scholars writing in the late 1960s to mid-seventies.

36. "The time had come for punishing him [Godunov] who had not believed in divine justice on earth, who had hoped to save his soul from hell by humble repentance. . . . A despicable tramp dreamed up this whole affair and carried it through in the name of a child long since laid to rest in his grave. . . . As if by some supernatural act, the shade of Dmitri went forth from his grave to strike terror in the heart of the murderer, to drive him mad, and to lead all of Russia into confusion. We begin a tale that is in equal part authentic and unbelievable" (XI, 74).

37. Pushkin identifies him as *Samozvanets* at all points in this scene except one, immediately after Marina ridicules him for his false oaths. Then he becomes Dmitri for one speech, in which he creates for himself his own biography: "The shade of the Terrible fathered me . . ."

38. In the early versions of the play, the "Night. Garden. Fountain." love tryst was even more of an interrogation about identity. It was preceded by a scene (later omitted by Pushkin from the published 1831 text) in Marina's dressing room, where the maid Ruzia rattles on to her mistress about the Tsarevich. "But do you know," Ruzia gossips, "what is said about him among the people? That he's a petty clerk who escaped from Moscow, a well-known rogue in his own parish." "That's stupid," Marina retorts, but then she rises, in her gorgeous attire, and says grimly to herself: "I must find out everything." "Zamok voevody Mnishka v Sanbore," *P:Pss* VII, 266–67.

Pushkin's ultimate exclusion of this scene, as well as the monastery scene between the "evil monk" and Grigory, moved the play toward a more subtle, "backstage" understanding of character motivation.

39. Vsevolod Meyerhold, "Notes at a Rehearsal of *Boris Godunov,"* in *Meyerhold at Work,* ed. and trans. Paul Schmidt (Austin: University of Texas Press, 1980), 126.

40. V. S. Nepomniashchii, " 'Naimenee poniatyi zhanr,' " in his *Poeziia i sud'ba* (Moscow: Sovetskii pisatel', 1983), 212–50. Quoted material appears on pages 224, 225, and 245.

41. In a letter to N. N. Raevsky *(fils),* 30 January or 30 June 1829, Pushkin calls his Pretender an "amiable aventurier" who resembles Shakespeare's Henry IV. *P:Pss* XIV, 47–48, draft in French. What Pushkin liked about the Pretender might have been an image of his own peculiar freedom. For an excellent discussion of the chameleonlike "social self" in Nikolaevan Russia, see William Mills Todd III, "A Russian Ideology," *Stanford Literature Review* (Spring 1984): 108–13.

42. S. N. Durylin, *Pushkin na stsene* (Moscow: AN SSSR, 1951), 71. Durylin continues: "The creative device of Pushkin the dramatist always follows the rule *pars pro toto* (the part instead of the whole); the broad flow of historical time, filled with a multiplicity of action, he compresses down to an

instant in which the action is revealed like a flash of lightning."

43. Yurii Tynianov, *Arkhaisty i novatory* (Leningrad, 1929; repr. edition Slavische Propylaen, Band 31, Munich: Wilhelm Fink Verlag, 1967), 262.

44. Ivan Kireevskii, "Obozrenie russkoi slovesnosti za 1831 god," in *Evropeets*, 1832, no. 2, cited here from *Polnoe sobranie sochineneii I. V. Kireevskogo*, ed. M. Gershenzon (Moscow: Tip. imp. Moskovskogo universiteta, 1911), Pt. II, 46.

45. This very interesting idea has been explored in several articles by Olga Arans (see ch. 1, n. 33, for specific citations). Arans points out that a superstitious mentality such as Boris's would not have distinguished sharply between desire and deed (such a blurring is, after all, the nature of witchcraft). She suggests, further, that Pushkin might have "trapped Boris in his own time" by making him the victim of a sixteenth-century understanding of personal guilt, that is, guilt as a projection of the people's collective unconscious. In this reading, the *narod* may indeed be the hero of this play—but not in the progressive sense that later Soviet Marxist critics had in mind.

46. Only one escape is possible from this sort of epic paralysis, Belinsky argues, and that is possession of genius. This is genius as the romantics understood it: the power to transcend, to be oneself in a hostile world, to commit a crime and then step over it. If Boris had simply seized power, punished openly and reformed openly like Peter the Great, he would have been both accepted and loved. His life (and Pushkin's play) would have been rescued from the realm of melodrama. Instead, Boris was obsessed with defending his legitimacy in traditional ways, and thus he never advanced beyond intrigue. Anticipating Dostoevsky's Raskolnikov, Belinsky calls Boris Godunov a "failed Napoleon," and this, he says, is fatal: "a *parvenu* must be a genius, or fall." "Stat'ia desiataia: Boris Godunov" first appeared in *Otechestvennye zapiski* 43, no. 11 (1845) cited here from V. G. Belinskii, *O drame i teatre*, vol. II (Moscow: Iskusstvo, 1983), 326–57. The quote occurs on 344.

47. In a letter to Katenin that has not survived (April or May 1826), Pushkin inquired if Aleksandra Mikhailovna Kolosova would be willing to play the role of Marina. Katenin responded (6 June 1826) that the actress "would willingly play the role in your tragedy, but we both fear the honorable Dame Censor won't permit it . . ." *P:Pss* XIII, 282. In his reminiscences of Pushkin, Katenin later wrote that Pushkin very much wanted to see his play on the stage ("Vospominaniia P. A. Katenina o Pushkine," *Literaturnoe nasledstvo* [Moscow: AN SSSR], nos. 16–18 [1934]: 641).

48. For a good survey of the shifting concept of "stageworthiness" and its effect on productions of *Boris,* see A. A. Gozenpud, "O stsenichnosti i teatral'noi sud'be *Borisa Godunova,*" in *Pushkin: issledovaniia i materialy,* vol. V (Leningrad: Nauka, 1967), 339–56. Productions of *Boris,* writes Gozenpud, have been at best "sporadic, connected for the most part with Jubilee celebrations, and then they fall out of repertory" (339). This can no longer be attributed to censorship or to the mechanical difficulties of production, Gozenpud claims; ever since the fast-paced and elaborate stagings of Rimsky-Korsakov's operas in the 1890s, stage technique has been adequate to Pushkin's play (346–47). What has been missing is the concept; at the center has been the concept of guilt, whereas in fact Pushkin's central motif was fate (348ff).

Among Western critics the play as a play still gets only lukewarm credits. For a blunt recent statement, see Briggs, 157–81. Briggs concedes that the play is better than its reputation but should be "tidied up" by appending a list of dramatis personae, numbering the scenes, and dividing the play into five acts (174).

49. "I would not have decided to stage Pushkin as drama, it is so difficult; perhaps Pushkin can only be properly revealed in opera, where singing and orchestra support Pushkin's verseline." Cited in G. Kristi, *Rabota Stanislavskogo v opernom teatre* (Moscow: Iskusstvo, 1952), 152.

50. For an excellent survey of the "revisionist" arguments defending the stageability of Pushkin's minimalist dramatic system, see S. Bondi, "Dramaturgiia Pushkina," in his *O Pushkine: Stat'i i issledovaniia* (Moscow: Khudozhestvennaia literatura, 1978), 169–71, 192–208. This new flexibility and innovation in the staging of Pushkin could be seen as part of a general European renewal of interest in the Elizabethan theater during the early part of the twentieth century. By the 1920s, Shakespeare's plays were being viewed not only as texts but as performances in the specific space of the Globe playhouse. The sort of director-actor-critic epitomized in England by Harley Granville-Barker had its counterparts on the continent, and was reflected in Meyerhold's stagings in the 1930s.

51. See, for example, the good discussion by K. I. Arkhangel'skii, "Problemy stseny v dramakh Pushkina (1830–1930)," *Trudy Dal'novostochnogo pedagogicheskogo instituta* (Vladivostok), seriia 7, no. 1 (6) (1930): 5–16. Arkhangelsky argues that Pushkin did not write his play for the stage of his time, and this is why *Boris* has been declared unstageworthy. The Elizabethan stage, with its traces of mystery-play structure still intact, would have made possible an intense, uninterrupted flow of events before the spectator's eyes— the very essence of Pushkin's dramatic principle (7–10).

52. For an intelligent discussion of this aspect of Pushkin's "Shakespearism," see Stephanie Sandler, "The Problem of History in Pushkin: Poet, Pretender, Tsar" (Ph.D. diss., Yale University, 1981), 107–20, 130–35. Addressing Pushkin's probable ignorance of the details of the Elizabethan stage, Sandler concludes: "[Pushkin] responds to the essential dynamism of Shakespearean theater, to something deeper in Shakespeare than the use of blank verse or the mixing of tragedy with comedy. Pushkin uses these techniques as he saw Shakespeare using them, to modernize and make less conventional the dramatic spectacle of his age" (130).

53. Efros discusses the production in his *Profesiia: rezhisser* (Moscow: Iskusstvo, 1979), I, 142–47. He first experimented with the play in the 1950s. "*Boris Godunov* has never succeeded in our theater," Efros writes of this early attempt. "A lot of noise and rubbish has resulted from this, from the play's 'boxed-in quality' [*sunduchnost'*]. So I went and staged it lightly in all its movements, without any extra accessories. . . ." Efros's return to *Boris* fifteen years later was his first excursion into television, a medium he had earlier regarded "with some irony." Although the realization in this new art form was very different, Efros's goal was the same: to achieve a simplified Boris that would make the audience think. "And that marvelous little box demanded that I suppress all fantasy and calm down a stormy imagination," he confessed. For contemporary opinions of the production, see the review by Rozov, "Dolgoe mgnovenie," in *Literaturnaia gazeta* (16 June 1971), and by Filippova, "Bezdonnost' pushkinskogo slova," in *Sovetskaia kul'tura* (5 June 1971).

54. Cf. n. 14, above.

55. G. O. Vinokur, "Iazyk *Borisa Godunova*," in Derzhavin, ed., *"Boris Godunov" A. S. Pushkina*, 127–58. Subsequent page references given in the text.

56. Cf. n. 26, above.

57. Cited in A. N. Glumov, "Proiznesenie stikha *Borisa Godunova*," in Derzhavin, ed., *"Boris Godunov" A. S. Pushkina*, 176.

58. N. N. Raevsky *fils* advised Pushkin to do just that in a letter of 10 May 1825, around the time Pushkin was experimenting with various meters (*P:Pss* XIII, 535). The one scene written in trochaic octometer, "Ograda monastyrskaia" (At the Monastery Wall), is generally considered a poetic failure and was removed from the final manuscript by Pushkin himself.·

59. In his oft-quoted lines from the letter to *Moskovskii vestnik* (1828), Pushkin wrote that in *Boris* he had "exchanged the venerable Alexandrine for pentametric blank verse, and in a few scenes even stooped to despicable prose." *P:Pss* XI, 67. In one of his draft prefaces to *Boris*, Pushkin dates the origin of blank verse in Russian drama to Kiukhelbeker's 1823 play *Argiviane* (*P:Pss* XI, 141), although in fact Zhukovsky and others had worked in this meter earlier.

60. Durylin, *Pushkin na stsene*, 89.

61. For an interpretation, see Sandler, 134–35:

Pushkin uses Shakespeare to proclaim the superiority of his artifice. Shakespeare used blank verse because of its affinities to spoken English, and the iambic pentameter line remains dominant in English verse patterns to this day. But Pushkin chooses blank verse because it sounds Shakespearean: in Russian, of course, it is the iambic tetrameter line which best follows the spoken language, as Pushkin proved definitely in *Evgenij Onegin*. Pushkin is not interested in making his characters sound like "real" people—*Boris Godunov* is, after all, a play.

62. "[Nabroski predisloviia k Borisu Godunovu]," *P:Pss* XI, 141.

63. Glumov, "Proiznesenie stikha *Borisa Godunova*," in Derzhavin, ed., *"Boris Godunov" A. S. Pushkina*, 162.

64. See Durylin, *Pushkin na stsene*, 85–89.

65. See, for example, Meyerhold's essays "The Naturalistic Theatre and the Theatre of Mood" and "The Stylized Theatre" in Edward Braun, *Meyerhold on Theatre* (New York: Hill & Wang, 1969), 23–34 and 58–64.

66. Vinokur, "Iazyk *Borisa Godunova*," 133–35. As Vinokur correctly notes, in its mixture of "language masks" Pushkin's text more resembles Karamzin's *History* than any eighteenth-century drama (135). Pushkin's innovation, Vinokur claims, lay not in reproducing an image of medieval speech but in "replacing the conventional language of drama, based on a detached high style, with the general poetic language of the epoch as Pushkin himself had understood and created it . . ." (134).

67. The literature is very large, but for a good critical survey and bibliography of major European studies, see M. P. Alekseev, "Pushkin i Shekspir," in *Pushkin: Sravnitel'no-istoricheskie issledovaniia* (Leningrad: Nauka, 1984), 253–92. The essay was written in the 1960s and first anthologized in 1972, so does not include work of the last two decades.

68. As Pushkin explained in a draft foreword to his play (1830):

I confess I would be upset by the failure of my tragedy, for I firmly believe that the popular tenets of Shakespearean drama are better suited to the Russian theater than are the courtly habits of Racine's tragedies, and any unsuccessful experiment might slow down the reform of our stage. (*P:Pss* XI, 141)

See also his discussion of the evolution of drama in his "O narodnoi drame i drame *Marfa Posadnitsa*," *P:Pss* XII, 178–79, where he distinguishes between the *narodnaia* (popular, national, folk) tragedy of Shakespeare and the *pridvornaia* (court) drama of Racine.

69. Like Macbeth, Boris sees ghosts and consults witches. Together with Richard III he has the blood of little princes on his conscience; like *Richard II*, the play openly explores the delicate issue of usurpation. As in *Othello* and *Romeo and Juliet* there are touching scenes of a doomed child-bride with her nurse. As does King Lear, Tsar Boris first hears the truth from a fool. Like Julius Caesar, Boris dies before the end of the play, and this premature death suggests a special understanding of the historical process. Actual "quotation" (lines so similar as to suggest a specific subtext) probably occurs from *Richard III* (III, vii), the deathbed monologue in *Henry IV Part 2*, and *Macbeth*.

70. A. L. Slonimskii, "*Boris Godunov* i dramaturgiia 20-kh godov," in Derzhavin, ed., "*Boris Godunov*" A. S. Pushkina, 45.

71. See, for example, Henry Ansgar Kelly, *Divine Providence in the England of Shakespeare's Histories* (Cambridge: Harvard University Press, 1970), and John W. Blanpied, *Time and the Artist in Shakespeare's English Histories* (Newark: University of Delaware Press, 1983). By examining the various "traditional defenses" of the ruling houses (the Lancaster Myth, the York Myth, the Tudor Myth) and their official mythographers, Kelly demonstrates how Shakespeare's characters play with providential time by "speaking" various myths to one another. Blanpied traces Shakespeare's maturing understanding of history (and the problems of portraying history dramatically) through the tetralogies, concentrating on the role of the King as surrogate dramatist and writer (or maker) of history.

I thank Phyllis Rackin of the University of Pennsylvania for alerting me to these and other texts of recent Shakespeare criticism that support this thesis of Pushkin's "revisionist" Shakespearism.

72. I draw here on Erich Auerbach's discussion of Shakespeare's "mixing of styles" in ch. 13, "The Weary Prince," of *Mimesis: The Representation of Reality in Western Literature*, trans. Willard R. Trask (Princeton: Princeton University Press, 1968), 312–16. Auerbach concentrates on Prince Hal, Hamlet, and Lear. The opening quotation (from *Henry IV Part 2*, II, ii) and indeed the very title of the chapter concern a prince's unprincely desire for "small beer"—a phrase whose very words are small, and contrast oddly with Poins's elevated mockery of his friend. But Auerbach asserts that Shakespeare's kings, once crowned, always sound like kings; "his conception of the sublime and tragic is altogether aristocratic" (315). Even Lear, whose childishness is everywhere apparent, retains kingly diction to the very end; Shakespeare meant us to take "aye, every inch a king" quite seriously, even from a madman (316–17).

73. L. Pinskii, *Shekspir: Osnovnye nachala dramaturgii* (Moscow: Khudozhestvennaia literatura, 1971), 50.

74. For a classic statement of this received image, see E. M. W. Tillyard, *Shakespeare's History Plays* (New York: Collier, 1962), Part I, 1 and 2. ". . . Shakespeare's Histories with their constant pictures of disorder cannot be understood," Tillyard concludes, "without assuming a larger principle of order in the background" (360).

75. For a good discussion, see L. S. Sidiakov, "Stikhi i proza v tekstakh Pushkina," *Pushkinskii sbornik*, vypusk 2 (Riga: Uchenye zapiski Latviiskogo gos. universiteta, 1974), 11ff.

76. *P:Pss* VII, "Boris Godunov," in scenes 6 ("Palata Patriarkha," p. 24) and 10 ("Tsarskie palaty," p. 42). Ksenia's lament is stylized and rhythmic, but significantly laid out on the page as prose. The lament was actually in verse in an earlier draft (*P:Pss* VII, 267).

77. Out of a full page of neutral narrative information in Karamzin (XI, 75), Pushkin molded one explosive dialogue that brings the Patriarch both

into focus and down to earth—which, in this context, increases his credibility vis-à-vis the chameleonic Pretender.

78. In translating this monologue, I have drawn liberally, with permission, on Paul Schmidt's excellent poetic re-creation in his *Meyerhold at Work*, 89–91.

79. *P:Pss* VII, 289.

80. See the brief discussion in K. V. Bazilevich, "Boris Godunov v izobrazhenii Pushkina," *Istoricheskie zapiski*, vol. I (Moscow: AN SSSR, 1937), 39–40. This monologue, Bazilevich reminds us, is all the play has to show for six years of Boris's reign and 100 pages of Karamzin's text. Pushkin "forces Boris to recall [only] the major failures, the times when all his measures, beneficial in themselves, were invariably turned against him. . . . Only as a *result* of the consciousness of total alienation and isolation do the pangs of a guilty conscience set in" (emphasis mine) (40).

81. See V. V. Vinogradov's discussion in his *Iazyk Pushkina* (Moscow-Leningrad: Academia, 1935), 145–47.

82. Mikhail Bakhtin, *Problems of Dostoevsky's Poetics*, ed. and trans. Caryl Emerson (Minneapolis: University of Minnesota Press, 1984), 198.

83. See, for example, A. L. Slonimskii, "Boris Godunov i dramaturgiia 20-kh godov," in Derzhavin, ed., *"Boris Godunov" A. S. Pushkina*, 71–72. Slonimsky argues that in *Boris* (and in "Poltava" soon after) this type of lyrical hero "serves as a convenient channel through which motifs of the author's lyricism penetrate both the drama and the poem." But surely the oddness of Boris's language serves a broader purpose than mere outlet for Pushkin's lyric gift, which scarcely needed romantic tragedy as its vehicle.

84. In his earlier drafts of the play, Pushkin made several references to Boris's virtues—all ultimately eliminated. In a draft of scene 1, Vorotynsky says to Shuisky: "Boris is intelligent; his rule / has calmed, enhanced Russia— / He's already Tsar; what will it be like without him? . . ." And in a draft of scene 2, a voice from the people comments on Boris's energetic campaigns against the khans: "Who will repulse the heathenish horde / [if Boris refuses the crown]?" (*P:Pss* VII, 271, 273). In the published text of the play, however, only Boris himself speaks in Boris's defense—and it is a crabbed embittered voice.

85. So argues John Bayley, for example, in his *Pushkin: A Comparative Commentary* (Cambridge: University Press, 1971), 109.

86. Pushkin to Raevsky *(fils)*, 30 January or 30 June 1829. *P:Pss* XIV, 47.

87. See, for example, Bondi, "Dramaturgiia Pushkina," 191, and Yu. D. Levin, "Nekotorye voprosy shekspirizma Pushkina," in *Pushkin: Issledovaniia i materialy*, VII (Leningrad: Nauka, 1974), 58–70. See also Tatiana A. Wolff, "Shakespeare's Influence on Pushkin's Dramatic Work," *Shakespeare Survey* (Cambridge) 5 (1952): 93–105, which purports to trace parallels but in the process makes much better points about differences.

88. John Blanpied, *Time and the Artist*, 247. Blanpied in fact argues that the nine history plays demonstrate Shakespeare's increasing sophistication in dealing with the *problem* of historical time in drama. Shakespeare begins with "a fairly conventional view of history as a more or less established body of facts and events, capable of assuming more or less direct expression" (12). But the playwright's own dramatic imagination soon reveals the fiction of presuming preexistent material. In an effort to achieve a "clear and unimpeded view of history," Shakespeare resorts to a series of devices. First he embodies the artistic presence, usually in the surrogate-dramatist figure of a *king*, and "uses the figure as a focus of energy that he can both control and observe" (13). But

the king-centered plays, with their focus on mechanisms of control, give way to another understanding of historical process: history comes to be seen as continual drama, originating on stage but carried over into the world of every potential audience. See Blanpied's introduction for more on his general strategy, 11–15.

89. *P:Pss* VII, 290. It should be stressed, however, that in Pushkin's time the genre of comedy was rather more broadly defined than it is today. Ostolopov's *Dictionary of Ancient and Modern Poetry* (St. Petersburg, 1821) defined comedy as "an imitation, presented in action, of the mores, vices, habits, and eccentricities noticeable among people." See N. F. Filippova, *"Boris Godunov" A. S. Pushkina* (Moscow: Proveshchenie, 1984), 71.

90. Fel'dman, *Sud'ba dramaturgii Pushkina*, 64.

91. Translation here and in the passages that follow by Paul Schmidt in Schmidt, ed., *Meyerhold at Work*, 83–88. Reprinted with permission of the University of Texas Press. Lines 43, 44, 143, 144, 145, and 152 of the Schmidt text have been retranslated to reflect certain aspects of the Russian original that are significant for my interpretation.

92. "Ograda monastyrskaia," *P:Pss* VII, 263–64. The source in Karamzin reads: "The marvelous idea had already settled and ripened in the soul of the dreamer, suggested to him (so it is claimed) by a certain evil hermit [*zloi inok*]: the idea that a bold pretender might make use of the superstitious nature of the Russians, moved by the memory of Dmitri, and in the name of Divine Justice put an end to the saint-killer!" (XI, 75).

93. See, for example, B. Varneke, "Istochniki i zamysel *Borisa Godunova*," in *Pushkin: Stat'i i materialy*, ed. M. P. Alekseev (Odessa: Odesskii dom uchenykh, 1925), 14–15. Varneke suggests that Pushkin's ultimate turning away from the Faust motif was a decisive step in the direction of a *Russian*, as opposed to a West European, concept of pretendership. It is significant that the impetus to pretend comes, in both of Pushkin's variants, from the clergy—a reference, perhaps, to a defect of conscience (rather than a noble desire for freedom) at the heart of Russian *samozvanstvo*.

94. See Meyerhold's notes on the Monastery Scene in Schmidt, ed., *Meyerhold at Work*, 112–33.

95. "Pis'mo k izdateliu *Moskovskogo vestnika*," *P:Pss* XI, 68.

96. It might be objected that Pushkin chose Pimen, a common ecclesiastical name, for his Monastery Scene with no intentional reference to Karamzin or to the historical Pimen. But this particular coincidence catches the eye, because Pushkin followed other details of Karamzin's text very closely in this section. The Patriarch's words are moved almost verbatim into the drama. The footnote on Pimen (#199) provides all the details for the Inn Scene and border-crossing. So I have presumed that the difference between historical and dramatic Pimen is a deliberate one.

97. The primary source for the historical Pimen is Patriarch Iov's *gramota* of 1605, cited by Karamzin in vol. XI *prim.* #199. More extensive use of the document is made by Kostomarov in his *Kto byl pervyi Lzhedimitrii?* (St. Petersburg: tip. Bezobrazova, 1864), 6–7, where Pimen is identified as a *chernets* of Smolensk Monastery.

After Pushkin's pious re-creation of Pimen it is something of a jolt to see the historical Pimen thoroughly secularized in other artistic transpositions. In the historical novel *Dimitri the Pretender*, Faddei Bulgarin portrays Pimen as a timid background voice, loyal to Tsar Boris when others are loyal but easily swayed by the crowd when defection becomes general ("It's not for us to judge . . ."). See F. Bulgarin, *Dimitrii Samozvanets*, 4 vols. (St. Petersburg: tip. Smirdina, 1830), vol. I, 31–32.

98. I. Z. Serman, "Pushkin i russkaia istoricheskaia drama 1830-kh godov," in *Pushkin: Issledovanie i materialy*, vol. 6 (Leningrad: Nauka, 1969), 118–49; the Pimen scene is discussed on 120–25. More recently Serman has refined his views in an unpublished essay, "Paradoxes of the Folk Mind in Pushkin's *Boris Godunov*," an expanded version of a talk delivered at Cornell University on 9 February 1981 ("Paradoksy narodnogo soznaniia v tragedii A. S. Pushkina *Boris Godunov*").

99. *P:Pss* VII, 269.

100. This idea is eloquently developed by Serman, "Paradoxes of the Folk Mind," 11:

> Pushkin's Pretender is not only a "poet" in the strict sense of the word: he is a poet in the larger sense as well; he has a poetic nature, a poetic, artistic attitude toward life, toward all its manifestations, its joys, its beauty and vitality. The Pretender has an immediate sensuous perception of life. It is this, and not any abstract ideas of a political or ethical sort, that determines his behavior, the choice of his way of life, the decisions he makes in critical situations.

101. See the good discussion in B. P. Gorodetskii, *Dramaturgiia Pushkina* (Moscow-Leningrad: AN SSSR, 1953), 111–12, and the analysis of Pimen in Filippova, *"Boris Godunov" A. S. Pushkina*, 22–26.

102. *P:Pss* VII, 280.

103. The "terrible denunciation," in an earlier draft, was the more neutral "Here [a hermit] is writing about you in a silent cell" (*P:Pss* VII, 281).

104. *P:Pss* XII, 306.

105. Gorodetsky has suggested, however, that Pushkin did have a model in mind for his Pimen: Avraam Palitsyn. In Karamzin's *History* (XI, 65) Palitsyn is presented as *bezpristrastnyi* (dispassionate), and his testimony on Boris's reign closely resembles Pimen's. See Gorodetskii, *Dramaturgiia Pushkina*, 154–55.

106. For an excellent discussion of the "conjunctive thinking" that makes this mixed testimony possible, as well as commentary on the general nature of chronicle creativity, see Igor P. Smirnov, "On the Systematic-Diachronic Approach to Medieval Russian Culture of the Early Period," trans. Ann Shukman, *New Literary History* XIV, no. 1 (Autumn 1984): 111–36, especially 121–23.

107. Serman, "Paradoxes of the Folk Mind," 11.

108. Thomas M. Greene, "History and Anachronism," in *Literature and History: Theoretical Problems and Russian Case Studies*, ed. Gary Saul Morson, Part III (Stanford: Stanford University Press, 1986), 210–11. Before discussing superannuated figures, Greene posits five types of anachronism. Cultures without a strong historical sense may commit innocent or *naïve* anachronism, not in itself an artistic blemish but merely a means for composing "the texture of the work without pretension to historical control." Cultures struggling for historical awareness can produce *abusive* or *serendipitous* anachronism, depending on the degree of awareness of the author. Complex cultures with a fully differentiated sense of time have at their disposal types of anachronism (*creative, pathetic,* or *tragic*) that can actually confront the problem of multiple times and the inevitability of datedness. Creative anachronism, Greene claims, can demonstrate awareness of historicity and thus enact a successful revival or rebirth.

109. D. Bernshtein, *"Boris Godunov* Pushkina i russkaia istoricheskaia dramaturgiia v epokhu dekabrizma," in *Pushkin: Rodonachal'nik novoi russkoi literatury*, ed. D. D. Blagoi (Moscow-Leningrad: AN SSSR, 1941), 247.

110. For a discussion of these specifically "slanderous" borrowings from

Karamzin (Boris's responsibility for the Moscow fires and for the deaths of the Danish prince, Fyodor, and Irina), see Gorodetskii, *Dramaturgiia Pushkina*, 162.

111. Interestingly enough, this detail was picked up in one of the earliest, and largely critical, reviews of the play, the pseudonymous "Conversation of Old Acquaintances" in *Teleskop* (1831). After an irreverent search for the heroes and genre of the play, one of the conversationalists makes the comment that Pushkin's piece is in fact more conventional than it at first seems. Despite the unruly mob scene at the end, the play *does* end on Boris's death—because Tsar Boris lived for, and in, his son, and therefore died only in him. See N. Nadoumko, "Beseda starykh znakomtsev," *Teleskop*, 1831, no. 4, 559.

J. Thomas Shaw has also noted the primacy of generations as a structuring principle for the play, stressing that "*Boris Godunov* is, unlike *Macbeth*, a play of dynastic, rather than personal, ambition." See his entry, "Alexander Pushkin," in *The Romantic Century* (European Writers, vol. 5), ed. Jacques Barzun and George Stade (New York: Charles Scribner's Sons, 1985), 678.

112. The first play of Tolstoy's *Trilogy*, *The Death of Ivan the Terrible* (1864), opens on a session of the Boyar Duma. Its members are abusing one another over matters of rank and seating priority. Finally Zakharin-Yuriev, brother of Ivan IV's first wife, tries to calm the quarreling assembly:

> Boyars!
> Have you forgotten why we're here?
> How can you? How? At this time
> When the Tsar, having killed his son,
> Is wracked with remorse, when
> He has decided to leave the world,
> And bypassing his second son,
> Fyodor, because of his illness,
> Has named us the most worthy to choose
> The man to whom all power shall be transferred . . .

A. K. Tolstoi, "Smert' Ioanna Groznogo," Act I, i, in A. K. Tolstoi, *Izbrannye proizvedeniia* (Leningrad: Lenizdat, 1980), 317.

113. D. D. Blagoi, *Tvorcheskii put' Pushkina (1813–1826)* (Moscow-Leningrad: AN SSSR, 1950), 472: "This is not a stage direction but a summing-up of the play's general meaning [*smyslovoe rezume*], the result of Pushkin's historical and political meditations."

114. For a discussion of the issue, see Jean Alter, "From Text to Performance: Semiotics of Theatricality," in *Poetics Today* 2, no. 3 (Spring 1981), especially 114–18.

115. For a good discussion, see M. Zagorskii, *Pushkin i teatr* (Moscow-Leningrad: Iskusstvo, 1940), 91–97.

116. Aleksandr Gladkov, "Meierkhol'd govorit," *Novy mir*, no. 8 (1961): 222.

117. See the afterword by Elizaveta Dattel' to the score of the incidental music, in S. Prokofiev, *Boris Godunov (op. 70 bis) Hamlet (op. 77): Muzyka k dramaticheskim spektakliam*, partitura i klavir (Moscow: Sovetskii kompozitor, 1973), 84–86.

118. For a survey of these readings and a persuasive demonstration of the power of closure on the heroes and ideology of the play, see M. P. Alekseev, "Remarka Pushkina 'Narod bezmolvstvuet,'" originally anthologized 1972, reprinted in M. P. Alekseev, *Pushkin: Sravnitel'no-istoricheskie issledovaniia* (Leningrad: Nauka, 1984): 221–52. The brief account in the text is summarized from Alekseev's survey.

119. "Sochineniia Aleksandra Pushkina, stat'ia desiataia, *Boris Godunov*," in V. G. Belinskii, *O drame i teatre*, vol. II, 357.

120. After an exhaustive survey of the evidence, Alekseev concludes that *narod bezmolvstvuet* most likely does not belong to Pushkin, and cannot be presumed to "organically conclude the author's text to the play" (224–25). G. O. Vinokur, in his extensive commentary to volume VII (the only extant volume) of the 1935 edition of Pushkin's collected works, disagrees. See G. O. Vinokur, "Kommentarii k *Borisu Godunovu*," in *Polnoe sobranie sochinenii A. S. Pushkina*, vol. VII (Moscow: AN SSSR, 1935), 430–31:

> There are no grounds for doubting the authorial origin of the celebrated *narod bezmolvstvuet*, which closes Pushkin's tragedy in the printed text in place of the "Long live Dmitri Ivanovich!" in the manuscript. The censor paid no attention at all to this place in the manuscript, so Pushkin could not have had any external reasons for correcting it. . . . [At any rate] the political content of *Boris Godunov* is not changed in the least by the ending of the tragedy, because that content is determined by the entire text of the tragedy and not by this one line alone.

Vinokur thus not only disagrees with Alekseev over the status of the ending but over the efficacy of end-determined readings in general. Also at issue between the two critics is a textological question: in the presence of known censorship pressure, can a line that has left no trace in any surviving drafts be presumed to be "authorial"?

121. Rassadin, *Dramaturg Pushkin*, 55.

122. See, for example, S. L. Frank, *Pushkin kak politicheskii myslitel'* (Belgrade/Novi sad: tip. Filonova, 1937), 22.

123. Engel'gardt, "Istorizm Pushkina," 67.

124. The most likely immediate source for the *narod*-as-hero idea was Andrei Filonov, *"Boris Godunov" A. S. Pushkina: Opyt razbora so storony istoricheskoi i esteticheskoi* (St. Petersburg: tip. Glazunova, 1899), a scene-by-scene comparison between Karamzin's and Pushkin's texts and a plea for the "fidelity" of the play to Karamzin's historical framework. Only several years later did the potential for such a progressive reading become clear. See Serman, "Paradoxes of the Folk Mind," 1–4, 17–19.

The thesis here differs somewhat from his earlier article. Serman's several key essays on *Boris*, both pre- and postdating his emigration, afford a fascinating glimpse of an eminent scholar reassessing his own data once freed from Soviet publishing constraints.

125. See M. Tikhomirov, "Samozvanshchina," *Nauka i zhizn'*, no. 1 (January 1969): 120.

126. See Yury Tynianov, "Dostoevsky and Gogol: Towards a Theory of Parody, Part One: Stylization and Parody" (1921), in *Dostoevsky & Gogol: Texts and Criticism*, ed. Priscilla Meyer and Stephen Rudy (Ann Arbor: Ardis, 1979), 104.

127. Willis Konick, "The Secrets of History: Pushkin's *Boris Godunov*," *Occasional Papers in Slavic Languages and Literature* (The University of Washington at Seattle) 1, no. 1 (Summer 1982): 53–62.

128. Pushkin to N. I. Gnedich, 23 February 1825. *P:Pss* XIII, 145.

Chapter 4: Boris in Opera

1. Hermann Laroche, "A Thinking Realist in Russian Opera," *Golos*, no. 44, 13 February 1874. As cited in A. Orlova, *Trudy i dni M. P. Musorgskogo: Letopis' zhizni i tvorchestva* (Moscow: MuzGiz, 1963), 366–67. A competent translation of this indispensable chronicle now exists: Alexandra Orlova,

Musorgsky's Days and Works: A Biography in Documents, trans. and ed. Roy J. Guenther (Ann Arbor: UMI Research Press, 1983). Since my translations frequently depart from Guenther's, however, both the Russian and the English reference will be cited, and in the following format: Orlova *Trudy,* 366–67/*MDW,* 388–89.

2. Nikolai Soloviev in *Birzhevye vedomosti,* no. 28, 29 January 1874. Orlova *Trudy,* 336/*MDW,* 362.

3. Nikolai Strakhov in his second letter to *Grazhdanin,* no. 9, 4 March 1874. Orlova *Trudy,* 379/*MDW,* 400–401.

4. Cesar Cui in *St.-Peterburgskie vedomosti,* no. 37, 6 February 1874. Orlova *Trudy,* 355–56/*MDW,* 378–79.

5. The pioneering general statement was by Joseph Kerman, *Opera as Drama* (New York: Vintage, 1952); more recently, see Gary Schmidgall, *Literature as Opera* (New York: Oxford University Press, 1977), Peter Conrad, *Romantic Opera and Literary Form* (Berkeley: University of California Press, 1978); and Herbert Lindenberger, *Opera: The Extravagant Art* (Ithaca: Cornell University Press, 1984). These authors offer various and incompatible theses. Kerman (chs. 6–7) sees libretti arranged along a continuum that privileges at one pole words ("opera as sung play") and at the other pole music ("opera as symphonic poem"); he argues that the nineteenth century worked out its operatic aesthetic between these two extremes, those respectively of Debussy and Wagner. Schmidgall and Conrad attempt more theoretical statements. The conservative argument is made by Schmidgall: opera, he insists, is in essence a conventionalizing, simplifying, "epiphanic" art form, and if it is to succeed dramatically it must draw its libretti from texts with much passion, little philosophy, and hard heroic surfaces (10–12). Conrad, on the other hand, argues that music complicates: it complements depth and dimension, and therefore the best sources for opera libretti are not dramatic texts but those in the category of "novel": allegory, epic poem, romance, and psychological narrative. Lindenberger's study contains very interesting ideas on the generic "border-crossings" experienced in opera and the special relationship between operas and novels, as well as a discussion of the "dialogicality" of the genre that draws on Bakhtin (91–95).

For a discussion of the merits—and shortcomings—of Conrad's and Schmidgall's texts, see the penetrating review by Joseph Kerman, "Reading Opera," *New York Review of Books* 25/1 (9 February 1978): 30–33.

6. Kerman devotes only one, albeit enthusiastic, page to Musorgsky's *Boris* (256–57). Schmidgall's single reading of a Russian opera, Tchaikovsky's *Eugene Onegin,* is a somewhat awkward attempt to read a libretto in light of its literary source text without, apparently, a knowledge of Russian. "Between the intentions of Pushkin and Tchaikovsky," Schmidgall writes (219), "lies a strange aesthetic warp that seems to divide—and make mutually exclusive—the essential qualities of poem and opera." Pushkin's *Onegin* is not a poem, of course, but a novel in verse, and Tchaikovsky was not rejecting this novel but recasting it into precisely a set of "lyrical scenes."

7. Patrick J. Smith, *The Tenth Muse: A Historical Study of the Opera Libretto* (New York: Schirmer, 1970). Smith's greatest regret in his "'libretto-eyed' view of operatic history" is "the omission, except for passing references, of the Slavic nineteenth- and twentieth-century librettos," since his "ignorance of Czech and Russian would cripple any systematic discussion" (iv–v).

8. B. M. Iarustovskii, *Dramaturgiia russkoi opernoi klassiki,* ch. 5 ("Rabota nad opernym libretto") (Moscow: GosMuzIzdat, 1953), 181.

9. For a good discussion, see Lindenberger, *Opera: The Extravagant Art,*

100–102. Lindenberger points out that changes in performance technique and the relative scarcity of printed scores until the mid-eighteenth century make quite problematic any assumption of "opera continuity"—at least continuity of the sort possible to trace in the more fully transcribable arts, such as literature or painting.

10. For an excellent survey of the creative relationship, see Emilia Frid, "Musorgskii i Golenishchev-Kutuzov," in her *M. P. Musorgskii: Problemy tvorchestva* (Leningrad: Muzyka, 1981), 125–71. See also my "Real Endings and Russian Death: Musorgskij's 'Pesni i pljaski smerti,'" *Russian Language Journal* 38, nos. 129–30 (1984): 199–216.

11. See, for example, M. S. Pekelis, "Musorgskii—pisatel'-dramaturg," in *Modest Petrovich Musorgskii: Literaturnoe nasledie/Literaturnye proizvedeniia*, ed. A. A. Orlova and M. S. Pekelis (Moscow: Muzyka, 1972), 5–6.

12. Iarustovskii, *Dramaturgiia russkoi opernoi klassiki*, 150–55. For Iarustovsky's own contribution to such a theoretical discussion, see 155–82. He selects from the second category of librettists several source-texts and their derived libretti (*The Queen of Spades* and *Boris Godunov* among them) and then compares brief excerpts, suggesting in the process possible principles for some future "poetics of the libretto line." Iarustovsky notes (178) that obligatory rhyme at the end of phrases, even for the musically rounded numbers, began to disappear from Russian opera during the 1860s—and this absence soon became characteristic of Russian-language libretti.

13. From Hermann Laroche's review of excerpts from *Boris* at the Mariinsky Theater, in *Golos*, no. 45, 14 February 1874. Orlova *Trudy*, 283/*MDW*, 303.

14. Hermann Laroche in "Musical Letters from Petersburg," *Moskovskie vedomosti*, no. 49, 25 February 1874. Orlova *Trudy*, 375/*MDW*, 397.

15. Cesar Cui in *St.-Petersburgskie vedomosti*, no. 37, 6 February 1874. Orlova *Trudy*, 355/*MDW*, 378–79.

16. From a letter to Musorgsky signed "D. Pozdnyakov," 31 January 1874. Orlova *Trudy*, 347/*MDW*, 371.

17. Richard Taruskin, *Opera and Drama in Russia as Preached and Practiced in the 1860s* (Ann Arbor: UMI Research Press, 1981), ch.5 ("*The Stone Guest* and Its Progeny"), 257. Taruskin's revisionist reading of Dargomyzhsky's oeuvre—and especially its relation to Musorgsky's work on *Marriage*—is a welcome corrective to the usual direct line of descent presumed between the two musicians.

18. Although Vladimir Stasov provided Borodin with a "scenario" for the opera in the spring of 1869, the composer ultimately became his own librettist. For an account of Stasov's scenario and its gradual simplification and condensation by Borodin, see Serge Dianin, *Borodin*, trans. Robert Lord (London: Oxford University Press, 1963), 58–63 and 271–81.

19. Thus Borodin continues in the tradition of Bestuzhev-Marlinsky, who a generation earlier had made a romantic *topos* out of the Caucasus and its "savage" tribes. Central to the orientalizing (and colonializing) project was the assumption that native material offered no resistance: the wild maiden falls in love with the "civilized" Russian officer, he teaches her to read and write, and their correspondence instantly resembles a Richardson novel. This is the scenario parodied by Pushkin in his "Mistress into Maid" and by Leo Tolstoy in his *Cossacks*.

20. Both culturally and politically Russia had genuine roots in (and boundaries with) Asia, which made the Orient both self and other. Khans and their offspring regularly allied and intermarried with the Russians; the

twelfth-century author of the Igor Tale refers to the Polovtsian khans as "our fathers-in-law," and with good reason. The historical Vladimir Igorevich was actually betrothed to Konchak's daughter *before* Igor undertook his campaign, during a period when Igor himself was in alliance with the Polovtsians; Vladimir brought his wife and their child home to Novgorod-Seversk two years after Igor's death. This detail was the basis for the final scene (a wedding feast) in Stasov's original scenario, but Borodin replaced it with Igor's own homecoming.

Despite this real historical interaction between cultures, during the 1860s and seventies Russian orientalism *in music* was formulaic and pointedly exotic. I thank Richard Taruskin for this reminder.

21. Borodin to L. I. Karmalina, 1 June 1876, cited in Dianin, *Borodin*, 278.

22. All scenes for Part I of the opera are taken from Book II, Parts Three and Five, of *War and Peace*.

23. In parallel development, Pierre Bezukhov of Part I is the functional equivalent of Kutuzov in Part II: a lumbering and implacable force, threatening but not given to unnecessary violence. Natasha is the violated homeland, full of promise but foolishly in love with Western fashion and artifice. Anatol, by extension, is the French, an identification made explicit by Akhrosimova in scene 6: "Who've you begun to hang around with?" she castigates Natasha. "With Bezukhova. What did you find there? French feelings, French fashions. The ladies sit around almost naked, like signs for the public bathhouse. . . . Their gods are Frenchmen, their heavenly kingdom is Paris." S. Prokofiev, *Voina i mir* (partitura), in *Sobranie sochineii*, vol. 6A (Moscow: GosMuzIzdat, 1958), 365–67.

24. See the excellent discussion in Malcolm H. Brown, "Prokofiev's *War and Peace*: A Chronicle," *Musical Quarterly* 63, no. 3 (July 1977): 297–326. Prokofiev's wife, Mira Mendelssohn, helped him select material from the novel but, in the composer's own words, "virtually all the lines belong to Tolstoy" (cited in Brown, 303). The opera has received its share of the criticism common for such prose-sensitive transpositions. "The singers 'speak' for the most part against a background of marvelous music in the orchestra," Nikolai Miaskovsky complained, ". . . again the usual thing, scene after scene (in short, like a play) wordy, etc., and almost no singing" (Brown, 302–303).

25. Pushkin to N. N. Raevsky *(fils)*, 30 January or 30 June 1829, draft in French. *P:Pss* XIV, 48.

26. A word is in order on the limits of this chapter. While admitting the indispensable "purely musical element" in the libretto, there will be no technical analysis of the score. The technical aspects of Musorgsky's music have been amply investigated by musicologists. The best study to date on the balance between the claims of music and the claims of the verbal text is Robert William Oldani, Jr., "New Perspectives on Mussorgsky's 'Boris Godunov'" (Ph.D. diss., The University of Michigan, 1978). Except in passing, those issues will not be touched upon here. This study will focus on the selection and development of libretto material as narrative sequence, and as grounds for a philosophy of history.

27. Igor Stravinsky, *Stravinsky: An Autobiography* (New York: Simon & Schuster, 1936), 202. Stravinsky, not altogether surprisingly, disliked the "polemical nationalists in music," preferring the cosmopolitan spirit of Pushkin—"the most perfect representative of the wonderful line which began with Peter the Great and which, by a fortunate alloy, has united the most characteristically Russian elements with the spiritual riches of the West" (151).

28. See two essays by Ulrich Weisstein: "The Libretto as Literature,"

Books Abroad: An International Literary Quarterly (Winter 1961): 16–22, and "Librettology: The Fine Art of Coping with a Chinese Twin," *Komparatistische Hefte,* Heft 5/6 (1982), "Literatur und die anderen Künste" (Universität Bayreuth): 23–42. This later essay, a spirited defense of librettology as a potential literary science, begins by systematizing libretto variables and grounding them in familiar literary categories. Weisstein discusses the word/music relationship as an aspect of Aristotelian poetics—that is, in terms of the six elements that, according to Aristotle, contribute to every drama (24–29). He then surveys the spectrum from "spoken" to "musical" extreme (from the prose dialogue of the *Singspiel* to aria and ensemble writing in opera), suggesting at each level the appropriate literary tasks for a librettologist (30–33). The essay ends with a discussion of those areas "where literary expertise is especially called for": genesis of the libretto and philological analysis of the text; comparison of the structural properties of opera as opposed to drama; and special problems raised by *Literaturoper,* by adaptations of existing texts, and finally by opera in translation—i.e., the interdependence of supranational (musical) and national (verbal) languages in a single artwork.

29. For a plausible list of reasons behind the cuts in the premiere performance, see Robert William Oldani, "*Boris Godunov* and the Censor," in *19th Century Music* II, no. 3 (March 1979): 251–53.

30. The Inn Scene had been highly praised in Petersburg productions as proof of Musorgsky's gift for realistic comic recitative. There, the harshest criticism was leveled against the serious roles, so without appropriate arias. The Paris production, however—with Chaliapin in the title role and with the death of Boris moved to the end—was a triumph for the tragic Boris. In that setting, the Inn Scene might well have seemed out of place. On the qualified success of the 1908 performance and the polemics it generated, see Robert William Oldani, "Mussorgsky and Diaghilev: Reflections on the Production of *Boris Godunov* at Paris, 1908," *Liberal and Fine Arts Review* 2 (July 1982): 1–13. For an account of the 1908 production in the context of the opera's performance history, see Vas. Iakovlev, "*Boris Godunov* v teatre," in *Musorgskii: Boris Godunov—Stat'i i issledovaniia* (Moscow: GosIzdat, Muzykal'nyi sektor, 1930), 216–19. This anthology of essays will henceforth be referred to as *Mus:BG1930.*

31. For the title page of this early version with scenario, see Jay Leyda and Sergei Bertensson, eds. and trans., *The Musorgsky Reader: A Life of Modeste Petrovich Musorgsky in Letters and Documents* (New York: Da Capo Press, 1970), 127. Although Soviet musicologists routinely confuse this issue in an effort to claim Musorgsky's most famous opera for the *narod,* there is no indication that Musorgsky intended *Boris* to be a "people's musical drama." That title was given first to *Khovanshchina,* and would doubtless have applied as well to Musorgsky's projected, but unwritten *Pugachevshchina.* The confusion dates from at least 1896, when the term "people's musical drama" appeared on the title page of Rimsky-Korsakov's first revision of *Boris Godunov.*

32. For a good introduction to music in this decade, see Robert C. Ridenour, *Nationalism, Modernism, and Personal Rivalry in Nineteenth-Century Russian Music* (Ann Arbor: UMI Research Press, 1981).

33. When Western musical modes and styles began to penetrate Russia they met with little resistance from native models. Petersburg society reflected the basic European trends. In 1731 the Empress Anna invited to court the first Italian troupe; later the Italian presence was supplemented by French comic opera and Viennese fairy-tale opera.

34. See Ridenour, chs. II and III. The issue is also intelligently discussed by David Brown in his "Balakirev, Tchaikovsky and Nationalism," *Music &*

Letters 42, no. 3 (July 1961): 227–41. For a critique of the bad habits and careless classifications Western scholarship visits on Russian music—and especially the overuse of the "Slavophile" label—see Richard Taruskin, "Some Thoughts on the History and Historiography of Russian Music," *Journal of Musicology* III (1984): 321–39.

35. Musorgsky to Balakirev, 16 January 1861, in M. P. Musorgskii, *Pis'ma i dokumenty*, ed. A. N. Rimskii-Korsakov (Moscow-Leningrad: MuzGiz, 1932), 67.

36. The question of Musorgsky's antisemitic and anti-Polish sentiments has been as awkwardly treated as that of Dostoevsky's. Some anthologies of his letters unabashedly censor them out, as Jay Leyda and Sergei Bertensson have done in *The Musorgsky Reader* (". . . we have omitted violently chauvinistic phrases directed against Jews and Catholics as groups. Musorgsky's anti-Semitism and anti-Catholicism derived from his unthinking adherence to the nationalist program laid down by Balakirev and Stasov. . . . And Musorgsky's anti-Semitic remarks are made eternally absurd by the living contradiction of his music [etc.] . . . ," xiv–xv). Others explain the remarks by Musorgsky's extraordinary sensitivity to the voice, and moral outlook, of his particular interlocutor (see A. Orlova, "Epistoliarnoe nasledie Musorgskogo," in *Modest Petrovich Musorgskii: Pis'ma, biograficheskie materialy i dokumenty* [Moscow: Muzyka, 1971], 13).

37. See Ridenour, 115–17.

38. In the 1840s Anton Rubinstein, famous throughout Europe as a virtuoso pianist, could not register in the census book as "Rubinstein, artist"; there was no administrative slot for it. He was eventually inscribed as "the son of a merchant of the second guild," and he never forgot it. See Ridenour, 27–28, and also the account in Catherine Drinker Bowen's very partial (but engaging) biography, *"Free Artist": The Story of Anton and Nicholas Rubinstein* (New York: Little, Brown & Co., 1939), 98–99.

39. It must be said that the conservatories in Petersburg and Moscow attempted to hire Russians as soon as qualified ones were found—qualified, of course, by conservatory criteria. Rimsky-Korsakov was astounded when he was offered the position of Professor of Composition and Instrumentation at the Petersburg Conservatory in 1871, and in his memoirs spends three pages professing his lack of qualifications for the post (Nikolay Andreyevich Rimsky-Korsakov, *My Musical Life*, trans. Judah A. Joffe [New York: Vienna House, 1972], 115–18).

40. Musorgsky to Balakirev, 11 & 31 March 1862; 28 April 1862. *Pis'ma i dokumenty* 76–77/*The Musorgsky Reader*, 42–44.

41. Musorgsky to Balakirev, 28 April 1862. *Pis'ma i dokumenty* 81/*The Musorgsky Reader*, 43–44; for an abridged version, Orlova *Trudy*, 102/*MDW*, 102.

42. Relevant here are Rousseau's campaign for simplification and artlessness in music, his own "peasant" operas, his innovations in musical pedagogy (sightsinging taught through movable solfege), and his arguments in *Emile* on behalf of the singing voice—which he perceived as a primary emotional outlet for the young child.

43. For an excellent discussion of its implications in music, see Richard Taruskin, "Realism as Preached and Practiced: The Russian *Opéra Dialogué*," *Musical Quarterly* 56, no. 3 (July 1970): 432–54. It should be noted that Taruskin substantially modifies the conclusions of this article in his later work;

see his *Opera and Drama in Russia as Preached and Practiced in the 1860s* (Ann Arbor: UMI Research Press, 1981), 329–30 [note 11].

44. In 1889, Chernyshevsky returned from twenty-five years of Siberian exile with only a few months to live. Stasov wrote him in January hoping to renew their acquaintance, and added that he valued "The Aesthetic Relations of Art to Reality" above all other Russian books on art (cited in T. Livanova, *Stasov i russkaia klassicheskaia opera* [Moscow: MuzGiz, 1957], 156). The Stasov-Chernyshevsky connection is emphasized in all Soviet biographies of Stasov, and perhaps to excess.

45. N. G. Chernyshevskii, "Esteticheskie otnosheniia iskusstva k de-istvitel'nosti," *Polnoe sobranie sochinenii* in 15 vols., vol. 2 (Moscow: GIKhL, 1949), 62.

46. Richard Taruskin, *Opera and Drama in Russia*, 307–14.

47. In letters from the Stasov-Balakirev correspondence that have since become notorious, Stasov refers to Musorgsky as "a perfect idiot" (17 May 1863), sentiments that Balakirev echoes exactly in his comment that "Musorgsky is practically an idiot" (3 June 1863). See *The Musorgsky Reader*, 47. For an interesting, if ideologically rigid, attempt to explain Musorgsky's differences with Stasov and Balakirev on grounds of social class and economic interests, see Yuri Keldysh, "Musorgskii i problema nasledstva proshlogo," in *M. P. Musorgskii k piatidesiatiletiiu so dnia smerti 1881–1931: Stat'i i materialy*, ed. Iu. Keldysh and Vas. Iakovlev (Moscow: GosMuzIzdat, 1932), 8–10. This anthology of articles will henceforth be referred to as *Mus:1932*.

48. For the differences between the *kuchkisty* and Wagner (and Wagner's Russian disciple Alexander Serov), see Taruskin, *Opera and Drama in Russia*, 281–94; Igor Glebov (Boris Asafiev), "Vvedenie v izuchenie dramaturgii Musorgskogo," *Mus:BG1930*, 6–8; and Ivan Sollertinsky's review of the original *Boris* as performed at the Maly Opera Theater in June 1939 (in the journal *Iskusstvo i zhizn'*, no. 7, 1939; reprinted as "Boris Godunov" in *I. Sollertinskii: Kriticheskie stat'i* [Leningrad: GozMuzIzdat, 1963], 21–23). Sollertinsky correctly indicates the two major differences between Musorgsky and Wagner: first, that Musorgsky built his operas on the dramatic, not the symphonic, principle, and second, that Musorgsky found Wagner's "poetics of hyperbole" completely uncongenial; his was always a "minimum of expressive means."

49. Letter of Dargomyzhsky to Lyubov Karmalina, 9 December 1857. See O. Levasheva, Yu. Keldysh, A. Kandinskii, *Istoriia russkoi muzyki*, vol. I (Moscow: Muzyka, 1980), 533; also Taruskin, *Opera and Drama in Russia*, 258.

50. For an excellent discussion of the problems inherent in Dargomyzhsky's credo about sound expressing the word, see V. A. Vasina-Grossman, "Muzyka i proza: k izucheniiu naslediia Musorgskogo," in *Tipologiia russkogo realizma vtoroi poloviny XIX veka*, ed. G. Yu. Sternin (Moscow: Nauka, 1979), 14–16.

51. Vasina-Grossman (23–24) attributes the term "speech genre" to Viktor Vinogradov, but the concept is more commonly associated today in the West with Mikhail Bakhtin (see his "Problema rechevykh zhanrov" in *Estetika slovesnogo tvorchestva* [Moscow, 1979], 237–45). The term "speech genre" was in fact a familiar one in the theoretical lexicon of the formalists in the 1920s, where it designated not only verbal categories but also modifications of literary forms.

52. See Vasina-Grossman, 21.

53. Taruskin, *Opera and Drama in Russia*, 269; for an analysis of the "rounded intonational periods" that characterize Dargomyzhsky's prosody, see 249–81.

54. From Musorgsky's brief autobiographical sketch for Hugo Riemann's *Musik-Lexicon* (June 1880). Orlova *Trudy*, 583–84/*MDW*, 617; for a full translation of the text, see *The Musorgsky Reader*, 416–20.

55. Musorgsky to Rimsky-Korsakov, between 8 and 30 July 1868. Orlova *Trudy*, 158/*MDW*, 169.

56. Musorgsky to Rimsky-Korsakov, 30 July 1868. Orlova *Trudy*, 158/*MDW*, 169.

57. Musorgsky to Cui, 3 July 1868. Orlova *Trudy*, 157/*MDW*, 168.

58. Georg Gottfried Gervinus, *Handel und Shakespeare: Zur Aesthetik der Tonkunst* (Leipzig, 1868). Musorgsky acknowledged his debt to Gervinus in his autobiographical note for Hugo Riemann's *Musik-Lexicon* (Orlova *Trudy*, 583–84/*MDW*, 617). For excellent discussions of the Gervinus connection, see Igor Glebov [Boris Asafiev], "Muzykal'no-esteticheskie vozzreniia Musorgskogo," *Mus:1932*, 33–50, and Taruskin, *Opera and Drama in Russia*, 309–13. More detail can be found in Richard Taruskin, "Handel, Shakespeare, and Musorgsky: The Sources and Limits of Russian Musical Realism," in *Studies in the History of Music*, vol. I (New York: Broude Brothers Limited, 1983), 250–55.

59. From an earlier version of the autobiographical sketch. Orlova *Trudy*, 584/*MDW*, 617.

60. Musorgsky to Vladimir Nikolsky, 15 August 1868. Orlova *Trudy*, 162/*MDW*, 173.

61. In his third-person autobiographical sketch, Musorgsky correctly notes that he "cannot be classed with any existing group of musicians, either by the character of his compositions or by his musical views." Orlova *Trudy*, 583/*MDW*, 617.

62. Cesar Cui in *Golos*, no. 98, 8 April 1881. Orlova *Trudy*, 625/*MDW*, 659.

63. Musorgsky to Liudmila Shestakova, 30 July 1868. Orlova *Trudy*, 159/*MDW*, 170.

64. Musorgsky to A. A. Golenishchev-Kutuzov, 15 August 1877, in M. P. Musorgskii, *Pis'ma k A. A. Golenishchevu-Kutuzovu*, ed. Iu. Keldysh (Moscow-Leningrad: GosMuzIzdat, 1939), 69–70; henceforth *Pis'ma k GK*. In English in *The Musorgsky Reader*, 360.

65. For analysis and creative commentary on the rationale underlying each Musorgsky version, see Richard Taruskin, "Musorgsky vs. Musorgsky: The Versions of *Boris Godunov*," in two successive installments in *19th Century Music:* VIII, no. 2 (Fall 1984): 91–118, and VIII, no. 3 (Spring 1985): 245–72. Hereafter referred to as Taruskin, "M vs M I" and "M vs M II."

66. See Pushkin's letter to N. N. Raevsky (*fils*), second half of July 1825: "I feel that my spiritual powers have reached their full development—I can create." *P:Pss* XIII, 198. Consider in comparison Musorgsky's letter to V. V. Nikolsky, 15 August 1868: "But through the gloom of uncertainty I see a glimmer of light, and this glimmer is the complete renunciation by society of its former (and still existing) operatic traditions. Impossible! Then why is this glimmer so bright? Because when you are blazing a new trail you feel your powers are doubled, and when power is doubled . . . then you can work, and work joyfully." Orlova *Trudy*, 163/*MDW*, 173–74.

67. Musorgsky to A. A. Golenishchev-Kutuzov, 6 September 1875. *Pis'ma k GK*, 55/*The Musorgsky Reader*, 308.

68. Musorgsky's skill at musical parody was famous, or infamous, in

Petersburg of the 1860s. His songs "Raek" (The peepshow) and "Klassik" (The classicist) were openly directed against conservative music critics and opera singers of the time; no less bold were his "improvisation evenings" at the piano, where no genre survived intact. In the words of one anonymous memoirist: "He would play some well-known aria with such changes in tempo and beat that it was impossible to hear it without laughing; or he would perform a different piece with each hand, the left would do 'Lieber Augustin' and the right a waltz from *Faust*. Then a potpourri would follow, out of various gay polkas and waltzes, solemn hymns, funeral marches, organ music, and so on. . . ." V. U. in *Istoricheskii vestnik*, March 1888, 686–87, cited in "Karikatura M. P. Musorgskogo," *Mus:1932*, 144.

69. Musorgsky to Vladimir Stasov (16 or 22 June 1872). *Pis'ma i dokumenty*, 217/*The Musorgsky Reader*, 186.

70. Vasina-Grossman, 10.

71. In scene 4 of Part I, Natasha receives and furtively reads the love note from Anatol Kuragin. Subsequently, and conventionally, she embodies her anguish in an aria; Sonia "hears" this aria and abruptly asks Natasha what she intends to do about Bolkonsky. This is Prokofiev's whimsical operatic solution to the novelistic scene where Sonia finds, and reads, Anatol's letter while Natasha sleeps on the sofa nearby. See S. Prokofiev, *Voina i mir* (partitura), in *Sobranie sochinenii*, vol. 6A (Moscow: GosMuzIzdat, 1958), 276–88.

72. Especially noteworthy are the chamber songs "Hopak," "The Goat" (Kozyol), "Svetik Savishna," "The Scamp" (Ozornik), "The Orphan" (Sirotka), and the song cycle "The Nursery" (Detskaia); see Vasina-Grossman, 23–26. For a good discussion of the performing aesthetic behind Musorgsky's realistic songs, see Alexander Tumanov's account of interviews with Maria Olenina-d'Alheim, one of the earliest popularizers of Musorgsky's vocal repertory in Europe. A. Tumanov, "U sovremennitsy Stasova," *Sovetskaia muzyka* 7 (July 1964): 48–52.

73. Shirinian, *Opernaia dramaturgiia Musorgskogo* (Moscow: Muzyka, 1981), 17.

74. The technique included a matching of spoken accent with musical pulse, an avoidance of melisma, a preference for quick repeated forms and triplet settings, and the preservation of the natural pitch contours of questions, exclamations, and declarative statements. See, in addition to Vasina-Grossman, Taruskin, *Opera and Drama in Russia,* 270.

75. See, for example, Oldani, "New Perspectives," ch. VI ("The Music"), 228–323.

76. The best discussions to date are both by Aleksei S. Ogolevets: *Slovo i muzyka v vokal'no-dramaticheskikh zhanrakh* (Moscow: GosMuzIzdat, 1960), with a chapter devoted to Musorgsky (5: "Normativy prozaicheskoi rechi v opernykh formakh," 255–306), and the more recent *Vokal'naia dramaturgiia Musorgskogo* (Moscow: Muzyka, 1966).

77. This methodology is developed by Ogolevets, *Slovo i muzyka,* 258–91.

78. Iarustovsky shows ingeniously how Musorgsky's principles shift as the line "quotes" other genres—say, prose and lyric. One example from the revised *Boris* occurs in the Pretender's courtship of Marina (Act III, scene 2), when recitative in expository prose switches in midsentence to romantic arioso. Fearing mere prose will not work on the hardhearted Marina, Dmitri summons both a lyrical and a musical genre to plead his case. The text of the arioso has no equivalent in Pushkin's scene 13, although the sentiments (and, at this point, the alignment of power) are the same. See Iarustovskii, *Dramaturgiia russkoi opernoi klassiki,* 177–78.

79. Robert Oldani has isolated twelve motifs in the second version of *Boris*, denoting characters, situations, even abstract ideas ("New Perspectives," 245–49). Oldani shows, for example, that the Polish Act—often abused as "one tedious mazurka"—is as subtly plotted musically as the Russian scenes. E major is the key for the "scheming Poles," and the six musical periods at the fountain reveal a shift of key in accordance with shifts in political, and amatory, power. Dmitri enters singing his motif in his own key; by the end of the scene he is still singing his motif, but it has modulated to Marina's E major. Their duel, in short, is a duel of keys (277–80).

80. These basic types are briefly defined in Ogolevets, *Vokal'naia dramaturgiia Musorgskogo*, 8–10.

81. For a demonstration of Musorgsky's progressive relaxation of *kuchkist* standards of declamation and his increasing openness to a lyrical line, see Taruskin, "M vs M II," 251–54.

82. For a good sample of these subtle adjustments, see R. Shirinian, "Pushkin i Musorgskii," *Sovetskaia muzyka* 33 (September 1969): 80.

83. D. S. Mirsky, *A History of Russian Literature* (New York: Vintage, 1958), 255. Mirsky does say, in opposition to the spirit of this study, that the literary historian "unfortunately has no right to appropriate him [Musorgsky] or to sever the dramatic from the musical texture of his dramas."

84. N. Strakhov, *"Boris Godunov* na stsene," a serialized three-part review for *Grazhdanin*, in N. Strakhov, *Zametki o Pushkine i drugikh poetakh* (Kiev: tip. Chokolova, 1897; reprint ed. Russian Reprint Series XLIII, The Hague: Europe Printing, 1967), 81. The essay is slightly abridged in Orlova *Trudy*, 372–73, 379–80, 385–87 (25 February, 4 March, 18 March 1874)/*MDW*, 394–96, 400–01, 407–08.

85. Ogolevets, *Vokal'naia dramaturgiia Musorgskogo*, 174.

86. Stasov found it: "Sanctissima Virgo Juva servos tuos." V. V. Stasov, "Modest Petrovich Musorgskii: biograficheskii ocherk," in V. V. Stasov, *Izbrannye stat'i o M. P. Musorgskom* (Moscow: MuzGiz, 1952), 98.

87. A. A. Golenishchev-Kutuzov, *Vospominaniia o M. P. Musorgskom*, written 1888, first published in *Muzykal'noe nasledstvo*, vyp. 1 (Moscow: OGIZ/MuzGiz, 1935): 4–49. The quotation appears on p. 22 and continues: "To this day I cannot understand how he [Musorgsky] ever agreed to write an opera on one of Pushkin's subjects. Perhaps if there had been no chance to independently rework the text, or no chance to include various episodes—like the nurses' spat over the parrot, or the tramps ridiculing a nobleman or hanging some Jesuits—perhaps, I say, without the chance to add all that intolerable garbage, Musorgsky, as he was at the time, would never have embarked on writing *Boris*" (22–23).

Kutuzov, a minor poet, roomed with Musorgsky from 1874 to 1875 and provided poetry for two of Musorgsky's song cycles, "Songs and Dances of Death" (1875–77) and "Without Sun" (1874). This memoir was written after Musorgsky's death, when Kutuzov had already become estranged from the composer and his artistic methods; although Kutuzov never published it, he hoped in the writing to counter some of Stasov's pronouncements about Musorgsky's development as a composer.

88. For a careful discussion of the extant versions, see Robert William Oldani, "Editions of *Boris Godunov*," in *Musorgsky: In Memoriam, 1881–1981*, ed. Malcolm Hamrick Brown (Ann Arbor: UMI Research Press, 1982), 179–213.

89. For a popular treatment that illustrates the problem of distinguishing

among versions, see Frank Merkling, "Boris the Ninth," *Opera News* (23 March 1953): 6–8, 29–31.

90. See Iakovlev, *"Boris Godunov v teatre," Mus:BG1930*, 208–20.

91. For a detailed, if polemical, account of the major categories of alteration in melody, harmony, and verbal text, see Pavel Lamm, "Vosstanovlenie podlinnogo teksta *Borisa Godunova*," *Mus:BG1930*, 13–38.

92. Consider this angry retort by Boris Asafiev, written the year that Pavel Lamm published his conflated edition of Musorgsky's versions (1928): "Just imagine that Michelangelo had 'edited' Rafael, Wagner had 'corrected' Debussy . . . Borovikovsky had restored Andrei Rublyov . . . just try to apply Turgenev's language to Gogol or Tolstoy's syntax to Dostoevsky—what would you get?" B. V. Asafiev, "Pochemu nado ispolniat' *Borisa Godunova* Musorgskogo v podlinnom vide," in Akademik B. V. Asafiev, *Izbrannye trudy*, III (Moscow: AN SSSR, 1954), 70. This volume of Asafiev's collected essays (all on the *kuchka*, and the majority on Musorgsky) will henceforth be referred to as Asafiev *Trudy* III.

93. The chapter on Musorgsky in Shostakovich's alleged memoirs describes the making of a third-generation *Boris* redaction. "This is how I worked," Shostakovich wrote. "I placed Mussorgsky's piano arrangement in front of me and then two scores—Mussorgsky's and Rimsky-Korsakov's. I didn't look at the scores, and I rarely looked at the piano arrangement either. I orchestrated from memory, act by act. Then I compared my orchestration with those by Mussorgsky and Rimsky-Korsakov. If I saw that either had done it better, then I stayed with that. . . ." *Testimony: The Memoirs of Dmitri Shostakovich*, as related to and edited by Solomon Volkov, trans. Antonina W. Bouis (New York: Harper & Row, 1979), 227. As the authenticity and veracity of these memoirs are in doubt, I thank Robert Oldani for pointing out that Shostakovich's statement first appeared almost contemporaneously with the event, in an article in *Izvestiia*, 1 May 1941. It is reprinted in *D. Shostakovich o vremeni i o sebe: 1926–1975* (Moscow: Vsesoiuznoe izdatel'stvo sovetskii kompozitor, 1980), 88.

94. The key defender of this reworking ethos is Rimsky-Korsakov himself, who was called upon soon after Musorgsky's death to put the composer's *Nachlass* in order. Rimsky justifies both Musorgsky and his own editorial activity in his memoirs: "If Moussorgsky's compositions are destined to live unfaded for fifty years after their author's death . . . an archeologically accurate edition will always be possible, as the manuscripts went to the Public Library·on leaving me. For the present, though, there was need of an edition for performances, for practical artistic purposes, for making his colossal talent known, and not for the mere studying of his personality and artistic sins." Rimsky-Korsakov, *My Musical Life*, 249. It should be stressed, however, that the changes Rimsky introduced into works left incomplete or fragmentary at the time of Musorgsky's death are much more easily justified than are his later alterations in *Boris*, an opera already published and performed.

95. For an excellent review of the censorship issue, see Robert William Oldani, *"Boris Godunov* and the Censor," *19th Century Music* 2, no. 3 (March 1979): 245–53. Oldani concludes that censorship played a smaller role than is usually assumed, but the issue has been distorted by later polemics. Hostility to "tsarist institutions" as curbs on creative talent was especially strong in the Soviet 1920s, when something like a cult of the 1869 *Boris* was born. For more on "the legend of the malign Directorate," see Taruskin, "M vs M I," 96–98.

Oldani also discusses the chronology of Musorgsky's work on *Boris* and the opera's official reception in his "Mussorgsky's *Boris Godunov* and the Russian Imperial Theaters," *Liberal Arts Review* 7 (Spring 1979): 6–24.

96. These seven scenes and their equivalents in Pushkin are: 1. Novodevichy Monastery (2, 3); 2. Coronation Scene (4); 3. Cell in Chudovo Monastery (5); 4. Inn on the Lithuanian Border (8); 5. Tsar's Quarters (7, 10); 6. Square outside St. Basil's (18); 7. Boyars' Duma and Boris's death (16, 21). Most general sources discuss the relationship between Pushkin's text and this first version, but for two representative treatments, see S. Shlifshtein, *Musorgskii: Khudozhnik. Vremia. Sud'ba.* (Moscow: Muzyka, 1975), 140–50, and (for an exemplary nondialogic reading that continually faults Mussorgsky for "infidelity") Gerald Abraham, "Mussorgsky's 'Boris' and Pushkin's," *Music & Letters* XXVI, no. 1 (January 1945): 31–38. The most persuasive account of the Pushkin/initial *Boris* nexus is also the most recent: Taruskin, "M vs M I," 98–115.

97. M. D. Calvocoressi, *Mussorgsky,* The Master Musicians Series (London: J. M. Dent, 1946), 37.

98. Pushkin to N. N. Raevsky (*fils*), 30 January or 30 June 1829: "A tragedy without love appealed to my imagination." *P:Pss* XIV, 46.

99. Georgii Khubov, *Musorgskii* (Moscow: Muzyka, 1969), 376.

100. Stasov considered this initial rejection very beneficial to the opera, but portrays Mussorgsky as an intransigent defender of his initial version: "Mussorgsky, always stubbornly defending what he had done (like any true author) since it was the fruit of careful thought and inspiration, did not agree with us for a long time, and finally submitted only to force . . . [that is, when he received a rejection from the Theater Committee]." V. V. Stasov, "M. P. Musorgskii: Biograficheskii ocherk," 97. For more on Stasov's role in the posthumous reputation of the opera, see Taruskin, "M vs M I," 93–95.

101. Mussorgsky's comprehensive reworking of the entire opera—when only specific piecework seems to have been required by the committee—is one good argument for treating the two authorial versions as separate, independently motivated transpositions. See Taruskin, "M vs M II," 245–48.

102. "We have effected a shortening on Pimen, and we've revised Grisha (let it be understood that we have composed Grisha anew) . . . ," Mussorgsky wrote Vladimir Stasov, 11 September 1871. Orlova *Trudy*, 224/*MDW*, 241.

103. "Zamok voevody Mnishka v Sanbore: ubornaia Mariny," *P:Pss* VII, 265–67. Mussorgsky's cast is the same as Pushkin's (Marina and her maid Ruzia), but almost none of Pushkin's text survives in the libretto. In the play the maid has almost all the lines, for Marina is too proud to descend to gossip or self-display. In the opera, however, Marina sings out all her hopes and resentments in an extended solo passage. The Polish scenes, after all, were created to give lines to the leading lyric soprano. Taruskin ("M vs M I," 110–12) argues that the initial version of the Fountain Scene, if indeed it did exist, would have borne little resemblance to the Polish Act we now know (there would have been no Rangoni, no love duet, no interpolated mazurka or polonaise).

104. Faddei Bulgarin, "Marina Mnishekh, supruga Dmitriia Samozvantsa," in *Sochineniia Faddeia Bulgarina,* vol. 1, Parts 1–2 (St. Petersburg: tip. Grecha, 1827), 1–83.

105. Here we have an example of Mussorgsky's concern for historically realistic detail: according to Karamzin (X, 111 and *prim.* #316), parrots and a chiming clock were among the gifts given to Boris's family on 22 May 1597 by the Austrian ambassador to the Russian Court.

106. Lamm, "Vosstanovlenie," in *Mus:BG1930,* 31–32.

107. Gary Saul Morson, "Literary Theory, Psychoanalysis, and the Creative Process," *Poetics Today* 3, no. 2 (Spring 1982): 165–66.

108. See, for an opening salvo, B. V. Asafiev, "Pochemu nado ispolniat' *Borisa Godunova* Musorgskogo v podlinnom vide," Asafiev *Trudy* III, 68–77, and Igor Glebov [Boris Asafiev], "O podlinnom *Borise Godunove*," *Mus:1932*, 57–81. It should be noted, however, that Asafiev retreated from this extreme position in his later work; see especially "*Boris Godunov* Musorgskogo kak muzykal'nyi spektakl' iz Pushkina," written in 1945–48 but published posthumously (1954), Asafiev *Trudy* III, 100–59.

109. Shirinian, *Opernaia dramaturgiia Musorgskogo*, 139. For musical examples demonstrating the great similarity between the initial *Boris* and the second (revised) version of *Marriage*, see Taruskin, "M vs M I," 98–105.

110. See Lamm's description of his method: "As the basis for work I assumed that it was *possible* to reestablish all versions, that every word of the libretto *had* to have its music, that every unfinished musical fragment *had* to have either its own ending or its transition to the next fragment" (Lamm, "Vosstanovlenie," in *Mus:BG*, 30). It should be noted that Lamm's piano-vocal score of *Boris* does distinguish, through a fabric of footnotes and editorial commentary, between initial and revised versions of the opera. The two authorial versions are much more difficult to disentangle in the orchestral score (produced by Lamm in collaboration with Asafiev).

111. For a good discussion, see Oldani, "New Perspectives," 21–26; also Shirinian, *Opernaia dramaturgiia Musorgskogo*, 137–50.

112. B. V. Asafiev, "Opyt obosnovaniia prirody i kharaktera tvorchestva Musorgskogo," Asafiev *Trudy* III, 28–29. One can see how such sentiments become dangerous loopholes in the critical literature, however, serving to perpetuate the idea that Musorgsky lacked a sense of form and thereby justifying any splice or conflation of his work. Yuri Keldysh, one offender in this tradition, has written: "In Musorgsky's opinion there could never be a best solution for any creative task, for he perceived life itself as an uninterrupted, ever-renewing stream of events, facts, impressions. . . ." Iu. Keldysh, "Velikii iskatel' pravdy," in Iu. Keldysh, *Ocherki i issledovaniia po istorii russkoi muzyki* (Moscow: Sovetskii kompozitor, 1978), 196.

113. The source for the readings will be the 1873 Bessel libretto, *Boris Godunov: Opera v 4-kh deistviiakh s prologom M. Musorgskogo* (St. Petersburg: V. Bessel & Co, 1873), henceforth referred to in the text as Bessel, and the 1928 Lamm edition of the revised (1874) version of the opera. The Lamm text appears in A. A. Orlova and M. S. Pekelis, compilers, *Modest Petrovich Musorgskii: Literaturnoe nasledie/Literaturnye proizvedeniia* (Moscow: Muzyka, 1972), 57–112, and will henceforth be referred to as *BG74*.

114. Taruskin, "M vs M I" and "M vs M II."

115. See, for example, the positive comments on the "glorious scenery" and "beautiful costumes" in the otherwise rather critical reviews by Nikolai Strakhov and Hermann Laroche (both 25 February 1874), in Orlova *Trudy*, 373/*MDW*, 395.

116. See Shirinian, *Opernaia dramaturgiia Musorgskogo*, 68–71.

117. Ivan Sollertinskii, "Boris Godunov" (1939), in I. Sollertinskii, *Kriticheskie stat'i*, 23–24.

118. Shirinian, *Opernaia dramaturgiia Musorgskogo*, 82.

119. For an excellent technical discussion of Musorgsky's orchestration principles, see B. Asafiev, "Opernyi orkestr Musorgskogo" and "Orkestr *Borisa Godunova* Musorgskogo," in Asafiev *Trudy* III, 32–67. A cogent, though not adulatory, defense of Musorgsky's original orchestration was made by one

of the best textologists of Musorgsky in the West, David Lloyd-Jones, in his "*Boris Godunov: A Critical Analysis of the Original Orchestration*," a paper read at La Scala's Convegno Internazionale Musorgskij in 1981. Lloyd-Jones argues that Musorgsky's poor reputation as an orchestrator stems from the improper application of mid-nineteenth-century norms (those of Verdi, Wagner, Bizet) to the sort of music that Musorgsky was orchestrating, and the effects he aimed to achieve. Rimsky reorchestrated the opera working from the piano-vocal (not the full) score, thus missing many of the changes introduced by Musorgsky during orchestration. "The fact is," Lloyd-Jones asserts, "much of the music of *Boris* militates against normal theater orchestration as practiced by Musorgsky's contemporaries." These "abnormalities" in the 1869 version included an orchestra that rigorously accompanied the voices (so much so that when a voice stopped or paused the orchestra often did too), a notable lack of counterpoint (made necessary by frequent modulations), the slow pulse of much of the music, and the generally underplayed, quiet endings to scenes.

For a good (and more accessible) discussion of the general principles behind the Musorgsky and Rimsky orchestrations, see Nigel Osborne, "Boris: Prince or Peasant: A Discussion of Orchestration and Style in Two Versions of 'Boris Godunov,'" in *Boris Godunov/Modest Mussorgsky*, Opera Guide no. 11, Series Editor Nicholas John (London: John Calder, 1982), 35–42.

120. On Musorgsky's infelicities as an orchestrator, see Rimsky-Korsakov, *My Musical Life*, 248–49 and 407.

121. If Tolstoy's *War and Peace* provides us with a central image of *un*real art—Natasha at the opera—then that novel is also the source of the perfect episode of inspirational amateurism: Natasha's singing, untrained and uncertain, as it began to sound that winter when her brother Nicholas and his fellow officer Denisov were home on leave. When Natasha unexpectedly "takes that high *si*," Rostov's very soul vibrates; when Denisov hears that voice he inadvertently proposes. Natasha's singing is *responsive*, Tolstoy intimates, in a way that the professional voice on stage could never be. See Leo Tolstoy, *War and Peace*, the Maude Translation (Norton Critical Edition, 1966), Book Four, chs. 14–15.

122. For this discussion of the aesthetic underlying the Musorgsky and the Rimsky sound, I am indebted to my father, David Geppert—whose many insights into music have permitted me over the years to enlarge my own amateur appreciation through his thoroughly professional ear.

123. B. V. Asafiev, "*Boris Godunov* Musorgskogo kak muzykal'nyi spektakl' iz Pushkina," in Asafiev *Trudy* III, 118.

124. What served Musorgsky as a thematic link in the opera has a real-life base: the historical Varlaam (or Thief Varlaam, as he was called in Boris's manifestos) was well known as a confederate of the Pretender. After both Boris and the False Dmitri were dead, this Varlaam came forth with a "Communication" to Shuisky's government describing his experiences with the Pretender in Poland. See Skrynnikov, *Boris Godunov*, 137–38.

125. See Emilia Frid, "Pushkin i Musorgskii," in her *M.P. Musorgskii: Problemy tvorchestva*, 85–86. See also Taruskin (to whom this paragraph is indebted) "M vs M I," 105–10, for an analysis of the psychological realism behind the various incarnations of the Dmitri theme in the intial version.

126. Richard Taruskin argues that this aggrandizement and patheticization of Boris was Musorgsky's attempt to distance his revised image of the tsar from the "bouffe" element so closely associated with the Inn Scene—and, in

fact, with most of Musorgsky's creative output up to 1872. See "M vs M II," 251–53.

127. Based on his analysis of this new use of the Dmitri motif, Taruskin offers a very strong defense of the cuts Musorgsky made in his revision. See "M vs M II," 261–64.

128. Mention has already been made of the childish games for Fyodor that Musorgsky inserted into the revised version. Consider also Shuisky's account of Dmitri's death to Tsar Boris:

> In Uglich, in the cathedral . . .
> I saw the corpse of the child . . .
> The childish face of the Tsarevich
> Was bright, pure and radiant,
> The deep, terrible wound gaped;
> But on his innocent lips
> A wondrous smile played,
> It seemed as if he were sleeping peacefully in his cradle
> Crossing his little arms, and in his right hand
> Grasping firmly a childish toy . . .
>
> (Bessel, 37–38/*BG74*, 88)

In the equivalent account in Pushkin (scene 10), the epithet "childish" occurs only once.

129. 21 January 1874, second version of the dedication in Musorgsky's hand. Orlova *Trudy*, 329/*MDW*, 354–55.

130. For an excellent survey of Musorgsky's choral technique with many observations relevant to *Boris*, see Vladimir Morosan, "Folk and Chant Elements in Musorgsky's Choral Writing," in Brown, ed., *Musorgsky: In Memoriam*, 95–133.

131. See Shirinian, *Opernaia dramaturgiia Musorgskogo*, 84–89.

132. B. V. Asafiev, "*Boris Godunov* Musorgskogo kak muzykal'nyi spektakl' iz Pushkina," in Asafiev *Trudy* III, 153.

133. Consider, for example, the exchange between the chorus and Bogdan Sobinin, romantic tenor, at the end of Act I in *A Life for the Tsar*. Sobinin has returned home from battling the Poles and hopes to wed Susanin's daughter Antonida:

SUSANIN: A hundred victories are not worth
      As much as that rumor [that Mikhail Romanov has been elected tsar]!
      A Tsar! A legitimate Tsar!
EVERYONE BUT SUSANIN: A Tsar! A legitimate Tsar!
SOBININ: After a brave battle
      We deserve a Tsar!
      For our victory over the enemy
      God gives us a Tsar!
NAROD: The Lord God gives us a Tsar! [etc.]

See *Zhizn' za Tsaria*, tekst Barona Rozena, muzyka M. Glinki; ed. M. Balakirev i S. Liapunov (Moscow: P. Iurgenson, 1906), 67–68. In 1939 the opera was reassigned Glinka's original choice of title, *Ivan Susanin*, and its legitimist, orthodox libretto was rewritten by the Soviet poet Sergei Gorodetsky to reflect a more secular patriotism ("Rus, your enemy shall perish!") better suited to the new regime. The antiphonal quality of the choral response is fully retained in the new text.

134. Even in his more conventional Polish Act, Musorgsky double-voices the crowd *against* the hero, using Pushkin as source. The basic tone of the

Polish choruses (both in the boudoir and around the fountain) is praise of Marina. But small groups of voices dispute and undermine her fame: "She can't do it. She's beautiful but dry, haughty, mean . . ." (Act III, 2, *BG74*, 95–96). This counter-chorus is inspired by Pushkin's scene 12, where the Cavalier calls Marina "a marble nymph, her eyes and lips without life. . . ."

135. Musorgsky's own anti-Polish and anti-Catholic sentiments doubtless play a role here; in any case, the direct source for scenes of violence against Poles was Glinka's patriotic *A Life for the Tsar*.

136. Soviet commentators tend to attribute the cut to censorship (*BG74*, 62); Oldani, on the other hand, has argued that the omission of the final episode was for practical and artistic reasons ("*Boris Godunov* and the Censor," 251).

137. *BG74*, 63. This exchange is absent from the 1873 Bessel libretto.

138. From ch. XV, "Boris Godounoff," in Henry Edward Krehbiel, *A Second Book of Operas* (Garden City, N.Y.: Garden City Publishing Co., 1916), 210.

139. See Frid, "Pushkin i Musorgskii," 112.

140. See Boris Eikenbaum, *Tolstoi in the Seventies*, trans. Albert Kaspin (Ann Arbor: Ardis, 1982), 71–76.

141. The term is Asafiev's. See Igor Glebov [Boris Asafiev], "Vvedenie v izuchenie dramaturgii Musorgskogo," *Mus:BG1930*, 11.

142. For a good discussion that focuses on the initial and revised versions of the second half of Act II (Boris's "verbal dueling" with Shuisky), see N. Isakhanova, "Put' k sovershenstvu," *Sovetskaia muzyka*, no. 7 (July 1966): 51–60. Isakhanova argues that Musorgsky's revision of the opera was not piece-work imposed by the Imperial Theaters but a thorough reconceptualization, in which the principle of the "illustrated text" gave way to that of dramaturgy. The Boris-Shuisky confrontation is exemplary of the shift. Pushkin's—and Musorgsky's initial—Boris is calm and shrewd in his sparring with Shuisky ("a battle of wits"); the revised Boris is openly melodramatic, unable to cover or control his guilt. Protagonists in the revised version do not develop but are juxtaposed with one another, in what becomes a highly dramatic "battle of characters" (54–55). A similar interpretation is developed by Taruskin in "M vs M II."

143. For details on the adjustment of this first monologue, see Shirinian, "Pushkin i Musorgskii," 77–79; and Abraham, "Mussorgsky's 'Boris' and Pushkin's," 32.

144. For the 1869 and 1874 texts of this aria and intelligent discussion of their differences, see B. V. Asafiev, "Muzykal'no-dramaturgicheskaia kontseptsiia opery *Boris Godunov* Musorgskogo," in Asafiev *Trudy* III, 89–91.

145. Richard Taruskin has argued that the hallucinations in *Boris* were inspired not only by the internal logic of Musorgsky's transposition of Push-kin but also by the operatic models and "genre scenes" familiar to the composer's generation—in this case, Holofernes' hallucination scene in Serov's opera *Judith* ("M vs M I," 102).

146. Taruskin, "M vs M I," 110.

147. The musicologist Viktor Beliaev uses this monologue, in fact, to illustrate Musorgsky's prose method. He points to the necessity of inserting a word in the third line, as the prose rhythm of the monologue is characterized by an increasing number of bars per melodic phrase—and "grammatical phrase" must overlap with musical phrase (4). See Viktor Beliaev, "*Boris Godunov* Musorgskogo, opyt tematicheskogo i teoreticheskogo razbora"

(1930), reprinted in V. M. Beliaev, *Musorgskii, Skriabin, Stravinskii* (Moscow: Muzyka, 1972), 20–23.

148. Shirinian, "Pushkin i Musorgskii," 78.

149. Musorgsky to Vladimir Stasov, 10 August 1871. The entire letter is written in a mock-archaic style, poorly served in translation, which suggests Musorgsky had precisely stylization in mind when referring to Boris's role. Orlova *Trudy,* 221/*MDW*, 238.

150. See Ogolevets, *Slovo i muzyka,* 468–71.

151. For an excellent discussion of this final song, "Polkovodets" (The field marshal), in the context of the other songs of the cycle, see M. Sokol'skii, "S dymom pozharov," in two parts in *Sovetskaia muzyka,* no. 9 (1969): 58–81 and no. 10 (1969): 71–79.

152. *BG74,* 104. The equivalent passage in Bessel, 59, contains what must be a misprint: *litsemernyi* (hypocritical) for the correct *nelitsemernyi* (not hypocritical). The 1874 Bessel vocal score shows *nelitsemernyi.*

153. Frid, "Pushkin i Musorgskii," 97.

154. Shirinian, *Opernaia dramaturgii Musorgskogo,* 101.

155. For the 1869 text of the Uglich events, see *BG74,* 69, fn.***.

156. Musorgsky to Vladimir Stasov, 11 September 1871. Orlova *Trudy,* 224 /*MDW*, 241. Taruskin interprets this deletion of Uglich as an attempt on Musorgsky's part to restrict the Dmitri motif solely to the Pretender, and remove it from the slain tsarevich ("M vs M II," 262–64).

157. From Nikolai Soloviev's review of the Free Music School's Subscription Concert, in *St.-Peterburgskie vedomosti,* no. 20, 20 January 1879. Orlova *Trudy,* 525/*MDW*, 557.

158. Cesar Cui in *St.-Peterburgskie vedomosti,* no. 37, 6 February 1874. Orlova *Trudy,* 357/*MDW*, 380.

159. According to a reliable nineteenth-century source (Father Pierling, Russian-born Jesuit historian), Rangoni was formally responsible for Dmitri's conversion but had almost nothing to do personally with the Pretender. Dmitri courted this dignified personage very carefully; Rangoni kept his distance, and turned most of the details over to his subordinate Jesuits. See Otets Pierling, *Dimitryi Samozvanets,* trans. into Russian from the French by V. P. Potemkin (Moscow: Sfinks, 1912), 59–113. Pierling draws the papal nuncio as a powerful and subtle figure, "both a cleric and a courtier . . . with an abundance of banalities appropriate to every situation" (59). Karamzin mentions Rangoni only briefly (XI, 79), and Pushkin does not portray him at all.

160. For discussions of the interaction between Pimen's motifs, see Ogolevets, *Vokal'naia dramaturgiia Musorgskogo,* 133–61, and Shirinian, *Opernaia dramaturgiia Musorgskogo,* 107–108.

161. See Richard Taruskin, "'The Present in the Past': Russian Opera and Russian Historiography, ca. 1870," in *Russian and Soviet Music: Essays for Boris Schwartz,* ed. Malcolm Hamrick Brown (Ann Arbor: UMI Research Press, 1984), 124–26. Taruskin's excellent essay, with its penetrating discussion of the Kromy Scene, came to my attention as this chapter was being completed and corroborates many of my hypotheses.

162. See the argument ascribed to Yuri Tiulin by Boris Iarustovskii in "K izucheniiu naslediia M. P. Musorgskogo: Stsena 'Pod Kromami' v dramaturgii *Borisa Godunova,*" *Sovetskaia muzyka,* no. 3 (March 1970), 102–103.

163. Golenishchev-Kutuzov, *Vospominaniia o M. P. Musorgskom,* 20.

164. Alexandra Orlova and Maria Shneerson, "After Pushkin and Karamzin: Researching the Sources for the Libretto of *Boris Godunov,*" trans.

Veronique Zaytzeff, in Brown, ed., *Musorgsky: In Memoriam,* 249–55.

165. Richard Taruskin advances this thesis in his "Russian Opera and Russian Historiography," 124–36. For a good sample of Kostomarov's approach, see his account of the 1602–1603 famine in "Smutnoe vremia Moskovskogo gosudarstva v nachale XVII stoletiia 1604–1613," *Sobranie sochinenii N. I. Kostomarova,* Book II, vol. 4 (St. Petersburg: tip. Stasiulevich, 1903), 38–45; for a vivid account of the brave and cunning defense of Kromy, conducted by peasants and Cossacks from underground tunnels or "burrows," see 111–112.

Kostomarov did not idealize the people, but he did sympathetically portray their sufferings and on that account pardoned them for their rebellion against Boris. This, we recall, was a step Karamzin was never willing to take, and an attitude clearly distinct from Pushkin's ironic, somewhat stylized cameo-portraits of "voices from the people." Kostomarov,. in contrast, made the *narod* into a hero by defining as heroic their pain and resistance. To a certain extent this does resonate with the events and spirit of Musorgsky's scene.

166. The major forums, which interrogate one another, are: "K izucheniiu naslediia M. P. Musorgskogo: Stsena 'Pod Kromami' v dramaturgii *Borisa Godunova,*" discussants Yu. Tiulin, E. Frid, B. Iarustovskii, A. Kandinskii, P. Aravin, in *Sovetskaia muzyka,* no. 3 (March 1970): 90–114; A. Tsuker, "Narod pokornyi i narod buntuiushchii," in *Sovetskaia muzyka,* no. 3 (March 1972): 105–109; I. Obraztsova, "K ponimaniiu narodnogo kharaktera v tvorchestve Musorgskogo" and M. Rakhmanova, "Musorgskii i ego vremia," both in *Sovetskaia muzyka,* no. 9 (September 1980): 95–110.

167. Exemplary of this position is Yuri Tiulin (above, *Sovetskaia muzyka,* no. 3 [1970]: 90–96). Tiulin argues that Kromy distorts Pushkin and lowers the ethical level of the opera.

168. See, for example, the incipient high-Stalinist rhetoric in P. S. Kogan, "Sotsial'nyi portret Musorgskogo," *Mus:BG1930,* 3.

169. Vas. Iakovlev, *Pushkin i muzyka* (Moscow-Leningrad: GosMuzIzdat, 1949), 86.

170. For Musorgsky's planned trilogy, see Khubov, *Musorgskii,* 367–68. Khubov endorses the standard Soviet *narod*-as-positive-hero interpretation.

171. N. Briusova, "Stsena pod Kromami," in *Mus:1932,* 90–105.

172. Between 1908 and 1911 Lenin wrote seven articles on Tolstoy. See as exemplary V. I. Lenin, "Lev Tolstoi, kak zerkalo russkoi revoliutsii," in *L. N. Tolstoi v russkoi kritike* (Moscow: GIKhL, 1960), 53–58.

173. Iu. Keldysh, "Musorgsky i problema nasledstva proshlogo," *Mus:1932,* 15–17. Keldysh explicitly cites, as authority for his "progressive" reading of Musorgsky, Lenin's reading of Tolstoy.

174. Frid, "Pushkin i Musorgskii," 86–87.

175. Ina Obraztsova, "K ponimaniiu narodnogo kharaktera v tvorchestve Musorgskogo," *Sovetskaia muzyka,* no. 9 (September 1980): 95–99.

176. See especially Mikhail Bakhtin, *Rabelais and His World,* trans. Helene Iswolsky (Bloomington: Indiana University Press, 1984), written in the 1940s and first published in Russian in 1965; and the collection of essays by Likhachev in D. S. Likhachev, A. M. Panchenko, N. V. Ponyrko, *Smekh v Drevnei Rusi* (Leningrad: Nauka, 1984), especially "Smekhovoi mir Drevnei Rusi" (7–25) and "Bunt kromeshnogo mira" (45–59). Here I would like to thank William Mills Todd for his reminder that both Bakhtin and Likhachev were themselves writing about carnival laughter from within their own, at

times terrifyingly rigid, Stalinist world—and quite possibly were investigating, under historical cover, the means by which such monologism could be challenged.

Both Bakhtin's and Likhachev's utopian carnivalesque has been cogently criticized by the Tartu semioticians Yury Lotman and Boris Uspensky. The image of a laughing, playful *narod* is quite foreign to medieval Russian culture, they argue; the guffaw was not ambivalent, it was the laugh of Satan. See Ju. M. Lotman and B. A. Uspenskij, "New Aspects in the Study of Early Russian Culture," in *The Semiotics of Russian Culture,* ed. Ann Shukman (Ann Arbor: Michigan Slavic Contributions 11, 1984), 36–52.

177. For a succinct discussion, see "An Impersonal Note" by Jay Leyda and Sergei Bertensson, prefacing their *Musorgsky Reader,* xi–xii. The authors quote a portion of the excellent commemorative essay on Musorgsky by Ivan Lapshin, neo-Kantian philosopher and occasional writer on music, with its comments on Musorgsky's "jesting and macabre" masks that recall Dostoevsky. For more on the Dostoevsky (and Tolstoy) connections in Musorgsky, see Ivan Lapshin, "Modest Petrovich Musorgskii," *Muzykal'nyi sovremennik* (Petrograd), nos. 5–6 (January–February 1917): 56–86.

178. Likhachev, "Smekhovoi mir Drevnei Rusi," 11.

179. Ibid., 13.

180. Likhachev, "Bunt kromeshnogo mira," 48–50.

181. Decrowning is frequently mentioned in connection with the Kromy Scene, but this is coopted by the much more common thesis that Musorgsky used the comic in a thoroughly political and sinister way (to expose, embarrass, threaten). See L. Zhuikovo-Minenko, "Tragicheskoe i komicheskoe v tvorchestve M. P. Musorgskogo," *Voprosy teorii i estetiki muzyki,* vyp. 14 (Leningrad: Muzyka, 1975), 45.

182. Constantin Stanislavski and Pavel Rumyantsev, *Stanislavski on Opera,* trans. Elizabeth Reynolds Hapgood (New York: Theatre Arts Books, 1975), 309.

183. A. M. Panchenko, "Drevnerusskoe iurodstvo," in D. S. Likhachev et al., *Smekh v Drevnei Rusi,* 77.

184. I draw here on Richard Taruskin's discussion of Kromy in "M vs M II," 255–61.

185. Ibid., 256–57.

186. Ibid., 257.

Concluding Remarks

1. "Roman vospitaniia i ego znachenie v istorii realizma," 1936–38, first published in M. M. Bakhtin, *Estetika slovesnogo tvorchestva,* 188–236. The typology of novels is discussed on 198–204. Translation of the essay as "The *Bildungsroman* and Its Significance in the History of Realism" is forthcoming by Vern McGee in Mikhail Bakhtin, *Speech Genres and Other Late Essays* (Austin: University of Texas Press, 1986).

2. "Discourse in the Novel," in *The Dialogic Imagination: Four Essays by M. M. Bakhtin,* 417–20.

3. Relevant here is Tynianov's concept of literary evolution not as development but as "displacement"; see his essay "Literaturnyi fakt" in Iu. N. Tynianov, *Poetika, istoriia literatury, kino* (Moscow: Nauka, 1977), 256. Also helpful is Jan Mukařovský's concept of aesthetic function and aesthetic norm in *Structure, Sign, and Function: Selected Essays by Jan Mukařovský,* trans. and ed.

John Burbank and Peter Steiner (New Haven: Yale University Press, 1978), chs. 3 and 4.

4. Mikhail Bakhtin, "Problema soderzhaniia, materiala i formy v slovesnom khudozhestvennom tvorchestve," in *Voprosy literatury i estetiki* (Moscow: Khudozhestvennaia literatura, 1975), 25.

Index

"About Dmitri the Pretender" (Suvorin), 20–21, 215–16
"About Tragedy" (Pushkin), 93
"Abstract time," 6
Adashev, Aleksei, 4
"Adventure time," 6
"The Aesthetic Relation of Art to Reality" (Chernyshevsky), 158, 249
Alekseev, Mikhail, 134, 215, 242, 243
Alexis, Tsarevich, 214
Amalrik, Andrei, 213
Anachronism. *See* Superannuation; Temporal layering
Ancient Russian History (Lomonosov), 35, 37, 221
Andropov, Yuri, 25, 218
"Answer to . . . *Novii Mir*" (Bakhtin), 213
Anti-Semitism, 214; Musorgsky's, 156, 248
Arans, Olga, 235
Argiviane (Kiukhelbeker), 237
"Aria time," 152, 153, 165–68
Aristotle, 2–3
Asafiev, Boris, 174–75, 178, 253
Assembly of the Land, xi, 12, 50, 52
Audience: presumed knowledge of, 8–9, 22, 149–52, 176; Russian and Western, differences in, 24; implicated, 25
Auerbach, Erich, 3, 238
Az i Ya (Suleimenov), 213

Bachtold, Rudolf, 82
Bakhtin, Mikhail, 3, 244; and Einstein, 5; on Pushkin; and multivoicedness, 98, 234; and posthumous life, 213
—Works of: "Answer to . . . *Novii Mir*," 9, 213; "The *Bildungsroman* and Its Significance," 207, 213; "Discourse in the Novel," 208–209; "Forms of Time and of the Chronotope," 5–8, 213, 227; "Notes of 1970–71," 88; "The Problem of Content," 210–11; "The Problem of Speech Genres," 249; *Problems of Dostoevsky's Poetics,* 116–17; *Rabelais and His World,* 202, 260–61

Balakirev and Balakirev Circle (and Mighty Handful), 142–43, 155–59, 205, 249
Basmanov, in Pushkin's *Boris,* 99, 115, 135, 194, 199
Batteux, Abbé, 31
Bayer, Gottlieb-Siegfried, 35, 36
Becker, Carl, 3
Bekbulatovich, Simeon, 52
Beliaev, Viktor, 258–59
Belinsky, Vissarion, 4, 28, 105, 134, 137, 235
Bells, in Musorgsky's *Boris,* 28
Belsky, Vladimir, 145
Benstock, Shari, 219
Berlioz, Hector, 156
Bernshtein, D., 130
Bestuzhev-Marlinsky, Aleksandr, 92, 231, 245
Bestuzhev-Riumin, Konstantin, 222
"The *Bildungsroman* and Its Significance" (Bakhtin), 207
Biography, 1, 7, 16, 19, 40, 97, 214, 227
Bitiagovsky, Danilo, 68
Bitiagovsky, Mikhail, 49, 68, 126
Bizet, Alexandre, 256
"Blackamoor of Peter the Great," 88
Blanpied, John, 238, 239–40
Bodenstedt, Friedrich, 214
Bogoliubsky, Andrei, 17
Bondarchuk, Sergei, 98, 233–34
Boris and Gleb, 17, 56, 214
Boris Godunov (Lobanov), 21
Boris Godunov (Musorgsky), 1–2, 4, 8, 23–29, 52, 53, 142–211, 247, 251, 252, 256, 257–58, 259; Rimsky-Korsakov's reworking of, 2, 23–24, 154, 170–71, 178, 183, 201, 256; and Karamzin's Boris story, 8, 175, 183, 184–92; and Pushkin's *Boris,* 23–24, 27–28, 105, 154–55, 168–80; performances and productions of, 23–24, 153–54, 183, 192, 193, 199–200, 204; Musorgsky's two versions of, 23, 143, 151, 161, 163, 166, 167, 168, 170–75, 180, 182, 186,

191, 192, 193–94, 198–99, 206, 208, 210, 250; Chaliapin in, 24, 247; and generic experimentation, 25–29, 146, 149, 154–55, 163–68, 177, 205; opening of, 52, 181, 182, 183, 198; populism of, 141, 180–84; initial reception of, 142–43; language, meter, and intonation in, 142, 167, 168–70, 176–77, 190–91, 196–97; dedication and subtitles of, 154–55, 180; hallucinations in, 164, 165, 179, 189–90; chronotope of, 165–68, 179, 186, 192, 206; and Shakespeare, 176–77; endings of, 178–83 *passim,* 198–206; violence and torture in, 181–83, 193, 198, 203–204; folklore and folk life, 198–206; carnivalization in, 202–206; and transpositions, 208–11

—Characters and scenes: Boris's monologues, 184–92; Boyar Duma, 181; choruses, 180–84, 186, 193, 195, 202, 203, 205; clock duet, 172–73; coronation monologue, 184–86; Dmitri of Uglich (mentions of death of), 179–80, 187–95 *passim;* Dmitri the Pretender, 168, 179, 180, 184, 189, 192–99 *passim,* 203, 205, 208, 251, 252, 259; Fyodor Borisovich, 172, 180, 190, 195; Fyodor (Tsar, mentioned), 187; heavenly chorus, 182–83, 195; holy fool, 173, 179, 182, 198, 199, 204, 206; Innkeeper and Inn Scene, 154, 168, 170, 171, 172, 177, 179, 247, 256; Irina (Godunova), 187; Krushchov, 181, 198, 199, 203, 204; Kromy, 173, 180–81, 183, 198–205, 208; Ksenia (Godunova), 173, 209; Marina (Mniszech), 172, 196, 251, 252; Misail, 198, 203; *Narod,* 173, 180–84, 186, 188–90, 191, 201–206, 257–58; Pimen, 166, 169, 172, 178, 179, 190, 192–97, 209, 254; police officer, 181–83, 203; Rangoni, 172, 196, 259; Shuisky, 168, 179, 189–90, 192, 257, 258; Varlaam, 168, 170, 179, 198, 203. *See also* Musorgsky, Modest

Boris Godunov (Pushkin), 1–2, 4, 8, 15, 21–29, 51, 86, 88–141, 142, 146, 163–64, 168–77, 184–200 *passim,* 204, 205, 207–11, 226, 230, 234–40 *passim,* 243; as "romantic tragedy," 1, 21, 91–96, 101, 104, 107, 141; playability, performances, and texts of, 2, 22–23, 24–25, 101, 105–107, 108, 109, 116, 122, 123, 133–35, 163, 176, 210, 235–36; and censorship, 2, 22–23, 133–34, 176; and Musorgsky, 8, 23–25, 105, 168–80; and Karamzin, 8, 115, 119–31, 243; miracles in, 8, 125–28 *passim;* soothsayers in,

24, 113, 114–15; and generic experimentation, 25–29, 88–93, 107–10, 146, 163–64, 205; and transposition, 25–29, 95, 208–11; metaliterary devices in, 25, 119–20, 125–26, 128–30, 241; ending of, 25, 121–41; silence in, 25, 131–41; opening of, 51, 52; rumor in, 51, 96, 104–105, 115–16, 187; dedication, variant titles, and draft prefaces of, 86, 90, 91, 94, 230; variant titles, 86, 230; absence of causal nexus and historical patterning in, 88–90, 96–103, 178–79, 190, 194; and Shakespeare, 91, 92, 97, 110–19, 176–77, 238; and historical drama, 94–96; and temporal layering, 94–96; chronotope of, 96–99, 104–107, 186; language and meter of, 107–10, 112–18, 133, 142, 146, 168–70, 176–77, 237, 239; Kromy rebellion, 199–200

—Chracters and scenes: Basmanov, 115, 194, 199; Dmitri of Uglich (death mentioned), 100, 103–105, 115, 120, 126–28, 129, 192–95 *passim,* 204; Dmitri the Pretender, 96–105 *passim,* 117, 120–31, 137, 141, 192–95 *passim,* 208, 239; "Dostig" monologue, 24, 113–17, 130, 186–90, 226; "evil monk," 122, 125, 196, 240; Fyodor Borisovich, 99, 102–103; Fyodor (Tsar, mentioned), 115, 185, 186, 187; holy fool, 103, 204; Inn, 123; Irina (Godunova), 115, 187; Ksenia (Godunova), 209; Marina (Mniszech), 98–99, 100, 118, 125, 234; Misail, 123; *Narod,* 106, 180–91 *passim,* 234, 257–58; Patriarch (Iov), 113, 179, 183, 185, 238–39; Pimen, 24, 85, 100, 102, 104, 113, 116, 119–31, 141, 183, 192–97, 209; Afanasy Pushkin, 100, 102, 117; Gavrila Pushkin, 135, 199; Shuisky, 15, 51, 98–99, 100, 104, 115, 118, 129, 130, 140, 185, 186, 194, 239; Varlaam, 100, 123; Vorotynsky, 100, 185, 239. *See also* Pushkin, Alexander

Borodin, Aleksandr, 145, 155; *Prince Igor,* 147–49, 245–46

Briggs, A. D. P., 97, 235–36

The Brothers Karamazov (Dostoevsky), 15, 104

Büchner, Georg, 91

Bulgarin, Faddei, 22–23, 34; *Dmitri the Pretender,* 23, 240; "Marina Mniszech," 172

Byron, George Gordon, Lord, and Byronism, 96, 101, 232–33; *Cain,* 233

Cain (Byron), 233

Canonization of Dmitri of Uglich, 16, 54

"Canonization" (Bakhtin's term), 208–209
The Captain's Daughter (Pushkin), 201
Carnival and "carnivalization," 7, 202–206, 214
Censorship, 10, 25, 101, 184, 235; of Pushkin, 22, 23, 34, 133, 134, 176, 193, 220; of Musorgsky, 171, 193, 253, 258
Červinková-Riegrová, Marie, 217
Chaadaev, Pyotr, 28
Chaliapin, Fyodor, 18, 24
Chatman, Seymour, 212
Chekhov, Anton, 133
Chepchugov, Nikifor, 68
Chernyshevsky, Nikolai, "The Aesthetic Relation of Art to Reality," 158, 249
Child-martyrs, 19, 131–32, 180, 195
Chistov, K. V., 54, 214–15, 225
Chorus, in Musorgsky's *Boris*, 180–84, 186, 193, 195, 202, 203, 205. See also *Narod*
"Chronicle chronotope," 45
"Chronicle line," in Musorgsky's *Boris*, 197
"Chronicle style," 123
"Chronicle time," 112
"Chronicle view of the world," 44, 67
Chronicles and chroniclers, 7–8, 16, 35, 37, 50, 224; and Karamzin, 42–48, 149; Likhachev's view of, 47; and Pushkin, 84–86, 118, 229. *See also* Pimen
Chronotope, 19, 25, 26, 210; term defined, 5–6; of Greek romance, 6–7; of Karamzin's *History*, 43–46, 61–62, 67, 69, 80–85 *passim*, 128, 208; nondevelopmental, 61–62, 227; of Pushkin's *Boris*, 96–99, 104–107, 186, 192; of Musorgsky's *Boris*, 165–68, 179, 186, 192, 206
"Chronotopicity," 7
"The Classicist" (Musorgsky), 251
Collingwood, R. G., 41
Conrad, Peter, 244
The Cossacks (Tolstoy), 245
"Counterversions," 9, 245
Crime and Punishment (Dostoevsky), 15, 235
Cromwell, Oliver, 60
Cui, Cesar, 142–43, 146, 155, 162, 193

Dargomyzhsky, Aleksandr, 145, 161, 245; *The Stone Guest*, 143, 159–60, 163, 197, 249
Dead Souls (Gogol), 29
Death of Ivan the Terrible (A. K. Tolstoy), 132, 242
The Death of Tsar Boris . . . (Pogodin), 215
Debussy, Claude, 244
Decembrists, 18, 94, 95, 232; response to

Karamzin's *History*, 34, 220, 223
The Decline and Fall of the Roman Empire (Gibbon), 36, 71
Decree of 1597, 12
Defamiliarization, 93, 167
Delvig, Baron Anton, 229
Demetrios (Ernst), 19, 214, 215
Demetrius (Hebbel), 132
Demetrius (Schiller), 14, 217
Diaghilev, Serge, 23–24, 154
The Diary of a Writer (Dostoevsky), 28, 218
Dictionary of Ancient and Modern Poetry (Ostolopov, 1821), 240
Dimitrij (Dvořak), 21
"Discourse in the Novel" (Bakhtin), 208–209
"Distant Lands" myth in Russia, 214
Dmitri of Uglich, xi, xii, 7, 12–19 *passim*, 48–50, 54–57, 70; as True Deliverer, 17–18, 55, 215; death of, in Karamzin's *History*, 45, 68, 71–75, 140; death of, historical, 48–50, 53, 225; death of, in Pushkin's *Boris*, 48, 103–105, 115, 120, 126–28, 129, 131–32, 192–95 *passim*, 204; death of, in Musorgsky's *Boris*, 48, 179–80, 187–90, 191; in seventeenth-century accounts, 56–57; Pogodin on death of, 83–85. *See also* *Sledstevnnoe delo*
Dmitri, Second False, xi, 13, 55
Dmitri the Pretender, xi, 12–13, 18, 19, 26, 60, 79, 216; and Godunov children, 13, 138–40; German and Russian versions of contrasted, 14, 18; in Karamzin's *History*, 26, 99, 100, 138–40, 234, 240; in Pushkin's *Boris*, 96–105, 117, 120–33, 135, 137, 141, 192–95 *passim*, 234, 239; in Musorgsky's *Boris*, 179–80, 184, 189, 251, 252, 259. *See also* Pretendership
Dmitri the Pretender (Bulgarin), 22–23, 240
Dmitri the Pretender (Khomiakov), 14, 21, 217, 218
Dmitri the Pretender (Sumarokov), 22, 131, 216
Dmitri the Pretender and Vasily Shuisky (Ostrovsky), 14, 217
Dmitriev, I. I., 30
Dostoevsky, Fyodor, 4, 116–17, 187, 261; *Poor Folk*, 4; *The Brothers Karamazov*, 15, 104; *Crime and Punishment*, 15, 235; *The Diary of a Writer*, 28, 218; "What Language . . . ?" 28, 218
Drafts, theory of, 174
Dramatic Trilogy (A. K. Tolstoy), 21, 132, 242
"Dual time," 97, 165–68
Dumy (Ryleev), 14

Durylin, S. N., 102–103, 234–35
Dvořak, Antonín, *Dimitrij*, 217

Efros, Anatoly, 106–107, 237
Eidelman, Natan, 41
Eikhenbaum, Boris, 85
Einstein, Albert, 5
Eisenstein, Sergei, 98, 223
Emile (Rousseau), 248
Endings of Boris stories: as general question, 25–28; and Pushkin, 25, 26, 131–41; and Musorgsky, 28, 178–83 *passim*, 198–206; of Sumarokov's *Dmitri the Pretender*, 131
Engelhardt, Boris, 89, 136
Ernst, Paul, *Demetrios*, 19, 214, 215
Estat de l'Empire de Russie (Margeret), 216
Eugene Onegin (Pushkin), 24, 88, 108, 154, 209, 216, 237, 244
Eugene Onegin (Tchaikovsky), 4, 9, 24, 149, 151, 154, 209, 213, 244
Even-Zohar, Itamar, 216

False Dmitri. *See* Dmitri the Pretender
Famine, great, of 1601–1603, xi, 12, 30, 105
Faust (Goethe), 122–23, 240
Fedotov, Aleksandr, *The Godunovs*, 21
Feldman, Oleg, 98, 234
Feodosia (daughter of Tsar Fyodor and Irina Godunova), 76
Fesler (historian), 222
Filaret (Fyodor Romanov), xii, 139. *See also* Romanov family and dynasty
Film and transpositions, 5
Filonov, Andrei, 243
Fletcher, Giles, *Of the Russe Commonwealth*, 66, 227
Folklore, folk song, and folk life, 11, 56–57; and Karamzin, 44, 46, 221; and Pushkin, 135, 142; and Musorgsky, 142, 158, 200–206
Footnotes, 8, 32, 33, 39, 219. *See also* Notes to Karamzin's *History*
Formalism, Russian, 93, 167
"Forms of Time and of the Chronotope" (Bakhtin), 5–8, 213, 217. *See also* Bakhtin, Mikhail; Chronotope
"The Fountain of Bakhchisarai" (Pushkin), 92
Free adaptations, 146–49
Free Music School, 156–57
Freud, Sigmund, and Freudian readings, 19
Frid, Emilia, 191–92, 202
"Fused time" (in opera), 166–68
Fyodor, Tsar, xi, xii, 11, 12, 48, 49, 50–51, 55–57, 63, 115, 116, 185, 187

Genre, 1–5, 9–10, 19–25; as category of consciousness, 5; and hero, 25–29; and ideology, 41–42; of speech, 160, 249; in Russian seventeenth century, 214
—Experimentation with and mixing of: 28–29, 46, 209–11; and nationalism, 1–2, 9–10; in Pogodin's *History in Voices*, 20; by Musorgsky, 27–28, 146–47, 163–68, 177, 205; by Pushkin, 27, 29, 88–96, 163–64, 107–10, 146, 205, 237; and Tolstoy, 28–29, 218; in *Dead Souls*, 29; by Karamzin, 33–35, 39, 205; and libretti, 143–52. *See also* Metaliterary devices
Genre/medium distinction, 4–8, 212
"German school" of historiography, 35–37, 38
Gervinus, Georg, 161, 250
Gibbon, Edward, *Decline and Fall*, 36, 71
Gifford, Henry, 97
Glinka, Mikhail: *Ruslan and Liudmila*, 145; *A Life for the Tsar*, 181, 257, 258
Gnedich, N. I., 141
Godunov, Fyodor Borisovich, xi, xii, 13, 15; in Karamzin, 26, 138–40; in Pushkin's *Boris*, 99, 102–103, 132–33; in Aleksei Tolstoy's *Trilogy*, 132; legitimacy of, 139–40; in Musorgsky's *Boris*, 166, 180, 190, 195
Godunova, Irina, xi, xii, 11, 12, 48, 51, 63; in Karamzin, 65, 75–76; in Pushkin and Musorgsky, 187
Godunova, Ksenia, xii, 13, 15, 139–40, 216; in Pushkin, 132–33, 238; in Karamzin, 139–40; in other writers, 20, 21, 131
Godunova, Maria, xi, xii; in Pushkin, 133; in Karamzin, 139–40
The Godunovs (Fedotov), 21
Goethe, Johann Wolfgang von, 213; *Faust*, 122–23, 240
Gogol, Nikolai: "The Overcoat," 4; *The Inspector General*, 20–133, 215; *Dead Souls*, 29; *Marriage*, 147, 160–63
"Going to the People," 184
Golenishchev-Kutuzov, Arseny, 144, 161–62, 164, 170, 199–201, 252
Gozenpud, A. A., 235
Graham, Stephen, 225
Gramota (of Patriarch Iov), 240
El Gran Duque de Muscovia (Lope de Vega), 14
Grand Inquisitor, Dostoevsky's, 15
Greek romance, chronotope of, 6–7, 213
Greene, Thomas, 128–29, 241
Grey, Ian, 225
Gronicka, André von, 216
Grunwald, Constantin de, 227

Guizot, François, 89; "Life of Shake-
speare," 110
Gukovskii, G. A., 232
Gulyga, A., 41
"The Gypsies" (Pushkin), 89

Hallucinations, 19, 189; in Musorgsky's
Boris, 28, 164, 168, 177, 184, 187, 205,
258
Hamlet (Shakespeare), 22, 177, 216–17,
238
Hamlet (Sumarokov), 22, 216–17
Hebbel, Friedrich, *Demetrius*, 132, 214
Heissler, Henry von, 216; *Die Kinder God-
unofs*, 21
Henry IV, Part 2 (Shakespeare), 130–31,
238
Henry V (Shakespeare), 131
Henry VIII (Shakespeare), 112
Herzen, Alexander, "The Russian People
and Socialism," 74
Histoire Physique . . . (Le Clerc), 36
Historical drama, 97, 210. See also *Boris
Godunov* (Pushkin)
"Historical Reminiscences . . ." (Ka-
ramzin), 40, 74
Historiography, 3; Russian, 35–37, 40
History in Voices (Pogodin), 20, 215
History of England (Hume), 31, 36
History of Hungary (Fesler), 222
History of Pugachev (Pushkin), 88
History of Russia . . . (Pokrovsky), 223
History of the Russian People (Polevoi), 89
History of the Russian State (Karamzin), 8,
16, 30–87, 91, 95, 137, 141, 194, 207–
11, 220, 222–23, 225; and problems of
genre, 1, 25–29, 39, 205, 208–11;
Notes, divergence from text, 20, 32–35,
38, 39, 42, 68, 69, 90, 219; Pushkin on,
27, 31, 34, 47, 223; foreword to, 27, 33,
40, 46; vols. 1–8, appearance and reception of, 30–31, 32, 34, 43–44, 218,
220; on Ivan the Terrible (IV), 30, 34,
62–83, 65, 81; politics of, 31–34, 220;
and Decembrists, 34, 220, 223; and
Pol'za/Istina distinction, 37–43; didac-
ticism of, 39–40, 90; narrative voices in,
42–48, 65–68, 82, 90, 137; chronotopes
of, 43–46, 61–62, 67, 69, 80–81, 83, 84,
85, 128; evolution in techniques of, 43–
48; and temporal layering, 43–48; and
sources, 43–48, 221; and chronicles, 45,
46, 82–86, 149; and earlier views of
Boris, 54, 57, 58–61; civil disobedience
in, 71–76; and historical patterning,
88–90; and Musorgsky, 141, 175, 189–
92 *passim*; and Kromy rebellion, 199–
200; and transpositions, 208–11

—Boris story, characters of: Dmitri of Ug-
lich, 61–75, 127, 140; Dmitri the Pre-
tender, 99, 100, 138–40, 234, 240;
Fyodor Borisovich (Godunov), 138–40;
Ksenia (Godunova), 139–40, 209;
Maria (Godunova), 139–40; *Narod*,
138–40, 183, 243; Pimen, 123–24, 126–
27, 240. See also Karamzin, Nikolai
History vs. poetry. *See* Poetry vs. history
Hofmannsthal, Hugo von, 144
Holy fool: in Lobanov, 21; in Musorgsky,
28, 182, 198, 199, 204, 206; in Pushkin,
103, 204
Hugo, Victor, 92
Hume, David, *History of England*, 31, 36

Iarustovsky, B., 245, 251
Ibsen, Henrik, 91
"Ideas for Vivid Pictures" (Lomonosov),
221
Imitation, genre of, 146
"Inner genres" (Bakhtin's concept), 5
Innkeeper, in Musorgsky's *Boris*, 166, 168
Inoe skazanie, 56, 69
"Inside-out" world, 205
Inspector General (Gogol), 20, 133, 215
Investigatory commission, 49–50, 53–57,
69–70
Iov. *See* Patriarch Iov
Ippolitov-Ivanov, Mikhail, 171
Ivan IV (the Terrible), xi, xii, 1, 11, 15,
116, 203; in Karamzin's *History*, 44–45,
62–63, 65, 81
Ivan, son of Ivan IV, 11; in A. Tolstoy's
Trilogy, 132
Ivan Susanin (retitled Glinka's *A Life for the
Tsar*), 257
Ivanhoe (Scott), 10
Ivanov, F. F., 91

Jakobson, Roman, 11
Julius Caesar (Shakespeare), 51, 77, 117

Kachalov, Nikita, 68
Kant, Immanuel, 5
Karamzin, Nikolai, 4, 8, 31, 32, 35, 39,
219, 220, 221–22, 238–39; death and
eulogies of, 1, 83, 86, 229; dislike of
French and German histories of Russia,
36–37; and Russian literary language,
36, 107, 110; correspondence with A. I.
Turgenev, 37, 219, 222; as sophisticated
narrator, 39–40, 43, 65–68, 90; evolution of view of Boris, 57–61; Pushkin
on, 82–87, 228, 229, 230
—Works of (excluding *History*): eulogies
to Catherine II, 59; "Historical Reminiscences," 40, 57–59, 74, 226; *Letters of*

a Russian Traveler, 39; "Marfa Posad-
nitsa," 39; Memoir on Ancient and Modern
Russia, 59–61, 227; "Natalia the Boyar's
Daughter," 39, 222; odes to Alexander
I, 59; "On Events and Characters . . . ,"
37, 221; translation of Julius Caesar, 77.
See also History of the Russian State (Ka-
ramzin)
Katenin, Pavel, 228–29, 235
Katyrev-Rostovsky, Ivan, 56
Keenan, Edward, 46
Kelly, Henry Ansgar, 238
Kerman, Joseph, 244
Kheraskov, Mikhail, 108
Khilkov, Andrei, Nucleus of Russian History
(Iadro), 68, 69, 227
Khomiakov, Aleskei, Dmitri the Pretender,
14, 21, 217, 218
Khovanshchina (Musorgsky), 201, 247
Khovansky, Ivan, 201
Khubov, Georgy, 172
Die Kinder Godunofs (Heissler), 21
King Lear (Shakespeare), 238
Kireevsky, Ivan, 19, 103, 179
Kiukhelbeker, Wilhelm, 59, 226; Argi-
viane, 237
Kleist, Heinrich von, 91
Kliuchevsky, V. O., 50, 53, 225
Kniazhnin, Iakov, Vadim of Novgorod, 95
Kolosova, Aleksandra, 235
Kostomarov, Nikolai, 200, 206, 225, 240
Kriukovskoy, M. V., 91
Kromeshnyi mir, 203, 260–61
Kromy, 203, 260–61; in Karamzin, 199,
200; in Pushkin, 199, 200
Kurbsky, Andrei, 100
Kuzmich, Feodor, 215

Lamm, Pavel, 171, 173, 174, 253, 255
"Language masks," 110
Lapshin, Ivan, 261
Laroche, Hermann, 255
"Lay of the Host of Igor," 10, 147–49,
213, 245–46
Le Clerc, Nicolas, Histoire Physique . . . ,
36
Lectures on Dramatic Art and Literature
(Schlegel), 232
"Legend of Saint Dmitri," 54
Legitimacy, 50, 52, 61, 71, 81, 84, 102,
139–40, 206; Russian concepts of and
Boris tale, 16–19
Lenin, V. I., 201
Lernet-Holenia, Alexander, 214
Letourneur (translator), 110
"Letter about the Novel" (Schlegel), 232
Letters of a Russian Traveler (Karamzin), 39
Libretto, 152, 160, 210; as quasi-literary

genre, 4; general theory of, 142–55,
159–67, 210, 244; and poetics of transposition, 143–52; "preexisting," 144; as
"free adaptations," 146–49; and three
principles of adaptation, 147–52; as
"scenes from classic works," 149–52; as
literature, 152–54; language and into-
nation in, 159–64; use of prose in, 159–
79; and chronotope, 165–68
A Life for the Tsar (Glinka), 181, 257, 258
"Life of Shakespeare" (Guizot), 110
Likhachev, Dmitri, 3, 47, 202–204, 214,
260–61
Lindenberger, Herbert, 244–45
Lipking, Lawrence, 219
Liszt, Franz, 156
Liubimov, Yuri, 24–25, 106, 217–18
Lloyd-Jones, David, 256
Lobanov, Mikhail, Boris Godunov, 21
"Local color," 44, 66, 85
Lomonosov, Mikhail, 108; Ancient Russian
History, 35, 37, 221; "Ideas for Vivid
Pictures . . . ," 221
Lope de Vega, El Gran Duque De Muscovia,
14
Lotman, Yuri, 18
Loyalty oaths, 52, 98–99
Luria, Ia., 33, 224
Luzianina, L. N., 42–44, 45, 223–24
LzheDmitri. See Dmitri the Pretender

Macbeth (Shakespeare), 77, 79, 97, 177,
228, 238
Mankiev, A. I., Nucleus of Russian History
(Iadro), 67, 68, 69, 227
Marfa, Nun, 14, 15
"Marfa Posadnitsa" (Karamzin), 39
Marfa Posadnitsa (Pogodin), 91, 94, 231
Margeret, Jacques, Estat de l'Empire de Rus-
sie . . . , 216
Marginal glosses, 33, 219
Marina Mniszech. See Mniszech, Marina
"Marina Mniszech . . ." (Bulgarin), 172
Marriage (Gogol), 147, 160–63
Marriage (Musorgsky), 160–63, 164, 174
Masons, 221
Medium/genre distinction, 4–8, 212
Memoir on Ancient and Modern Russia (Ka-
ramzin), 59–61, 227
Metaliterary devices, 165–67, 251; in
Pushkin's Boris, 25, 119–20, 125–26,
128–30, 241
Metastasio, Pietro, 144
Meyer, Michael, 91, 92
Meyerbeer, Giacomo, 177, 217
Meyerhold, Vsevolod, 24, 110, 217; pro-
ductions and views of Pushkin's Boris,
24–25, 101, 106, 133–34

Michael of Tver, 17
Mighty Handful. *See* Balakirev and Balakirev Circle (and Mighty Handful)
Mikovec, Ferdinand, 217
Miliukov, Paul, 36, 37–38, 82, 220, 221
Miracles, 7–8, 104, 125–26, 127, 128, 137, 193–95
Mirsky, D. S., 170, 252
Mniszech, Marina: in Pushkin's *Boris*, 26, 98–99, 100, 118, 125, 234; in Khomiakov, 26; in Musorgsky's *Boris*, 170, 172, 196, 251, 252
"Monarchical school" of historiography, 35–36
Monas, Sidney, 219, 220
Morozov, P. O., 134–35
Morson, Gary Saul, 174
Moscow Art Theatre, 109
Moscow fires: of 1591, 56, 57, 75, 105, 221; of 1812, 32, 219
Mstislavsky family, 12, 48
Müller, G. F., 227
"Multivoicedness," 98, 234
Muraviev, Nikita, 220
Musicians, Russian, economic and legal status of, 156–57
Musin-Pushkin, Aleksei, 32, 219
Musorgsky, Modest, 1, 155, 160, 162, 249; anti-Semitism of, 156, 248; and role of language in music, 157–59; and Golenishchev-Kutuzov, 162–63, 164, 252; skill at parody, 250–51
—Works (excluding *Boris Godunov*): chamber songs of the 1860s, 166, 251; "The Classicist," 251; *Khovanshchina*, 201, 247; *Marriage*, 147, 160–63, 164, 175, 245; "Peepshow," 251; *Pugachevshchina* (planned), 201, 247; "Songs and Dances of Death," 144, 191, 252; "Without Sun," 144, 252. See also *Boris Godunov* (Musorgsky)
Musset, Alfred de, 91

Nagoi family, and Maria Nagaia, xi, xii, 11, 49–50, 55, 68
Napoleon, 9–10, 15, 59–60, 235
Narod (the people), 71–74, 136, 137; in Pushkin's *Boris*, 132–41, 173, 180–84 *passim*, 186, 188–90, 191, 234, 243, 257–58; in Karamzin, 138–40, 183, 243; in Musorgsky's *Boris*, 173, 180–84, 186, 188–90, 191, 201–206, 257–58; in Glinka's *Life*, 181; in Ernst's *Demetrios*, 215; in Pogodin, 215
"Natalia the Boyar's Daughter," 39, 222
"Nationalism," musical, 157–58, 246, 247–58
Nekrasov, Nikolai, 145

Nepomniashchy, Valentin, 101
Nikolai Mikhailovich Karamzin (Pogodin), 35, 42, 220, 222–23
Nikolsky, Vladimir, 162, 198, 250
Norman question, 10, 213
Northern Flowers (periodical), 220
The Notebooks of Malte Laurids Brigge (Rilke), 14
"Notes of 1970–71" (Bakhtin), 88
Notes to Karamzin's *History*, 20, 32–35, 38, 39, 42, 68, 69, 90, 219
"Novel of emergence," 207
"Novel of ordeal," 207
Novy letopisets, 56
Nucleus of Russian History (Iadro), 67, 68, 69, 227

Oaths, 52, 98–99
Oedipus Rex (Stravinsky), 152
Of the Russe Commonwealth (Fletcher), 66, 227
Ogolevets, Aleksei, 169
Oldani, Robert, 252
Olenina d'Alheim, Maria, 251
"On Classical and Romantic Poetry" (Pushkin), 93, 232
"On Events and Characters" (Karamzin), 37, 221
"On Tragedy" (Pushkin), 93
Opera. *See* Libretto
Ostolopov, N., *Dictionary of Ancient and Modern Poetry* (1821), 240
Ostrovsky, Aleksandr, *Dmitri the Pretender and Vasily Shuisky*, 14, 217
Otello (Verdi), 154
Othello (Shakespeare), 154, 238
"The Overcoat" (Gogol), 4
Ozerov, Vladislav, 91, 107, 108

Palitsyn, Avraam, 56
Parody, 26, 39, 160, 164, 165; Tynianov on, 4, 140; medieval folk, 202–206; in Musorgsky's songs, 250–51
Passion-sufferer, 17, 214
Patriarch Iov, 50–52, 64, 123, 125, 240; in Pushkin's *Boris*, 183, 185, 193, 238–39
"Peepshow" (Musorgsky), 251
People. *See Narod*
"People's musical drama," 154, 201
"People's tsar," 50
Peter, False, 55
Peter the Great, 1, 15, 64, 214, 235, 246
Pimen, 8, 47, 240; in Pushkin's *Boris*, 24, 25, 85, 94, 100, 102, 104, 192–97, 209; in Karamzin's *History*, 25, 123–24, 126–27, 240; in Musorgsky's *Boris*, 25, 166, 169, 172, 178, 179, 190, 192–97, 209, 254

—Pimen's monologue, in Pushkin, 119–31; metaliterary devices in, 119–20, 125–26, 128–30, 241
Pinsky, Leonid, 112
Plagiarism, 22–23
Platonov, Sergei, 16, 49, 53, 54, 57, 225, 226
Plutarch, 7, 97
Poetry vs. history, 20–21, 53–54, 90, 125–26, 212, 228; and Aristotle, 2; and Tolstoy, 2–3; Karamzin on, 40–41
Pogodin, Mikhail, 4, 20, 59, 83–85, 108, 226, 229; History in Voices about Boris Godunov, 20, 215; Nikolai Mikhailovich Karamzin, 35, 42, 220, 222–23; "On Godunov's Participation . . . ," 83–84; Marfa Posadnitsa, 91, 94, 231; The Death of Tsar Boris, 215
Pokrovsky, Mikhail, 223
Polevoi, Nikolai, 41; History of the Russian People, 32, 38, 89
Poliakov, Ia., 97, 233
Polosin, I. I., 53, 225, 226
"Poltava" (Pushkin), 88, 239
"Poly-perspectival drama," 97
Pol'za/Istina distinction, 36–43, 82
Pomar, Mark, 231
Poor Folk (Dostoevsky), 4
Populism, 141, 157–58, 191, 200
"Posthumous life" (Bakhtin's phrase), 213
Pretendership, 16–19, 55, 214; fiction as, 21; in Pushkin's Boris, 99–103, 122–23, 124, 234, 240; in Karamzin's History, 99, 234. See also Dmitri the Pretender
Primechaniia. See Notes to Karamzin's History
Prince Igor (Borodin), 147–49, 245–46
"The Problem of Content" (Bakhtin), 210–11
"The Problem of Speech Genres" (Bakhtin), 249
"Problem play," 92
Problems of Dostoevsky's Poetics (Bakhtin), 116–17
Program music, 212
Prokofiev, Sergei, 24, 134, 217; War and Peace, 4, 149–51, 165, 246, 251
Pskovitianka (Rimsky-Korsakov), 198
Pugachev, Emilian, 1, 50, 201
Pugachevshchina (Musorgsky, planned), 201, 247
Pushkin, Afanasy, in Pushkin's Boris, 100, 102, 117
Pushkin, Alexander, 29, 84–97, 123, 134–36, 141, 151, 231–37 passim, 246, 250; and "romanticism," 27, 29, 91–96, 231–32; on Karamzin, 27, 31, 34, 47, 82–87, 90, 94, 220, 228, 229, 230; on chroni-

cles, 84–86, 229–30; on generic idiosyncrasy, 88–96; on historical drama, 94–96; and Shakespeare, 91, 97, 228
—Works (excluding Boris Godunov): "About Tragedy," 93; "The Blackamoor of Peter the Great," 88; The Captain's Daughter, 201; epigram on Karamzin's History, 34, 220; essay on Pogodin's Marfa Posadnitsa, 91, 94; Eugene Onegin, 29, 88, 108, 209, 237, 244; "The Fountain of Bakhchisarai," 92; "The Gypsies," 89; The History of Pugachev, 88; letter (drafted) to Moskovskii vestnik, 93–94, 123, 222, 232; "Mistress into Maid," 245; notes on Pogodin's article, 83–85; "On Classical and Romantic Poetry," 93, 232; "On Tragedy," 93; "Poltava," 88, 239; "The Queen of Spades," 154; review (draft) of Polevoi's History, 89; "Scene from Faust," 122; The Stone Guest, 147, 159, 163; Vadim, 95–96. See also Boris Godunov (Pushkin)
Pushkin, Gavrila, in Pushkin's Boris, 135, 199

"The Queen of Spades" (Pushkin), 154
"The Queen of Spades" (Tchaikovsky), 245

Rabelais and His World (Bakhtin), 202, 260–61
Racine, Jean, 91
Rackin, Phyllis, 238
Raevsky, Nikolai (fils), 91, 93, 151, 237, 250
Rangoni, in Musorgsky's Boris, 172, 196, 259
Ranke, Leopold von, 3
Raskolnikov, compared with Boris, 15
Rassadin, Stanislav, 136, 233
Rathaus, Karol, 171
"Reaccentuation" (Bakhtin's concept), 208–209, 210
"Recitative time," 152, 153, 165–68, 205
"Reflections" (Ryleev), 14
"Repentant noblemen," 184
Richard III (Shakespeare), 77, 228, 238
Richardson, Samuel, 245
Riemann, Hugo von, 205
Rilke, Rainer Maria, Notebooks of Malte Laurids Brigge, 14
Rimsky-Korsakov, Nikolai, 235; reworkings of Musorgsky's Boris, 2, 23–24, 154, 155, 160, 170–71, 182, 201, 253, 256; Pskovitianka, 198
Romanov family and dynasty, 12, 13, 19, 55, 56, 78, 184, 225; Michael, xi, xii, 13, 139; Filaret, xii, 139; others, xii

"Romantic tragedy," 29, 104, 107, 141, 154, 175, 191, 231; and endings, 131–32

Romeo and Juliet (Shakespeare), 238

Rousseau, Jean-Jacques, 157, 248; *Emile*, 248

Rubinstein, Anton, 155–57

Rudakov, A. A., 54, 57, 225, 227

Rumor and rumors: historical, 51, 52, 225; in Pushkin's *Boris*, 51, 67, 96, 104–105, 115–16, 140, 187; in Karamzin, 66, 67

Rumiantsev, Nikolai, Count, 35

Ruslan and Liudmila (Glinka), 145

Russian Musical Society, 156–57

Russian Opera Company, 157

"The Russian People and Socialism" (Herzen), 74

Rybakov, V. A., 224

Ryleev, Kondraty, 34; *Dumy* (Reflections), . 14

Saint Petersburg Conservatory, 155–57

Saints' Lives, 8, 19, 68–69, 80, 214; and shape of Karamzin's treatment of Dmitri of Uglich, 126–28

Samozvanstvo. See Dmitri the Pretender; Pretendership

Sandler, Stephanie, 236, 237

"Scene from Faust" (Pushkin), 122

"Scenes from classic works," opera, 149–52, 176

Sceptical School, of Russian historiography, 40, 222

Schiller, Friedrich von, 21, 91, 217; *Demetrius*, 14, 217

Schlegel, August Wilhelm, *Lectures on Dramatic Art and Literature*, 232

Schlegel, Friedrich, "Letter about the Novel," 232

Schlözer, August Ludwig, 29, 35, 37, 229–30

Schmidgall, Gary, 244

Schmidt, Paul, 230–31, 239–40

Schumann, Robert, 156

Scott, Walter, *Ivanhoe*, 10

Scribe, Augustin-Eugene, 144

Self, nature of, and Boris story, 6–7, 14, 16, 19, 214; and chronotope, 6–7; in Pushkin's *Boris*, 99–103, 117–18, 208. *See also* Dmitri the Pretender; Pretendership

Self-calling. *See* Pretendership

Sentimentalism, Russian, 35, 107

Serfdom, xi, 12, 156

Serman, Ilya, 125–26, 136–37, 202, 241

Shakespeare, William, 103, 105, 149, 213, 234, 236; Karamzin's debt to, 77, 79,

80; and Pushkin, 91, 94, 110–19, 176–77, 238; language of, 108–109, 237
—Works of: *Hamlet*, 22, 177, 216–17, 238; *Henry IV, Part 2*, 130–31, 238; *Henry VIII*, 112; *Julius Caesar*, 51, 77, 117; *King Lear*, 238; *Macbeth*, 62, 77, 79, 97, 177, 238; *Othello*, 154, 238; *Richard III*, 77, 228, 238; *Romeo and Juliet*, 238

Shakhmatov, Aleksei, 47

Shakhovskoy, A. A., 92

Shcherbatov, Mikhail, 35, 37

Shestakova, Liudmila, 162

Shevyrev, S. P., 229

Shirinian, R., 166–67, 192

Shlovsky, Viktor, 93

Short Course (Stalin), 30

Shostakovich, Dmitri, 171, 253

Shuisky, Vasily, and Shuisky family, xi, 12, 13, 16, 48, 49, 53–57, 216; Karamzin on, 26, 60–61, 70; in Pushkin's *Boris*, 51, 98–99, 100, 104, 115, 117, 118, 129, 130, 140, 184, 185, 186, 194, 239; in Musorgsky's *Boris*, 168, 179, 184, 189–90, 192, 258

Sidney, Sir Philip, 3

Sigismund, King of Poland, 13

Silence: and Pushkin's *Boris*, 72–73, 131–41; in Karamzin's *History*, 72–73, 138–39; in Gogol's Inspector General, 133; in Chekhov's plays, 133

Sipovsky, V., 231–32

Skazanie of Tsar Fyodor, 57

Skrynnikov, R. G., 48–53, 69, 225, 226

Skuratov, Maliuta, 15, 63. *See also* Godunova, Maria

Slavophilism, 14–15, 19, 21, 155–57

Sledstvennoe delo, 49–50, 53–57, 70, 83, 225, 228

Slonimsky, A. L., 111, 239

Smith, Patrick J., 244

Sollertinsky, Ivan, 177, 249

Soloviev, Nikolai, 193

Soloviev, Sergei, 53, 177

"Some Words about *War and Peace*" (Tolstoy), 29, 212, 218

"Songs and Dances of Death" (Musorgsky), 144, 191, 252

Soothsayers and sorcerers, 57, 66, 113, 114–15

Spaun, Wilhelm von, 214

"Speech genre," 160, 249

Srednii-Kamyshev (critic), 221

Stalin, Joseph, *Short Course*, 30

Stanislavsky, Konstantin, 105, 110, 204

Stasov, Vladimir, 155, 164, 170, 172, 245, 249, 252, 254

Sterne, Laurence, 82; "Story of Le Fever" (in *Tristram Shandy*), 39

The Stone Guest (Dargomyzhsky), 147, 167; language in, 159–60, 197, 249
The Stone Guest (Pushkin), 147, 163
"Story of Le Fever" (Sterne), 39
Strakhov, Nikolai, 4, 142, 170, 255
Strastoterpets, 17, 214
Strauss, Richard, 144
Stravinsky, Igor, 246; *Oedipus Rex*, 152
Striedter, Jurij, 90, 230
Suetonius, 7
Suleimenov, Olzhas, *Az i Ya*, 213
Sumarokov, Aleksandr, 95; *Dmitri the Pretender*, 22, 131, 216–17; *Hamlet*, 22, 216
Superannuation, 128–29, 241
Suvorin, Aleksei, 20–21, 215–16; *Tsar Dmitri the Pretender and Tsarevna Ksenia*, 14, 20–21; "About Dmitri the Pretender," 20–21, 215–16
Sviatoubiitsa, 16, 140

Taganka Theatre, 24–25, 217–18
"Tale of 1606," 56
Taneev, Sergei, 213
Taruskin, Richard, 158, 160, 175, 179–80, 187, 205–206, 245, 246, 249, 250, 251, 256–60 *passim*
Tatishchev, Vasily, 35
Tchaikovsky, Modest, 145
Tchaikovsky, Pyotr: *Eugene Onegin*, 4, 9, 24, 149, 151, 213, 244; letter to Taneev, 213; *The Queen of Spades*, 245
"Temporal color," 44
Temporal layering: in chronicle and Karamzin, 43–48; Pushkin's, 94–96
Tillyard, E. M. W., 111, 238
Todd, William Mills, 220, 234
Tolstoy, Aleksei K., *Tsar Boris*, 15, 21; *Dramatic Trilogy*, 21, 132, 242; "Death of Ivan the Terrible," 132, 242
Tolstoy, Leo, 2–3, 28, 201, 212, 218; *War and Peace*, 2–3, 29, 150–51, 158, 212, 218, 234, 246, 256; "Some Words about War and Peace" (and draft prefaces), 2–3, 28, 212, 218; *The Cossacks*, 245
Toomre, Joyce, 216–17
Translation, 11, 22, 146–47, 216, 217. *See also* Transposition
Transposition, 5, 9–10, 91, 105, 244; term defined, 3; theoretical poetics of, 3–11,

90, 95, 159, 208–11; and opera, 142–54
Trans-sense verse, 152
Tristram Shandy (Sterne), 39
"True Deliverer," 17, 214–15
Tsar Boris (A. K. Tolstoy), 15, 21
Tsar Dmitri the Pretender and Tsarevna Ksenia (Suvorin), 14, 20
Tumanov, A., 251
Turbin, Vladimir, 17, 214
Turgenev, A. I., 219, 222
Tynianov, Yuri, 4, 103, 140, 212, 261

Uspensky, Boris, 214
Uvarov, S. S., 222

Vadim of Novgorod (Kniazhnin), 95
Value and evaluation, 1, 4, 11, 131; and chronotope or genre, 3, 4, 6, 8; and transpositions, 9, 149
Varlaam: in Pushkin, 123; in Musorgsky, 168, 170, 179
Verdi, Giuseppe, *Otello*, 154
Viazemsky, Pyotr, 20–21, 218, 229
Vinogradov, Viktor, 249
Vinokur, G. O., 107–108, 110, 117, 237, 243
Volokhov, Osip, 68
Voltaire, 36
Vorotynsky, in Pushkin's *Boris*, 185
Vowles, Judith, 222

Wagner, Richard, 143–44, 158, 177, 244, 249, 256
War and Peace (Prokofiev), 4, 149–51, 165, 246, 251
War and Peace (Tolstoy), 2–3, 29, 150–51, 158, 212, 218, 234, 246, 256
Weisstein, Ulrich, 152–53, 246–47
"What Language . . . ?" (Dostoevsky), 28, 218
White, Hayden, 3, 5, 38, 213
"Without Sun" (Musorgsky), 144, 252
"Writing theme" in Musorgsky, 197

Zagriazhsky, 68
Zemsky sobor, xi, 12, 50, 52
Zhitie of Dmitri, 56, 68–69
Zhukovsky, Vasily, 30, 227, 228

Editor: Risë Williamson

Book designer: Matthew Williamson

Jacket designer: Matthew Williamson

Production coordinator: Harriet Curry

Typeface: Baskerville with Erbar display

Typesetter: Coghill Book Typesetting

Printer: Murray Printing Co.

Binder: Murray Printing Co.

Caryl Emerson is Associate Professor of
Russian Literature at Cornell University.